DEAN B. ELLIS LIBRARY

WITHDRAWN
From the
Dean B. Ellis Library
Arkansas State University

ARTIFICIAL INTELLIGENCE IN BUSINESS, SCIENCE, AND INDUSTRY

Volume I: Fundamentals

WENDY B. RAUCH-HINDIN

President, Hi-Tech Editorial, Inc.

PRENTICE-HALL, Englewood Cliffs, New Jersey 07632

Library of Congress Cataloging-in-Publication Data
(Revised for vol. 1)

Rauch-Hindin, Wendy B. (date)
    Artificial intelligence in business, science,
and industry.

    "Computer vision, chapter 11 in volumn II,
by Harvey J. Hindin."
    Includes bibliographies and indexes.
    Contents: v. 1. Fundamentals—v. 2. Applications.
    1. Artificial intelligence. I. Hindin, Harvey J.
II. Title.
Q335.R38 1985   006.3   85-19252
ISBN 0-13-048893-3 (v. 1)
ISBN 0-13-048901-8 (v. 2)

Editorial/production supervision: **Lisa Schulz**
Interior design: **Christine Wolf**
Cover design: **20/20 Systems, Inc.**
Manufacturing buyer: **Gordon Osbourne**

Portions of this book are based on special reports and newsletters that have been published in *Systems and Software* magazines. Reprinted by permission of Hayden Publishing Company.

© 1986 by Prentice-Hall
A Division of Simon & Schuster, Inc.
Englewood Cliffs, New Jersey 07632

All rights reserved. No part of this book may be
reproduced, in any form or by any means,
without permission in writing from the publisher.

Printed in the United States of America

10 9 8 7 6 5 4 3 2 1

ISBN 0-13-048893-3 025

Prentice-Hall International (UK) Limited, *London*
Prentice-Hall of Australia Pty. Limited, *Sydney*
Prentice-Hall Canada Inc., *Toronto*
Prentice-Hall Hispanoamericana, S.A., *Mexico*
Prentice-Hall of India Private Limited, *New Delhi*
Prentice-Hall of Japan, Inc., *Tokyo*
Prentice-Hall of Southeast Asia Pte. Ltd., *Singapore*
Editora Prentice-Hall do Brasil, Ltda., *Rio de Janeiro*
Whitehall Books Limited, *Wellington, New Zealand*

To Harvey,
With love and thanks for his help and endurance

Contents

Preface *xi*

Acknowledgments *xvii*

INTRODUCTION TO ARTIFICIAL INTELLIGENCE

1 Introduction to AI and Dispelling AI Myths *1*
    Three AI branches *3*
    What is AI? *6*
    Why word processing is not symbolic *8*
    Eminent domains *10*
    AI misconceptions corrected *14*

2 AI Trends and Applications *23*
    AI good for non-AI tasks *27*
    Borrowing benefits from business *30*
    Popularity at last *31*
    Market trends *33*
    Applications repeat themselves *35*
    Cautions *36*

3   AI Technology: Getting It from Here to There *38*
         Turnkey AI systems *39*
         Importing AI technology *40*
         Pioneers *41*
         Perceived versus actual risk *43*
         Copy a success story *43*
         Communicating on management's terms *44*
         Getting started in AI *44*
         Technology transfer *45*
         A problem of culture *45*
         Involve management *47*
         Learning AI *48*
         Tooling up for AI *49*
         Better than video games *50*
         Graphics for AI development *52*
         Digital Equipment Corp. imports AI *54*
         AI's reception at DEC *59*
         A knowledge network *61*

EXPERT/KNOWLEDGE-BASED SYSTEMS

4   Identifying Expert/Knowledge System Applications *63*
         Expert system characteristics *65*
         Knowledge bottlenecks *65*
         Knowledge systems *66*
         Choosing an application *68*
         Knowledge system prerequisites *69*

5   Knowledge Bases *71*
         Knowledge bases and databases *73*
         Fuzzy facts *74*
         Who does the updates? *74*
         Handling common sense *75*
         Semantic networks *76*
         Frames *77*
         Rules *78*

6   Knowledge System Reasoning Strategies *83*
         The problem to solve *83*
         Human experts solve the problem *85*
         The knowledge-based system solves the problem *85*
         Inference strategies *88*

Backward chaining *88*
Control mechanisms *90*
Confidence in knowledge system conclusions *91*
Recommending treatment *91*
What's the payoff? *92*
Getting the answer *93*
Forward chaining *96*
Setting up personal computers *97*
Forward or backward *103*

7 Knowledge Representation: Frames, Rules, and Processes *104*
Frames *105*
Hierarchies of frames *108*
Two types of frames *109*
Frame-based inheritance *111*
Both expert and apprentice *112*
Knowledge system architecture *113*
From one program to another *114*
Enter AI *114*
Frames are educational *115*
From the generic . . . *122*
. . . to the specific *123*
Teaching and explaining procedures *124*
Many ways to explain *127*
Combining frames and rules *128*

8 Logic, Semantic Networks, Inheritance, Object-Oriented Programming *129*
A logical application *130*
Two more representations *132*
Inheritance *132*
Object-oriented programming *134*
Object-oriented inheritance *135*
Inheritance and trucking *138*
Exploratory programming *139*

9 Acquiring Knowledge from an Expert *142*
Living through ordeals *143*
Preliminary knowledge engineering stages *144*
In the field *144*
Coding the system *146*
Knowing what knowledge looks like *146*
Translating from human expert to computer *147*
Challenge the system *149*

AI APPLICATION DEVELOPMENT TOOLS

10 A Guide to Building Expert/Knowledge Systems with Microcomputer-Based AI Tools *151*

    Microcomputer-based tools *152*
    The knowledge system building cycle *153*
    Building a prototype *157*
    M.1 *157*
    Incrementally adding rules *160*
    Controlling a consultation *163*
    Debugging *167*
    Expanding the knowledge system *168*
    Adding extra features *168*
    Larger knowledge systems *172*
    Prompt tools: The Personal Consultant *174*
    How to build a system *175*
    Running the system *178*
    How it solves problems *178*
    Table-based AI tools *179*
    Expert-Ease *182*
    Building a system with a table-based tool *183*
    Inducing rules *186*
    Procedure and table tools *191*

11 A Guide to Building Expert/Knowledge Systems with Large-Scale Application Development Tools *195*

    Multiple paradigms *196*
    Environments for tools *198*
    Who uses the tools? *198*
    Frames *202*
    Hierarchies *205*
    Inheritance *207*
    Building a knowledge system *208*
    Attaching graphical images *211*
    Using the KEE-created knowledge system *212*
    Many viewpoints *215*
    A knowledge base tool with database features *217*
    More about databases *219*
    Menu-driven tools for vertical markets *219*

UNDERSTANDING LANGUAGE

12 Natural-Language *224*
- Natural-language-system innards *229*
- Recognizing words *231*
- Analyzing sentences *232*
- Parse trees *234*
- Parse trees are not a bed of roses *236*
- Understanding what is said *238*
- Exceptions abound *238*

13 Natural-Language Goes Commercial—For Mainframes through Micros *240*
- Choosing a natural-language system *242*
- Density of coverage *243*
- Ambiguity *244*
- Navigating the database *245*
- Series information *245*
- Commercial systems *246*
- Teaching natural-language systems new words *252*
- Trust the user *254*
- Interfacing a natural-language system to a database *256*
- Writing a grammar *257*
- The grammarian *258*
- Lexicons . . . *259*
- . . . and the lexicographer *259*
- The ScreenBuilder *260*
- Put it together *260*
- Natural-languages and fourth-generation languages *261*

14 Unconventional Natural-Language Technologies for Micros *264*
- Integrating knowledge systems with syntax analysis *265*
- Microcomputer processing *267*
- Nongrammatical ATNs *268*
- Limits of ATNs *269*
- A knowledge system approach *270*
- Database searches *271*
- Displaying the appropriate data *272*
- From query to response *273*

Talk like the animals *275*
The biology angle in natural-language processing *278*
Inside a language/speech recognition system *278*
Scrambling the bits *279*
Shrinking the language system *281*
Training the language system *282*

15 Natural-Language through Meaning *286*
Understanding meaning *287*
Stereotypes and scripts *288*
Underneath scripts *288*
Understanding with conceptual dependencies *291*
Understanding with scripts *292*
Using scripts and MOPS *292*
Scripts go commercial *294*
Between syntactic analysis and scripts *296*
Natural-language systems tell tales *300*

Selected Vendors of AI Hardware and Software *305*

Bibliographies and References *312*

Index *317*

Preface

The technological side of artificial intelligence is in place, pioneer applications have demonstrated that AI can provide great leverage for a company, and AI stands poised to deliver its first round of commercial applications. The success of AI as a mass-market technology, however, depends on a number of practical factors. These include cost, personnel, training, corporate management attitudes, and most important, the demonstration of a variety of commercial AI success stories to be a role model for more.

Some issues are being addressed. Decreasing prices of AI hardware and the availability of AI languages and environments for conventional computers and engineering workstations make AI accessible to large numbers of corporate and technical people. AI application tools make it possible for programmers, computer scientists, and some application experts, with no previous AI training or experience, to build expert systems and natural (native) language interfaces to their applications and databases.

These cost, availability, and tool developments, together with demonstrated AI leverage, are the ingredients for a technology in which just about all major businesses and industries should be interested. And they are. The aerospace and automotive industries, banking and insurance companies, scientific and engineering organizations, and government agencies all have major involvement in AI projects—some public and some under wraps. Still, there are some other facts and remaining problems that will influence AI success. For example, AI is commercially feasible only if the right applications are chosen. But it is too early to be certain about all applications that may be suitable.

Assessing an application may be confusing because many people's perceptions of AI have been biased by misleading terms such as "artificial intelligence" and "expert system." Exacerbating the problem is the lack of sufficient AI knowledge on the part of potential AI users. Because commercial AI is so new, most corporate, organizational, and technical people received their training and degrees at a time when AI courses and training programs were only for the AI expert, specialist, and researcher. Consequently, the adoption of AI technology seems a risky proposition. It is difficult to make a decision to invest money, resources, personnel, and possibly a career in a new technology, based on claims of already convinced experts, when one's own knowledge is too vague to properly evaluate the claims or technology.

This book is intended to bridge the technology gap between AI experts and potential AI users, programmers, and managers in business, science, engineering, and industry. The book is technically-as well as commercially-oriented. It has two goals. One is to provide both a general overview and technical knowledge of artificial intelligence, its software, hardware, and applications, in addition to general and technical information about what to do with the new technology and how to do it.

The other goal is to present AI in perspective, without hype. Pains are taken to point out the benefits of AI, as well as its problems, what AI can do and what it will not do, and the difficulties of getting started in AI. The technology is presented in a straightforward manner with the dual aims of educating readers in the subject, and establishing credibility for AI by providing the basic knowledge needed to distinguish between claims for AI which are true and those which are naive, misleading, or puffery.

Geared to the AI nonexpert, the technical material in the book assumes no prior knowledge of AI. It begins with the basic concepts of AI and builds on them. As new concepts and ideas arise, they are explained with a view toward communicating an in-depth technical understanding, knowledge of how the ideas can be used in AI systems, and how they apply to different types of users.

Sections and topics in the book, and in the two volumes are independent. Each section and topic begins with general interest information and gradually gets into greater technical depth. This organization avoids the need to read the book sequentially. Less technical readers can get a basic understanding of the different AI suubfields (expert or knowledge-based systems, natural-language, and computer vision) and the applications they need to be aware of, while skipping the nitty gritty technical details. More technical readers can get an in-depth knowledge of the technical details they need for their work, while skipping chapters dealing with applications or commercial information.

Volume I deals with the fundamentals of AI. The first two chapters introduce the basic concepts explain what AI is and what it is not, the market, applications, the commercial future of AI, its limitations, pitfalls, and cautions.

Chapter 3 discusses getting started in AI, and the strategies and problems of bringing AI out of the research labs and into an organization.

Chapter 4 through 9 are concerned with expert systems. The range of topics discussed include how to choose a suitable expert system application, the differences between a knowledge base and a database, methods of representing knowledge, the techniques of reasoning with this knowledge to come up with AI solutions, and how to extract knowledge from an expert in some application area in order to encode it in an expert program.

Chapters 10 and 11 explain how to build expert systems, using the different kinds of

Preface

application development tools available for microcomputers, large-scale conventional computers, and specialized Lisp computers.

Chapters 12 through 15 are about natural-language. They explain the various techniques that language understanding systems use to understand a user's language, how to interface natural-language systems to a database so users can query the database in their native language and what to look for, and beware of, when choosing a natural-language system. A sampling of various types of commercial natural-language systems illustrate these chapters.

Volume II is divided between AI applications and in-depth technical material. The applications sections focus on applications that are suitable for AI solution, particularly those with field experience. The applications are discussed with a view toward explaining exactly what they do, how they do it, what benefits they provide that cannot be achieved with conventional programs, and why.

Chapters 1 through 4 discuss a variety of knowledge-based manufacturing applications, such as planning, scheduling, monitoring, project management, distribution, and diagnosis.

Requirements for knowledge-based business systems are analyzed in Chapters 5 through 7. Application examples comes from fields such as investment planning, financial statement analysis, assets and liabilities management, data processing, and office automation.

Chapter 8 covers AI applications in scientific research, mechanical engineering, seismic analysis, and knowledge-based interfaces to scientific instruments and complex software, oil-well logging analysis, and mechanical engineering.

Chapter 9 discusses medical applications, some developed by AI experts and some by physicians.

Chapter 10 concentrates on the role of AI in VLSI and circuit design, and circuit board troubleshooting.

Chapter 11 is about computer vision, its current state, how much AI content it really contains, and its future.

Chapter 12 is devoted to AI programming languages.

Chapters 13 and 14 are about AI computers and their associated system development environments.

Chapter 15 explains what must be done to develop AI systems that write programs, or help programmers write programs by taking over some of the programming chores, and it discusses the work done so far in this field.

Chapter 16 deals with programs that learn by experience or analogy, or that discover things for themselves. These types of programs are still in the research stages, but some moderate successes have already been achieved in the laboratory.

If this fundamental AI research turns out to be successful enough to produce practical AI programs that learn, three things can happen. AI will advance to a new level of achievement. AI may have as great an effect on commerce and industry as the industrial revolution. We will succeed in learning a great deal about the human mind and how it works.

What AI programs will not do is create an AI-based superior being, with a mind of its own, an ability to defend itself, and a desire to take over the world. Even when viewing the enormously powerful, sophisticated, and human-like capabilities that a technology such as AI can provide, it is essential to distinguish between AI and science fiction. So the last goal of this book is to provide a basis for the reader to make this differentiation and expect not too much and not too little, but just the right amount.

VOLUME II APPLICATIONS CONTENTS

Expert/Knowledge-Based Systems in Industry

1. AI in Industry: Planning and Scheduling: Issues in manufacturing; Planning systems: printed circuit board production; Fuel to start; What Opgen knows; The knowledge base; How it works; Learning unknown parts; Rule system evolves to frames; The military business viewpoint; Factory scheduling: planning on a large scale; Enter ISIS; How ISIS works; Representing constraints; Constructing a schedule; Evaluating its own schedule; Computer-based scheduling issues

2. AI in Industry: Project Management, Factory Monitoring, Long-Term Planning, and Integration of Knowledge Systems: Factory automation architecture; A user interface for factory systems; Knowledge-based project management; Industry interest; Factory monitoring; Long-range planning

3. AI in Industry: Sales, Design, Manufacturing, Distribution, Field Services, and Expert System: Integration; The configuration system; How XCON configures; Walking through XCON; Conflicts; Why bother?; A knowledge network; Sales; Sharing expert systems; Scheduling manufacturing; Scheduling the shop floor; Distribution; Field services; From the customer back to the customer

4. AI in Industry: Diagnosis and Troubleshooting: The diagnosis problem; The diagnosis solution; Reliable trains; Getting started; Testing the system; Diagnosing; The forward chainer; Don't stop at just one fault; Help; Generating power reliably; Knowledge systems fix many faults; Telephone repair

AI in Business and Finance

5. AI in the Financial Industry: AI-based interest-rate swaps; The role of AI; Inside K:Base; Knowledge Engineering in K:Base; AI on the exchange trading floor; A knowledge-based network; AI in finance; Suiting businesses to AI

6. Financial Expert/Knowledge-Based System Applications: Natural-language requirements; Fuzzy business-requirements; Application types; Financial statements; Reading financials; Financial statement knowledge-based systems; Portfolio management; Assets and liabilities; The way it is done now; Where knowledge-based systems fit in; Knowledge-based asset and liability benefits; Financial services

7. AI in Business and Data Processing Applications: Expert database systems; Understanding human motivation; Searching for ships; Knowledge-based systems as reporters; The problem with reports; A knowledge-based solution; Who writes the AI

Preface   XV

system; Tools help; Starting up with AI; AI in publishing; AI enters the office; Congress speaks: a scenario

AI in Science, Medicine, and Engineering

8. AI in Science: Confusion; Smart control panels; Knowledge-based process control programs; Object-oriented communications; How to write a real-time knowledge system; Smart instruments; What's in the interface; Using complex software; Structural analysis; A software guide to finding oil; Statistical analysis programs; Math; Designing experiments

9. AI in Medicine: Puff; Physician's management systems; Help; Care; The database factor; Physician acceptance; Advice for future developers; Anatomy of a medical knowledge-based system; Physiology of Care; How Help works; Walking through a Bayesian sector; Help and Care continue growing

10. AI in Engineering: Chip layout; Design synthesis; What AI does not do; What AI can do; AI/VLSI spin-offs; A design assistant; Acquiring VLSI design knowledge; A cardboard solution; Top-down VLSI design; VLSI design catalogs; Verification; Smalltalk has few words and many pictures; The circuit-board expert; Smalltalk knowledge system tools; Building a knowledge system

Computer Vision

11. Computer Vision: A quick overview; The first step: pictures; Applications galore; The first systems; Multiple technologies; Technical details; Choosing a threshold; Training schemes; Edge detection; Edge system architecture; Object recognition; Dynamic analysis; Many experts; Composite model; Still other problems; Shape and recognition; Surface identification; 2½ dimensions; Mathematics to the rescue; A chicken by any other name; AI's place

Advanced Technical Details

12. AI Programming Languages: Backtracking: control by looking for dead ends; History may repeat itself; Lisp; Tree surgery; Many versions of Lisp; Prolog; Parallel processing?; High level AI languages; Working memory; OPS5 rules; Reasoning; Who's in control?; Conflict resolution; Specificity; Why rule-based languages?; Block-structured AI languages; OPS83 is like Pascal; Procedures are in

13. AI Computer Hardware: The Software Environments: Of mice and windows; Very large personal computers; The age of the Lisp computer; Size; Multipurpose; Networking; Programming languages; Object-oriented programming; Windows; Supporting software development; Speeding software development; A program development example; Dynamic linking and loading; Garbage collection; A rapid prototyping example; More exploratory programming tools

14. AI Hardware Issues: Environment and performance; Long words; Speed through microcode; Unique toolkits; The changing Lisp computer market; Lisp chips; More is less; AI on minicomputers; AI on engineering workstations; AI computers that

run Smalltalk; AI on Risc Machines; Board-level AI; AI on PCs; Prolog; Fifth-generation computers

Future Directions for AI
15. Automated Programming: Code while you wait; Near term solutions; The Programmer's Apprentice; What makes it tick?; Whereto from here?
16. AI's Future: Programs That Learn and Discover: A learning experience; How computers learn; Hail, Thane of Cawdor!; Making rules; Programs that use what they have learned; Human-learning laboratories; Learning in industry; Discovery and creativity; Bacon; Two theories for one; But is it intelligence?

Acknowledgments

It is difficult to provide appropriate acknowledgments to individuals in a book which was written with the cooperation of many people. One person, Mark Fox, stands apart from all others who gave their time and advice, and I am at a loss for words to thank him adequately. An authority in the AI field, he read and criticized every chapter in both volumes of this book. I owe him a great intellectual debt for making many comments and suggestions that improved the book.

I would also like to thank Beau Sheil for critiquing the hardware chapters, Charles Forgy for reviewing the programming language chapter, and George Gagliardi for reviewing the computer vision chapter.

Although the book bears the name of a single author, it has been influenced by many people and would not have happened without their help, ideas, and cooperation. It is my pleasure to acknowledge and thank the following people:

James Alexander, Bradley Allan, Howard Austin, Robert Balzer, Ram Banim, Harry Barrow, David Barstow, Roger Bates, Daniel Bobrow, Piero Bonissone, Kenneth Bosomworth, John Seely Brown, Jaime Carbonell, Maria Celocruz, Eugene Charniak, Gregory Clemenson, Mache Creeger, Simon Curry, Stanley Curtis, Jim Dowe, Scott Fahlman, Robert Fallat, Aryeh Finegold, Bernard Finzi, Horace Flatt, Charles Forgy, Mark Fox, Bud Frawley, Roy Freedman, Michael Freiling, Eric Frey, William Gale, Thomas Gannon, Bruce Gras, Abraham Gutman, Stephen Hardy, Larry Harris, George Heilmeier, Carl Hewitt, Peter Hirsch, Erna Hoover, Alex Jacobson, Peter Jones, Alan Kay, Jerrold Kaplan, Thomas Kehler, Charles Kellogg, Ted Kowalski, Arnold Kraft, Karen Kukich, Fred Luconi, Francis Lynch, John McDermott, Clement McDonald, Marvin Minsky, Jack Munson, John Nairn, Sal Nuzzo, Dennis O'Connor, Marcel Pahlavan, Jeffrey Perrone, Charles Rich, Charles Rieger, Bruce Roberts, Charles Rosen,

Roger Schank, Beau Sheil, Herbert Simon, Howard Shrobe, Kenneth Sloan, James Spoerl, Mark Stefik, Albert Stevens, John Stickland, Jay M. Tenenbaum, Christopher Tong, John Vermes, Geoffrey von Limbach, David Walden, Homer Warner, David Warren, Daniel Weinreb, Gio Wiederhold, Karl Wiig, Chuck Williams, Douglas Williams, Michael Williams, Nels Winkless, Patrick H. Winston, and Stephen Wyle.

My apologies to anyone who has been inadvertently left out. Needless to say, any errors of fact, interpretation, or emphasis that may have crept into the book are mine.

I also extend special thanks:

To Eric Hindin for performing the logistics work and preparing the art and manuscript for submission

To David Trowbridge, Susan Metzler, and Gail Jacobs for expediting information transfer.

To Eileen Zanni for hours of patient tape transcriptions

To Wordstar

Introduction to AI and Dispelling AI Myths

CHAPTER 1

At 4:00 one morning, the $100,000-a-day drilling operations grind to a halt as an offshore rig automatically shuts down. The foreman holds a brief consultation with the on-site, experienced drilling advisor to explain the manner in which the problem occurred and the characteristics of the rock formations in the drilling area.

The drilling advisor advises that in all likelihood, liquid under high pressure is seeping out of the permeable rock surrounding the drilled hole and forcing the drilling assembly against the side of the hole, thus causing it to stick. The drilling advisor then recommends that the foreman circulate the drilling fluid (mud) at a normal flow rate to homogenize the mud, but at the same time decrease the filtrate and add lubricant products. This procedure frees the stuck drill bit and avoids a half-a-million dollar delay. In addition, the drilling advisor makes some suggestions about how to avoid a recurrence of the same problem.

Later that day, in another part of the world, the chief engineer of a large military/industrial complex company is worried about meeting the shipping dates scheduled for several different nonstandard printed-circuit (PC) boards. Technicians to build the boards are plentiful. The engineer's worry exists because the planning of installation procedures that the technicians must follow are time consuming and tedious to do for so many different boards.

The chief engineer confers with the company's industrial engineer. The industrial engineer assigns the PC board planning chores to a skilled assistant. The assistant (a veteran with 12 years' experience) examines the parts list and schematic diagrams output from a computer-aided design program and rapidly draws up complete sets of plans for several technicians to assemble the different PC boards. The industrial engineer remains on hand to answer questions about those components the assistant does not yet know.

With help from this assistant, the installation procedures are planned in less than a day, the technicians get to work, and the company meets its calendar obligations.

Still another company has a 6-foot bookshelf of fully documented rules and regulations that pertain to the activities and requirements of a particular government agency. The contract administrator of the company must understand these rules and regulations in order to bid successfully on contracts for the government agency. Although the rules and regulations have been documented correctly and are beautifully bound, their length and wordiness makes them effectively inaccessible.

With help from a government regulations consultant, an expert in the agency's activities who also previously worked as a planner for the agency, the contract administrator extracts the agency's rules and regulations relevant to the contract proposal in question and explores their ramifications. Since time is pressing, the administrator's assistant calls up the cognizant people in the government and industry to ask for any extra data that would be helpful in evaluating the proposal. With this information in hand, the administrator weighs the benefits of bidding against the cost and resources for his company and begins to outline the proposal.

In these examples, the on-site drilling advisor, the industrial engineer's assistant, the government regulations consultant, and the cognizant people in the government and industry have one thing in common. They are not people. The drilling advisor, engineer's assistant, and government consultant are computer programs called "expert systems." The cognizant people are computer programs called natural (native)-language systems. All three expert systems/natural-language systems are real programs at work in commercial environments.

Expert systems and natural-language systems got their names because they contain knowledge of human experts or respond to people's native language. The concepts and techniques used in building these types of systems are part of a larger field, known as artificial intelligence (AI), whose programs exhibit behavior normally identified with human intelligence.

Many people associate AI only with thinking and learning programs. These programs, exotic by nature, form the basic research and leading edge of technology and are largely under study in universities.

But underneath this exotica, a host of more practical AI programs have emerged and stand poised to make their mark in business, industrial, and scientific organizations. The practical AI programs mimic human behavior and reasoning and perform tasks that previously could be performed only by human beings. The internal software operations may not correspond to the activities of the human mind. Nonetheless, AI programs seem to understand English, concepts, and ideas, and they can infer new information. They do not substitute for people, but they give people leverage. The people leverage occurs because AI systems have the knowledge and reasoning powers to advise and consult with people so that the people perform their jobs more expertly and appear smarter than they would otherwise.

The leverage for people translates to leverage for companies. For example, Schlumberger Ltd. had in mind $200 million a year worth of economic and competitive leverage when, back in 1978, it decided to develop AI capabilities. The AI programs de-

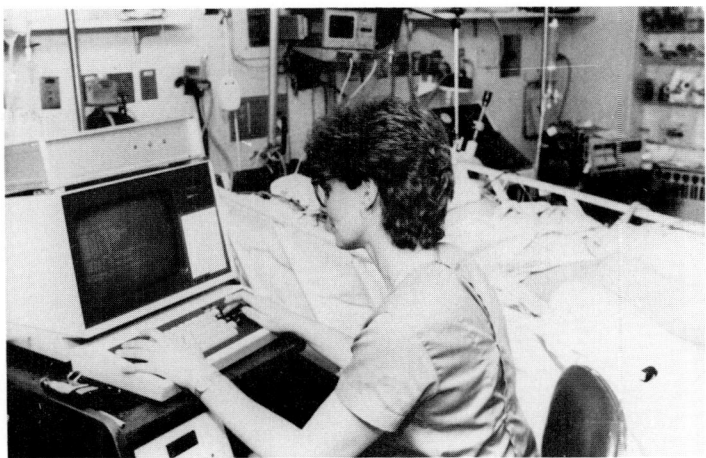

Figure 1-1 At LDS hospital, a computer is wheeled into a patient's room and hooked up to an expert system via a modem. (LDS Hospital)

veloped help the firm's oil-exploration experts evaluate seismic data to locate oil. The seismic data are measured with proprietary tools. The firm's AI objective was to improve its competitive position and generate an additional $200 million a year in sales-of-service revenues for the use of just one particular tool.

Another group of AI systems provides intellectual leverage. AI-based medical diagnostic and consultation systems at the Pacific Medical Center, Regenstrief Institute for Health Care, and LDS Hospital perform diagnoses and offer treatment recommendations (Figure 1-1). Because these medical systems make sure that routine cases get their due care, they leave physicians freer to spend more time on the difficult, challenging cases.

As for manufacturing and sales operations, Digital Equipment Corporation, a company that markets its computer systems based on components that customers specify and order a la carte (a time-demanding marketing option), uses AI programs to configure these computer systems. The firm has now placed similar AI systems in the hands of its sales people who use them to configure orders and quote prices in the customers' offices.

THREE AI BRANCHES

AI systems fall into three basic categories: expert (or knowledge base) systems (and the tools to build them), natural-language (everyday native language) systems, and perception systems for vision, speech, and touch (Figure 1-2). Expert systems are programs that use humanlike reasoning processes rather than computational techniques to solve problems in specific problem domains. These programmed, humanlike reasoning processes, in turn, rely on experiential human knowledge, or expertise, which is encoded in the program in a structure called a knowledge base (Figure 1-3).

With this encoded knowledge and reasoning mechanism, expert systems can tackle

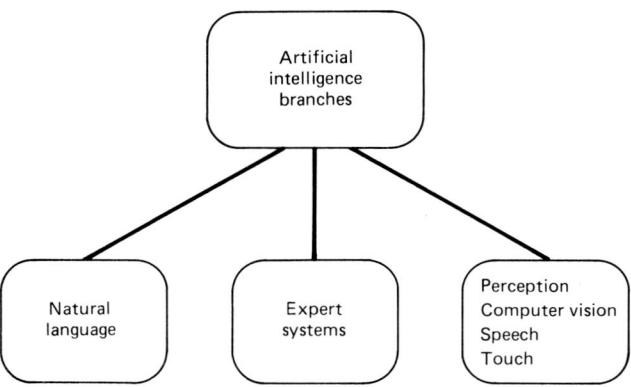

Figure 1-2 The three branches of AI

problems that are beyond the reach of conventionally programmed computers. A number of expert systems have already demonstrated their commercial successes in fields such as equipment and medical diagnosis, computer configuration, oil exploration, and data-processing operations.

The second AI area, called natural-language systems, encompasses programs that understand the natural language of the user, such as English. These programs provide an easy-to-learn means of communication with computers, because they eliminate the need to learn a stylized, formal computer language.

The most popular natural-language systems, which address the most immediate need, are those that act as an interface to databases. These natural-language systems allow database users to query databases in fairly unconstrained English instead of formal query languages. These systems can determine ambiguities and resolve them in a variety of ways (Figure 1-4). In this way, natural-language systems make database information accessible to noncomputer professionals who require or desire access to computers.

The third type of AI programs are simple perception systems for vision, speech, and touch. Computer vision systems, for example, can interpret visual scenes or can make inferences about the quality (not broken or bent) or physical orientation of some object that is passing under a television camera.

Computer vision capabilities are still fairly limited. Consequently, computer vision systems can only be used under controlled lighting and simple scene conditions. Such

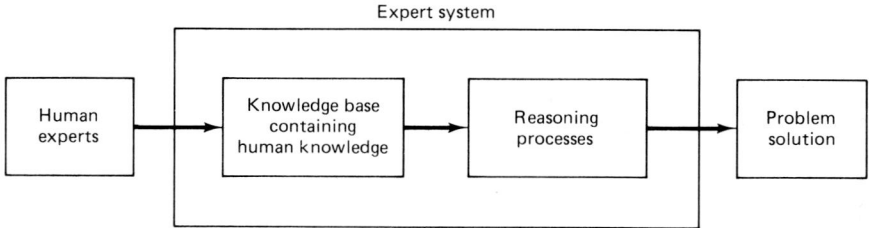

Figure 1-3 Expert systems solve problems by reasoning with knowledge acquired from human experts.

```
HOW MANY COOKS ARE BAKERS
YOUR REQUEST IS AMBIGUOUS TO ME.  DO YOU WANT:
   1): CURRENT JOB TITLE = COOK & LAST NAME = BAKER.

   2): LAST NAME = COOK & CURRENT JOB TITLE = BAKER

PLEASE ENTER THE NUMBER OF THE INTERPRETATION YOU INTENDED.
```

Figure 1-4 Language understanding systems can understand fairly unstrained English, determine some ambiguities and resolve them. (Artificial Intelligence Corp.)

conditions exist, in factories. There, vision capabilities added to robot systems eliminate the necessity for constant reprogramming and readjustment of robots whose arms perpetually get out of alignment (Figure 1-5).

One of the most important types of AI programs are AI application development tools. Introduced first in 1983, these tools help AI novices (experts also) build and maintain their own expert systems. And therein lies their value—because these tools are availa-

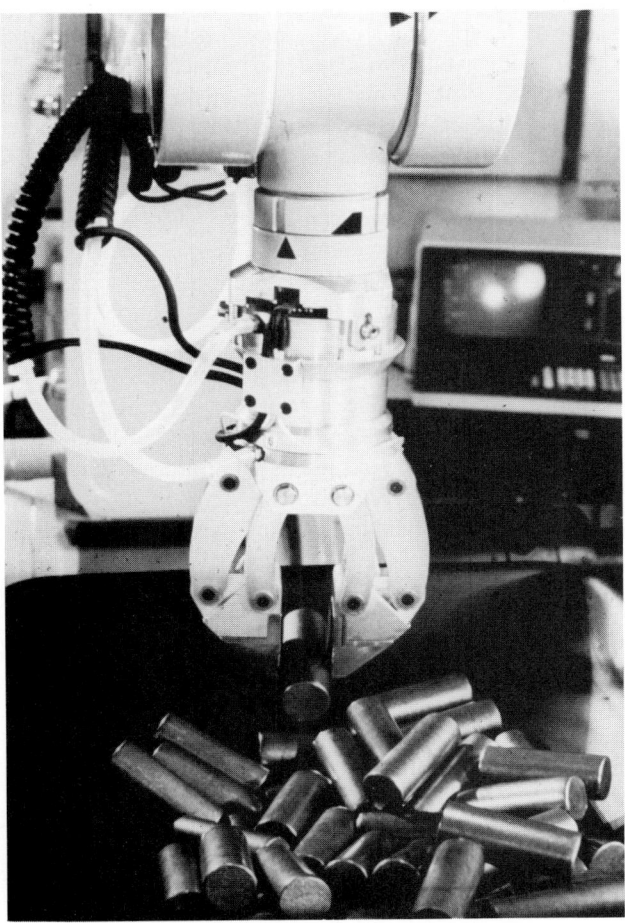

Figure 1-5 Computer Vision capabilities allow robots to select randomly spreadout items from a bin. (Photos courtesy of General Electric Company, Robotics and Vision Systems Department)

ble to the AI nonexpert, they facilitate the spread of AI technology and AI applications into interested organizations.

Users of these AI application development tools are likely to be computer programmers and software engineers. They also may be experts in some subject area, such as biology, equipment repair, or financial analysis. The important thing is that they need not be experts in AI. To build an AI application, however, the tool users must understand what AI is and what kinds of problems it can solve. AI application development tools have already been used commercially by computer scientists and application experts who work for management consulting companies, financial firms, scientific and instrumentation corporations, and corporate data-processing departments.

With these tools now available to help build AI applications, the potential payoffs are so great that most large companies have already formed AI departments. The initial commercial AI applications have been developed in large, high-technology industries, such as the oil and computer industries. Large industries embraced AI first because they could most afford, in terms of dollars, to pioneer the new technology. High-technology industries embraced AI first because technology pioneers are most likely to appear first in companies that are constantly closely involved with new technologies.

The next wave of commercial AI applications has been gradually emerging in equipment-fault diagnosis, data interpretation, and a variety of manufacturing applications in companies that comprise the military- and consumer-industrial complex. The Department of Defense insists that companies bidding on government contracts examine the possible productivity and capability gains that bidders can achieve with AI techniques. The aerospace, automotive, and other manufacturing companies have been investigating and piloting new technologies to use to help them integrate their diverse operations on the factory floor, data center, engineering office, and business office. AI is one of the major new technologies they are piloting.

AI companies indicate that the next target markets for AI applications will be in the financial industries, for several reasons. Activities in the financial industries are fairly uniform, and therefore it is easy to identify activities suitable for AI systems. In addition, the financial industries already recognize the importance of, and rely on, information technology. This makes it relatively easy to get the attention of financial company decision makers to talk technology and leverage opportunities without needing to first educate them as to the importance of high technology.

The acquisition of an AI capability will put pressure on rival companies to develop or purchase some AI capability in order to compete. When that time comes, managers and professionals will need to understand some AI basics in order to cope with emerging questions and decisions about how AI will affect them personally, their present and future jobs, their departments, and their companies.

WHAT IS AI?

As a subfield of computer science, AI is a software technique that programs use to solve symbolic rather than numeric problems. Symbolic problems, which are the problems encountered in common everyday life and work, deal with symbols and symbolic concepts rather than numbers.

Symbols are, for example, names of objects or attributes, such as "hair," "brown," "eyes," "blue." As will be more fully explained throughout this book, symbolic concepts are ideas about these symbols. Psychologists consider the ability to understand symbolic concepts fundamental to human intelligence.

A good way to understand what is meant by AI, or symbolic processing, is to contrast it with more conventional computer programs that perform computational or arithmetic operations. A conventional program's strongpoint is, for example, its ability to multiply or add two 10-digit numbers together. It may perform complex computations very fast, and it may use highly complex algorithms to process that numeric data, but the processing is numerically oriented.

In contrast to numeric-oriented programs, an AI program's strength is its ability to solve problems that involve symbols and symbolic and conceptual ideas. Like numeric-oriented computer programs, AI programs handle the familiar arithmetic and algebraic symbols such as 7, 325.6, X, and M. More important, they group symbols like these together to form still other symbols such as: dog, desk, typewriter, telephone-network, contract-1215, and scheduling.

The intelligent behavior that AI programs exhibit, which makes them different from numeric, database, and word-processing programs, comes from the ability to handle these symbols as concepts and ideas rather than as a collection of meaningless symbols that only human beings can interpret.

As will be explained in later chapters, AI programs seem to understand concepts such as that of a screwdriver or ideas such as scheduling because they are designed to understand the relationship between these concepts and ideas and others. Because their design allows them to know how a screwdriver is related to a screw or a conveyer belt, and how scheduling is related to its sequences of operations which are related to resources, they can interpret various symbols so that they make sense in view of the relationships represented in the program. Relationships like these are not handled by databases, whose job is to store data so they can be retrieved efficiently. The ability of AI programs to understand symbols in terms of concepts, ideas, and relationships makes AI programs seem to possess, at least to some small degree, common sense.

Examples of symbolic concepts and ideas that AI programs understand include "all dogs are mammals" and "typewriters are generally found on desks but desks are not found on typewriters." Because AI programs can deal with symbolic concepts and ideas, the output of expert systems consists not of numbers or lists of names as do numeric and data-processing programs, but of opinions, analyses, and recommendations based on the concepts and ideas.

For example, a sample output from ACE (Automated Cable Expertise), an expert system that supports management analyses for telephone cable maintenance, reports that since a particular telephone cable had 15 troubles, mostly of a certain type, in the past 30 days, the problem is most likely in one crossbox, for which ACE then indicates specific maintenance steps. Steamer, an educational expert system that trains Navy personnel to operate ship steam plants, knows the ramifications of each step of a steam plant operation procedure and can answer questions and generate explanations about any of its operation procedures, violations, and consequences. SMP, a computer algebra (not computation) program from Inference Corp., can differentiate and integrate most mathematical expressions, solve linear and nonlinear equations, and perform matrix and tensor algebra.

A number of developing AI programs offer opinions about business. Among them are AI systems from Syntelligence (Menlo Park, California) that advise underwriters at commercial insurance companies about various aspects of customer risks and premiums. At Brattle Research of Boston, programs have opinions about investment portfolio management. Culver City, California's Inference Corp. is developing programs that offer opinions about banking.

Some AI goals at Applied Expert Systems (APEX in Cambridge, Massachusetts) are programs that examine and offer opinions about provisions in proposed contracts. ISIS, a job shop scheduling expert system from Carnegie–Mellon University and Westinghouse Electric Corp., generates factory schedules by weighing the trade-offs and juggling the constraints imposed by the large numbers of people and departments that could impact a factory schedule.

In natural language, the meanings of words such as "manager," "employee," and "drill bit" are symbolic concepts. Language is a symbolic activity and the natural-language systems that process these symbols reason about the symbols and relate them to their meanings.

Computer vision systems need to understand both symbolic concepts and patterns. For example, a computer vision system might glean patterns of a screwdriver and screw from TV camera pictures and represent them as photographic dots (pixels) on a screen. The concept of a screwdriver and screw, however, is represented symbolically, just as it is in expert systems.

By integrating this photographic and expert system information, as well as reasoning strategies, vision systems can analyze a scene and decide if objects meet inspection standards and quality control criteria, or move a robot to the proper location to grasp an automobile part. Currently, however, most vision system analyses use numeric and pattern-recognition techniques, and few have any AI content.

WHY WORD PROCESSING IS NOT SYMBOLIC

Some people might argue that word-processing programs and databases handle textual as well as numeric information and therefore process symbols. Word-processing programs manipulate words. A database might contain employee or inventory information in textual form. So why aren't word-processing programs, databases, and database management systems that manipulate words and database information equivalent to the symbolic reasoning capabilities that characterize AI technology?

One answer is that word-processing programs do not see characters that make up words as characters. Instead, they see each character as an equivalent code number (called ASCII code value). For example, upper case "A" equals ASCII code 65 and lower case "d" equals ASCII 100 (Figure 1-6).

Why Word Processing Is Not Symbolic

ASCII value	Character	ASCII value	Character	ASCII value	Character	ASCII value	Character
000	(null)	045	−	073	I	101	e
007	(beep)	046	.	074	J	102	f
009	(tab)	047	/	075	K	103	g
010	(line feed)	048	0	076	L	104	h
011	(home)	049	1	077	M	105	i
012	(form feed)	050	2	078	N	106	j
013	(carriage return)	051	3	079	O	107	k
024	↑	052	4	080	P	108	l
025	↓	053	5	081	Q	109	m
026	→	054	6	082	R	110	n
027	←	055	7	083	S	111	o
028	(cursor right)	056	8	084	T	112	p
029	(cursor left)	057	9	085	U	113	q
030	(cursor up)	058	:	086	V	114	r
031	(cursor down)	059	;	087	W	115	s
032	(space)	060	<	088	X	116	t
033	!	061	=	089	Y	117	u
034	"	062	>	090	Z	118	v
035	#	063	?	091	[	119	w
036	$	064	@	092	\	120	x
037	%	065	A	093	]	121	y
038	&	066	B	094	≙	122	z
039	'	067	C	095	.	123	{
040	(	068	D	096	`	124	!
041	)	069	E	097	a	123	}
042	*	070	F	098	b	126	~
043	+	071	G	099	c		
044	,	072	H	100	d		

Figure 1-6 Partial table of 8-bit ASCII codes

The ASCII codes, representing characters, are strung together to form words. But word-processing programs do not represent or understand the relationships between words. They do not even represent or understand the relationship of words to a paragraph. As a person types, a word-processing program stores the ASCII values of all the typed characters into arrays. Special ASCII code numbers mark the end of a document file. As such, a word processor sees a document mostly as a bunch of numbers. In addition, typical word-processing operations, such as search for a certain character and replace it with another, is a clever but number-crunching operation where the program merely matches and substitutes one number for another. Hence word-processing programs are mostly numerically oriented programs.

For their part, while databases contain textual information, the actual processing and manipulation involved in database management operations, such as adding payroll information together, are numerically or computationally oriented. As far as handling the textual information is concerned, database systems mostly store and retrieve that information.

The process of locating the database information in computer memory uses a system of addresses whereby each piece of data, such as employee name, has its own address

Information	=	Collection of separate words or characters
Knowledge	=	· Interconnection of words · Structure present · Relationships indicated

Figure 1-7 The difference between information and knowledge is in the relationships represented between parts in a program.

in memory. The addresses are just plain numbers. Therefore, the processing of the information is numeric.

AI programs differ from conventional programs in that they contain knowledge as well as information. The difference is that in a program that contains knowledge, the information, such as words, data, patterns, or something else, are interconnected and related. The interconnections, which form various structures, are used to represent relationships. Relationships, in turn, are related to what human beings interpret as meaning, or knowledge (Figure 1-7).

Of course, it is true that all computer programs, AI or otherwise, eventually boil down to bits and bytes in memory. However, unlike with conventional programs, both AI users and programmers are far removed from the need to handle these bits and bytes or the addresses they represent. In AI programs, the location of data in memory is handled by the programming language. The programmers work with symbolic concepts, or with interconnected words that represent some relationship or concept that implies meaning. The ability of programmers and programs to work with these symbolic concepts, or interrelated words, makes a vast difference in the type of program that can be written and the types of tasks the program can perform.

EMINENT DOMAINS

AI programs, based on symbolic processing, are finding their way into real systems in a variety of problem areas (Figure 1-8). For the manager or engineer, an understanding of these systems is important because their concepts can be copied and applied to similar problems.

Successful AI systems that are transferable to different problem domains fall into several general categories. These include configuration, design, diagnosis, interpretation, analysis, planning, scheduling, intelligent interfaces, database intermediaries, natural language, vision, and automatic programming (Figure 1-9).

Computer configuration programs select and arrange components for computer systems. They were among the first commercial expert systems. In fact, they proved so successful that computer configuration expert systems are currently in use or under development by almost every large computer manufacturer in the United States.

Design systems perform planning or layout of an object or system to meet specified requirements, in addition to evaluating the consequences of design decisions. Computer configuration systems are actually a simple type of design problem. Electronics firms hope to incorporate artificial intelligence techniques into much more complex design systems to design the next generation of chips. Engineers hope to use similar systems to

Eminent Domains

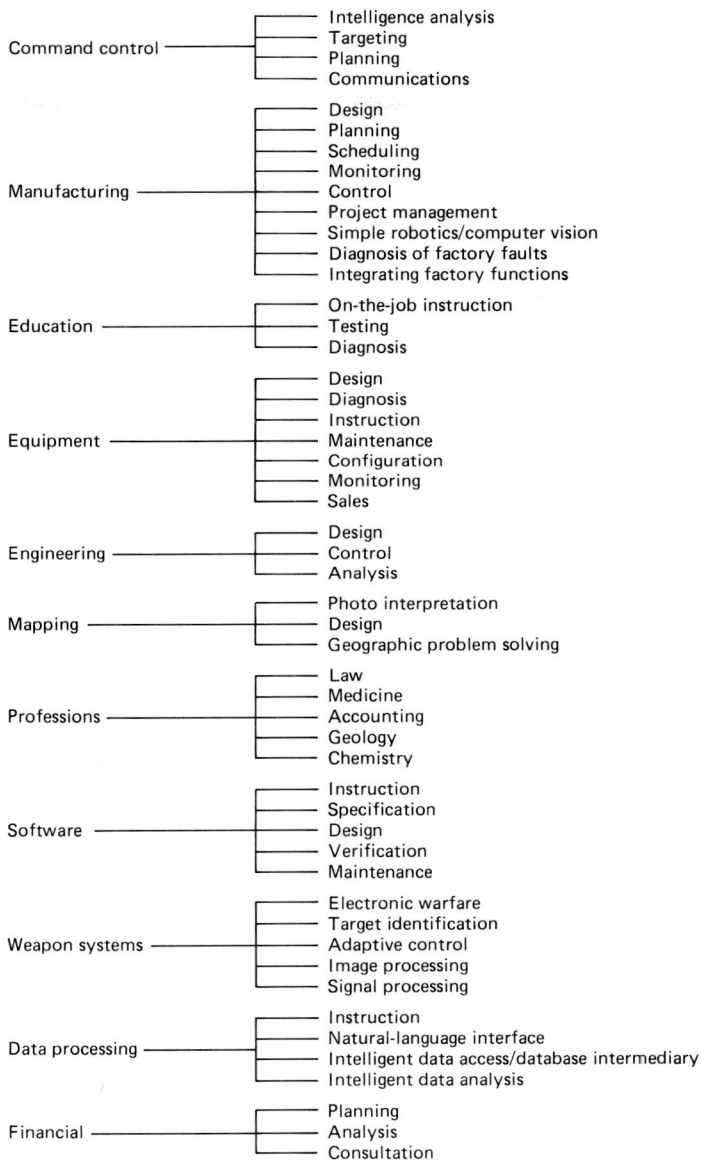

Figure 1-8 Artificial intelligence application areas

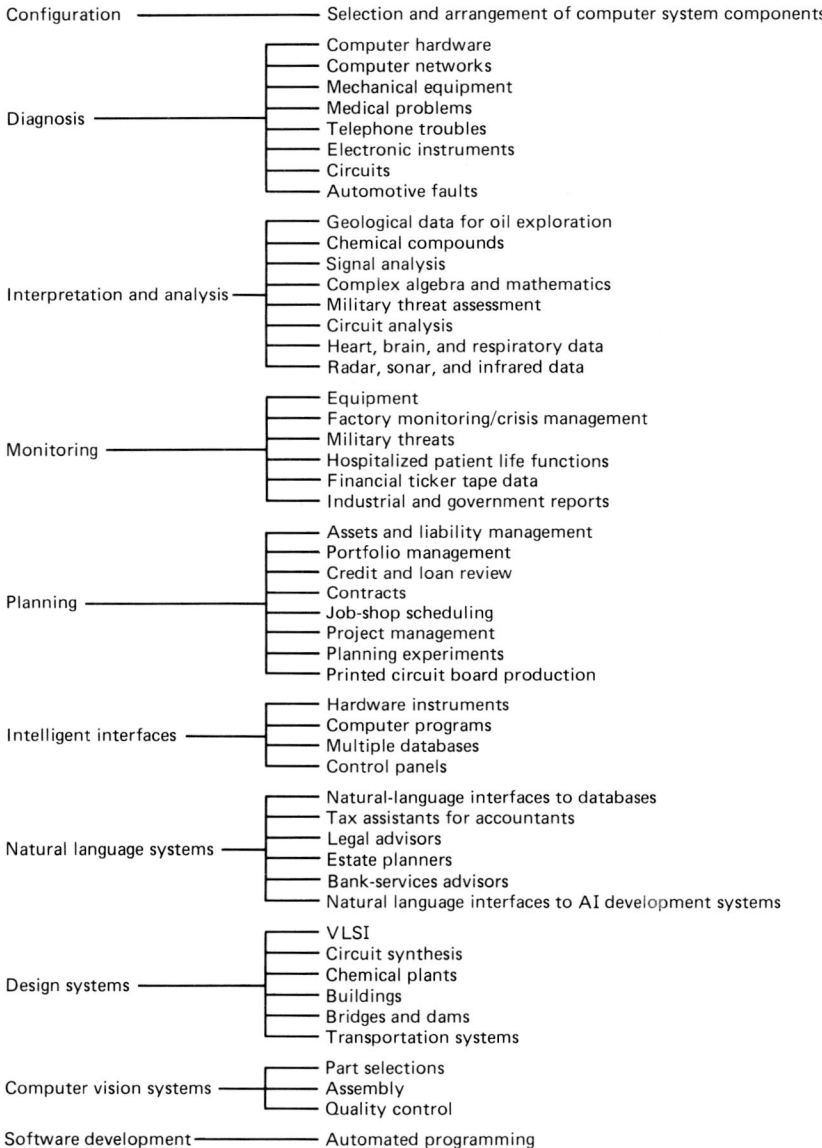

Figure 1-9 Commercial AI applications

design systems and structures, such as chemical plants, buildings, bridges, dams, and transportation systems and circuits.

Design systems generally perform some system design themselves and check the design performed by engineers for potential problems. This is particularly useful in the design of large systems, where it is easy to forget the reasons for some design decisions and difficult to evaluate a change in part of a design.

Diagnostic systems that incorporate AI technology include expert systems that apply similar techniques to diagnose different types of problems. For example, expert systems in use in the field perform diagnosis of mechanical equipment, computer networks, medical problems, telephone troubles, and factory systems.

Interpretation and analysis systems sift through and make sense out of reams of data. The data to be interpreted may be received, in the form of graphs that resemble electrocardiograms, as the result of electrical or acoustical signals transmitted, nuclear bombardment, infrared, radar, or sonar scans, or magnetic fields. Interpretative expert systems help experts interpret these data to infer diverse features such as underground geological structure, arrangement of atoms in compounds, or the presence of threatening objects on land, sea, or air.

Analysis systems also evaluate data to help assess earthquake damage for structures, perform military threat assessment, tactical targeting, monitor equipment, monitor factories, and mathematically manipulate and symbolically solve algebraic problems. In addition to their monitoring functions, analysis systems frequently must be able to make a critical judgment in a very short time to avoid a potential disaster. Such crisis management systems are likely to be found, for example, in nuclear power and process control plants.

Planning systems are closely related to analysis systems. Expert planning systems are found in the financial, industrial, and scientific arenas. There, they use knowledge acquired from interviewing experts in the field to perform assets and liabilities management, portfolio management, financial planning services, credit loan review, job shop scheduling, project and organization management, and planning of molecular genetics experiments.

Intelligent interfaces are AI-based computer programs that insulate users from complex, difficult-to-use hardware or software. Unfortunately, most hardware and software systems, especially complex ones, are not blessed with friendly interfaces. As a result, useful systems often become less useful because they require an expert with detailed knowledge of the system to operate it properly.

Experts, in any field, are scarce. Intelligent interfaces to the unfriendly system make them easier to use by the nonexpert. For example, intelligent interfaces make complex laboratory instruments accessible to a broader group of scientists because they perform some of the chores necessary to use or to tune the instruments.

Database intermediaries are expert systems that sit between users and database management systems and interface to one or more databases. Their job is to intercept database information requests from users or programs. Then they use their knowledge of what is contained in one or more databases and what is the best way to search them to generate intelligent strategies to get information out of the databases.

Searching a database may be a difficult task, especially if more than one database is involved. Upon receiving a request for database information from a user, the expert intermediary would not only choose which database to search. It also might use its database knowledge to retrieve information from one database to use subsequently as a key to retrieve information from another.

Natural-language interfaces act as front ends to database management systems. The front ends accept users' queries in users' natural language, English or otherwise, and translate them into the formal, more difficult-to-learn database query language. Currently, almost every database company in the United States is working on natural-language front ends to databases because end users and office managers are pushing for them.

Computerized vision systems can guide robots to select parts, drill holes, spray paint, or spot weld. Without the vision system, robots must be carefully programmed to perform these jobs in an exactly specified position. Moreover, the robots must be constantly reprogrammed as their parts get out of line. There is no leeway for error on either the robot's or manipulated objects' parts.

If the robot has even a simple vision system, it becomes an intelligent and adaptive machine because it can identify a piece, locate it, adjust itself for different positions, and then perform manipulations.

Quality control and visual inspection are other important areas for computer vision systems. Some vision inspection systems merely check parts as they pass by on a conveyer belt. When checking these parts, they ensure, for example, that the parts are correct ones; are not broken, chipped, or bent; and have four holes drilled in the correct place.

Expert programmer systems are under development to create AI programs to automate the creation of other programs. Current automatic-programming systems handle only very simple and narrow problem domains, such as database retrieval or update. In the near future, it will be possible to combine traditional programming with AI techniques such as natural-language and expert system capabilities to create moderately complex programs that reliably meet specifications.

AI MISCONCEPTIONS CORRECTED

A number of misconceptions surround the field of AI, possibly because commercial AI is still young and not personally known to most people. Here is the real story about some of these misconceptions.

- Contrary to what many people think, AI is not a black art. Instead, it is a software technique which is very "do-able" provided that it is applied to the appropriate problem.
- AI systems provide their economic leverage by performing the types of tasks that occupy a high percentage of highly paid people's time, rather than by handling "far-out" tasks which are a figment of science fiction. In fact, AI systems cannot perform tasks or solve problems that human beings do not know how to do.
- AI systems do not replace people. They augment them.

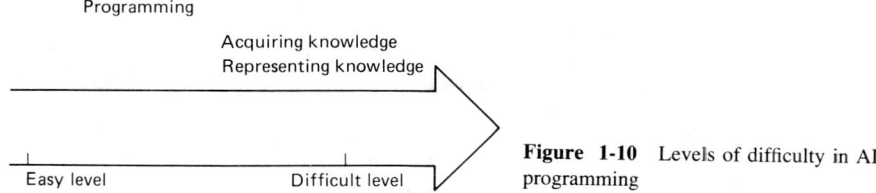

Figure 1-10 Levels of difficulty in AI programming

AI IS A SOFTWARE TECHNIQUE WHICH IS DO-ABLE: Although programming is still considered an art, AI techniques are not only do-able, but programming is the simplest part of creating most AI applications. The more difficult task is finding some way to represent knowledge in a computer program (see Figure 1-10). If the AI program is an expert system, an equally difficult task is getting the knowledge from an expert in the first place.

The latter task—acquiring the knowledge to represent in the program—in many respects is not a technical task. Often, it requires more diplomatic than technical skill, some knowledge of cognitive psychology, and an ability to get along with people, talk to them, draw them out (Figure 1-11).

It turns out, in fact, that once many of the programming techniques are explained, many people feel that they have been duped by the name "artificial intelligence." This is an unfortunate feeling because, in reality, expert systems can emulate experts such as doctors, geophysicists, and computer and locomotive equipment diagnosticians. Such experts are paid high salaries for reading and interpreting electrocardiograms or oil-well logs (graphs of seismic data that help determine the presence of oil), or for diagnosing equipment malfunctions.

Their compensations are considered to be deserved because the human experts think, reason, and call on knowledge that they have diligently acquired over time in order

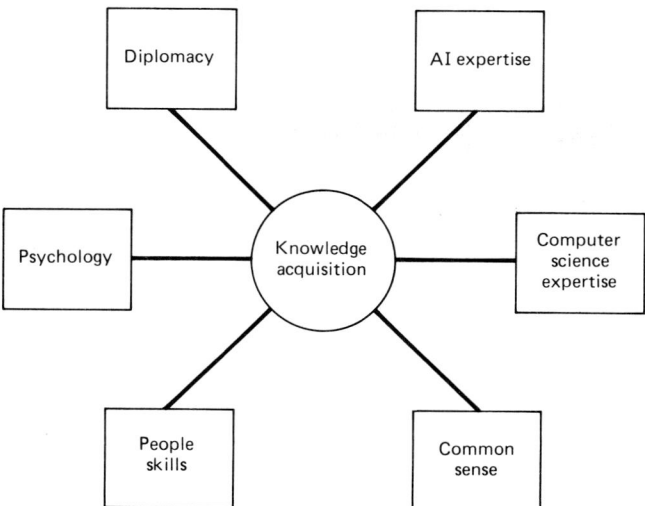

Figure 1-11 Knowledge acquisition relies on many skills

to perform their interpretative and diagnostic duties. In the minds of many people, however, the remuneration is further considered deserved because of a human foible known as the "witch-doctor" syndrome. This syndrome takes the view that since no one knows how human beings think or reason, the human experts must be performing truly intelligent activities. Are these activities any less intelligent when incorporated into computer programs just because we understand their techniques?

The answer to the question is yes, if the populace's general attitudes are to be believed. People view a lot of behavior as intelligent if it is mysterious. But once they understand the elegant algorithms underlying this behavior so that the mystery is stripped away, it is questionable whether they still want to call the behavior intelligent or not.

In fact, people often think of intelligent behavior as encompassing the things for which they do not have a good explanation. This view of intelligence affects the general view of AI. AI ideas are subconsciously defined by many as bizarre, flaky, harebrained, and questionable ideas at the forefront of technology. But what is radical AI today is apt to become obvious tomorrow and find its way into the computer systems after that. When that happens, the boundary of AI shifts. Yesterday's AI then becomes something else—ordinary computer functionality—but not intelligent (Figure 1-12).

AI SYSTEMS PERFORM TASKS THAT OCCUPY A HIGH PERCENTAGE OF HIGHLY PAID PEOPLE'S TIME: As mentioned, unlike conventional programs which perform computation or arithmetic operations, AI programs manipulate nonnumeric quantities, such as symbols, concepts, and ideas. Computational processing is indeed a necessity for most companies and organizations to carry on their activities today. However, most of what people do in their daily business lives is symbolic- rather than numeric-oriented.

For example, a visit to an accounting firm or the back office of a bank—organizations that deal primarily with numbers—reveals that from a percentage point of view, very little information that these organizations deal with is actually handled numerically. Instead, aside from communicating with people, highly paid employees spend most of their time reasoning, understanding, discussing, and making judgments about concepts, subjective issues, and organizational structure—all symbolic ideas. For example, both decision makers and workers constantly need to make judgments in their jobs.

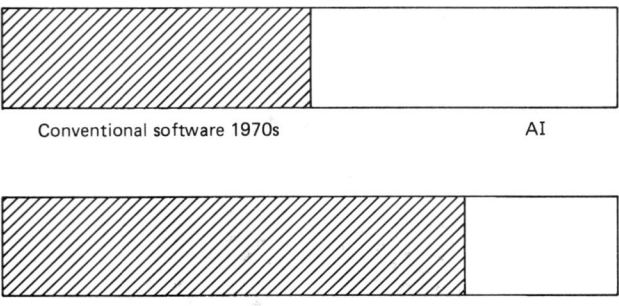

Figure 1-12 The shifting AI theme

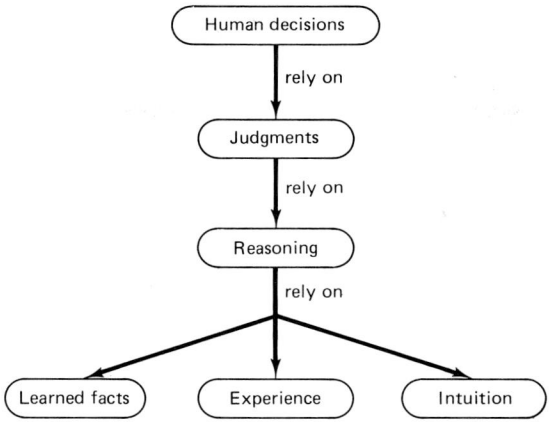

Figure 1-13 Human decisions rely on heuristics

To make these judgments, they rely on reasoning. Their reasoning, in turn, is based on learned facts, experience, and intuition, which collectively are called heuristics (Figure 1-13).

True, both the accounting firm and bank most likely use electronic spreadsheets—a prime example of numeric-oriented processing. They also use computerized decision support programs which were formulated originally on mathematical models, and they perform various kinds of regression analysis. These techniques, however, deal with only a small set of the world's problems.

An AI program's strength is its ability to solve the more common problems that involve symbols and symbolic and conceptual ideas. In fact, just the ability to deal with symbols (names, for example) has been associated with knowledge, strength, and power throughout the known history of life on earth. For example, members of some primitive societies will not tell strangers their names because they believe that to know the names of objects is also to have power and dominance over them. Similarly, some societies change the names of dying persons or will not tell the names of infants (until they have passed the critical stage of mortality) to confuse the angel of death. And the Bible tells us that one of Adam's first jobs was to name all the animals, including himself—a task which, according to Biblical commentators, implies recognizing the nature of the animals, separating them by species, and clarifying which are fit to mate with one another. These are symbolic processing activities which require superior intellect and provide much more information and power than simply counting the animals (although the human beings were told to be fruitful and multiply).

These symbolic activities require the ability to reason about causality, which implies the ability to discern relationships between objects, concepts, and ideas. The humanlike ability to discern relationships is what allows an AI system to relate a set of symptoms to equipment failure or medical diagnosis, plan the best way to configure a computer system, or interpret and analyze a collection of data, understand language ambiguities—in short, to perform activities thought to require human intelligence.

By their nature, computationally oriented programs are not up to solving these everyday, symbolic types of problems. As will be seen, symbolically oriented AI programs can handle a much broader range of problems than can numerically oriented computer applications. In that sense, it is far more suited to the operations that people in business, industrial, and scientific organizations constantly deal with.

AI SYSTEMS DO NOT REPLACE PEOPLE: Although current, practical AI systems can emulate intelligent behavior, they emulate only a shallow imitation of intelligence. True, AI systems can see, understand English, and apply knowledge to some problems and come up with a solution. But, unlike people, vision systems can only see simple scenes under controlled lighting conditions where objects in the field of vision do not overlap. They cannot use knowledge of situations, environments, or experience to figure out what an object is. Natural-language systems can only understand or answer queries about a specifically designed, narrow domain of knowledge, such as a particular database or database application. And expert systems cannot give a solution for problems that cannot be done by human beings.

What AI systems can do well is to augment people. Vision systems, for example, add humanlike seeing capabilities to robotic systems that operate in environments that are inhospitable to people. These environments include radiation and very cold environments, where people cannot or do not want to work, and in "clean room" environments such as in VLSI inspection areas of chip fabrication plants, where it is difficult for people to achieve the desired sterility.

Natural-languages systems enable executives and managers who need timely access to a database to avoid having to learn a formal query language. It turns out that even the simplest, English-like language to query a database still requires users to learn and remember stylized commands. Furthermore, some queries are quite complex. Then it often happens that the manager moves to another department which uses a different query language, and the learning process must begin again.

For their part, expert systems do not replace experts. Instead, expert system developers clone an expert in some specific problem area and then make that expert available to other experts to help them improve their work.

In fact, it is very premature, and perhaps presumptuous, to think that machines that emulate human behavior can ever take the place of people. Human experts are good at intuitively leaping to conclusions about hypotheses. For example, as doctors examine patients, they perceive subtle signs and symptoms that remind them of a case they saw 10 years ago. For them, these recollections point in the direction of a diagnosis.

No machine can perceive and diagnose in this manner. Machines do not have "gut" feelings, nor can they substitute for warm bodies needed to perform work. What expert systems do well, however, is to follow an expert's line of reasoning systematically to ensure that reasonable hypotheses have not been overlooked. Or they check to see whether or not the expert's intuition is consistent with the actual evidence. As part of this checking procedure, many expert systems perform their analyses at the same time as the experts and arrive at their answers before the expert does.

For these analyses, expert systems apply encoded knowledge provided by an actual expert. Experts then use the knowledge-based system as an advisor and consultant to help them diagnose, plan, and analyze, and to speed up and reinforce their own decisions.

With the help of these advisors and consultants, experts can work at more of their potential capabilities. Several industry figures indicate that those experts who normally work at a level of 75 percent of what it is humanly possible to do can raise their expertise to the 85 percent level; those who work at the 85 percent level can up their capabilities to 90 percent; and those top experts who work at the 90 percent level can reach the 92 percent mark.

Although these gains in expertise may appear small by some standards, they save companies millions of dollars. With these gains, companies can also provide better answers and analyses for the same money it cost them using traditional means, and therefore they can compete more effectively. Better answers and analyses help ensure more satisfied customers. They also help prevent unnecessary work as the result of misdiagnosis of equipment faults.

Schlumberger has converted the knowledge and experience of its oil well experts into an expert system called the Dipmeter Advisor. The Dipmeter Advisor interprets seismic data to construct a picture of subterranean geology to determine with some certainty if oil is present. Oil-well experts normally perform these seismic data interpretations manually at the drilling site. These field interpreters are trained as geologists and geophysicists. Only a small number of them exist in the first place. In addition, many of the most accurate and reliable interpreters have 30 years' experience and are about to retire.

The geological and geophysical experts that perform the data interpretation procedures manually are learning to use the Dipmeter Advisor. The Dipmeter Advisor will not replace these experts. But the expert system will augment their capabilities, improve their ability to interpret data, and enable them to give better answers, predictions, and recommendations about the presence of oil and oil-drilling procedures.

Similarly, CATS-1 (Computer Aided Trouble Shooting), General Electric's expert system for locomotive troubleshooting, does not replace GE's human experts who diagnose locomotive faults. But as happens in so many industries, the best troubleshooters, computer configurers, engineers, and business workers tend to be promoted, especially as they gain experience, to jobs where they no longer perform the functions for which they showed great talent.

GE developed its locomotive troubleshooting expert system because too many technicians in its repair shops were tying up a million dollars worth of gear by scheduling locomotives with minor problems for major overhaul. So the firm captured the expertise of one of its most experienced troubleshooters in CATS-1.

The GE mechanics still must go through the routine rigamarole necessary to check out symptoms and suspected faults. But now they can consult with a clone of a GE expert locomotive diagnostician and gain some of the benefits of his experience (Figure 1-14). As is the case with the oil-well data interpreters, the locomotive mechanics can now provide a better, more accurate, more reliable diagnosis.

There is an endless list of experts, skilled workers, and companies who have lots to gain from expert systems that can provide the advisory and consulting services of an experienced expert, much as CATS-1 and the Dipmeter Advisor does. For example, anyone who has had difficulty finding a good automobile mechanic can well imagine the benefits of an on-premises expert advisor and consultant to an automotive service department, ga-

Figure 1-14 GE mechanics can consult with an expert system to help diagnose locomotive faults (General Electric)

rage owner and mechanic, and automobile owner. Expert system benefits become important, even for a first-class automobile mechanic who runs into problems with automobile electrical work which often requires a different type of expertise.

Before such applications can become widespread, however, two ingredients must become plentiful: people to write the AI software and affordable computers that can run the AI software. AI people are currently a scant resource. Many more people who can develop expert systems must be initiated into the AI field. Tools to develop these systems will help attract potential developers, as well as speed up the expert system development process.

But sufficient people are not the whole story. Most AI applications are developed on specialized computers designed to execute the Lisp or Prolog programming languages fast and to facilitate AI program development. Lisp is a symbolic programming language suited to developing AI applications. Prolog is based on formal logic.

AI applications that simulate human behavior tend to be quite large and complex. Therefore, in addition to Lisp, these specialized Lisp-execution machines feature an entire application development environment, replete with powerful programming tools, networking, high-resolution graphics, and overlapping windows (Figure 1-15).

Although Lisp machine environments are ideal for the development of AI applications, they are currently too expensive to place at many business sites. However, like most hardware and electronic equipment, as AI becomes popular, the volume of Lisp ma-

Figure 1-15 Specialized Lisp machines feature a graphical application development environment (Xerox Corp.)

chines sold increases and the purchase price decreases. In addition, there is a move underfoot to convert many AI applications, once developed, to a form that can run on standard computers found in typical business environments. Standard computers are less expensive and, unlike Lisp machines, operate in a manner that most business personnel find familiar.

Expert systems provide leverage for experts. Replacing them is a different ballgame. To replace people, expert systems need many more people capabilities. In particular, they must be able to learn and to reason from first principles.

Currently, expert systems are limited to capturing and reasoning about knowledge only in a specific, narrow domain. If a new event occurs that the expert system has not seen before, the expert system is stymied because it does not know about that event. It can infer some new information, but only based on the knowledge that has been encoded into it. In order to include the ability to handle the new event, it is generally necessary for human beings to extend the expert system by adding new knowledge.

In contrast, when doctors, for example, encounter conflicting symptoms that do not fit standard textbook cases, they fall back on deeper conceptual knowledge of how the body's physiological and enzyme systems work. In other words, when doctors recognize that something is new or unusual, they can go back to first principles and reason from previously learned information. If their reasoning is successful, they add the newly learned information to their knowledge bases.

The ability to do this highly original, creative thinking, based on underlying conceptual knowledge of a domain, is characteristically human. There is ongoing work to develop programs that likewise learn and reason from first principles. For example, with an eye to improving its wafer production, Fairchild is developing a consultant system that learns new rules about the wafer-fabrication process by deriving them from first principles. Wafers are the circular slices of polished silicon that are the basis for semiconductor chip manufacture. Atari would like to make its fantasy games more exciting with the help of artifically intelligent "agents" that learn the players' idiosyncrasies and synthesize game responses accordingly. General Telephone and Electronics hopes to use AI-based telecommunications software that learns from experience how to manage itself, to ensure reliability and coordination of its increasingly more complicated and remotely located telecommunications network. Several AI computer programs developed at MIT learn by past precedent. A program developed at Carnegie–Mellon University can discover knowledge in the same way as many scientists and, indeed, given the same data the scientists had available have rediscovered some of the great laws of science.

The maturity and availability of such learning programs, which might replace human beings, is premature. In fact, the current generation of expert systems is still a long way from knowing the best way to represent knowledge in a computer program or even to acquire that knowledge. Knowledge acquisition is still a very labor intensive activity. Because AI is so labor intensive, it is not likely to be the basis of an economic revolution.

AI clearly has, however, a lot of economic potential. As will be discussed in this book, there are numerous applications for business, sciences, and industry, particularly in analytic, diagnostic, and planning areas that are amenable to the limited capabilities of the current AI computer vision, natural-language, and expert systems. Using AI techniques to solve these applications should provide an evolving profitable industry for years to come.

AI Trends and Applications

CHAPTER 2

Artificial intelligence has always had an attraction and appeal for people who have dreamed of building machines that think. Toward that goal, in the early nineteenth century, a chess playing machine was presented to the public. It turned out, however, that rather than AI, the intelligence was supplied by a midget inside a large machine-like box.

When the Eniac computer was created during World War II, followed by the Maniac and then other digital computers, several researchers revived the idea of machines that think—without, however, defining what it means for a machine to think. Bypassing this still unanswered question, the British mathematician/scientist Alan Turing devised a test that has come to be know as the Turing test. It is reminiscent of the story of "The Lady or the Tiger."

In this test, a person is required to communicate with a "thing" behind a closed door. The person is unaware of whether the "thing" is a human being or a machine. A typewriter outside the closed door provides the only means of communications. Through the typewriter, the person can ask any questions of the thing, which also responds through the typewriter. The Turing test requires the person to identify, after some period of interrogation, whether the "thing" is a human being or a machine.

As Turing points out in his paper "Can a Machine Think?", which discusses the feasibility of programming a machine to think, any program that deceives a person into believing that a machine is a human being requires more than just knowledge and reasoning capabilities (Turing, 1950; discussed further in Beckman, 1981). For example, to deceive human interrogators, the machine would have to make periodic errors since human beings are not infallible. Also, it would need to know how much time to delay before returning an answer, as well as when to throw up its hands and claim ignorance. The machine would even need to know when to refuse to answer a question by feigning a lack of taste for, say, certain art forms about which the question is predicated. And so on.

In 1956, John McCarthy convened a 10-scientist conference at Dartmouth College to devise the techniques necessary to produce intelligent computer programs, and thus thinking machines. From this meeting, the present field of AI emerged.

In those early days, optimistic AI experts first defining the field promised the moon and the stars, and needless to say, could not deliver them. Among the AI goals then was a program that could mimic the full range of human problem-solving abilities—a kind of superman, if you will. One of the earliest and best known AI programs, called the General Problem Solver (GPS), was written by Allen Newell and Herbert Simon of Carnegie–Mellon University and J. Clifford Shaw of the Rand Corp. GPS, the basis of most AI programs today, views problems to be solved in terms of a current situation and a desired goal. Its underlying problem solving strategy, known as "means–end" analysis, was to reach a goal (solution) by defining and selecting steps that would reduce the difference between the current and goal states (Figure 2-1).

Alas, the dream failed miserably. Except for the simplest cases, the generalized AI programs were overwhelmed by the complexity of the problems and the number of possible paths between the current and goal states.

Another tarnished dream was the AI program that would be able to translate accurately any language into any other. The stories say that when this language program, overwhelmed by language subtleties, translated the statement "THE SPIRIT IS WILLING, BUT THE FLESH IS WEAK," into Russian and back into English, the translated version came out as "THE WINE IS GOOD, BUT THE MEAT IS ROTTEN."

From the heights of hope and optimism, artifical intelligence plunged into an era of disillusionment. Labeled a useless discipline and esoteric science (or art), companies by and large ignored the field. AI progress was left to a few universities and research groups mostly supported by government grants.

Out of these years of obscurity came a number of practical and popular by-products of the quest for intelligent machines. These include time-sharing computer systems, graphic displays, word processing, computer-aided design techniques, and the modern, visually exciting computer interfaces adorned with windows, mice, pop-up menus, and icons. During these dark ages, a great deal was learned and the groundwork was laid to make AI successful. Based on the new knowledge, a number of prototype AI systems were built and tested. To accomplish this system building, the AI community came up with a development environment which is the most productive environment for producing any type of complex software program.

Only in the 1980s did AI tentatively emerge from the depths of obscurity, being very careful this time about what it promises. And the times they have a-changed from the early faddish days.

For the first time in the history of AI, affordable hardware with large enough memories is available to support AI systems. AI developers have learned not to expect perfection. Practical AI systems have been successfully demonstrated. Some are customized systems for in-house use where they were developed. A newer trend is to develop off-the-shelf AI systems for sale.

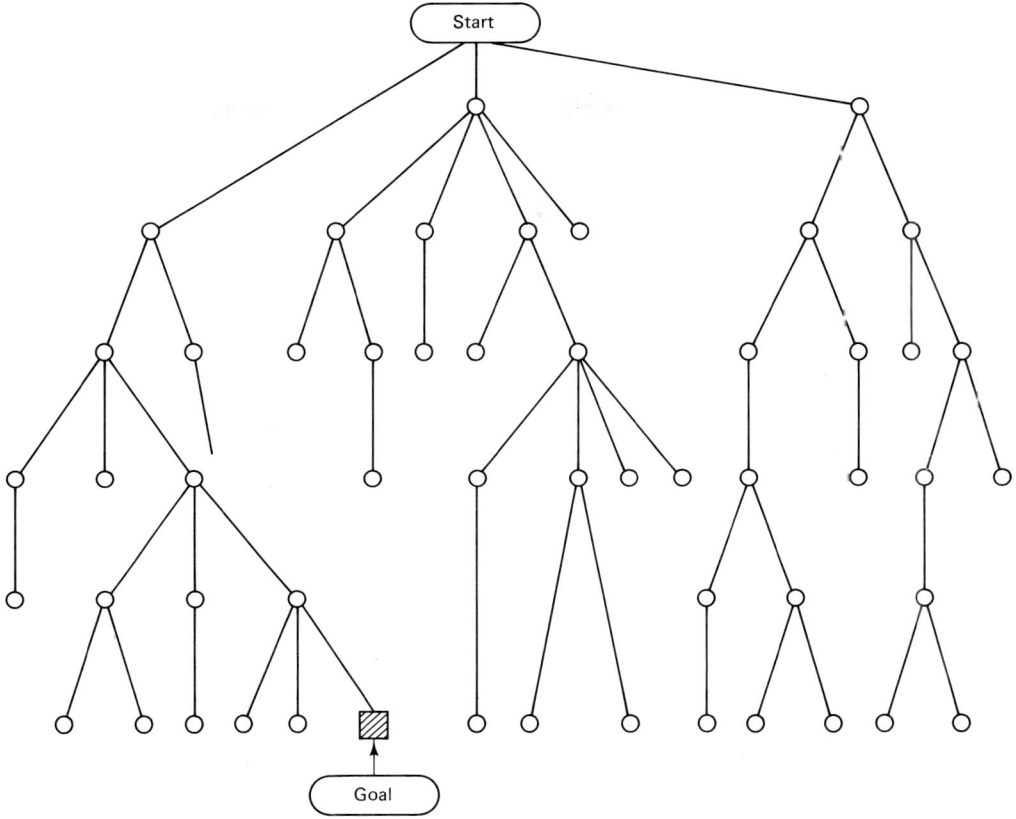

Figure 2-1 The means-end analysis strategy attempts to reach a goal by defining and selecting steps that will reduce the difference between the current and goal states.

Application development tools have been introduced to ease both AI system development and technology transfer. No longer need AI be the province and possession of a select few brainy scientists. The time is ripe for that technology transfer because AI is now appearing in the wake of programs such as VisiCalc, which prepared previously computer-naive users for the next wave of technology.

For all these reasons, industry analysts and AI suppliers agree that the commercial AI field will grow explosively and rival that of the data-processing industry. The fastest commercial AI growth for any market segment is expected to be in expert systems, although the largest magnitude increase in dollars will be in the natural-language interface area. Military systems are estimated to consume the largest share of the early AI market, but it is difficult to tell how large the military market is because military AI expenditures are generally embedded in a comprehensive contract. Market experts estimate, however, that quantification of the military AI figure would reveal that the level of AI-based software and systems in the military establishment is multiple orders of magnitude (possible 8 to 10 times) higher than that in the commercial marketplace. Venture capitalists and investment and market analysts expect that as AI catches on, industrial and business-oriented AI systems will dominate the AI market.

AI is already finding its way into real systems in a variety of problem areas. Troubleshooting and data interpretation applications are among the pioneer commercial AI systems. Other AI programs include planning, scheduling, and design systems; intelligent interfaces for complex equipment; database intermediaries that efficiently retrieve information from multiple databases; and natural-language systems. Among the last fields to be penetrated by AI are vision, speech, VLSI, and circuit design. The delay is partly due to complexity of these applications. A further difficulty that affects many areas of VLSI is the pattern recognition required. For example, VLSI design expert systems exist, but they cannot pack their designs into minimal space as well as human beings can, nor can they do their designs well enough to be competitive.

AI systems are up and running, or under development, in factories, computer manufacturing organizations; the aerospace, automotive, power, and petrochemical industries; financial, insurance, medical, scientific, and educational institutions; and government agencies. The least AI information is known, however, about the largest early AI user, the military. The major AI challenge for the military is in the areas of signal and image processing. The military tries to figure out, from radar, sonar, or infrared scans and photographs, just what is likely to be happening either on land, sea, or in the air.

For example, military experts might suspect a foreign nuclear submarine. In a very short time period, they must figure out from photographs and sonar scans of the ocean surface and underwater just what is likely to be going on. Does the submarine exist and, if so, where exactly is it?

In one technique used for detecting submarines, pilots fly an aircraft over the surface of the ocean. Of course, the surface of the ocean usually has a lot of waves. Fast submarines, even if they are a couple of hundred feet below, create a shock-wave effect as they travel. Russian nuclear submarines, for example, can travel at 50 or 60 knots under water. They produce a shock wave that causes some modulations on the ocean's surface waves.

These modulations to the ocean waves are imperceptible to the eye. But signal-processing and image-processing equipment can detect them after going through a complex series of image enhancement steps. The image enhancement steps are dictated, in part, by the image-processing system's knowledge about what basic waveforms are involved in the creation of a complex ocean wave pattern and what sort of wave shapes can be changed by objects moving under the water, and in part by what does not look right in terms of the system's understanding of what a wave pattern ought to look like. The challenge is to use this knowledge to determine if somewhere, built within this pattern, is the characteristic shock-wave effect caused by the submarine and to generate some analysis of what is under the water, how fast is it going, and in what direction.

This analysis requires signal-processing capabilities to recognize such a large variety of wave patterns that the image analysis system really needs to include AI capabilities to perform the analysis reliably and efficiently.

What an AI program actually does is to go down a series of multiple decision paths to finally arrive at an answer. Following road maps when traveling has this flavor since roads often fork, with only one road being the shortest way to a destination.

Unfortunately, with complex applications such as image analysis, as with more complex games such as chess, the number of potential paths through the tree of possible decisions (called the solution search space) is so great that an ordinary algorithmic computer strategy to investigate all the paths would take the fastest computer centuries. For such programs, more intelligent methods of choosing an appropriate path must be considered. The intelligent aspects of many AI programs has a lot to do with picking which paths are more likely than others to be appropriate.

Similar searches through decision trees are used in medicine, equipment diagnosis, computer configuration, and assets and liability management. In medicine, for example, an AI program is presented with a group of symptoms, followed by a series of diagnoses correlating these symptoms. The program then figures out that for somebody with a particular type of symptom and a particular circumstance, a certain set of diagnoses are most likely. Based on this likelihood, the program figures out the appropriate recommended next test for the patient. It then looks for the results of that test to refine its diagnosis further.

AI GOOD FOR NON-AI TASKS

It is not just AI applications like expert systems, natural-language systems, and computer vision systems that have commercial uses. The tools and techniques that are used to build AI applications also lend themselves to building applications that have nothing to do with AI. In particular, AI tools and techniques are suitable for problems that are ill-specified and ill-understood because they (the tools) are designed to allow programmers to change their minds. Consequently, they allow exploration of programming strategies.

An exploratory program construction environment that supports mind changing is necessary to build AI systems because AI systems solve problems that are, by definition, uncertain and not well defined. For example, an AI system might advise about ways to maximize a company's net profit margin or play a game of chess. But who knows the best way to maximize a company's net profit margin or the best strategy to get an opponent's king in checkmate? And how should an AI system handle problems that have many correct answers?

Human experts solve such problems by intuition which AI experts can encode in expert systems. To write a program to solve problems that are uncertain and ill-defined to begin with, by the technique of "gut" feelings and intuition, AI system developers need an environment that is easy to work with, easy to change, and which supports the exploration of strategies and ideas.

This is opposite to the ideas of classical software engineering. In software engineering contractors or end users decide what they want and communicate their requirements to software engineers. The software engineers design an overall system to meet the contractor's requirements. They partition the system into small, but interdependent modules that many individuals can work on. Then they check out the system requirements and design with the contractor, freeze those requirements and design, and implement, test, and deliver the system (Figure 2-2).

Clearly, if the contractors do not know what they want, the program design will be incorrect. If the software engineers misunderstand the requirements that the contractors intended, their completed system will be unacceptable. If after the system is built, the builders and contractors discover new features that are important to have because these newly discovered features make the system far more suitable, they must tear down the system and rebuild it at great expense.

A change in even one part of a program generally necessitates a rebuilding effort because in conventional programming, a change in one place is likely to affect the rest of the program. As seen, the classical programming environment is oriented toward the idea of defining a system's requirements, designing and partitioning the program based on those requirements, getting both requirements and design right, and then adhering to those ideas.

In contrast, AI languages and tools have several features that allow developers to explore ideas and change their minds (Figure 2-3). First, AI systems are the most modular software systems in existence. The program structures and mechanisms that contain knowledge, infer information, and control the way the program infers information are separate and independent. Moreover, the substructures that hold each individual piece of knowledge that is encoded in the program are largely independent of each other. Separation of these program mechanisms and knowledge structures makes it relatively easy to modify one part of an AI system and to add new knowledge without requiring program redesign.

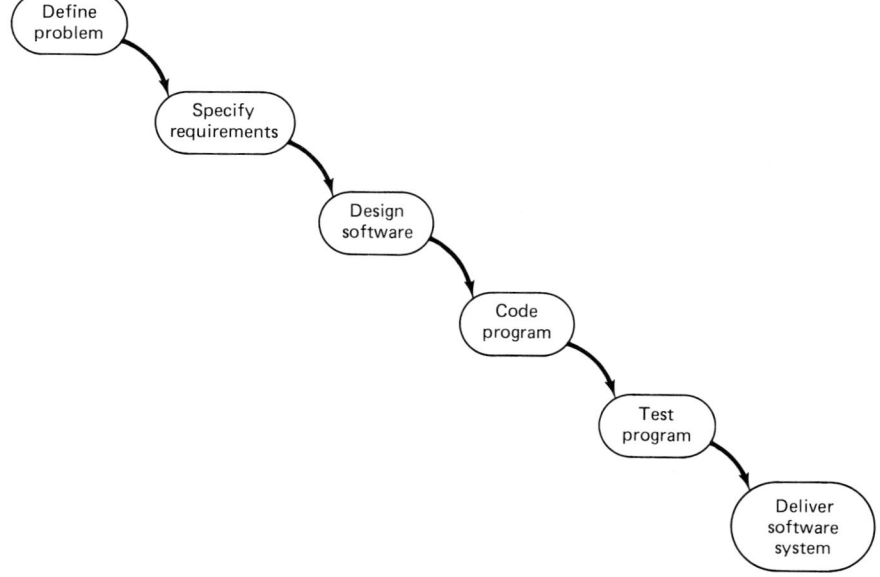

Figure 2-2 Classical software engineering.

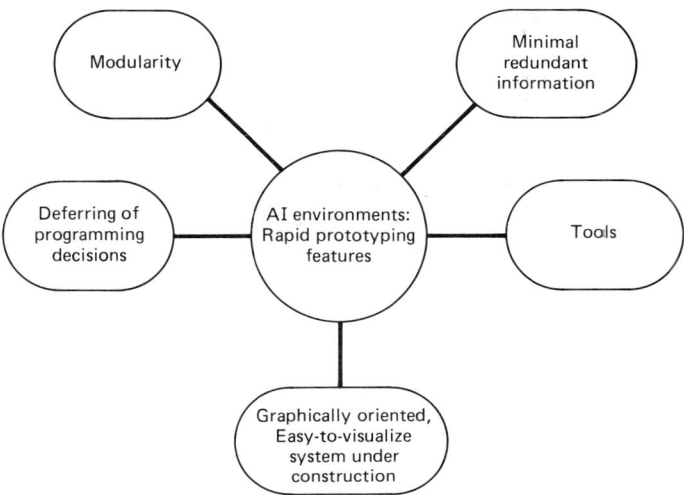

Figure 2-3 Exploratory programming features.

A second feature that allows exploratory programming stems from the ability of AI languages to defer many final programming decisions until the last minute when the program actually is running. Programming decisions that can be deferred include allocation of memory, associating a name of a variable with information that describes that variable, and deciding on the most appropriate procedure that a piece of code should invoke and use. As a result, AI application developers can easily change the behavior of a module and know that their changes will be properly implemented when the program runs.

In contrast, in conventional programming languages, programmers make all the aforementioned programming decisions in advance. If they are wrong, they must remake their decisions, implement them, and be sure that the new module runs correctly without impacting any other modules.

A third exploratory-programming feature is the graphical orientation of AI environments. They help AI system developers to visually see the framework of the system they are building, the structures they create within it, and changes they make. In addition, as programmers edit and explore their programs, AI tools keep track of all types of changes they make. These graphical and program management tools not only help programmers figure out how to make changes, but they can also then unmake them in a single step.

The fourth exploratory-programming feature is that AI environments have a large number of tools that allow AI systems developers to build programs that understand other programs and automatically make transformations in them.

This inherent ability to explore ideas, rapidly build prototypes, and easily change them makes AI particularly useful for designing and producing applications such as physician's and lawyer's workstations, and office information and industrial automation systems. In these applications, even the cognizant people have strong but poorly formulated ideas about what they want. They do not know what characteristics professional workstations or office information systems should have; these types of systems are likely to evolve with use.

Although physician's workstations and office systems do not necessarily contain AI components, it is difficult to build such first-time systems using conventional structured programming approaches. Changing such programs once they are built is just too expensive.

AI tools and techniques, on the other hand, invite developers to explore different designs for such systems without great grief or expense. Users or system developers can start with only a few requirements and rapidly build a prototype system. Trying out the prototype system on themselves or on selected users helps them crystallize other ideas, add extra niceties, and discover and dump any potential disasters early-on.

BORROWING BENEFITS FROM BUSINESS

Until now, rapid prototyping and experimenting with new ideas and products has been advocated but not widespread in the software industry. The concept, however, is not new to business. Experimentation with new ideas and involving customers in the shaping of new products has proven successful in many innovative and competitive businesses. It requires the ability to transform an idea rapidly into something that people can see, feel, or experiment with.

A rapid prototyping ability fosters creativity and innovation. This, in turn, leads to a certain number of new and successful products, new uses for products, new ideas, and increased long-term profits (Peters and Waterman, 1982).

Despite these benefits, most often innovation is reserved for smaller companies and startups. Industry leaders tend to be very conservative about building something that involves a new idea or technology because it is too costly to tolerate a mistake. The risk is amplified when developing products for new markets whose requirements have not yet completely evolved. The likelihood of costly consequences becomes still greater when the products involve, as so many products today do, labor-intensive software development.

Under these risky conditions, most innovations are to be avoided unless a facility is available that makes it easy to build and try out the new ideas. And it is. Where development of software-base products are concerned, such as professional workstations, automated office systems, and new types of decision support systems, AI environments offer the prototyping capabilities that other industries assume, and then throw in the tools to support evolution and adaptation.

The greater ease of developing AI and non-AI programs in AI environments, together with the potential payoffs, has led a variety of vendors to introduce subsets of AI languages, tools, and environments on standard mainframes, minicomputers, workstations, supermicros, and PCs. Commercial commitment has become great indeed, and the environments and hardware have become available to support the accelerated growth of rapidly prototyped projects. Examples include an AI-based process control system, built on a Lisp computer which also runs Unix (from LMI), in 4½ months. Another three-month effort produced an expert system prototype, running on a Tektronix computer with AI hardware and software added, for simple instrumentation and circuit-board diagnosis at Tektronix. A three-week AI project produced the Lehman Brothers/Shearson/American Express AI-based interest-rate-swap system, which runs on IBM PCs with added AI software all linked to a Lisp computer from Symbolics.

Texas Instruments also took advantage of AI tools and exploratory programming environments when it developed NaturalLink, its language understanding system that runs on PCs, and Arborist, its PC-based decision-tree software. Decision-tree software is not new, but Arborist differs from other decision-tree software in that it allows users to interact directly with the decision tree instead of with tabular data from which the computer program draws and redraws a decision tree.

Since both natural language systems and direct interaction with decision trees were new capabilities for conventional programs and had ill-defined software functionality, TI chose to prototype both systems in Lisp on Lisp machines. NaturalLink was then translated into the C programming language but Lisp was retained as Arborist's run-time language. Using Lisp as a base language, TI will interface Arborist not only to standard spreadsheet and other conventional productivity packages, but also to expert systems for in-depth analysis.

TI admits that some of the problems of migrating the programs to conventional PCs were more difficult than the initial program development, particularly when PCs did not support the kinds of graphics supported by Lisp machines. However, the firm claims, significant productivity efficiency was gained because it took only four months to develop Arborist (even though the primary developer was an inexperienced Lisp machine user), and the migration to the PC was facilitated by the Lisp language. But even the migration difficulties are expected to be alleviated as a standardized version of Lisp with graphics and related capabilities is specified and implemented both on Lisp machines and standard computers.

POPULARITY AT LAST

No major intellectual breakthroughs have occurred to justify the radical interest and commercialization of AI. Instead, a combination of economic, attitude, and interface factors has evolved to make commercial AI systems possible.

For example, on the economic side, until recently, a dedicated million-dollar machine was needed to make an expert system that could duplicate the functionality of a professional making $50,000 to $100,000 per year. Clearly, this is not a cost-effective approach. Despite the benefits that can accrue, the cost to perform tasks manually placed a ceiling on how much a company was willing to pay for automated functionality.

Worse, in the past, most AI was done on large mainframes such as PDP-10s and 20s. Although large and powerful, these multiuser machines were limited in the memory that could be assigned to or used by any particular program without a lot of inconvenient reallocation and coordination of others users' memory-mapping registers—burdens that are supposedly removed from programmers by Lisp. AI programs, however, are very processing intensive and frequently are 1 to 2 million words in length. The software tricks that got around the large memory requirements unfortunately resulted in extra overhead and decreased performance for the already processing intensive AI programs.

Out of a growing need for cost-effective, efficient AI hardware, a small group of companies (Xerox, Symbolics, Lisp Machine, Inc., and later, Texas Instruments) developed relatively inexpensive (compared to DEC PDP-10s and 20s), dedicated minicomputers that support AI languages, environments, and systems. Called Lisp machines, these computers, which have larger memory address spaces than the older mainframes and provide greater performance for lower price, have made AI cost-effective for a variety of applications. The Lisp machines also provide high-quality graphics interfaces. These improve the people/machine communications and make it far easier to develop large, complex AI programs.

When development is complete, some companies are reimplementing the AI systems so that the final versions run on cheaper, more standard machines (Figure 2-4). GE had price, availability, and general use in mind when it designed its CATS-1 locomotive troubleshooting expert system. The firm switched from its original Lisp version to a more common, portable language, called Forth, and completed and implemented the expert system on a Digital Equipment Corp. computer, the DEC PDP-11/23. GE's ultimate aim in making this switch was to get as many small, portable systems as possible out in the field at their locomotive maintenance ships to supply leverage to their locomotive mechanics. Similarly, PUFF, a respiratory medical diagnosis expert system used at Pacific Medical Center (San Francisco, California) started life on a Sumex mainframe computer, made its way to a DEC PDP-11 minicomputer, and now, under the name of Micropuff, runs on a variety of microcomputers.

Almost all natural-language systems run on ordinary mainframes, minicomputers, and micros. Most of the AI tool companies are committed to implementing the expert systems developed with their tools on standard, commonly available computers.

Conventional-computer manufacturers have not been content to watch Lisp computers get all the AI action either. So a myriad of vendors are merging Lisp and conventional programming technologies within one machine with communications pathways provided between the two environments. This merge will allow standard programs to be enhanced with AI capabilities. Toward this end, the standard DEC VAX minicomputer, Data General Eclipse minicomputer and DS family of engineering workstations, and the Apollo, Tektronix, Hewlett-Packard, and IBM computer lines now support a Lisp environment; LMI's Lisp computers host a standard Unix environment.

Another factor that has affected the recent commercial feasibility of AI has been the increasingly practical attitudes of many AI experts. In AI's early days, ambitious AI researchers thought in terms of learning enough about the cognitive and computer sciences to enable them to build supermen that could do what human beings could not do. That still out-of-reach goal was followed by attempts to learn how to build systems that can perform as well as human beings.

More recently, AI experts have changed their point of view and narrowed their focus to a smaller, more practical domain of problems that can improve human productivity

Figure 2-4 Reimplementation of AI systems

and performance. As a result, they have come up with achievable solutions to problems that cannot be solved by traditional programs.

It is not just the changed attitudes of AI developers that have contributed to the growing commercialization of AI. Many potential AI users have also undergone a drastic change of computer attitudes which increases their likelihood of becoming AI users.

VisiCalc, the other Calcs, and fourth-generation English-like languages such as Ramis, Focus, and Nomad are to thank for this change in computer attitude. The electronic spreadsheet programs and English-like fourth-generation computer languages have been major factors in getting nonprofessional computer operators to use computers.

Two events involving VisiCalc happened simultaneously to involve users in computing. For one, VisiCalc first appeared on the Apple computer. For another, it was designed to be so natural to use that a nontechnical person who knew something about spreadsheets and numbers could quickly learn to use it productively. Both events squashed the idea that only experts could directly access the processing power of computers.

Fourth-generation languages also helped break down the idea that the only way to get a program that works is to send a shop requirement to build an application to a central computer capability in a company. These languages opened up the door that allowed the people with the problems to develop the programs with the solutions.

As a consequence of this exposure to personal-corporate computers (in addition to home computers), increasing numbers of people are becoming comfortable in dealing with the computer directly. Computing is no longer just a back-office thing. AI systems are evolving at a time when society is becoming more cognizant of and more ready to accept, use, and make decisions about computing in their lives.

This effective end-user computer revolution means that a lot of people in corporate America are ready to accept AI because they can think about it in terms of how it will directly affect them and what it will do for them. The situation would be different if expert systems were being evaluated and thought of only by people who ran data-processing centers. Such professionals would be likely to think of expert systems mostly in terms of the technology. With a situation instead where end users are viewing AI in terms of personal benefits, AI firms have a better chance of catching the ear of the corporate and organizational decision makers. These reasons increase the chances that the time is ripe for AI to become widespread instead of a passing curiosity.

MARKET TRENDS

As the commercialization of AI technology gains in popularity, four trends are emerging which indicate the way in which expert systems will be developed and marketed in the foreseeable future. Expert systems and other types of AI applications can be developed either as salable commodities or for in-house use. A trend toward tool-based strategies overlaps both the salable commodity and in-house-use market segments. One of the most major trends may turn out to be traditional proven systems with value-added AI capabilities (Figure 2-5).

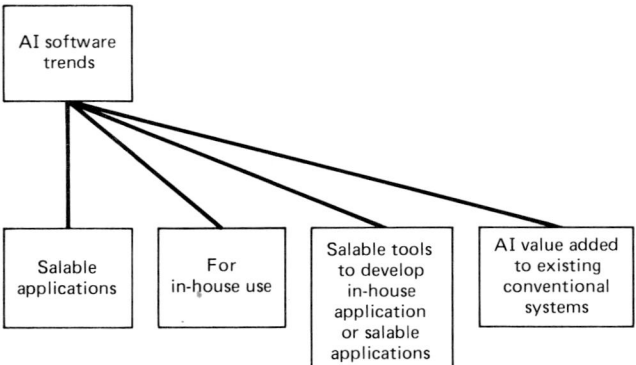

Figure 2-5 AI software market trends

One major problem that in the past has confronted the development of expert systems for external sale is their tendency to be customized, one-of-a-kind applications. Such customized applications are labor intensive and likely to be outrageously expensive. This limits the number of expert systems that can be sold.

To compound the problem, firms that purchase a customized expert system frequently train a core staff of people to understand, use, and maintain it. The training of that core staff often sprouts seeds that result in the formation of an in-house AI department. Such a highly trained department may continue its own AI development work. This seed effect is good for the spread of AI. It may or may not be profitable for expert system development companies.

A different AI company strategy trends toward development of expert systems for internal use only. Such internally developed and internally used expert systems provide leverage for critical skills within firms. In this context, expert systems may not directly generate new revenues. Instead, they reduce costs, enhance performance, and add new capabilities. By doing so, they enable a firm to improve its competitive position.

Still another significant AI product trend is a shift toward selling AI application development tools. These tools enable firms to build their own expert systems internally.

It is not only large user companies that are considering the purchase of these tools. Many AI firms are also undergoing a shift toward a tool-based strategy for constructing the expert systems that they sell. A tool-based strategy meets all the criteria necessary to make a good product candidate. From the viewpoint of the tool seller, many clones of the same product can be manufactured and sold within the same or different company. Clearly, such sales will drive down the price and create a wider AI market. From the viewpoint of the AI application developer/tool user, many more expert systems can be created faster, more predictably, and with less expert but more available labor, thus making both in-house and packaged expert systems feasible.

However, no matter how beneficial the AI capabilities, they cannot substitute for computational, algorithmic software that has long been the mainstay of business and engineering organizations, nor is it worthwhile to replace these existing systems. Yet, to varying degrees, AI can address problems that operators of these systems swear have been their nemesis.

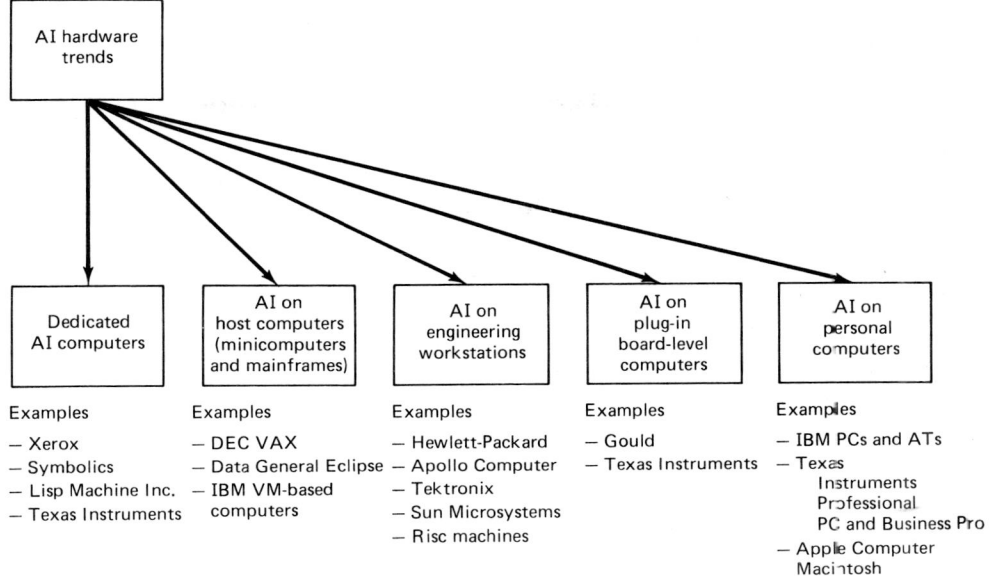

Figure 2-6 AI hardware market trends

For situations involving existing hardware and software systems, the trend is toward adding AI languages, environments, and even optimized hardware to conventional computers (Figure 2-6). By also adding a means of communications between the AI and conventional components of computers, standard systems can perform their tasks in normal mode but switch to the AI mode for performing AI tasks that have been added to the standard system.

APPLICATIONS REPEAT THEMSELVES

All in all, there are a number of reasons and a good deal of evidence that AI is poised to make its mark in the commercial, industrial, and scientific worlds. True, it has taken more than 20 years of development to reach this point. After an initial spurt of development, to outsiders the AI field seemed to have reached a plateau. Actually, it needed those years to define the first level of problems it could and should address, as well as to build its various techniques for representing and manipulating knowledge.

Now, the AI research that has built up over the last 20 years has overflowed into an accelerating number of applications. It is not likely, however, that development of new applications will continue at that rate. Instead, the AI community will learn from and repeat these applications, in various forms, over the next several years.

In other words, many computer companies will build computer configuration systems similar to DEC's XCON (eXpert Configurer). Various versions of Schlumberger's Dipmeter Advisor will be independently developed at most oil companies. Numerous repetitions of diagnostic systems will appear for a multitude of types of equipment. And every database company will (in fact, have already started to) acquire a natural-language facility.

Still another type of application repetition will occur because the ability to interpret one kind of graph, which represents signals in one domain, is at least partly transferable to the interpretation of other kinds of graphs of signals in other domains. Thus some of the techniques used to interpret seismic data, a pioneer application, can be used to interpret other graphed data, such as brain waves and radar signals.

The AI field, paced by the repetition of applications, will expand in terms of dollars until at some point it once again hits a plateau. For example, AI is largely barred from most problems that involve spatial and temporal reasoning because it knows very little about how to handle such reasoning. Ultimately, AI researchers will make another technological breakthrough that will enable them to handle many problems they cannot handle now. When that breakthrough occurs, it will open up a new area of AI applications and the AI field will again shift from a plateau to a rise.

CAUTIONS

Some words of caution regarding AI are necessary here. Although AI systems can give companies a lot of leverage and can solve complex problems that are not solvable with alternative techniques, they still have limited capabilities. They do not, and will not, replace human beings; they augment them.

AI is appropriate only for certain types of applications, and there are surprisingly few of them. For example, many real-time processing problems (those that have critical time constraints), as well as problems that involve modeling of space and time (such as aircraft flying in radar environments and constantly shifting position coordinates in real time), are particularly difficult. Worse, AI systems must be hand-crafted by both AI, and applications experts. As such, it is not the stuff of economic revolutions. Any AI-induced economic revolution will have to wait until the AI researchers figure out how AI systems themselves can learn some of the expertise they need without requiring so much help from professionals.

There is a scarcity of AI talent. AI experts are not the kind of people picked off the streets or found, in most personnel offices, looking for jobs. A Ph.D. in AI generally goes for about $70,000 a year to start (Master's-degreed AI specialists start at $50,000 to $60,000) and, even then, they are a scant resource. This cost and scarcity is difficult to reconcile with the labor-intensive requirements needed to develop current AI systems.

Resistance to AI exists in many segments of the programming community, and the reasons for the resistance contain several elements of logic. It is difficult to convince traditional programmers who have been programming in Fortran or Cobol or C for 15 years that a new technology will increase their productivity. It may increase it, but only after they learn and become experienced with the Lisp programming language, AI concepts, and a variety of new techniques. Under these circumstances, it is easy to understand why many programmers will not see the gain; they will react by claiming that they work pretty productively right now.

The science of knowledge extraction—trying to interview experts to get at their knowledge to encode in an expert system—is another labor-intensive activity. Worse, it is a poorly understood science. No one yet knows how to get someone to tell them everything he or she knows about a subject.

Despite these problems, AI can provide many intellectual and economic benefits. Yet its history has involved passage through several fads where it has been presented to the public with much fanfare and hype. As a result, people have expected a lot from AI which has never been delivered.

Now it can deliver something that people can see, touch, feel, and understand in terms of their personal benefits. A sure-fire way to be disappointed in AI, however, is to expect more of it than it can deliver.

AI Technology: Getting It from Here to There

CHAPTER 3

No matter what the benefits are, artificial intelligence cannot reach its full potential if only a select group of people are able to understand it or use it. Under these circumstances, insufficient numbers of people would exist who are able to build AI systems. Worse, insufficient numbers of people or organizations would be amenable either to supporting the development of AI applications or to spending the time learning to use AI systems.

When AI was in its early stages, pioneers in a few large companies and universities were enough to support its research and development. But AI has reached the point where its researchers have amassed enough knowledge to build several powerful and practical AI systems. Most of these systems have so far been limited to academic research projects. For AI to enter the marketplace and achieve success on a wide scale, interested parties must devise methods to transfer the AI technology between the universities inhabited by select groups of AI researchers and industrial environments where the bulk of the world resides.

There are actually two different levels of AI technology transfer which must be understood before it is possible to discuss technology transfer in a meaningful manner. One level involves the sale of turnkey AI-based applications. The other level involves the transfer of the technology necessary to build AI-based applications (Figure 3-1). Several AI hardware and software vendors have undertaken the job of transferring AI technology on both levels, on a wide scale, to both programmers and users.

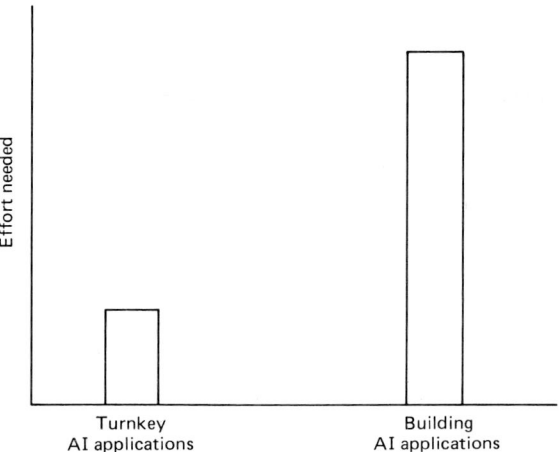

Figure 3-1 A technology transfer

TURNKEY AI SYSTEMS

The first level, off-the-shelf, turnkey AI-based applications that users can buy, install, and maintain themselves, are still in the early stages of development. Their underlying philosophy is to eliminate the need to transfer any AI technology in order to use the application. Instead, the application developers will use AI technology to hide the complexity of both the problem to be solved and the AI system used to solve it. Consequently, end users will see only functionality and not even know that the application contains any underlying AI (Figure 3-2).

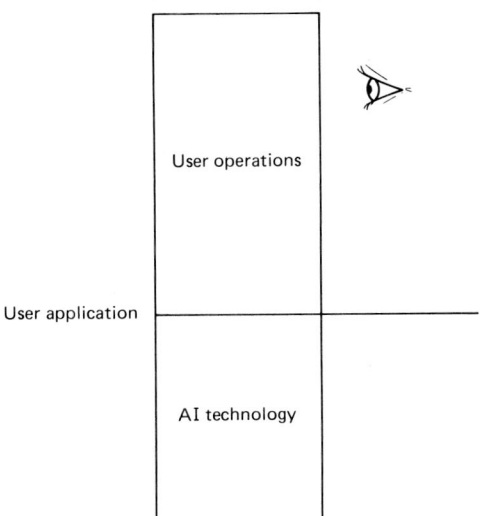

Figure 3-2 For AI market success, AI technology must be used to hide the AI.

The aim of turnkey AI application developers is to make their systems as easy, and sometimes easier, to use as mainframe decision support systems that are currently in widespread use by analysts. Several AI turnkey application developers choose mainframe decision support systems, rather than microcomputer spreadsheets, as a comparison to turnkey AI applications because of the more complex functionality offered by these mainframe systems. More complex functionality is generally associated with more training needed to use a system. Indeed, while mainframe decision support users are not computer scientists, neither are they casual, first-time users.

The simpler electronic spreadsheets are most known for their ability to recalculate many numbers quickly in response to questions such as: "What if the interest rate is 8 percent instead of 7 percent?" or "What if the sales for March were $100,000 instead of $90,000?" In contrast, AI applications will be targeted at more complex problems in the public accounting, equipment diagnosis, planning, design, and signal interpretation areas. They will attempt to answer questions such as "Should I buy or lease this equipment?" or "What went wrong in my manufacturing process to cause this batch of semiconductor wafers or potato chips to be defective?"

In view of these complex capabilities, at least for the immediate future, AI developers expect users of turnkey AI applications to be neither computer scientists nor novices. They may be financial analysts, supervisors of an assembly line, or in some way experts in some application area. Although their AI application systems is turnkey, the system developers describe the training time needed to learn the system as comparable to the training time that airline reservation clerks need to learn to use their airline reservation systems.

There are exceptions to this need for training. The earliest, major examples of off-the-shelf AI systems are the natural-language interfaces to databases. These interfaces, which allow users to request information from databases in their native language, are targeted at novices and casual computer users. Clearly, they are easier for novices to use than are fourth-generation database languages (database languages that are English-like but still highly stylized and that require users to learn specific syntaxes).

It is interesting to note that although great for novices, natural-language interfaces are not always easier for analysts and computing professionals to use. The reason is that trying to describe in words requests for such things as a mathematical operation, or the look, size, and format of a complex combination report and series of graphs and tables, may be an exercise in frustration and require many iterations until the desired result or printout is obtained. A stylized computer and application-oriented language is more likely to contain terms specific to the desired operations and allow users who know the language to represent their requests more concisely and with less chance of error.

IMPORTING AI TECHNOLOGY

Turnkey AI applications provide fine solutions for organizations that need to solve problems that are amenable to off-the-shelf solution. Many problems, however, are not so amenable. They may be specific to an organization, its products, or its techniques, or they may be standard problems for which there just are no off-the-shelf products available.

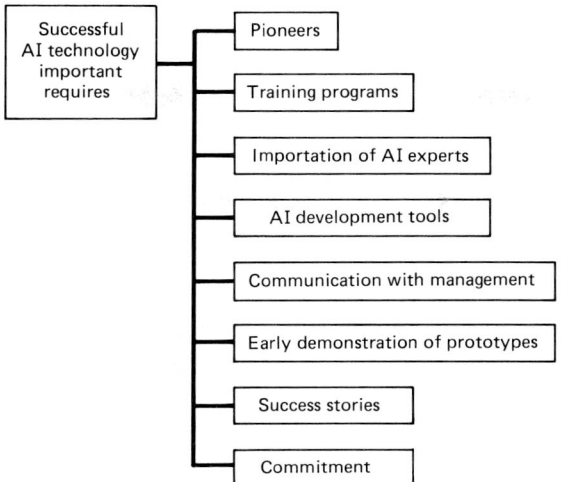

Figure 3-3 AI technology transfer guidelines

Under these conditions, the organization may consider either forming an AI department to develop its own AI applications, or contracting with an AI company to develop the application. Either method involves importation and diffusion of technology—a difficult feat for any technology to accomplish. How much more difficult, then, is the making of a decision to import AI technology and then managing the AI technology transfer simply because the technology is still so new and there are so few precedents to learn from.

Experience in many technologies has shown that technology alone does not provide the answer to an organization's problem, even if the technology is suitable and can solve the problem. For example, the existence of suitable technology does not help to make people aware of the new technology or get them to accept it into the mainstream of their organizational activities. It is, rather, the management of the technology transfer that ultimately determines the success or failure of the new technology and therefore the problem solution within an organization.

Despite the newness of the technology, some observations and guidelines for getting an organization into the AI business and diffusing AI ideas throughout the organization have been noted and established. These observations and guidelines cross several different areas, including getting started, personnel, training, money, management involvement, tools, hardware, and attitudes (Figure 3-3).

PIONEERS

In AI, as in any other field that is new, very different, and which requires big steps to adopt, there are people who pioneer and there are other people who copy. The process of adopting AI technology into an organization usually requires a pioneer—a person with some sort of gleam in his or her eye. That pioneer might have heard that AI is a glamorous subject, but is also aware that it might do something for the organization.

AI pioneers generally have read some of the available AI literature. This reading is not enough to inform them how to integrate AI into their everyday workplace. However, it does provide them with enough background knowledge so that what they have heard about how AI might solve their organization's problem makes a modicum of sense to them. Therefore, they are willing to investigate the subject further.

AI technology pioneers are most likely to turn up in high-technology industries where there are a large number of people who are used to dealing with and reading about new technology. They also tend to turn up in large organizations because most large organizations have technology scouts that keep an eye out for new technologies.

It is the technology scouts and pioneers that often make the initial contacts with AI tool or hardware firms or academic institutions. For importation of AI technology into an organization, that contact must be followed by more comprehensive training and education (Figure 3-4).

Most AI tool and AI application development vendors, AI hardware suppliers, and several universities offer some sort of educational and training programs in AI. Educational seminars also provide some general AI education, as well as insight into the identification of AI opportunities, roadblocks, and how an organization might get into the AI business. Some educational programs are geared to the use of a particular AI tool. Other programs teach the basic concepts of AI, expert systems, or Lisp programming. In addition, videotapes available from many AI companies promote the transfer of AI concepts.

But some handholding is necessary for anyone first learning to walk. Therefore, the AI tool and application companies have support provisions to review potential AI applications with customers on a contractual consulting basis. At the same time, many AI hardware companies provide services where they refer a customer to one or more appropriate AI application or tool firms, based on discussions about the customer's application.

For still more intensive technology transfer, combined with application development, some universities have joint programs with commercial and government institutions. Under these programs, organizations sponsor research at the universities. Aimed primarily at development or study of specific applications, the research is performed jointly with company personnel. They are required to spend enough time at the university to learn, acquire, and transfer the AI technology, as well as the application, back to the sponsoring organization.

For example, Digital Equipment Corp., Westinghouse, the Air Force Office of Scientific Research (AFOSR), Gulf, and Alcoa sponsored research at Carnegie–Mellon University (CMU). The Digital, Westinghouse, AFOSR, Gulf, and Alcoa apprentices attended courses and worked on their projects with CMU's AI professionals. Some typical

— Commercial AI vendor educational programs
— Academic institutions' seminars and courses
— Contractual consulting
— Videotapes
— Inexpensive, exploratory tools
— Joint programs with universities

Figure 3-4 AI technology training available from many sources

projects that were developed under this apprenticeship program include the CMU/Digital's XCON (eXpert CONfigurer), which configures computer systems, and the CMU/Westinghouse/AFOSR ISIS, which performs factory scheduling.

A key point for organizations to bear in mind when teaming up with a university is the necessity to match up the research interests at the university with the central research interests at an organization. For example, knowledge can be represented in a variety of computer memory structures, such as rules, frames, and others. Trying to talk a researcher into a project where its knowledge will be represented in "frames," when the researcher's area of expertise is "rule-based" systems, is the wrong thing to do.

PERCEIVED VERSUS ACTUAL RISK

Because the importation of AI technology is a big and costly step, the impetus and approval for AI projects must come from an organization's top management. It is the pioneers and scouts who involve their organization's top management in the AI effort. These pioneers and scouts are also the ones who continue to maintain the relationship between their organization and the AI company or university after the initial briefings are over and a decision has been made to pursue the possibility of implementing an AI project.

The managers who negotiate and approve the entry of an organization into the AI arena must perceive a relative advantage for AI over the organization's present way of operating. Many factors—financial, training, experience—influence whether or not an AI solution to a problem is the best one. Most important, however, the perceived risk associated with adopting an AI solution, in terms of accomplishing a particular task or achieving a specified goal, must lie within acceptable limits.

An AI solution may have a very high perceived advantage. However, the risk perceived may also be very great because the AI field is still relatively uncharted. For this reason, widespread AI acceptance and high-volume AI activity will not take place until there has been a number of success stories.

COPY A SUCCESS STORY

The tendency to copy-a-success-story can already be seen in the computer manufacturing and oil exploration industries. There, venturesome engineers at Digital Equipment Corp. and Schlumberger pioneered XCON and the Dipmeter Advisor (an expert system that interprets oil-well logs and tries to infer the presence of underground oil from them). It was no accident that once these expert systems demonstrated their feasibility and benefits, almost every other computer manufacturer began development of computer configuration programs, and almost every other oil company began to develop oil-well log interpretation and other oil exploration programs.

Each of the successor programs is different from its ancestor. But they were developed after company management understood concretely what such a program could do and observed personally that such programs were feasible. Then they were able to translate what they understood and observed into their own situations.

COMMUNICATING ON MANAGEMENT'S TERMS

Once the feasibility of an AI solution to an organization's problem is understood, management needs to be convinced that the new technology will benefit the organization in several ways, but particularly financially. Most organization's management is generally composed of nontechnical people who are trying to achieve a certain business result. It is up to the organization's pioneers and scouts to create the image and vision of what AI can do for a problem so that management will feel that the benefits are worth the risk.

Upper management generally regards the idea of employing any new technology as any other business investment. Since commercial organizations cannot be run as charitable enterprises, discussions with management reveals that they are pretty matter of fact about what facets of the new technology concern them most. Simply put, one question is foremost in their minds: "What is my return going to be?" The answer to that question mostly determines why they want to make that investment.

Therefore, the believers—the pioneers, technology scouts, and AI firms—must sell management objectively or subjectively on why AI technology will net the company a return on its investment. Which of several ways to represent knowledge or infer information, and the elegance and simplicity or sophistication of a solution, are issues for the early research and later implementation stages. But when the decision to import AI technology is being made, the major issues are chances of success (whether it works) and bottom line (what the return is). Some understanding of AI concepts is necessary to equip management to evaluate both of these issues.

GETTING STARTED IN AI

Once a decision to import AI technology has been made, a host of difficult-to-resolve details must be addressed. For example, AI is a technology that has a very limited number of practitioners. There is a shortage of competent knowledge engineers. They are difficult to locate and to hire.

An organization cannot expect to just plunge into the AI field by hiring a few programmers. Any organization that wants to get into the AI business must be prepared to make a substantial investment in education—in other words, to train technical people.

Because of the substantial investment needed, many companies importing AI technology start with a small system to see if AI is suitable for their needs. Although the first application may not be a company's most meaningful one, most new-to-AI companies use it as a learning experience. During this experience, they develop some expert system building skill and they learn how they can use AI technology on a whole range of company problems waiting in the wings.

Some firms elect to experiment with an AI system before building a department by contracting to have a small expert system built for them. By contracting externally, the firms are able to see how expert systems solve a problem and how applicable and worthwhile expert systems are to the firm's specific problems before they invest in staffing a department and training the staff. The one-time contract cost is modest compared to building a knowledge engineering group with several technical people and the associated computing equipment to support them.

TECHNOLOGY TRANSFER

Most technology importation ideas are intuitive and the product of common sense, but unfortunately, they are not always followed. Still, a day of reckoning arrives. Regardless of a company's technology pioneers or the type and size of its entry-level AI applications, eventually it must confront the difficult question of how to train the staff of an organization so that its members are capable of employing technologically new AI concepts in products and applications that they build. To compound the problem, as discussed in Chapter 2, many people who are part of the traditional programming staff of an organization are quite likely to be resistant to the new technology. It is difficult for experienced programmers to imagine how taking their time to learn and gain experience in a new technology will increase their productivity.

The most successful technology transfer technique (and perhaps the only successful one) used at System Development Corp. (SDC) is to physically transfer the people who already have the technology into the organization so that they can personally transfer the technology to the uninitiated.

"Past software experience shows that technology does not transfer well either from the written word or from discussion about technology theory," claims Jack Munson, a vice president of SDC. Munson explains that cases where a technology is so obviously good that people seek it out are rare. Cases where engineers and software professionals learn the technology almost in a vacuum because the technology is its own reward generally are trivial cases. The notion that a company can import a technology based on a research organization's reports that explain a technology and its benefits just does not work.

In summary, Munson says that a newly formed group will not employ new technology concepts in an application unless they are sure they know how to do it. They will simply go back to techniques they understand. Unless an organization brings in people who already know the new technology and can distribute it throughout the organization, the organization will have a tough time getting its people to seek out, learn, and apply the technology.

A PROBLEM OF CULTURE

Another technology transfer issue to address is how to manage technology transfer between different types of cultures—for example, the different cultures that abound in computer science, manufacturing, engineering, or MIS domains. This issue is of particular importance in AI because AI is such an interdisciplinary subject. More than most subjects, AI involves computer-oriented experts working with and training experts in a variety of application fields.

Each of those fields has its own culture; and one of the biggest problems that impedes the flow of technology between the different cultures stems from cultural resistance. The cultural resistance that occurs is based on how the different cultures understand, preceive, or identify with goals, terminology, and the technology to be transferred. The people in each culture think about the technology in terms of how it affects them. They have different criteria for success. They talk about their functions and processes differently, even when they overlap.

Often, people in the different cultures do not even understand each other's terminology. Software professionals have been criticized for their jargon. But they should not be singled out. As frustrated observers can attest, the aerospace industry sports "leads" and "lags." The communications industry is filled with "acks" and "naks." And the financial industry's "puts," "calls," "liquidity risks," and "margins" are enough to cause the "bulls" and the "bears" to hide in their portfolios. Yet these cultures must decide together whether success of a project means a million dollars, a Nobel prize, easier-to-perform jobs, increased efficiency, more jobs able to be run, or fewer jobs that have to be run.

The implications of the various attitudes among heterogeneous cultures is best exemplified by an interesting situation that developed at Daisy Systems. Daisy makes computer-aided engineering workstations that use AI, as well as other technologies, to create intelligent circuit design assistants. The use of AI as one of the underlying technologies gave the Daisy system some modifiability and ease-of-interfacing-to-other-design automation systems benefits that are not common. Yet for the first few years of the firm's existence, Daisy refused to be known as an AI company or even to label its technology as AI. Instead, the firm called itself a "solution" company and called its technology "advanced programming." When pressed for an answer about its use of AI, it described itself only as a firm with an engineering problem to solve and a willingness to apply a multiplicity of solutions—AI or otherwise—to solve it.

Daisy's founder and president, Aryeh Finegold, blames the difference in research and commercial cultures for his refusal to set up business under an AI aegis. Simply put, researchers emphasize ideas and methodologies. In contrast, commercial organizations are interested in products that can be repetitively manufactured and result in a profit.

Until recently, to label the business AI automatically meant to associate it with advanced research cultures. Unfortunately, according to Finegold, because of the style with which certain circles within this culture operate, AI has traditionally been used as an excuse not to deliver. For many people in these circles, the aura of advanced research frequently legitimized excuses for writing software that was not of production quality. These researchers excused themselves and expected customers not to get angry when software was late or did not do the job because "the problem is complicated," "the problem is too big," "AI is still new technology and it will improve in the future."

The delivery and production quality problems cropped up because instead of concentrating on the problem they needed to solve, some AI people tended to concentrate on the methodologies they were using to solve it. In other words, they concentrated on ideas, not on solutions or products.

Daisy was aware of this "idea" emphasis and did not want to attract these kinds of researchers. Moreover, the firm shied away from being an AI company because it wanted to avoid any hint of the problems associated with the only-ideas-are-important contingent of the AI culture.

It turns out, Finegold maintains, that people who concentrate on solutions find that it may or may not be necessary to use AI to solve a problem. These are the kinds of people that Daisy wanted to attract—people who do not hesitate to use any kinds of ideas as a means to an end. If a problem solution demands AI techniques, then AI techniques should be used as they become available. If the problem can be solved better, faster, or cheaper with traditional or other new techniques, those techniques should be the ones of choice. There is nothing intrinsic about AI as a solution. It is only a means to an end. Practicing what it preaches, Daisy's workstations are indeed a conglomeration of both traditional and AI techniques.

INVOLVE MANAGEMENT

It is not sufficient simply to be aware of the training, personnel, cost, and attitudinal obstacles and then let nature take its course. To a large degree, the importation and diffusion of technology throughout an organization, in the face of the obstacles discussed and resistance to change, is dependent on effective planning for change.

For example, an important variable in the process of successful technology transfer and diffusion is who gets the technology to transfer. If the first people who receive the new technology are chosen for their flexibility and rationality, while those who are more dogmatic and rigid are eliminated from the newly forming AI team, the chances are that mental attitudes will be better, resistance to change will be minimized, and as a result, the technology diffusion time will be compressed.

Because AI is so new, technology transfer is facilitated if the senior managers responsible for the new technology are picked because they value and like to nurture innovation. Also, in the experiences of Digital Equipment Corp. and Teknowledge (a firm that develops expert systems under contract for several companies), since technology transfer depends on management's commitment, it is most important that both senior and corporate management are involved in the projects they are managing or supporting. It takes dedication on the part of organizations to stick with the new and unfamiliar when, instead of products or services, only potential benefits will be produced for a long time. Under these circumstances, the organization's managers should have something to back up their dedication. They are also entitled to know what they are getting for their money.

To keep managers involved, informal networks between AI experts and management should be developed to communicate the status and progress of the new technology. In addition, AI people must be prepared not only to give presentations on their projects, but also to provide hands-on experience for managers while the project is still under development. Fortunately, in AI, there is nothing farfetched about the idea of operating a partially complete system. It is standard practice to develop AI systems incrementally. Unlike with conventionally developed software, AI developers create simple prototypes relatively quickly. Then they use these prototypes as vehicles to determine what new knowledge needs to be added.

Three classes of people concerned with the expert system development should be able to try out these prototype systems to get a firsthand feeling for the project. One, as discussed, is management, because their support and commitment is absolutely necessary. Application domain experts also need to try out the system because their heuristic knowledge is encoded and they need to evaluate the system's performance as an expert throughout development. Moreover, application domain experts who are being cloned by these expert systems can become attached to them. Finally, end users need to be involved early with expert system development because expert systems are user-driven tools. The final product expert system must satisfy user needs because it is the users whose abilities they amplify and leverage.

The end users also need to be involved because of the fear and insecurity that may otherwise be generated. DEC discovered these fears in its initial trials of XCON, its computer configuration program. Just when the firm thought it had its AI importation program under control and expected its computer configurers to send the XCON-generated configuration outputs to the factory floor with each order, none appeared. After much discussion with the configurers, accompanied by a lot of hemming, hawing, and hedging, DEC management realized that its supposedly convinced configurers were afraid for their jobs. Since then, the firm has involved the end users in expert system development so that they realize early just how it will affect them.

It turns out that DEC's configurers have not been made redundant. They have become XCON supervisors or have gone on to similar challenging jobs. However, part of the reason for no layoffs was DEC's growth; new configurers who might have been hired were not.

In other DEC expert system development efforts, such as XSEL, which helps sales people use XCON to configure orders and quote prices at the point of sale, the sales representatives were involved at the very beginning. From the first, the salespeople were able to weigh the idea of visiting customer sites carrying their computer, telephone link, and keyboard, and also the image of typing while talking, against the potential for getting more orders and resulting greater commission dollars. Consequently, XSEL has enjoyed a high level of support from its users.

LEARNING AI

Convincing management solves the problem of support for AI projects. But the problem of a shortage of AI practitioners remains. Several solutions to alleviate the shortage are likely to occur, especially as the AI field gains acceptance. First, what generally happens when a new field arises is that schools start training people. In fact, a number of schools, other than those known for their AI departments, have already instituted AI courses in computer science departments.

Second, many of the AI companies feel that there are presently enough AI-trained people to seed companies. With these people as the seeds, it is possible to train sufficient people to build systems.

The people that AI companies plan to hire and train are people with some sort of computing background. These people include computer scientists, electrical engineers who have been working with computers, software engineers, and business data-processing professionals. People who understand a particular application domain and who have no computer anxiety and some computer experience are valuable because of the interdisciplinary nature of AI. Data-processing people fall into this category both because they have programming experience and because they know the problems of large database applications and of interfacing to intelligent, but not technically savvy people.

TOOLING UP FOR AI

AI tools improve the ability to transfer the technology and shorten the training time. So, in an effort to make knowledge-based programs and programming more widely accessible, a number of AI companies have simplified knowledge programming methods and designed AI application development tools that incorporate the simplified methods. The power of these tools lies in their ability to be used by people with no AI expertise. Most commonly, the tool user turns out to be a person who is an expert in the application domain in question. He or she works in conjunction with another person with some computer or programming background. An example is the chemist at Lawrence Livermore Laboratories and her computer scientist colleague. Working together, the pair used KEE, an AI application development tool from IntelliCorp, to build an intelligent interface to a triple-quadripole mass spectrometer—a complex instrument used in the determination of chemical structures.

The AI companies' goal, however, is to provide tools so that domain experts can eventually build their own expert systems. In fact, cases already exist where persons ranging from managerial personnel to biology experts have done so.

AI's accessibility has been possible only recently because tools have been developed that enable someone without an extensive AI background to build expert systems. By analogy, there was a time when a company that needed a computer hired a group of physicists and electrical engineers, who understood how parts such as vacuum tubes and relays worked. At that stage of computer technology development, there could only be a small number of computers built, such as for the U.S. Bureau of the Census or at an occasional university.

As the technology matured, computer technology became accessible because people had to know less and less to be able to use it. The AI field is now following the same pattern. Until recently, it was not possible to build an AI system without at least the equivalent of a masters degree in AI. That is no longer true because it is now possible to buy tools with which, after a relatively short training period, a competent software professional can build expert systems without having to know how to build the tools themselves.

Relatively inexpensive, easy-to-use application development tools are even appearing on personal computers. These tools allow users to explore AI technology, languages, and environments and learn firsthand whether it is worthwhile continuing to learn.

While AI application development system users need not be AI experts, they must understand some of the basic precepts of AI and expert system building. As mentioned, common methods of acquiring this knowledge are through training programs, formal courses, consulting and support services, videotapes, and as always, experience.

BETTER THAN VIDEO GAMES

Xerox has gone one step further in its technology transfer efforts with a method unusual for the software industry. The firm has devised a game, called Truckin', to teach potential AI users how to build small expert systems. Truckin', really an expert system, is a board-type game, in which players simulate independent truckers, buying and selling commodities and trying to make the greatest profits.

The game is played by computers, but the expert system that plays it is programmed by people. The players program the game in Loops, a knowledge programming language, environment, and application development system (also intended for serious project work) developed at Xerox. The value of the game, besides providing entertainment, which is certainly a by-product, is to seduce players (potential AI users) into learning the AI concepts needed to program their part in the game. Programming their part in the game entails building and modifying a small expert system.

Its designers chose Truckin' as the domain for this game/learning experience because it draws on most people's real-world experiences (buying, selling, making profits). Therefore, players need not take time to learn the application domain in order to build the expert systems that play the game. At the same time, the Truckin' domain is complex enough to exhibit many of the problems that turn up in real AI application areas. Consequently, players can transfer the techniques they learn to their own systems.

The game board (displayed on a computer screen) has numerous road stops (Figure 3-5). Players drive trucks around the board, stopping at these roadstops to buy and sell commodities, such as luxury goods or foodstuffs, and to buy gas when needed.

The object of the game is to make the most profit. To make their profit, players plan the best route to do their buying and selling while avoiding hazards. Hazards include bandits who move around the board and running out of gas. In addition, players must avoid pitfalls such as bumpy roads that damage fragile merchandise and spoilage of perishable foods that are trucked too long before they are sold.

The AI learning enters the picture because Xerox provides simple preprogrammed players who only know how to buy gas and to travel around the board. To win the game, users must modify these players' actions to make them smarter in their buying/selling and avoiding hazards strategies.

To modify the players' actions, users modify or create rules that govern the players' moves and strategies. A rule in AI is a conditional statement (similar to a traditional if-then statement, but much more modular) that specifies an action to take place under a

Better Than Video Games

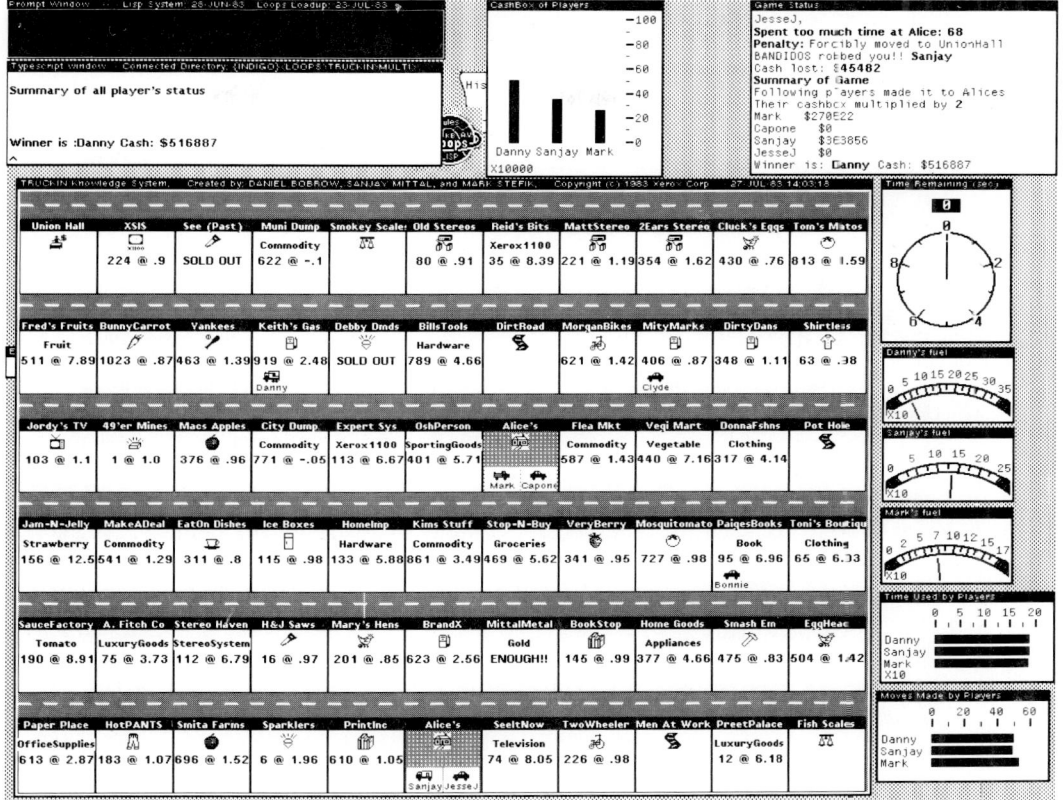

Figure 3-5 Computer games teach AI concepts. (Xerox Corp.)

certain set of conditions (Figure 3-6). Because AI systems are designed to be far more modular than conventional programs, users can easily add and change rules. If they add too many rules, however, they may slow down their system. If they do not add enough, their system is not smart enough.

Besides rules, in order to play the game, users learn several other AI paradigms. For example, they learn to build AI procedures. They also learn how to organize and work with game information taxonomically. A taxonomic organization would show, for example, that diamonds and gold are special cases of luxury goods, whereas apples and grapes are special cases of fruits, a special case of groceries (Figure 3-7). In such a taxonomic organization of information, users know that everything which is true of objects in a higher taxonomic level, such as that luxury goods have high prices, is also true of objects lower in the taxonomic hierarchy, such as that gold and diamonds have high prices. This taxonomic organization paradigm is commonly used in AI and is discussed later in the book.

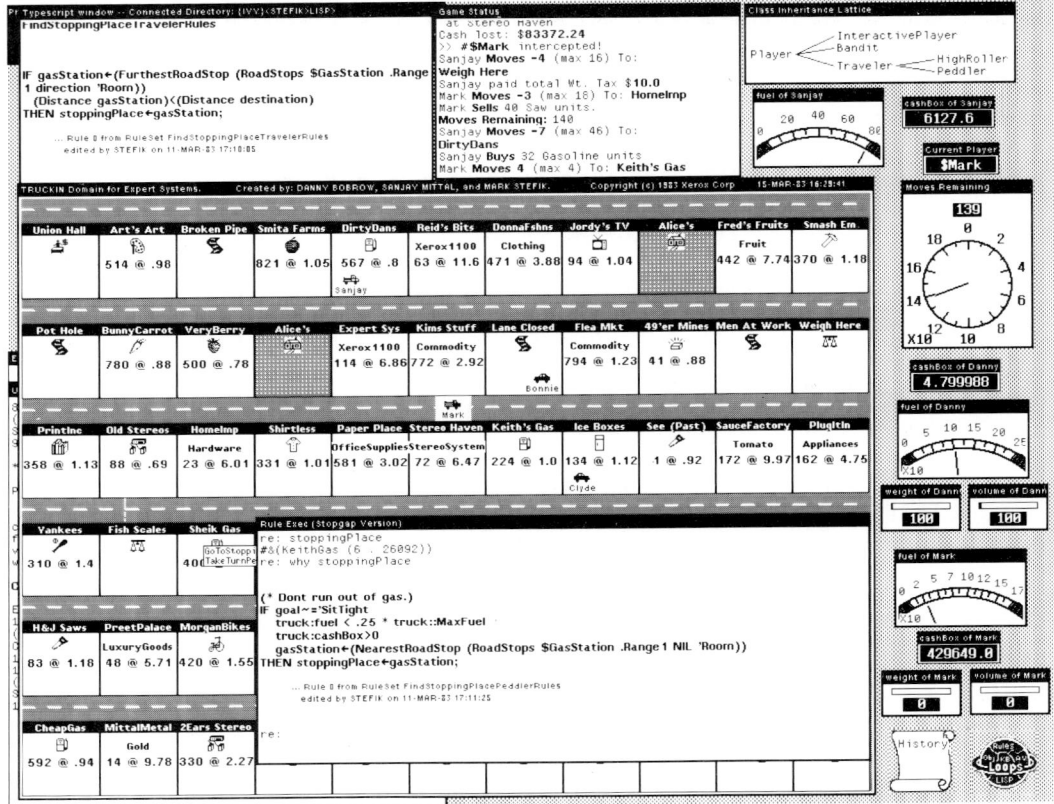

Figure 3-6 The game of Truckin' requires players to write rules to buy and sell commodities to ensure that they make the highest profits. (Xerox Corp.)

Finally, to play Truckin', users learn how to build gauges that graphically display, in real time, the changing value of variables and to handle structures that notify users or invoke procedures when variables are accessed.

GRAPHICS FOR AI DEVELOPMENT

Most of the AI application development systems currently run on Lisp-oriented machines with high-resolution, bit-mapped displays and integrated graphics environments. However, many tool vendors are committed to implementing the expert systems developed with the tools, and eventually, some of the tools, on standard machines such as IBM mainframes, DEC VAXs and high-end micros.

These standard computers already proliferate in users' environments. Moreover, they may give better run-time performance than that of many Lisp systems. Notwithstand-

Graphics for AI Development

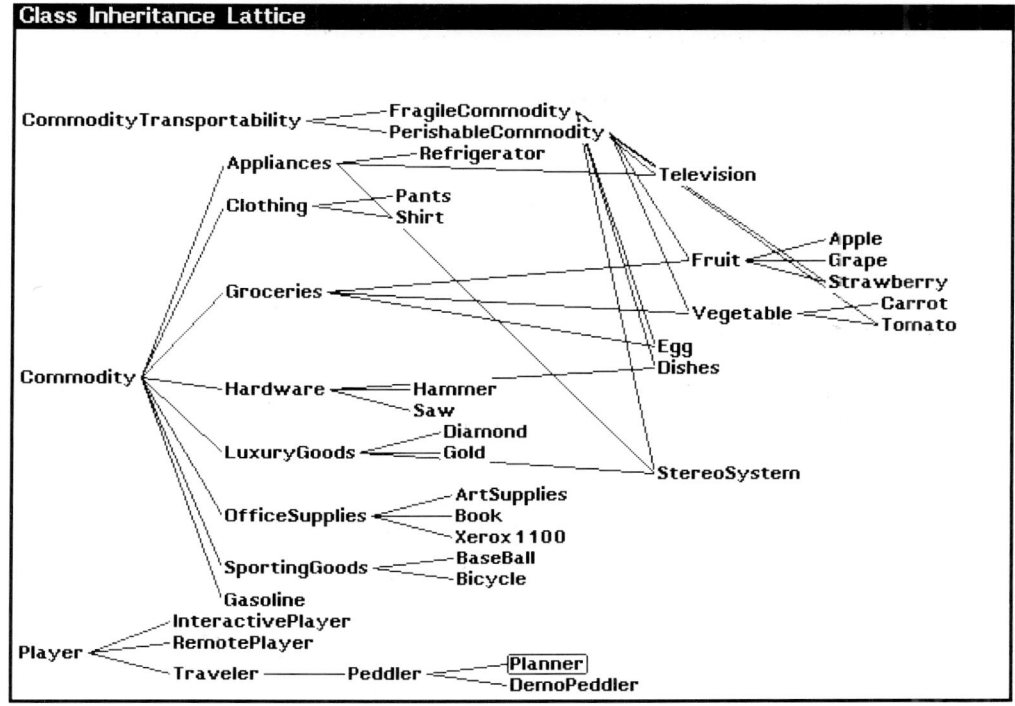

Figure 3-7 Taxonomic organization of game information shows relationships between game objects. (Xerox Corp.)

ing these benefits, most AI vendors agree that bit-mapped graphics environments are very important for AI development.

More important, these graphics environments have even more significance for AI novices and organizations that are first importing AI technology. The integrated AI and graphics capabilities make it easier for less sophisticated users to grasp quickly the complex ideas and techniques within AI.

There are several reasons for this greater ease of use. For one, a graphics environment provides developers with instant feedback about what their system knows, can do, and why it makes suppositions. In addition, as developers create knowledge-representation structures within an expert system framework, the graphics environment allows the developers to move about within that framework and view the structures they have built.

These kinds of capabilities are not generally available on the more common 24- by 80-character screen. Consequently, expert system development on a standard terminal demands a great deal of visual imagery within the minds of developers about what is happening as they build their expert system.

Because of the feedback and visual benefits, although IntelliCorp has KEE, its application development tool, running in-house on a standard DEC-20 as well as a Lisp computer, the firm does not recommend that AI novices attempt to use the former implementation. In fact, the argument is that given the cost of hardware versus the cost of people's time, from the company's viewpoint, an AI tool implementation without an integrated graphics environment is not cost effective and also risks the success of the expert system development project.

DIGITAL EQUIPMENT CORP. IMPORTS AI

The best way to understand the planning, learning, and support issues in AI technology importation, as well as the need for demonstration and early user involvement, is to examine a case of a company that has imported and established an AI capability, and in so doing has dealt with these issues. The development of XCON at Digital Equipment Corp. is one of the best examples of a successful technology importation and transfer.

XCON, named R1 at Carnegie–Mellon University (CMU) where it was originally developed, configures VAX-11 and some PDP-11 computers. Given a customer's order, XCON determines what, if any, substitutions and additions need to be made to build a complete and functional computer system with the best possible performance. In response to user input, XCON produces printouts showing the components chosen, reasons for adding or deleting others, cable lengths, vector addresses (physical addresses of devices on a computer bus), and a series of diagrams showing the spatial and logical relationships among the devices and modules in a computer system (Figure 3-8).

Computer configuration at DEC is time consuming and complex because DEC does not offer only a limited number of standard computer systems. Instead, DEC's computer system offerings are based on components that customers specify and order a la carte. The task of configuring a computer system involves examining the components that the customer has selected, and deciding whether the set of components is complete as is or if additional components must be added to make the system functional. In addition, a human configurer must determine the spatial relationships between the components in order to integrate them.

"It used to take an expert configurer about 25 minutes to configure a system manually," says Dennis O'Connor, group manager of DEC's AI Technology Center and a pioneer in applied AI at DEC. When that time is multiplied by 10,000 slightly different VAX orders per year, and adjusted both for the number of customers who change their minds so that the order needs to be reconfigured, as well as for other customers who want to know "what if I added this or did that," the configuration time problem becomes almost intractable.

In his article describing XCON's development and evaluation at DEC, John McDermott, XCON's designer, names three factors that contribute to making the computer configuration task difficult (McDermott, 1981). First, determining completeness is a very tedious task. To determine whether the set of components that has been ordered is complete, it is necessary to descend to a level of detail that is difficult for people to handle. As a result, completeness is not always determined satisfactorily.

```
C-NUMBER 08TEST780   test   12-MAY-82 PRODUCT LINE NIL XCON RELEASE AS OF   21-FEB-
 1983   BLISS v2.3

ULL SYSTEM CONFIGURATION ( WITH ADDITIONS AS REQUIRED )

NE   QTY   NAME               DESCRIPTION              COMMENT

 1    1    SV-AXHHA-CA        PACKAGED SYSTEM
           KA780-AA           PROCESSOR
           QE001-AV           OPERATING SYSTEM
           H9602-MA           UBX-CABINET
           RK07               LOAD DEVICE
           RK07               SYSTEM DEVICE
           LA120-DA           CONSOLE
           256 KILOBYTES OF MEMORY
 2    2    DZ11-E             ASYNC-COMM BUNDLE
 3    2    DMR11-AC           SYNC-COMM BUNDLE
 4    1    DD11-DK            BACKPLANE BUNDLE
 5    1    REM05-AA           DISK BUNDLE
 6    1    RM05-AC            DISK BUNDLE

COMPONENTS ADDED

 7    1    BA11-KE            BOX BUNDLE               INSUFFICIENT BOX SPACE FOR UNIBUS MODULES
 8    1    H9602-MF           UBX CABINET              NEEDED TO PROVIDE PANEL SPACE FOR THE UNIBUS MODULES
```

Figure 3-8

number 08test780   Customer name   test   Order Run   Date 12-May-82

NET LAYOUT

```
 ----------      ----------      ----------                           ----------      ----------
|11780-ca  |----|h9602-mf 1|----|h9602-mt 2|                         |rm05-aa   |----|70-17613-00|----|rm05-ac|
|          |    |          |    |          |                         |          |    |70-18322  2|    |       |
|          |    |          |    |          |                         |          |    |1 mba 0    |    |       |
|          |    |          |    |          |                         |          |    |70-18322  1|    |       |
|          |    |          |    |          |                         |          |    |0 mba 0    |    |       |
 ----------      ----------      ----------                           ----------      ----------

 ----------      ----------      ----------
|ba11-ke  1|----|ba11-ke  1|
|uba 0     |    |uba 0     |
 ----------      ----------

 ----------
|Console   |
|LA120-da 0|
 ----------

 ----------
|rk07-ea   |
|     2    |
 ----------
```

FREE STANDING DEVICES

11780-ca

k	d	ms780-ca	r	m
a	w	256 kb	h	9
7	7		7	0
8	8		8	4
0	0		0	3
-				
a	a			e
a	0		0	n
				d

UNUSED CAPACITY
   THE MEMORY CONTROLLER IN CABINET 0 COULD SUPPORT 3840 BYTES MORE MEMORY
   RK611 * 1 CAN SUPPORT 6 MORE DISKS
   MBA 0 CAN SUPPORT 6 MORE CONTROLLERS

CABLING

1 BC03M-25   FROM THE CPU-CABINET TO THE CONSOLE - LA120-DA
                   LENGTH: 25 FEET
                   LENGTH-REQUIRED: 15 FEET
3 BC05L-15   FROM UBA 0 TO BOX 1 ON UBA 0
                   LENGTH: 15 FEET
                   LENGTH-REQUIRED: 8 FEET
1 BC11A-10   FROM BACKPLANE 2 IN BOX 1 IN CABINET 1 TO BACKPLANE 1 IN BOX 1 IN CABINET 2
                   LENGTH: 10 FEET
                   LENGTH-REQUIRED: 8 FEET 6 INCHES
1 BC55A-10   FROM DMR11-AC* 2 TO NETWORK-INTERCONNECT PANEL 2 IN CABINET 1
                   LENGTH: 10 FEET
                   LENGTH-REQUIRED: 8 FEET
1 BC55A-10   FROM DMR-11-AC* 1 TO NETWORK-INTERCONNECT PANEL 1 IN CABINET 1
                   LENGTH: 10 FEET
                   LENGTH-REQUIRED: 8 FEET
1 BC05W-15   FROM DZ11-B* 3 TO MULTIPLEXER PANEL 2 IN CABINET 2
                   LENGTH: 15 FEET
                   LENGTH-REQUIRED: 8 FEET
1 BC05W-15   FROM DZ11-B* 4 TO MULTIPLEXER PANEL 2 IN CABINET 2
                   LENGTH: 15 FEET
                   LENGTH-REQUIRED: 8 FEET
1 BC05W-15   FROM DZ11-B* 1 TO MULTIPLEXER PANEL 1 IN CABINET 2
                   LENGTH: 15 FEET
                   LENGTH-REQUIRED: 8 FEET
1BC05W-15   FROM DZ11-B* 2 TO MULTIPLEXER PANEL 1 IN CABINET 2
                   LENGTH: 15 FEET
                   LENGTH-REQUIRED: 8 FEET
1 BC05W-15   FROM DZ11-B* 5 TO MULTIPLEXER PANEL 3 IN CABINET 2
                   LENGTH: 15 FEET
                   LENGTH-REQUIRED: 8 FEET

```
ADDRESS

UNIBUS 0
  DMR11-AC* 1    760070    M8207-ADDRESS E127 CLOSE SWITCHES FOR ZERO IN BITS: 2 6 7 8 9 10 11 12
  DMR11-AC* 2    760100    M8207-ADDRESS E127 CLOSE SWITCHES FOR ZERO IN BITS : 2 3 4 5 7 8 9 10 11 12
  DZ11-B* 1      760120    M7819-ADDRESS E81 CLOSE SWITCHES FOR ONE IN BITS: 4 6
  DZ11-B* 2      760130    M7819-ADDRESS E81 CLOSE SWITCHES FOR ONE IN BITS: 3 4 6
  DZ11-B* 3      760140    M7819-ADDRESS E81 CLOSE SWITCHES FOR ONE IN BITS: 5 6
  DZ11-B* 4      760150    M7819-ADDRESS E81 CLOSE SWITCHES FOR ONE IN BITS: 3 5 6
  DZ11-B* 5      760160    M7819-ADDRESS E81 CLOSE SWITCHES FOR ONE IN BITS: 4 5 6
  RK611* 1       777400    M7900-ADDRESS BITS PRESET IN VOLUME MFG TO ZERO: 2 3 4 5 6 7

VECTORS

UNIBUS 0
  RK611* 1       210       M7900-VECTOR BITS PRESET IN VOLUME MFG TO ZERO: 2 4 5 6 8
  DMR11-AC* 1    300       M8207-VECTOR E28 CLOSE SWITCHES FOR ONE IN BITS: 6 7
  DMR11-AC* 2    310       M8207-VECTOR E28 CLOSE SWITCHES FOR ONE IN BITS: 3 6 7
  DZ11-B* 1      320       M7819-VECTOR E14 CLOSE SWITCHES FOR ZERO IN BITS: 2 3 5 8
  DZ11-B* 2      330       M7819-VECTOR E14 CLOSE SWITCHES FOR ZERO IN BITS: 2 5 8
  DZ11-B* 3      340       M7819-VECTOR E14 CLOSE SWITCHES FOR ZERO IN BITS: 2 3 4 8
  DZ11-B* 4      350       M7819-VECTOR E14 CLOSE SWITCHES FOR ZERO IN BITX: 2 4 8
  DZ11-B* 5      360       M7819-VECTOR E14 CLOSE SWITCHES FOR ZERO IN BITS: 2 3 8

END OF FULL SYSTEM CONFIGURATION ( WITH ADDITIONS AS REQUIRED )
```

Figure 3-8 A partial output from XCON. (Digital Equipment Corp.)

Second, equally good configurers tend to configure the same sets of components in different ways. So the DEC system configurations are not consistent.

Third, it is difficult to keep skilled, experienced configurers. Such people tend to be promoted to other jobs. Consequently, configurers are often not as experienced or as knowledgeable as DEC would like.

AI'S RECEPTION AT DEC*

To solve its configuration problem, DEC made several unsuccessful attempts to automate the configuration process by developing a program using traditional software techniques. In 1978, Sam Fuller, who was then a faculty member in the computer science department at CMU, accepted a position at Digital. As he became aware of the problems that Digital was having in automating the configuration task, he proposed and began the negotiations between management at Digital and researchers at CMU.

After half a day of discussions about Digital's computer configuration, the CMU group believed that the configuration problem had characteristics that made it amenable to an expert system solution. So the group proposed that Digital Equipment support an effort at CMU to develop a configuration expert. John McDermott, senior research computer scientist at CMU and inventor of Digital Equipment Corp.'s expert computer configuration program, describes the initial reactions of the people at DEC to the idea of an expert system that configures VAX-11/780 computer systems as ranging from radical skepticism to moderate disbelief.

"The only reason we were asked to build the expert system was that the problem was bothering some people enough so that they were willing to try anything," McDermott says. "Yet, despite the seriousness of the problem, no one at Digital was prepared to fund the development of a knowledge-based configurer until after the demonstration version of XCON had been implemented."

In fact, this ability to try out the configuration system during its development stages was necessary both to convince enough doubtful people of the expert system's promise and to conjure up enough commitment to fund the project to its successful completion. After the first version of XCON was demonstrated, some people's skepticism was replaced not with belief but with caution and hope. And after each succeeding developmental stage and demonstration, a few more people became less cautious. Some even committed themselves to making XCON a success. Finally, after about a year, as XCON was able to demonstrate its increasing configuration expertise, staunch believers and supporters began to emerge.

Five factors, according to McDermott, enabled XCON to stay afloat in the sea of caution that surrounded it. First, at each stage in its development, and with each demonstration, XCON convinced a few people who were in a position to assist in its development that it had real promise. Second, the task of developing a computer configuration

*This discussion is based on McDermott (1981).

was of just the right degree of difficulty. As a result, XCON was able to develop at a reasonable enough rate so that anyone who looked could see progress.

Third, only occasionally did XCON do less than was expected of it. Therefore, it never made any enemies. It turns out that not having enemies was just as important as having strong supporters. XCON's place at Digital Equipment was tenuous enough that if a few people had believed that it was a serious mistake, the exploration and development efforts would have stopped.

The fourth factor that kept XCON adrift is actually a corollary to the third. The group of people who were close enough to the program to know about it firsthand was quite small and possessed the characteristics of not being resistant to change or new technologies. They believed that XCON had promise and therefore were willing to accept the times that it stumbled.

The fifth factor entailed maintaining XCON in a proper perspective by not allowing the hyping of any people's expectations for XCON. Keeping the right perspective is particularly important because, after a buildup of expectations, AI has flopped on this score in the past. To prevent such a recurrent experience, "the spokespeople for the project at Digital Equipment Corp. worked hard to manage people's expectations to insure that no one would count on more from XCON than it could deliver," McDermott says.

The initial contact between Digital Equipment Corp. and CMU occurred in 1978. From December 1978 through April 1979, a strategy for attacking Digital's configuration problem was formulated and a minimal expert system to demonstrate the potential of the knowledge-based approach was written and demonstrated. From May through September 1979, a large amount of more computer configuration knowledge was added to the program. From October through November 1979, Digital tested XCON extensively and determined that it was sufficiently expert to be used on a regular basis to configure its VAX-11/780 computer systems.

By January 1980, the chief question had become how to integrate the expert configurer into Digital's operational environment without disrupting the existing operations. It took the first half of 1980 to define the type of organization that should support XCON and the functions the group should perform. The second half of that year was spent recruiting people, none of whom had any background in AI, to learn enough AI so that they could continue the development and maintenance of XCON when CMU's involvement was completed.

Since that time, Digital Equipment Corp. has expanded this AI group. Using this initial CMU-trained group as the seed, the computer firm has grown its own internal expertise in AI, and it has grown that expertise without bringing in people who have formal credentials in AI.

However, it is Digital Equipment's usual computer system configurers, rather than this home-grown AI group, who actually operate the expert system. Normally, to operate without an expert system, in each of Digital's final assembly and test plants, people called technical editors configure each system to be built. Then they give their configuration diagrams to technicians, who actually assemble the systems.

Once XCON was ready for routine use, the person who had been the technical editor for VAX-11/780 systems become XCON's supervisor. The supervisor's role was to review XCON's output configuration diagrams for correctness. The output, if correct, was then given to the technicians for use in assembly.

The AI group that Digital formed when XCON was getting ready for routine use was given three principal functions: data collection, process development, and program maintenance and development. The data collection task, performed by engineers, involved extending XCON's database of component descriptions. The process development task was to invent ways to facilitate information flow and XCON's accessibility between the XCON development group and people in other Digital Equipment organizations, such as manufacturing, engineering, and sales. For example, the process development group formalized the reporting of problems with XCON, such as an incorrect configuration performance, and the checking of reported problems, such as "was the configuration produced by XCON indeed incorrect?"

The people responsible for data collection and for process development needed no special training. But the people responsible for program maintenance and development were slated to take over the role that CMU played. They were the people who, in the future, would modify XCON's rules as inadequacies in its knowledge were discovered, and they would extend XCON so that it could configure systems other than VAX-11/780s. Clearly, to take over this role, they needed to become proficient in OPS5, the specialized programming language used to program the expert system.

On the average, it took each of the new AI group's members about three months of learning and practice to achieve enough OPS5 proficiency to be able to make appropriate modifications and extensions to the program. With this proficiency, however, the group became self-sufficient enough to subsequently extend XCON's capabilities. First the group extended XCON so that it could also configure VAX-11/750 systems. Later, the group focused on extending XCON to configure PDP-11s. Configuring PDP-11 systems is a more difficult problem than configuring VAX-11s because PDP-11s support a significantly greater number of components.

A KNOWLEDGE NETWORK

XCON is now firmly entrenched at Digital. Since its acceptance, the Digital AI group has added a series of other expert systems which it is integrating with XCON. Most of these were developed by or in conjunction with CMU. Some are under development with other academic institutions, and some extensions to the expert systems are the products of Digital's AI technology importation and transfer. These integrated expert systems will eventually form what Digital calls a knowledge network to integrate sales, engineering, manufacturing, and field service.

The new expert systems encompass the fields of sales, engineering, manufacturing, distribution, and installation. XSEL (Expert Sales Person's Assistant), the sales system, sits on top of XCON. It uses XCON to help perform configuration chores, but not at such a detailed level as to include cable lengths and screws. However, XSEL is an interactive system that helps salespeople quote prices on multiple versions of configured system orders at their point of sale.

Once the computer system is purchased, detailed order information is supplied to XCON. Various expert systems in engineering, manufacturing, and field service use the product information that is resident in XCON. Altogether, seven integrated expert systems at DEC now perform not only configuration, but also manufacturing jobs to schedule computer system orders against the available material, schedule floor capacity, and create a flexible construction plan. Some are in daily use; others are still being tested. Finally, moving out of the factory, expert systems then help manage and distribute the product from the plant to the customer and help with the layout of the computer system installation at the customer site.

Identifying Expert/Knowledge System Applications

CHAPTER 4

It is probable that within the next 30 days yet another company will form an artificial intelligence department or yet another new artificial intelligence company will start up. Most likely, both the department and the company will investigate, build, use, or market an expert system.

Expert systems are computer programs that capture the expertise of human experts who are knowledgeable in a particular application domain. As such, human experts are in very short supply; they are expensive and difficult to get.

Since getting the real human expert has proved to be a problem, the alternative, the expert system scheme, is to represent an expert's knowledge in a form that a computer can use. A computerized model of the expert's reasoning and problem-solving abilities then uses that knowledge to solve problems in humanlike fashion.

The expert's knowledge is contained in what is aptly called a knowledge base. An inference mechanism also does what its name implies. It makes inferences based on its interpretation of the representation of the expert's knowledge (Figure 4-1). These expert

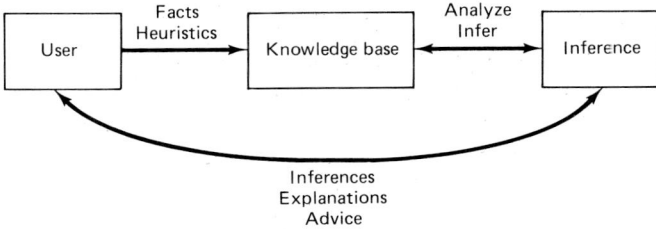

Figure 4-1 Expert systems infer and advise based on interpreting human experts knowledge.

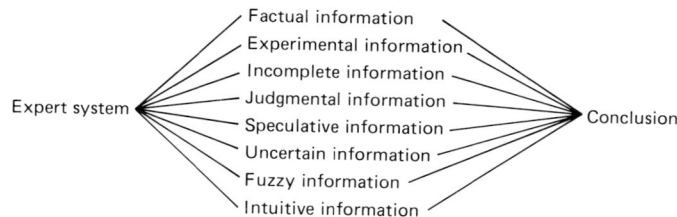

Figure 4-2 Expert systems solve problems for which there is no practical algorithmic solution by reasoning with heuristic as well as factual information.

systems (or knowledge-based systems), which incorporate these experts' reasoning and problem-solving models, augment the experts' capabilities and are similar to having a consultant on call.

It is important to realize, however, that while expert systems can reason from knowledge in a limited domain and can approach (in some cases, even exceed) human performance, they cannot provide solutions for problems that human beings do not know how to solve. Instead, expert systems contain, in encoded form, the existing knowledge of experts and use that encoded knowledge to reason like a human being. Therein lies the power of expert systems—in that knowledge, not in clever programming.

To reason like a human being, expert systems rely not only on factual knowledge as do conventional programs, but also on uncertain knowledge and observations based on experience and intuition (collectively called heuristics). The facts and heuristics are extracted from experts in a specialized subject area. They are then coupled with methods of analyzing, manipulating, and applying the encoded knowledge so that the program can make inferences and explain its actions.

Expert systems differ from computer programs because their reasoning is not straightforward. Their tasks have no practical algorithmic solutions, and they must often make conclusions based on incomplete, judgmental, speculative, uncertain, or fuzzy information (Figure 4-2). For example, most human beings would interpret the statement, "the boss is never in his office" to mean "the boss is frequently out of his office." "Fire him" would be an unthinkable conclusion to most human beings (and expert systems), who know that bosses are frequently at meetings held elsewhere in the organization.

Typically, to build an expert system, the developer chooses a form to represent the

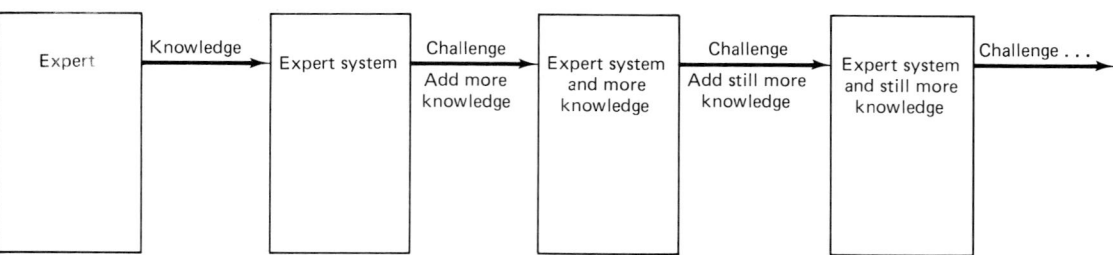

Figure 4-3 Expert system development

expert's knowledge. The developer and the expert work together to encode some of the expert's basic knowledge and reasoning techniques in that form. Then the developer and the expert together challenge that expert system with a lot of problems and cases. As the fledgling expert system makes mistakes, its developers add more knowledge and thus try to improve on the model of the expert (Figure 4-3).

EXPERT SYSTEM CHARACTERISTICS

There are several characteristics that expert systems must exhibit to be useful. First, in order to add more knowledge and to improve on the model of the expert developed, expert systems must have the capability to update their knowledge easily. The update capability is necessary not only to correct mistakes that the expert system makes, but to keep pace, for example, with new knowledge that an expert learns or new items that a company decides to handle. Ultimately, expert systems may be able to learn new facts themselves and, in this way, increase their knowledge. For the time being, they are dependent on acquiring their knowledge from human beings, either directly or through data entered into databases by people.

Second, to be able to cope with real-world problems, expert systems must have flexible problem-solving strategies, just as do human experts. This feature is necessary because each problem to be solved, as well as the information available to solve it, may be slightly different each time.

Third, expert systems need to exhibit high performance in terms of their ability to solve their assigned problems correctly. Just as human beings who have difficulty getting the right answer are not considered experts, expert systems that blunder when dealing with the basic problems they were designed to solve are not considered expert systems. Fourth, expert systems need to have the capability to explain what they have done and why, in the same way that human experts explain their actions.

A number of expert systems with these characteristics have successfully handled real problems in areas such as medical diagnosis and treatment, oil and mineral exploration, industrial automation, and product quality control (Chapters 1 and 2). Other commercially feasible expert systems have been built for domains that include equipment diagnosis, planning, scheduling, signal interpretation, financial analysis, accounting, computer configuration, and supervising the use of complex software.

KNOWLEDGE BOTTLENECKS

Not all fields of knowledge are currently suitable for expert system applications. In general, expert system applications are suitable for tasks about which people are more knowledgeable and perform a lot better if they have had years of experience. Usually, the number of such people is relatively small. As a result, their knowledge is scarce, poorly distributed in an organization, often distributed among many people, and unavailable with any degree of reliability. This scarcity, poor distribution, and unavailability results in a knowledge bottleneck for an organization (Figure 4-4).

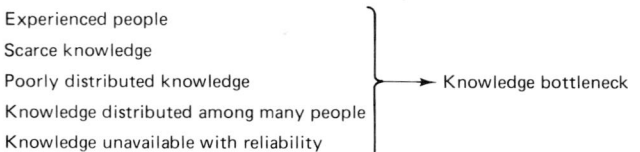

Figure 4-4 When selecting knowledge system applications, look for the knowledge bottleneck.

The high-payoff expert system applications occur where the knowledge bottlenecks are. Therefore, to identify what is a good expert system application in an organization, it is necessary to analyze the flow of information in the organization and locate the knowledge bottlenecks.

Unfortunately, instead of looking to locate these bottlenecks, there is a tendency among many people when considering potential expert systems to focus on the word "expert." These people frequently overlook excellent candidate expert system applications because they are misled by their perceptions of the word "expert."

Clearly, a geophysicist who interprets geological and oil-well log data is easily recognizable as an expert. The geophysicist is recognized as an expert because most people associate geophysicists with such characteristics as university degrees, intellectual sophistication, and the ability to perform tasks that the average person could not conceive of learning—a kind of witch-doctor syndrome if you will. For most people, the combination of the academic associations, together with the ability to perform tasks that are as unintelligible to most people as witch-doctor's methods, adds up to "expert." By this characterization, a physician and a geophysicist are clearly experts.

But knowledge bottlenecks frequently encompass ordinary types of knowledge, such as the planning performed by a travel agent, rather than the more intuitive and academic expertise often associated with expert systems. For example, in the case of expert systems that perform computer configuration, the knowledge bottlenecks comprised some moderately paid, experienced technicians/clerks who were expert at their jobs.

High-payoff expert systems have also been implemented to perform locomotive diagnostic tasks. Migrating to a less technical area of expertise, the loan advice domain has the characteristics of a possibly good expert system application. Knowledge about loans certainly exists in organizations that issue them. However, the information is generally poorly distributed, difficult to use, and difficult for most people to communicate to others. Therefore, loan organizations make a larger number of undesirable loans than they would like. Even something as simple as filling out various forms within an organization may require a fair amount of knowledge to avoid their bouncing back from the accounting department. Making an expert system out of such an application may be a valuable time and money saver. Yet people do not generally view the latter as a "real" expert system application.

KNOWLEDGE SYSTEMS

Because the term "expert system" often suggests misleading notions and features about what these systems can do and what kinds of applications are appropriate, "knowledge system" is the preferred label by many in the AI community. Knowledge systems suggest

Knowledge Systems

greater variety of ordinary knowledge than the intuitive and academic expertise associated with the label "expert" (Figure 4-5).

Knowledge systems that perform more ordinary tasks than, say, oil-exploration systems have several advantages, some of which are particularly relevant to organizations first getting into AI. First, the problems caused by knowledge bottlenecks affect an organization economically. Second, many AI companies claim that compared to systems with intuitive and academic expertise, it is easier to estimate the amount of time, cost, and effort to build ordinary knowledge-based systems. As such, they entail a much lower risk and are more practical.

The ease of estimating development time, cost, and effort are related to the ease with which the non-application expert can understand the subject matter of the application. This ease is important because to build an expert system, the knowledge engineer, who extracts knowledge from an application expert and converts it into a form that a computer understands, must to some degree acquire an understanding of the subject.

Clearly, there is much more to learn for a subject based on academic expertise rather than one based on ordinary knowledge. For example, an intelligent person can sit in a room full of books and figure out how to get from here to Tahiti. It may take time, it may not be convenient, and certainly it would be easier to find a route if either a travel agent or a travel information expert system were available. But sitting in a room filled with geology texts is a different ball game. In contrast to travel agents or other people who possess ordinary knowledge, experienced, expert geologists are more likely to have learned vast amounts of facts and have spent years in training and apprenticeship.

Because of the combination of their vast storehouse of facts and intuitive knowledge, an expert's expertise is difficult for a knowledge engineer to understand at the onset of a project. How, then, can a knowledge engineer estimate how long it will take, how much it will cost, and how much effort it will involve to build an expert system that per-

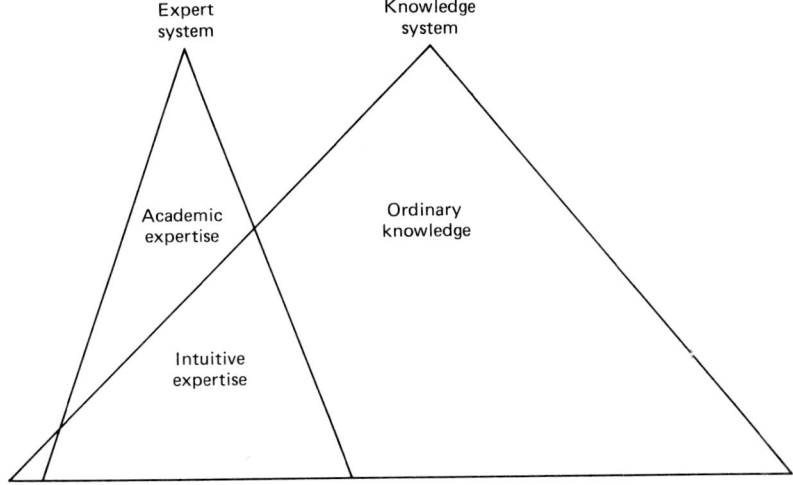

Figure 4-5 Connotations of "expert system" compared to "knowledge system."

forms the geologist's job? Knowledge engineers can, however, estimate and quantify such parameters for applications that incorporate ordinary knowledge simply because they understand them better.

A third advantage in building ordinary-knowledge systems is the ability to easily find experts who can systematically communicate their knowledge. Systematic communication of knowledge is a much more difficult task when building expert rather than knowledge systems. Expertise tends to be amorphous, unstructured, and intuitive. Like artists, experts, follow a classical pattern of accomplishing their work without ever thinking to any extent how they perform it systematically. These characteristics make it difficult for experts to articulate their knowledge.

In contrast, ordinary knowledge tends to be more structured and systematic. The structure and systematic nature of such knowledge makes it easier for knowledgeable people to make their knowledge explicit enough to be incorporated into a computer system.

Finally, more people exist who have ordinary knowledge than those who have expertise. This makes it easier to find the experts in a field. Because of the greater abundance of experts in ordinary knowledge, there is no danger that a knowledge system will not be able to be completed because the only articulate, experienced expert at a company has left.

While knowledge systems containing ordinary knowledge are in some ways more practical than academically oriented expert systems, they too have their failings and should not be considered simple to develop or run compared to their more complex conterparts. The problem is that simple systems, such as expert travel planners, may need to contain hundreds of heuristic rules about shortcuts, discounts, and so on. These systems frequently rely on search through a large search space of solutions to find the best solution—a strategy considered a "weak," not necessarily efficient method. In contrast, complex systems are likely to concentrate on representing more knowledge in ways that require less search to arrive at a solution and provide more efficient performance. Thus they classically rely on what is considered to be "strong" methods.

CHOOSING AN APPLICATION

Teknowledge, Inc. suggests eight common situations where a knowledge-based system can be of value.*

- The knowledge required to perform a particular task effectively is available only at a central location. Requests for advice are channeled to a small group of people who are always in demand. For example, a key product design team may be spending an excessive portion of their time on the phone advising repair personnel.
- A written document or flowchart is intended to facilitate the use of a program, procedure, or piece of equipment. However, it is so long and detailed that it is useless

*"Evaluating Knowledge Engineering Applications," Knowledge Engineering, Teknowledge, Inc., Palo Alto, Calif., 1983.

in practice. In actuality, the users develop folklore-like methods for accomplishing the task. They rely excessively on previous methods that were determined empirically to work. For example, a flexible and sophisticated computer simulation program goes unused in favor of building expensive models because its user manual fills a shelf of three-ring binders.

- An organization turns away work or loses business to competitors because an overworked human expert is required to make judgments or recommendations, even in routine cases. For example, to reduce unnecessary, expensive work, a locomotive repair center requires a supervisor to approve all diagnoses and recommendations before work is undertaken. Although costs are controlled, the average down time increases to a point where it is economical for customers to tow broken equipment to other centers for repair.

- Due to turnover in equipment or personnel, an excessive amount of time is spent training rather than doing. For example, a company updates its line of test equipment each year, and field engineers must spend an average of two months annually attending training sessions.

- A large amount of mainly routine data must be scanned by a highly trained expert on a continuing basis. For example, a high-energy physics laboratory employs a crew of 10 people to look for rare events in bubble chamber images.

- A variety of information from heterogeneous sources must be monitored and integrated to determine the possibility of an important event. For example, a government agency must constantly examine information from multiple sources to determine if a military threat is present.

- A critical judgment must be made in a very short time interval to avoid a potential disaster. For example, a nuclear power plant control center must decide quickly to shut down or cut back a particular unit when a potential problem is detected.

- An optimal solution to a routing, planning, or configuration task is too expensive or time consuming to determine. Instead, a minimally effective process of guesswork has been substituted. For example, a computer company has to configure orders for its equipment, with the proper cables, components, and mounting arrangement, on an individual basis. Errors and delays in this process become a serious problem as orders increase.

KNOWLEDGE SYSTEM PREREQUISITES

To build a knowledge-based system for any problem domain, certain prerequisites concerning the human beings involved and problem characteristics must be met. For example, prerequisite conditions concerning human experts require that there be at least one person who performs the task well enough to be classified as an expert in that task. The experts must be able to articulate their knowledge and explain how to apply that knowledge to a particular task. It is possible to bring the knowledge of several human experts to bear on a problem. Dealing with more than one expert, however, can cause inconsistencies in the knowledge extracted for computer use because different experts often arrive at the same or equivalent answer by what seems to be very different means.

Prerequisite conditions that apply to the problem, rather than the human expert, require that the application area be well bounded. In other words, the problem limits that the knowledge system can handle should be well defined because most knowledge systems today do not deal well with problems at the limits of their knowledge; in fact, many do not even know that a problem is beyond their knowledge. In addition, the chunks of knowledge encoded within the program must be relatively well defined so that when solving a problem the knowledge system can select from its various alternative pieces of knowledge. Finally, the problem chosen for a knowledge system application should be solvable by human beings within a period of three minutes to three weeks.

Knowledge Bases

CHAPTER 5

Although we can recognize intelligent behavior to some degree when we see it, no one has yet succeeded in defining what intelligence is. The lack of a definition of intelligence makes it difficult to attribute intelligence to computer programs. However, AI researchers have developed a number of ways to represent human knowledge and structure computer programs so that the programs exhibit behavior that we normally associate with intelligence. The computer programs that incorporate these knowledge representations and structuring techniques are our present-day expert or knowledge systems.*

Expert/knowledge systems contain three basic components (Figure 5-1). These components are in addition to the user interface, which varies with the knowledge-based system and insulates the end user from the AI technology. One basic component, called a knowledge base, in some symbolic manner represents knowledge of facts and general information, as well as heuristics such as judgments, intuition, and experience, about a particular narrow problem area. The second component, known as an inference mechanism, interprets the knowledge in the knowledge base and performs logical deduction and certain knowledge base modifications. The third component, the control mechanism, organizes and controls the strategies taken to apply the inference process.

Some components and characteristics are common to knowledge systems and conventional computer programs. For example, conventional computer programs also contain data (facts, as opposed to heuristics) and a means to manipulate those data algrorithmically and to control the strategies that the program applies to solve its problem.

---

*The terms ''expert system'' and ''knowledge system'' are synonymous. However, ''knowledge system'' is considered by many in the AI community to be more descriptive of what these AI systems are and will be used throughout most of the rest of this book.

71

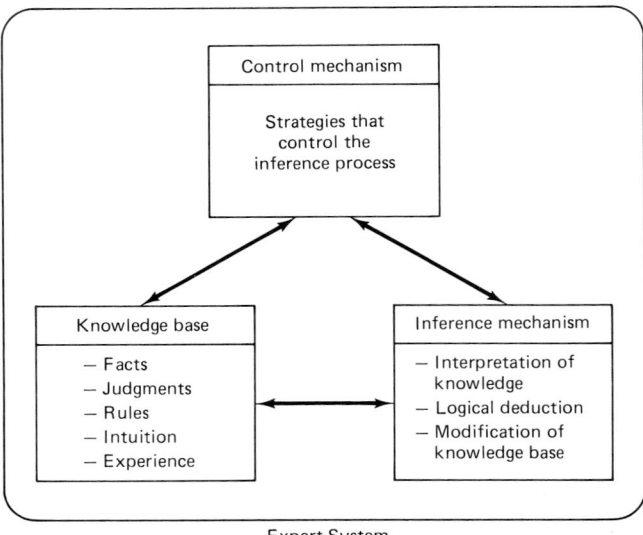

Figure 5-1 Three components of expert systems

However, conventional programs differ substantially from knowledge-based systems because in conventional programs, the data, manipulation, and control capabilities are all buried together and distributed throughout the program (Figure 5-2). In comparison to conventional programs, knowledge systems modularize the knowledge base, inference mechanism, and control mechanism. In other words, these three mechanisms are separate and independent of each other.

This separation of the knowledge base and the inference and control mechanisms contributes to the easy modifiability of knowledge systems and makes it possible to change the system just by modifying the knowledge base. For example, one knowledge-based system for oil exploration was converted to a knowledge system in the area of public accounting by substituting a public accounting knowledge base for the one containing oil exploration knowledge. Similarly, two other knowledge systems, one for medical diagnostics (Mycin) and one for speech understanding (Hearsay II), have been converted to general-purpose knowledge systems that can be used with a variety of knowledge bases in different application fields.

Even the chunks of knowledge within the knowledge base are separate from one another. This separation allows new chunks of knowledge to be added fairly easily to knowledge systems. As a result, the knowledge base lives and grows as the expert behind

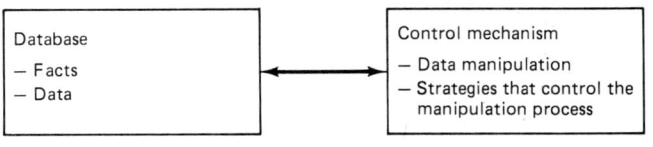

Figure 5-2 Components of conventional programs

it adds more knowledge to it. In contrast to the knowledge base, the inference and control mechanisms are essentially static. They do not generally change with time.

KNOWLEDGE BASES AND DATABASES

Both knowledge bases and traditional databases are designed to store information. They differ significantly from each other in the types of information they can store, the types of interrelationships between data they can handle (that indicate either application-specific or commonsense knowledge), and in what kind of training is needed for the person who updates the stored information.

To illustrate one difference, databases store only facts (Figure 5-3). Moreover, database facts are straightforward and definite. Typical facts found in databases include information such as "Liu is a male," "Karen is an employee in the sales department," and "the sales department contains 30 employees."

A major strength of databases is the ability to use this type of straightforward, definite information to respond to queries such as "what are the names of all the female employees in the sales department" and "how many departments contain greater than 25 employees?" However, databases cannot deal with complex descriptions of real-world situations, rules that state causal relationships, or uncertain knowledge about the stored facts. Neither can databases handle what seems to be commonsense relationships between the stored facts.

Knowledge bases, like databases, also store straightforward definite facts. But, in addition, knowledge bases store cause-and-effect knowledge, rules, and imprecise and probabilistic information. Typical knowledge found in knowledge bases includes information such as "smoking is bad for your health." Or else, knowledge bases handle observed or proven rules, such as "if you smoke, you are more likely to get lung cancer."

DATABASE TABLE FOR EMPLOYEES

EMPNO	ENAME	JOB	HIREDATE	SAL	DEPTNO
5124	ADAM	CLERK	15-DEC-81	800.00	20
5436	PUCCINI	SALESPERSON	28-FEB-82	1,600.C0	30
5499	NADER	SALESPERSON	04-MAR-82	1,250.C0	30
6012	BING	MANAGER	13-APR-82	2,975.00	20
6078	LYONS	SALESPERSON	23-JUN-82	1,250.00	30
7134	MARTIN	MANAGER	17-OCT-82	4,850.00	30
7488	FLYNN	MANAGER	25-NOV-82	2,450.00	10
7793	FERMAT	ANALYST	09-FEB-83	5,000.00	20
8005	KING	PRESIDENT	12-MAR-83	8,000.00	10
8035	KAREN	SALESPERSON	24-APR-83	1,900.00	30
8456	BACH	SALESPERSON	01-JUL-83	1,500.00	30
8888	ESCHER	CLERK	22-SEP-83	1,100.00	20
8900	EINSTEIN	CLERK	10-OCT-83	950.00	30
9116	GODEL	ANALYST	07-JAN-84	5,000.00	20
9130	JACKSON	CLERK	16-APR-84	1,300.0C	10

Figure 5-3 Typical facts stored in databases.

FUZZY FACTS

The latter is an example not only of a rule, but also of an imprecise, uncertain, or "fuzzy" chunk of knowledge. Fuzzy knowledge is knowledge quantified by words such as most, several, many, few, almost, unlikely, more frequently, almost impossible, very, quite, and extremely. It is difficult to describe real-world knowledge without the ability to deal with fuzzy, as well as probabilistic, knowledge because almost everything in the real world is a matter of degree.

In other words, the real world does not contain facts that state that smokers get lung cancer. Instead, the medical rules that doctors, insurance companies, and government agencies use for their statistics and decisions are couched in terms of "more likely to get lung cancer."

Knowledge bases, and the inference mechanisms that manipulate and infer new information from knowledge bases, are designed to handle fuzzy or probabilistic information. Databases are not. In the database (Figure 5-3), Karen either is or is not an employee. She is not almost an employee. She is not mostly in the sales department. Database applications understand that the sales department has 30 employees, not many employees.

WHO DOES THE UPDATES

The update requirements for databases contrast sharply with those for knowledge base updates because of the differences in the type of information and in the cause-and-effect relationships contained in knowledge bases. Typical database types of data, such as employee name, sex, department, and parts lists, are generic, traverse many types of applications, and are superficially understandable by the general populace. When new names or parts need to be added to a particular department listed in the database, a variety of people can add them.

For example, databases may be updated by workers in a data-processing department who are knowledgeable about databases. The data-processing workers do not, however, need to know about the mechanics of running a department or about the devices that will use the parts in a database. With the development of English-like, easy-to-use database update languages (fourth-generation languages), an increasing number of clerical workers can also update databases. All that is necessary for them to perform the update is some knowledge of how the data are structured, or else a tool or language that eliminates even that need.

In contrast to database information, the knowledge and rules found in knowledge bases include both data and heuristics of a professional and engineering nature, specialized for a particular application area. The application area they are specialized for determines who can update the knowledge base.

For example, one typical Mycin diagnosis rule indicates that if a blood culture shows an organism with a gram-negative stain and a rod morphology in a compromised-host patient, it suggests that the identity of an organism found in a blood culture is

```
IF  The site of the culture is blood
    The gram stain of the organism is gramneg
    The morphology of the organism is rod, and
    The patient is a compromised host,
THEN There is suggestive evidence (0.6) that the identity of
     the organism is Pseudomonas-Aeruginosa.
```

Figure 5-4 Mycin diagnosis rule

Pseudomonas aeruginosa (Figure 5-4). A knowledge base that contains this type of information needs to be modified or new rules added by a doctor or expert with comparable knowledge in this diagnostic area. Similarly, knowledge in an expert automotive troubleshooting system must be added or modified by a person with automotive troubleshooting expertise.

Easy-to-use languages and application development tools make the knowledge-base-update process easier. However, unlike with databases, the nature of knowledge contained in knowledge bases requires experts in the knowledge base's application area to perform the updates of causal knowledge and beliefs, because only they have the necessary knowledge.

HANDLING COMMON SENSE

It is not only the ability to store general knowledge, rules, and uncertain information that differentiates knowledge bases from databases. Knowledge bases store and handle far more complex and sophisticated relationships between facts, or chunks of information, than databases can. AI's goal is to identify and codify the variety of relationships that may exist. The ability to store these interrelationships makes it possible to build and infer a great deal of causal and commonsense knowledge about the world, as well as knowledge about what is possible in a given application area, into a knowledge base.

Two things make it possible to represent causal and commonsense information in a knowledge-based system. One is the representation of knowledge symbolically. The other is the various types of knowledge base structures that have been developed to represent and store both the knowledge and the relationships between the knowledge items in the knowledge base. These types of knowledge base structures do not exist in databases. Indeed, traditional databases do not deal with either causal or commonsense knowledge and are more limited in their ability to handle relationships between information than are knowledge bases.

Most often, a database is a fairly rigidly structured set of records and items within records, comparable to what is found in a file cabinet. For example, an inventory database for corporate offices might contain a list of office desks along with their cost, location, and owners. Each office desk and the information about it is a separate database record, just as it would be a separate record on an index card or inventory form in a file drawer. With such a database, users can answer such questions as "how many desks cost more than $1200?"

Interrelationships in this database are fairly simple. It is easy to represent, for example, a relationship that concludes that both these typewriters and desks belong to David. But certainly there will not be a lot of information about what is sensible in the world. For example, database users cannot deduce that typewriters tend to sit on desks; desks do not tend to sit on typewriters; desks tend to sit on floors; typewriters do not tend to sit on floors.

SEMANTIC NETWORKS

In contrast to database mechanisms that represent relatively straightforward relationships, knowledge bases contain a system of "predicate functions" and "symbolic data structures" which have meaning, or "semantics," built in. A function is a kind of procedure that is performed on certain input values, called arguments, and produces or is associated with a set of admissible values. For example, "3 plus 4," which is written in Lisp programs as (plus 3 4), is an example of the "plus" function. The function (plus 3 4) evaluates to 7. Times, Difference, Quotient, Min (to find a minimum) and Max (for maximum) are examples of other functions.

A predicate is a function that evaluates to either true or false. For example, in the function (on typewriter desk), "on" is a predicate, and the function, which states that the typewriter is on the desk, is either true or false.

Besides predicates, the other type of item in a knowledge base is a symbolic data structure. A symbolic data structure is a structure that is used to represent symbolic knowledge and that can also be stored in a computer's memory. One knowledge representation structure is called a semantic network.

A semantic network is a node-and-arc graphical notation that represents objects (or actions or events) and contains built-in real-world meaning about the objects (Figure 5-5). The nodes represent the objects. They could also represent actions or events. The arcs between the nodes represent predicates or attributes that indicate relationships between the objects (or actions or events) shown in the nodes.

The semantic network shown in the figure uses both predicates, such as "on" and "isa," as well as attributes, such as material, to represent objects in an office and to show relationships between the objects. A trace of the arcs that connect the nodes in this network shows that among other things, this knowledge structure can infer information such as "a particular object can't be a typewriter because it has a desk sitting on it."

The semantic network also enables a knowledge system to infer information such as "a particular desk sits on the floor because, as shown, desks sit on floors." With a semantic network representation, the knowledge system can also infer that "desk 1 and desk 2 have flat tops and are used for writing because desks 1 and 2 are both types of (instances of) desks, and desks in general have flat tops and are used for writing.

This type of inference is based on a principle called "inheritance." Here "inheritance" means that since desks 1 and 2 are types of desks, they inherit the characteristics of that desk. Since the purpose of desks is writing and their description is flat-topped, both instances of a desk inherit the purpose of writing and the description of flat-topped.

This inheritance principle in AI, and inferences that can be made because of inheritance, are similar to the assumptions that are made based on the classification of biological organisms. For example, it is known that mammals have hair and dogs are mammals. Therefore, it is possible to infer that dogs have hair.

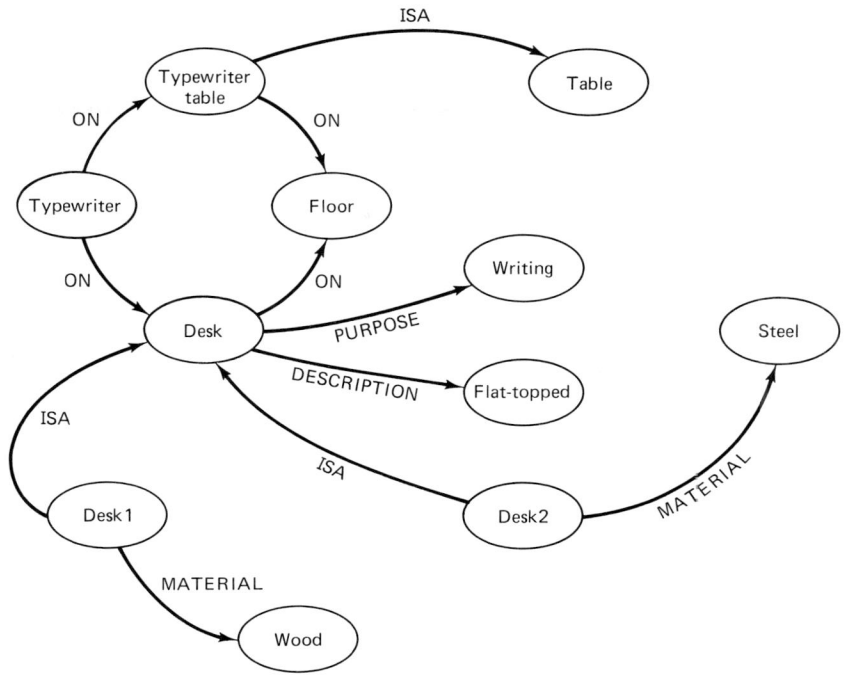

Figure 5-5 A semantic network

FRAMES

Another symbolic knowledge representation structure used to represent knowledge in knowledge bases is known as "frames." Like databases, frames store information. However, a database stores information about its data in what are called "fields." A field is the memory area that contains each item in a record. For example, an employee record might contain an employee's number, name, job, date of hire, salary, and department number. The area of memory allocated to employee number is one field; employee name, job, date of hire, salary, and department number are the other five fields in the employee record. The record is actually the collective group of fields for a single employee.

Instead of memory areas called fields, which a database uses to hold information about its data, frames are data structures that contain variable-sized memory areas called slots. The slots may contain standard attributes, such as are found in databases. But slots may also contain other types of information, such as hypotheses that relate to the expert program's function. In addition, slots can contain rules about application area situations and actions to take under certain conditions. They can contain subprograms, or "pointers," that point to and link the slots of one frame to other frames. Finally, individual slots in one frame may also be independent frames, with their own complete sets of slots of attributes, hypotheses, rules, and processes. This slot-to-other-frame link creates a hierarchy of relationships not found in databases.

The relationships that can be indicated with hierarchies of frames are similar to those shown in semantic networks. They are different primarily in the way programmers view the knowledge—groups of text and pointers instead of graphical nodes and arcs. Frames, how they are used, and why are described in more detail in Chapter 7 and later in the book.

There are several other methods used to represent knowledge in a knowledge base. Besides semantic networks and frames, knowledge-based systems employ representation methods known as rules, processes, logic, and scripts (used mostly in natural-language systems). These knowledge representation structures are discussed later, in Chapters 5 to 8, and 15 and in other chapters in conjunction with associated applications.

Despite knowledge representation differences, in general anything that one representation can do can be done by the others. Ultimately, a representation choice boils down to how the chooser thinks about the knowledge in question and which representation method lends itself most efficiently to retrieval and deduction of facts.

The representation of knowledge so that a computer understands it is one of the major problems in building a knowledge-based system. It may take months to represent the relationships in a simple world such as an office. How, then, can an AI expert represent the entire building? And once the knowledge has been represented, how is it possible to search it quickly and make inferences?

RULES

Although there are many ways to represent knowledge, the most common form of knowledge representation is with "rules." As in real life, a rule is a conditional statement that specifies an action that is supposed to take place under a certain set of conditions.

In some respects, rules are similar to the conditional "if-then" statements of conventional programming languages. If-then statements are statements of the form, "IF this is the case, THEN do that" or "IF this happens, THEN do that" or even "IF this is the case, THEN that is true." For example, IF Fido is a dog, THEN Fido is an animal. Rules differ from conventional IF-THEN statements because of their extreme modularity. A set of rules is an unstructured group of IF-THEN statements that control themselves in terms of knowing when they should be applied to solve a problem.

This difference between rules and IF-THEN statements is major and has significant implications for the building of knowledge-based systems. In fact, despite their similarities, experience has shown that it is very difficult—often impossible—to develop a knowledge-based system using conventional IF-THEN statements. The difficulties exist because knowledge systems require both greater conditionality and greater need to make changes during program development than do conventional software systems. Writing programs that satisfy the greater conditionality and modifiability requirements of knowledge-based systems is hampered by using conventional branching programming styles.

Concerning the first requirement for conditionality, it turns out that most instructions in conventional programs are unconditional. The program executes its instructions sequentially—first one, then the next, and so on. In addition, the conditional statements that conventional programs encounter contain only a relatively small number of possible paths at each step that calls for branching to perform one or another procedure (Figure 5-6). For example, during execution of conventional programs, when the conditions in the IF part of the statement are true, the program then branches to a particular set of procedures. If the conditions in the IF statement are not true, the program branches to a different set of procedures. Other types of conditional statements in conventional programming specify that depending on whether the results of some computation are equal to this, that, these, those, or the other thing, the program branches to this, that, these, those, or the other place and performs the procedures specified there.

In contrast to the two, three, or five possibilities usual in conventional programs, the conditionality embedded in AI problems is so great that the number of paths that can be exploited grows explosively. Typical conventional programs contain a smaller number of paths because they solve problems algorithmically and therefore contain little uncertainty about what the appropriate next step is. If uncertainty does exist, it is generally uncertain as to whether or not to do one of only a few possible things. The determination of which possible choice to take can be made on the basis of only a few critical pieces of information. On the other hand, when solving tasks heuristically, based on experience and intuition, it is not always clear what the next reasonable step is. So at every step during a heuristic problem solution, it is necessary to consider a number of alternative steps.

Unfortunately, human programmers who must specify the sequences of alternative steps that a knowledge-based system must execute are immediately confronted by the necessity to specify, at every step of a problem, several possible paths, each of which depends on several possible conditions. Each of the paths specified also necessitates further specification of several possible paths depending on a variety of conditions. Similar procedures are needed to specify still further paths.

All in all, a mental picture of such a program resembles a very branchy tree with a huge number of possible paths to follow to get to a solution. It is very difficult for human beings even to visualize, much less lay out in advance and write, such branchy AI programs using conventional software methods. Because of this difficulty with the visualization and layout of programs, traditional programming methods and languages are not well suited to the development of highly conditional knowledge systems.

Even worse, conventional algorithmic programs are very difficult to change. The difficulty exists because the architecture of conventional programs is highly structured. Even in supposed modular programs, the various modules and procedures depend on one another enough so that a change in one procedure may affect another. Most of the time, a change in one module that reflects, for example, a change in the state or strategy of a business, is a big undertaking and time consuming. As a result, once conventional programs are designed and coded, they become static.

But business activities and problem-solution requirements are not static. They often change, and computer programs based on these activities must reflect the changes. Unfortunately, conventional programs that have all the permutations of business activities or solutions encoded in them are not able to meet the change demand in a timely, cost-effective manner.

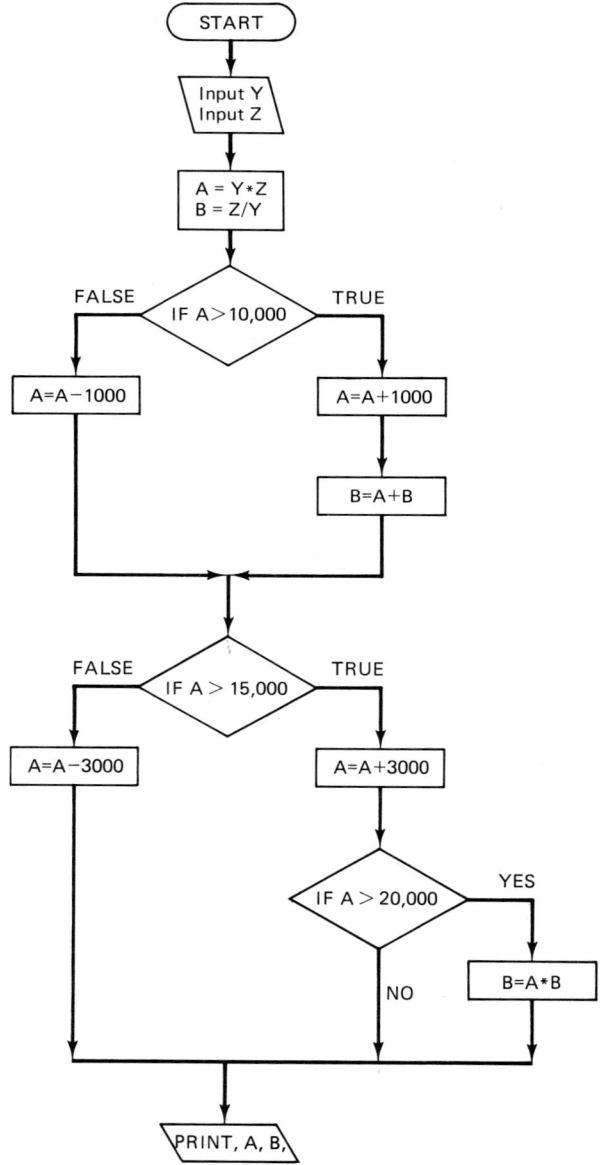

Figure 5-6 Conventional programs have a small number of paths compared to knowledge-based systems.

In fact, Digital Equipment Corp. made three unsuccessful attempts to automate its computer configuration with traditional software techniques before switching to a rule-based approach. Programs based on conventional techniques ran into difficulties because they could not keep pace with DEC's product offerings or engineering changes.

With conventional programming, every time DEC added, removed, or changed the possible mix of components in its computer system offerings, a program rewrite was needed. The conditionality expressed by the expert computer configuration system was so great that the rewrite was particularly difficult.

To compound the problem, changes occurred repeatedly within short time frames. Because of the large amount of conditionality, the changing components, and the short time frames, the conventionally styled computer configuration program never reflected the current state of business. In the end, the firm decided that what it needed, instead, was a programming tool or language that itself considers what to do at each step of solving a problem and then selects the best alternative choice on the basis of which action is most appropriate in the context of a particular situation. In other words, for success, the tool or language, rather than the programmer, must consider and select the alternative choices.

The ability for the program to control the consideration and selection of the alternatives while the program is running is an important characteristic of rules and the rule-based languages in which they were written. Rule-based languages do not require programmers to specify a sequence of steps for a program. Instead, programmers need merely describe conditions indicating some situation, specify the action that should take place if that situation is true, and then dump the whole set of unstructured rules into the program.

When the program runs, a rule interpreter applies its own rules to structure the program dynamically. To apply rules, the rule interpreter uses a "pattern-matching" procedure. The rule interpreter checks to see if the conditions specified in the IF part of a rule (it views the conditions as patterns) match similar patterns in a knowledge system database set up elsewhere in the computer's memory. For example, if the database contains a pattern which states that "there is an object called a monkey and there are bananas on the ceiling," the rule interpreter looks through the "rule base" for a rule whose IF part contains the same pattern about the object called a monkey and bananas on the ceiling.

If it finds a rule with that pattern in its IF part, the rule interpreter applies the rule. "Applies the rule" means that it modifies the database to create a new pattern. A typical rule might modify the database to create the pattern, "the object 'monkey' gets an object called ladder." The rule interpreter then performs this type of pattern-matching procedure all over again to handle the changed program and database state with the new pattern about the monkey, bananas, ceiling, and ladder.

The net effect of this pattern-matching technique is that each rule is fairly independent. Even better, each independent rule is always watching the world around itself which is simulated in the knowledge system database. The rule watches its world to see if it is applicable, which means to see if it matches a database pattern. Whenever the rule sees that it is applicable, it applies itself.

Although rule languages work in the manner described, clearly, the description given is simplistic. For example, many rules can apply at one time. There are different techniques for applying the rules. And it is unnecessary and inefficient to try out every rule every time a rule is applied. Rule-based systems in operation are discussed later in more detail.

Because the rule language does not impose any organization on the rules—the rules are applied based on pattern matches—knowledge system designers can add, modify, and delete rules with ease. In addition, since there is no need to bother about proper sequencing and consistency, system designers can explore and rapidly prototype complex, ill-specified, changeable systems.

It is important to note that although the symbolic manipulation language called Lisp is most commonly known as an AI language, most AI programming is not done directly in Lisp. What is used, instead, for example, are a number of specialized languages, such as rule-based and frame-based languages and languages associated with knowledge system development tools. These languages operate on top of Lisp, may translate into Lisp during program execution, and use various Lisp features.

With a rule-based language, which DEC now uses for its expert computer configuration system, whenever new components are added to the DEC computer system line, the company only needs to add new rules about how the new components will interconnect. In contrast, disasters would occur if programmers moved lines of code around a program written in conventional languages such as Fortran, Pascal, or Cobol.

Also, because rules can just be written and dumped into a rule-based system, it is easy to explore techniques and try out a system early. True, disorganized dumping of rules can contribute to the inefficiency of a system. On the other hand, it is a mistake to worry about structuring a system for efficiency and speed too early, because early structuring causes a system to become rigid. The technique in knowledge system development is to defer efficiency and speed issues until the end of the development time and give the developers as much flexibility and computational leverage as possible because the problems that knowledge systems seek to solve are so difficult. Only after the knowledge system has evolved and developed to a satisfactory point and developers are ready to freeze and deliver the system can they afford to go back and reimplement it. For example, DEC's XCON originally required $\frac{1}{2}$ hour to run a single-configuration case. That was considered fine because the goal then was to develop a program to assemble a computer system. When the developers were ready to freeze and deliver the system, the goal also became efficiency. After the reimplementation, XCON ran 200 times faster and required only a few seconds per configuration case.

Knowledge System Reasoning Strategies

CHAPTER 6

Since the power of a knowledge-based system is in its knowledge, a major concern of knowledge systems is the representation of that knowledge. The most common way to represent knowledge is in rules. Once the rules are in place, there are various ways of manipulating them to produce useful knowledge systems. A good example of rule manipulation is found in AI systems for the oil-exploration industry. Because the process of drilling a production oil well is such a complex, expensive undertaking, as measured in money, time, personnel, equipment, and materials, oil exploration companies were among the pioneer supporters of commercial rule-based expert systems.

One oil exploration system, developed by Teknowledge for the French oil company Elf Aquitaine, provides consultation services and advice on problems encountered during the drilling of oil wells. Called the Drilling Advisor, the knowledge-based system questions the drilling supervisor, who is in charge of an oil rig or set of oil rigs, in a natural language. Using the answers to the questions and its own knowledge, the Drilling Advisor then reasons about the drilling problem, identifies the cause of the problem, and finally offers, in text form, both advice on actions to solve the current problem and preventative measures to avoid a recurrence of the accident.

THE PROBLEM TO SOLVE

Sticking of the drill bit is a common oil-well drilling problem which the Drilling Advisor is designed to solve. Drill-bit sticking problems occur when the drilling assembly cannot turn, thereby preventing further drilling or the return of equipment to the surface.

Six major causes of sticking have been identified. However, it takes an expert to determine which of the six major causes of sticking is the problem in a particular drilling episode because problem determination is not done directly. There are no telemetry data from sensors at the bottom of the hole that transmit information to the surface about what is happening in the hole. The drilling engineer at the surface knows only that the drill will not turn. By examining the drilled rock pieces, mud, and lubricant material that comes out of the drilled hole, he or she then determines the reasons that it stopped turning. This procedure is a little like archaeology techniques—we read the present to determine the past.

As Figure 6-1 shows, the drilling assembly that actually drills the well passes through several geological formations. Each formation is composed primarily of a single rock type, perhaps interbedded with a secondary rock type.

The drilling assembly has two major parts: the bottom-hole assembly, which performs the cutting process, and the drill pipe, which connects the bottom hole assembly to

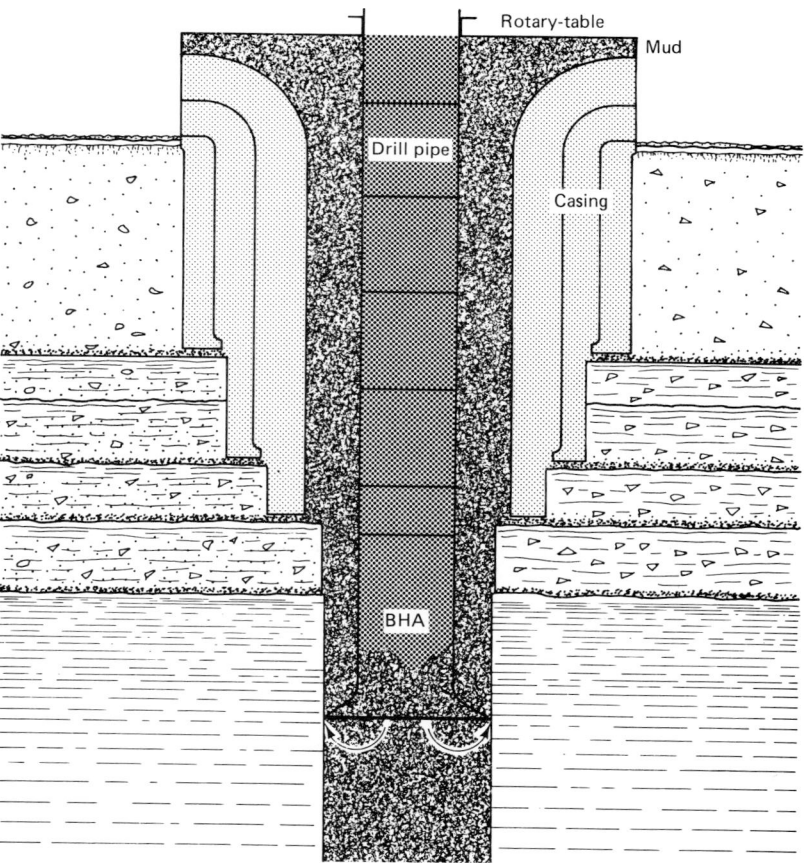

Figure 6-1 Down-hole environment (Teknowledge Inc.)

surface equipment. Stabilizers reach out of the bottom-hole assembly to touch the edges of the walls of the well and try to hold the drilling assembly in the center of the hole.

The characteristics of the underground rock, such as hardness and permeability, the drilling assembly itself, and the behavior of the drilling assembly as it passes through certain types of rock formations, affect the operation of the drilling assembly. For example, particularly hard rock in one place might cause the drilling assembly to be diverted away from a vertical path and stick as a result—a situation called "key seating." Another cause of sticking, known as "differential pressure," may happen if the bottom-hole assembly is in contact with a permeable formation. Under these conditions, the pressure from the rock formations may be higher than the pressure from the hole—a condition that happens with artesian wells. The differential pressure causes liquid to seep out of the rock and force the drilling assembly against the side of the hole. Even the stabilizers that are part of the bottom-hole assembly can cause sticking. Since as part of their function of stabilizing the drilling assembly in the center of the hole, they touch the side walls, they may scrape off (or slough off) material from the walls. This sloughing off of material from the sides of the well may cause caving in the sidewalls of the well and cause the drill bit to stick, a condition known as "sloughing."

HUMAN EXPERTS SOLVE THE PROBLEM

Usually, to determine the cause of sticking, the drilling supervisor examines the recirculated drilling fluid that comes up to the surface from the bottom of the hole. This fluid contains, among other things, cuttings from the rock drilled out of the exposed hole below any protective steel casing already in place. Based on knowledge and past experience, the drilling supervisor integrates information about the rock type, formation, drilling assembly, and drilling procedures to come up with an answer.

But experienced, knowledgeable drilling supervisors do not grow on trees. Generally, they got their jobs through having 20 years of experience drilling fancy wells and having better success than other drilling engineers. This amount of experience and success instantly makes them a scarce commodity. Therefore, they are on call seven days a week, 24 hours a day, for drilling engineers on several different rigs who need to call their supervisors out to their rig to bail them out of problem situations. The scarcity of drilling supervisors and potential unavailability when they are needed for an urgent situation results in a knowledge bottleneck for the oil exploration organization and makes the diagnosis of drilling problems a candidate for a knowledge system application.

THE KNOWLEDGE-BASED SYSTEM SOLVES THE PROBLEM

For these reasons, Elf Aquitaine decided to incorporate the knowledge of its top drilling experts in a knowledge-based system aptly called the "Drilling Advisor." The knowledge-based Drilling Advisor conducts an interactive dialogue in the native language and oil-drilling terminology that is used in the field, in order to consult with the drilling supervisor and the drilling engineers on the rig (Figure 6-2). During the dialogue, the Drilling Advisor requests a small amount of data in order to seed its reasoning process. These initial data may be nothing more than the name of the well, the depth of the hole, and the type of action being performed immediately prior to the drill getting stuck. Later, the system asks more detailed questions about circumstances surrounding the onset of sticking and historical data pertaining to previous activities, conditions, problems, and treatments in the well. These data requests are the same procedures that not only drilling supervisors, but also diagnosticians in other fields, follow.

Based on the knowledge incorporated in rules in its knowledge base, the Drilling Advisor offers two types of advice. The first is a diagnosis that indicates the most likely cause or causes of sticking, together with reasons to support its conclusions. The second consists of two sets of treatment recommendations aimed at alleviating the sticking condition and reducing the likelihood of its recurrence.

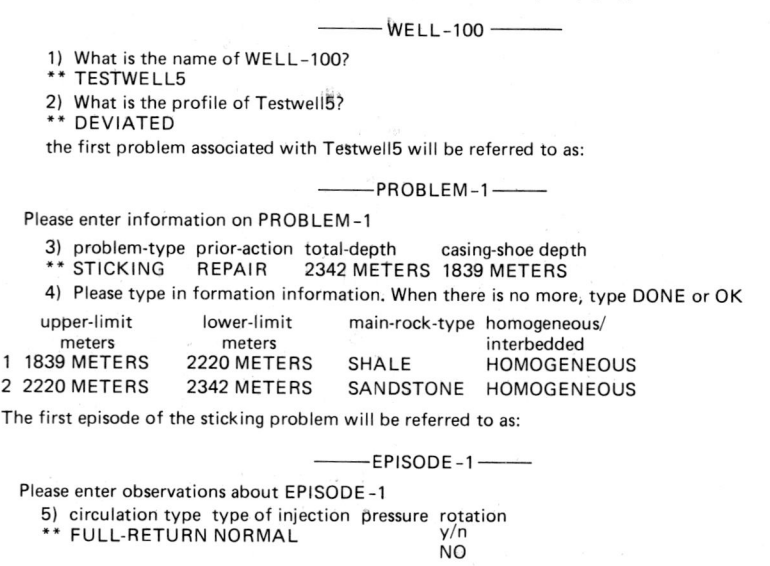

```
                    Welcome to the DRILLING ADVISOR
   I will now proceed to ask you a series of questions pertaining to the sticking problem(s) which you are
   experiencing. Each sticking problem is considered in terms of one or more episodes. Each episode is
   individually characterized with respect to BHA, drilling and mud parameters and observable symptoms.
   Successive episodes correspond to stages in diagnosing and treating the sticking problem.

   At present, the Drilling Advisor diagnoses sticking problems into one of six cause classifications:
   BALLING-UP, CONICAL-HOLE, DIFFERENTIAL-PRESSURE, KEY-SEAT, SLOUGHING AND
   TIGHT-HOLE. It then offers two types of therapy advice: CURATIVE TREATMENTS to alleviate
   the current sticking and PREVENTIVE TREATMENTS to prevent its recurrence.

   This session will be most successful if you can accurately answer all of the questions which I pose. For
   a full summary of your options, at any point in the consultation, simply type HELP.
                           ──────── WELL-100 ────────
     1) What is the name of WELL-100?
     ** TESTWELL5
     2) What is the profile of Testwell5?
     ** DEVIATED
   the first problem associated with Testwell5 will be referred to as:

                           ──────── PROBLEM-1 ────────
   Please enter information on PROBLEM-1
     3) problem-type  prior-action  total-depth    casing-shoe depth
     ** STICKING      REPAIR        2342 METERS    1839 METERS
     4) Please type in formation information. When there is no more, type DONE or OK
        upper-limit    lower-limit    main-rock-type  homogeneous/
        meters         meters                         interbedded
     1  1839 METERS    2220 METERS    SHALE           HOMOGENEOUS
     2  2220 METERS    2342 METERS    SANDSTONE       HOMOGENEOUS
   The first episode of the sticking problem will be referred to as:

                           ──────── EPISODE-1 ────────
   Please enter observations about EPISODE-1
     5) circulation type  type of injection  pressure  rotation
     ** FULL-RETURN       NORMAL                       y/n
                                                       NO
```

Figure 6-2 Drilling Advisor interactive dialog and consultation (Teknowledge, Inc.)

The Knowledge-Based System Solves the Problem 87

6) Please enter the composition of the drill-string starting from the bit (type * ? for assistance):
** BIT9"5/8 STAB9"5/8 KM7"3/4 STAB9"5/8 KM7"3/4 SDC7"3/4 STAB9"5/8 4SDC7"3/4 STAB9"3/8 4SDC7"3/4 STAB9"3/8 SDC7"3/4 JAR7"3/4 21HWP5" DP5"
7) What was the depth of bit at the time of the sticking problem
** 2325
8) Was the BHA motionless when the problem occurred?
** YES
9) What is the depth of the freepoint?
** UNKNOWN
10) What is the specific gravity of the mud?
** 1.24
11) What is the fluid specific gravity of the SANDSTONE formation between 2220 meters and 2342 meters?
** 1
12) What is the thickness of the cake?
** 0.03937008

The causes of sticking in EPISODE-1 are as follows:
DIFFERENTIAL-PRESSURE (0.5).
The reason(s) that DIFFERENTIAL-PRESSURE was concluded as the cause of sticking in EPISODE-1 are as follows:

The BHA was motionless at the time that sticking occurred. There is one or more potentially sticking BHA element in contact with a permeable formation. The total calculated sticking force is 52 tons.

13) What is the filtrate?
** 5.1
14) What is the type of mud?
** SEA-WATER
15) Is the jar currently in the BHA upward or both-directions?
** BOTH-DIRECTIONS

The list of possible curative treatments for EPISODE-1 are as follows:

Circulate to homogenize the mud with a normal flow.
During the circulation, you may consider changing the parameters as follows:
Decrease the filtrate.
Add lubricant products.
You should work on the drill-string both upward and downward, and work on rotation.
Jar both upward and downward, using the jar currently in the BHA.
You may consider pumping a lubricant and surfactant slug. (It could require over 2 or 3 days before the slug is actually effective.)
Run a freepoint measurement to determine the back-off depth, then -if possible- back-off and run a fishing jar able to work both upward and downward.
If you cannot get the pipe free using one of the previous techniques, and depending on the results of the freepoint, you may consider setting a cement plug and side-tracking.

The possible preventive treatments for EPISODE-1 are as follows:

If you can get the pipe free, you should now proceed to the following treatments during the next trip down:
Circulate at the bottom of the well, slowly increasing the mud injection pressure till reaching the desired flow rate.
The mud characteristics should be changed according to the curative treatments recommendations stated above.
You should change the BHA composition according to the following recommendations:
You should incorporate a safety joint in the BHA.
When resuming drilling, keep a normal flow.

16) Are there any other episodes of the sticking problem?
** NO
17) Are there any other problems associated with Testwell5?
** NO

Figure 6-2 (Cont.)

INFERENCE STRATEGIES

A knowledge system's advice and recommendations are produced by the system's inference strategies, which operate on the knowledge encoded in the knowledge base. Inference strategies in rule-based knowledge systems can be goal driven (a method called backward chaining) or data driven (a method called forward chaining), or a combination of these.

Backward-chaining inference strategies start off with a known goal and try to use the expert program's rules to get to that goal. In contrast to backward-chaining procedures, which plan the rules to use to reach an identified goal, knowledge systems that use a forward-chaining paradigm react to externally or internally simulated conditions or data. Some particular data or condition may cause certain rules to be invoked. The reaction, directed by the rules that happen to be invoked by the current data or conditions, may change the knowledge base or the knowledge system's environment.

The new data in the changed knowledge base or environment may cause other rules to be invoked and other changes in the knowledge base and environment. The object of a forward-chaining system is to trigger these reactions until it produces an end situation that satisfies a particular goal.

BACKWARD CHAINING

To establish its diagnosis and recommendations, the Drilling Advisor uses backward-chaining techniques to reason and interpret the knowledge encoded in its rules. For example, to determine if the cause of sticking in a particular drilling episode is sloughing, the Drilling Advisor postulates that the cause of sticking is indeed sloughing. The verification of sloughing as the cause of sticking becomes the goal at this point. Therefore, the Drilling Advisor looks for rules that lead to that conclusion, or goal.

Rule 038, a typical Drilling Advisor rule shown in Figure 6-3 is one of several rules that has sloughing as its conclusion. There are two different parts to rule 038 which are used to get to a goal: the IF part, also called the antecedent, and the THEN part, also called the consequent. The IF part, or antecedent, contains three clauses. The THEN part, or consequent, is true only if all the antecedent clauses are true.

The balance of the rule contains what are called "confidence factors," which tell how much evidence exists for the sloughing conclusion and therefore how much confidence should be placed in that conclusion. In this case, the evidence for the conclusion, on a scale from 0 to 1, depends on the number of stabilizers in the bottom hole assembly.

As mentioned, rule 038 concludes that the cause of sticking is sloughing if all the antecedent clauses in the rule are true. So first, the knowledge system tries to substantiate the information in clause 1 (whether the action before the problem occurred was drilling or reaming) directly from some other rule in the rule base. If it cannot do that, it checks to see if this clause of the antecedent has already been concluded while the program was

RULE 038

[This rule applies to episodes, and is tried in order to find out about whether the cause of sticking in the episode is sloughing]

If: 1) The action being done just prior to the occurrence of the problem was either drilling or reaming,
2) There is sloughing material in the well, and
3) The upspeed of cutting is slow

Then: The cause of sticking in the episode is sloughing; the strength of evidence for this conclusion depends upon the number of stabilizers in the BHA:
a) less than 1 then (0.2);
b) between 1 and 4 then (0.4);
c) greater or equal to 4 then (0.6).

<< Comments: Reaming is a kind of re-drilling.
Sloughing material is side-wall rocks which fall into the well from layers which have already been drilled.
Upspeed refers to the rate at which the drilling fluid, containing loose side-wall material, is circulated back to the surface.
Stabilizers are elements of the drilling assembly (BHA) whose function is to keep that assembly properly centered within the whole. They also tend, unfortunately, to be places at which sloughing material accumulates, plugging the annular space around the BHA and resulting in a sticking accident.>>

Figure 6-3 Drilling Advisor rule (Teknowledge Inc.)

executing. Failing that, the system asks the user whether the action prior to the problem occurrence was drilling or reaming.

If the system cannot find support for clause 1 of rule 038, it abandons that rule, but not the goal of sloughing. It looks for another rule that also concludes that the cause of sticking is sloughing and tries to substantiate that rule. If the user types in "unknown" in response to the Drilling Advisor's question about the action prior to the problem occurrence, the Drilling Advisor goes on to check out other rules, with the aim of returning later to fill in missing information.

It is possible that clause 1 is actually the conclusion of a second rule. In that case, clause 1 would be true provided that the clauses in the second rule are true. This situation causes what is known as a subgoal to be established. The aim of the subgoal is to prove the clauses of the second rule. Of course, a subgoal may generate another subgoal, and so on, which is why backward chaining is often called subgoaling. The knowledge system continues to work the chain of reasoning backward until it reaches a state or clause that it knows. At that point, it about-faces and unravels itself to conclude its originally postulated goal.

If the system never finds any rules to support sloughing, it postulates a different cause (a new goal), whose applicability it tries to conclude. As can be seen, although the backward-chaining technique can solve problems that are not solvable by alternative, algorithmic methods, it can turn out to be an exhaustive search technique. If luck holds, the knowledge system runs out of items to examine at an early stage and gives up. Otherwise, it may spend a lot of time trying to prove something that is false.

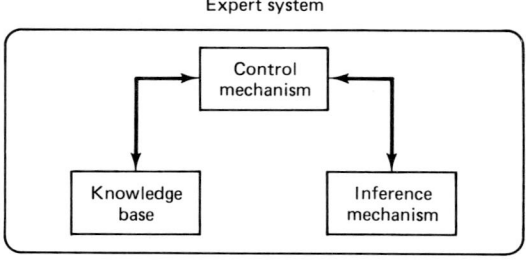

Figure 6-4 The control mechanism controls a knowledge system's search for a solution.

CONTROL MECHANISMS

The knowledge system search picture, however, is not quite as bleak as it appears because the knowledge system does not randomly search through its rules. Instead, in addition to an inference mechanism, knowledge systems of any size generally also have a control mechanism (Figure 6-4). The control mechanism controls the search and prevents the knowledge system from wasting its time exhaustively searching through irrelevant rules at random.

Both rules and strategies are inherent in a knowledge system's control mechanism. The rules, known as meta-rules, are rules about rules and how best to apply them, rather than about subject application knowledge. Most commonly, they are used to direct the order in which both hypotheses and different lines of reasoning should be pursued.

For example, a meta-rule might say that "to find out why a car does not start, first use the system rules to try to determine whether there is gas in the car, print the conclusions found, and only afterward check the starter motor." This meta-rule establishes system priorities. Another meta-rule might indicate that "if the starter motor turns over the engine vigorously, there is no need to check the battery or the alternator."

Meta-rules such as these facilitate knowledge system performance because knowledge systems view problem solving as a search through a space of possible solutions. Therefore, if there is a large space of possible solutions to a problem, meta-rules help narrow the search space.

In the Drilling Advisor, one way the rule-based interpreter controls searches is by selecting the most relevant rules. It determines relevancy based on its own rules about how to search rules and by building an index system based on information extracted from experts into the rules.

In another technique, some knowledge-based systems (for example, Mycin, a medical diagnosis system) avoid an exhaustive search by using heuristics to score the rules that they use to confirm the truth of a hypothesis. As the knowledge system proceeds through its search, it eliminates the highest-scoring rules from its search space of possible conclusions. It then retains and bases its further search for a conclusion only on the lowest-scoring rules that most support the goal. Thus a knowledge system uses confidence factors to direct a search through the most-likely-to-succeed rules while "pruning" unlikely paths from a problem's decision tree of possible solutions.

A common method of representing control knowledge, especially in large programs, is with conventional procedures. A control structure to diagnose a fault in a computer disk drive might look something like this:

```
Procedure
Begin
   Display a welcome message
   Determine the disk drive symptoms
   Check that the disk drive cable plugs in securely
   Check the disk controller board
     . . .
End
```

CONFIDENCE IN KNOWLEDGE SYSTEM CONCLUSIONS

In rule 038, the parenthetical .2, .4, and .6 is a scoring or confidence factor that indicates the strength of a rule. The confidence factors range from 0.0 to 1.0. A confidence factor of .2 indicates very weak evidence; .4 indicates moderate evidence; greater than or equal to .6 is the strongest evidence that rule 038 allows.

Confidence factors in knowledge systems correspond to the way human experts often think about conclusions that they reach. For example, most human experts faced with the Drilling Advisor's drill bit sticking problem to solve would probably not have 100 percent confidence in their conclusion, but would act anyway—a common situation. Physicians also base their conclusions on a certain probability or confidence factor; in fact, that is all the medical literature will allow.

Rule 038 is actually one of many rules that attempt to accumulate evidence that a particular cause is, in fact, the real cause of sticking. In the Drilling Advisor, as with many other knowledge-based systems, all the evidence that can be accumulated for different causes is compared in the end. At that time, the knowledge system may come up with one conclusion. Or it may decide to offer two conclusions, such as sloughing with a confidence factor of .6 and differential pressure with a confidence level of .5. This presentation of conclusions and evidence is similar to the way human experts reach conclusions and react.

Of course, it is possible that the Drilling Advisor's conclusion may turn out to be wrong, just as a human expert may reach the wrong conclusion. There are three ways that people usually deal with human experts who are wrong. One is to reexamine, or ask the human expert to reexamine, the data. A second way is to collect more data and try again. The third and last way is to get a better expert. All three ways are used by the Drilling Advisor, as well as by other knowledge-based systems.

RECOMMENDING TREATMENT

The Drilling Advisor not only diagnoses the cause of sticking but also recommends curative and preventative therapy. To avoid exhaustive searching, the knowledge system rules about sticking are organized in several ways. First they are grouped according to the major subjects, such as sloughing, key seating, and differential pressure, and then they are subdivided into groups of rules categorized according to causes of sloughing and treatment.

Once the Drilling Advisor has reached a conclusion about the cause of sticking, say sloughing, it examines a different set of rules relevant to sloughing and asks several more questions. In this manner, the system identifies what types of curative action are appropriate to correct the sticking problem and possibly prevent its recurrence.

WHAT'S THE PAYOFF?

Elf Aquitaine is an oil company whose cost of doing business illustrates the typically large payoffs that can accrue from using knowledge-based systems to alleviate knowledge bottlenecks. Elf Aquitaine drills large numbers of oil wells in scattered locations simultaneously. An offshore rig might cost an average of $100,000 per day to operate, with a low of $50,000 per day for land rigs and one-half million dollars per day for offshore deepwater drilling. The costs are primarily the rental of the rig itself (generally, these are rented pieces of equipment), associated operating costs for the machinery, and the cost of people on the rig. These costs are incurred 24 hours a day, seven days a week.

The number of people on the rigs varies. There are, at least, the drilling engineers with drilling backgrounds based mostly on experience, a company engineer with a general engineering background, a drilling rig captain highly experienced in drilling operations, and several "roughnecks." In addition, there is a drilling supervisor who creates and carries out the drilling program—how fast to drill, how hard, what lubricant to use—and supervises the drilling on one or a set of rigs. Depending on the company, the drilling captain and drilling supervisor may or may not be the same person.

Drilling supervisors are very experienced personnel with a high success rate at drilling wells. When the drilling rig encounters trouble that cannot be solved quickly by the drilling and company engineers, it is the drilling supervisor who gets called for help.

Drilling rig troubles are serious because they frequently cause work stoppages on the rig and require several weeks or more to correct the problem. It is not unusual for the costs attributable to forced work stoppages on drilling rigs to be about 2 percent of a company's total drilling costs.

Two percent of the total drilling costs turns out to be an enormous figure because a major oil company may be drilling as many as 100 wells at the same time. Arithmetic calculations show that it costs a company drilling 100 wells simultaneously, at $50,000 a day per rig, $5 million a day just for the rigs. If the rig were the only cost involved in drilling operations, a 2 percent rate would cost the company $100,000 for one-day work stoppages, a half million dollars if a stoppage lasted for five days, and 36.5 million dollars annually. These figures are exclusive of the costs of having the drilling program delayed.

Figures this high make the drilling supervisor who can avoid or solve drilling rig problems and reduce the downtime for oil rigs a very valuable resource to an oil company. Alas, such experienced and knowledgeable drilling supervisors are a scant resource and constitute a knowledge bottleneck and therefore a potential knowledge system application candidate.

The high costs incurred for oil drilling losses, the scarcity of expert drilling supervisors, and the identification of a knowledge bottleneck are the reasons that Elf Aquitaine, working with Teknowledge, developed the Drilling Advisor. Naturally, Elf Aquitaine does not expect the Drilling Advisor to avoid all accidents, any more than a human drilling expert could. It is, however, reasonable to expect the knowledge system to avoid a lot of them because, as in so many industries, many oil rig accidents result from "dumb" mistakes. Either an expert drilling supervisor or a system such as the Drilling Advisor would be able to avoid such mistakes. Thus Elf Aquitaine's motive when it decided to develop the expert drilling diagnosis system was to reduce the downtime of its oil rigs and keep the dollars in its pockets.

GETTING THE ANSWER

An example of how a knowledge system uses backward chaining to arrive at an answer is illustrated by a crisis management expert system (developed by IntelliCorp) that diagnoses nuclear power plant accidents. The system contains nine rules (Figure 6-5) to diagnose four possible types of nuclear reactor accidents. The four possible causes of accidents are loss of feedwater, loss of coolant, steam generator tube rupture, and steam line break.

To show which of the four possible causes is the cause of an accident, the knowledge system hypothesizes each cause, in turn, and then attempts to verify the validity of each through backward chaining. The audit, in Figure 6-6, of an execution of the system shows how the knowledge-based system attempts to verify all four hypotheses. First, it hypothesizes that the accident is loss of feedwater, then it chains backwards from that goal to verify this hypothesis.

Rule 5 concludes that this first hypothesis (ACCIDENT TYPE IS LOSS-OF-FEEDWATER) is true if the first two clauses of rule 5 are true. Rule 5, clause 1's assertion (THE SECONDARY-COOLING-SYSTEM HEAT-TRANSFER IS INADEQUATE) happens to be the conclusion of rule 2. Therefore, to conclude rule 5, clause 1, it is necessary to chain backward to rule 2.

The system is able to conclude the precondition of rule 2 (PRESSURE-CONTROL-SYSTEM IS INCREASING) because, as indicated in the audit trail, that condition is known to be true for the current knowledge base state. So the system applies rule 2 and then returns to try to conclude clause 2 of rule 5.

The system cannot conclude the second clause because, as the audit shows, the knowledge system has previously determined (from sensor reading, past information, or asking the user) that the assertion FEEDWATER-PUMP FLOW IS LOW is false for the current state. Consequently, it abandons rule 5, but notes that rule 6 also concludes that ACCIDENT TYPE IS LOSS-OF-FEEDWATER. To prove the hypothesis in question using rule 6, the knowledge system chains back to rule 3, which concludes clause 1 of rule

```
(OUTPUT) The ACCIDENT unit
Slot: RULES       (OVERRIDE)   From ACCIDENT type: LIST Value:
[(RULE 1 (IF (PRIMARY-COOLING-SYSTEM PRESSURE IS DECREASING)
             (HIGH-PRESSURE-INJECTION-SYSTEM STATUS IS ON))
         (THEN (PRIMARY-COOLING-SYSTEM INTEGRITY IS CHALLENGED)))
 (RULE 2 (IF (PRIMARY-COOLING-SYSTEM TEMPERATURE IS INCREASING)
             )
         (THEN (SECONDARY-COOLING-SYSTEM HEAT-TRANSFER IS
                                  INADEQUATE)))
 (RULE 3 (IF (STEAM-GENERATOR LEVEL IS DECREASING))
         (THEN (STEAM-GENERATOR INVENTORY IS INADEQUATE)))
 (RULE 4 (IF (CONTAINMENT-VESSEL RADIATION IS HIGH)
             (CONTAINMENT-VESSEL PRESSURE IS HIGH))
         (THEN (CONTAINMENT-VESSEL INTEGRITY IS CHALLENGED)))
 (RULE 5 (IF (SECONDARY-COOLING-SYSTEM HEAT-TRANSFER IS
                                  INADEQUATE)
             (FEEDWATER-PUMP FLOW IS LOW))
         (THEN (ACCIDENT TYPE IS LOSS-OF-FEEDWATER))
         (UNITPUT SELF (QUOTE TYPE)
              (QUOTE LOSS-OF-FEEDWATER)))
 (RULE 6 (IF (STEAM-GENERATOR INVENTORY IS INADEQUATE)
             (FEEDWATER-PUMP FLOW IS LOW))
         (THEN (ACCIDENT TYPE IS LOSS-OF-FEEDWATER))
         (UNITPUT SELF (QUOTE TYPE)
              (QUOTE LOSS-OF-FEEDWATER)))
 (RULE 7 (IF (PRIMARY-COOLING-SYSTEM INTEGRITY IS CHALLENGED)
             (CONTAINMENT-VESSEL INTEGRITY IS CHALLENGED))
         (THEN (ACCIDENT TYPE IS LOSS-OF-COOLANT))
         (UNITPUT SELF (QUOTE TYPE)
              (QUOTE LOSS-OF-COOLANT)))
 (RULE 8 (IF (PRIMARY-COOLING-SYSTEM INTEGRITY IS CHALLENGED)
             (STEAM-GENERATOR LEVEL IS INCREASING))
         (THEN (ACCIDENT TYPE IS STEAM-GENERATOR-TUBE-RUPTURE))
         (UNITPUT SELF (QUOTE TYPE)
              (QUOTE STEAM-GENERATOR-TUBE-RUPTURE)))
 (RULE 9 (IF (STEAM-GENERATOR INVENTORY IS INADEQUATE)
             (STEAM-GENERATOR STEAM-FLOW IS HIGH))
         (THEN (ACCIDENT TYPE IS STEAM-LINE-BREAK))
         (UNITPUT SELF (QUOTE TYPE)
              (QUOTE STEAM-LINE-RUPTURE]
```

Figure 6-5 Rules from a knowledge-based crises management system. (Program copyrights © 1983, 1984 by Intellicorp. All rights reserved).

Getting the Answer

```
Top level typescript window
Attempt to verify (ACCIDENT TYPE IS LOSS-OF-FEEDWATER)
Attempt to verify (SECONDARY-COOLING-SYSTEM HEAT-TRANSFER IS INADEQUATE)
Attempt to verify (PRESSURE-CONTROL-SYSTEM TEMPERATURE IS INCREASING)
(PRESSURE-CONTROL-SYSTEM TEMPERATURE IS INCREASING)
 is true for the current KB state.


(RULE 2 (IF (PRESSURE-CONTROL-SYSTEM TEMPERATURE IS INCREASING))
       (THEN (SECONDARY-COOLING-SYSTEM HEAT-TRANSFER IS INADEQUATE)))
 applied.

Attempt to verify (FEEDWATER-PUMP FLOW IS LOW)
(FEEDWATER-PUMP FLOW IS LOW) is false for the current KB state.

Attempt to verify (STEAM-GENERATOR INVENTORY IS INADEQUATE)
Attempt to verify (STEAM-GENERATOR LEVEL IS DECREASING)
Is it true that (STEAM-GENERATOR LEVEL IS DECREASING)? YES

(RULE 3 (IF (STEAM-GENERATOR LEVEL IS DECREASING))
       (THEN (STEAM-GENERATOR INVENTORY IS INADEQUATE))) applied.

Attempt to verify (FEEDWATER-PUMP FLOW IS LOW)
(FEEDWATER-PUMP FLOW IS LOW) is false for the current KB state.

Not verified: (ACCIDENT TYPE IS LOSS-OF-FEEDWATER)
Attempt to verify (ACCIDENT TYPE IS LOSS-OF-COOLANT)
Attempt to verify (PRESSURE-CONTROL-SYSTEM INTEGRITY IS CHALLENGED)
Attempt to verify (PRESSURE-CONTROL-SYSTEM PRESSURE IS DECREASING)
(PRESSURE-CONTROL-SYSTEM PRESSURE IS DECREASING)
 is true for the current KB state.

Attempt to verify (HPIS STATUS IS ON)
(HPIS STATUS IS ON) is false for the current KB state.

Not verified: (ACCIDENT TYPE IS LOSS-OF-COOLANT)
Attempt to verify (ACCIDENT TYPE IS STEAM-GENERATOR-TUBE-RUPTURE)
Attempt to verify (PRESSURE-CONTROL-SYSTEM INTEGRITY IS CHALLENGED)
Attempt to verify (PRESSURE-CONTROL-SYSTEM PRESSURE IS DECREASING)
(PRESSURE-CONTROL-SYSTEM PRESSURE IS DECREASING)
 is true for the current KB state.

Attempt to verify (HPIS STATUS IS ON)
(HPIS STATUS IS ON) is false for the current KB state.

Not verified: (ACCIDENT TYPE IS STEAM-GENERATOR-TUBE-RUPTURE)
Attempt to verify (ACCIDENT TYPE IS STEAM-LINE-BREAK)
Attempt to verify (STEAM-GENERATOR INVENTORY IS INADEQUATE)
Attempt to verify (STEAM-GENERATOR STEAM-FLOW IS HIGH)
(STEAM-GENERATOR STEAM-FLOW IS HIGH) is true for the current KB state.


(RULE 9 (IF (STEAM-GENERATOR INVENTORY IS INADEQUATE)
            (STEAM-GENERATOR STEAM-FLOW IS HIGH))
       (THEN (ACCIDENT TYPE IS STEAM-LINE-BREAK))) applied.

Verified: (ACCIDENT TYPE IS STEAM-LINE-BREAK)
^
```

Figure 6-6 The knowledge system attempts to verify four hypotheses. (Program copyrights © 1983, 1984 by Intellicorp. All rights reserved)

6. Information about rule 3 is not in the rule base, nor has it been concluded previously. Therefore, the system asks the user.

Although in this example the user answers yes, the system still cannot verify clause 2 of rule 6. It therefore abandons the LOSS-OF-FEEDWATER hypothesis and tries to prove the second hypothesis, ACCIDENT TYPE IS LOSS-OF-COOLANT.

To use rule 7 to prove that ACCIDENT TYPE IS LOSS-OF-COOLANT, the system chains back to rule 1, which concludes clause 1 of rule 7, which concludes that the PRIMARY-COOLING-SYSTEM-INTEGRITY IS CHALLENGED (listed in the audit as PRESSURE-CONTROL-SYSTEM INTEGRITY IS CHALLENGED). Concluding rule 1 first requires the system to show that the PRIMARY-COOLING-SYSTEM PRESSURE IS DECREASING (rule 1, clause 1), and the system shows this to be true for the current knowledge base state. The audit indicates, however, that the second clause of rule 1, HIGH-PRESSURE-INJECTION-SYSTEM STATUS IS ON, has been shown to be false for the current knowledge base state, and therefore the system abandons the LOSS-OF-COOLANT hypothesis.

Attempting to prove the third hypothesis, the system tries rule 8, which concludes that the hypothesis in question (ACCIDENT TYPE IS STEAM-GENERATOR-TUBE-RUPTURE) is true if the two clauses of rule 8 are true. Rule 1 concludes clause 1 of rule 8, but the system has already been shown, when trying to verify the last hypothesis, that rule 1's second clause (HPIS IS ON) is false for the current state. Therefore, the STEAM-GENERATOR-TUBE-RUPTURE hypothesis fails and the system tries to prove the last hypothesis, ACCIDENT TYPE IS STEAM-LINE-BREAK.

With similar hypothesis verification techniques, the expert system chains from rule 9 to rule 3, discovers that clause 1 has already been verified, clause 2 is shown to be true, and finally verifies that the accident type is indeed a steam line break.

FORWARD CHAINING

The same types of solutions are possible with forward-chaining knowledge-based systems. The difference is that the backward-chaining-oriented Drilling Advisor and nuclear reactor crisis management systems work by hypothesizing a conclusion and working backward to find existing evidence via rules or information inferred from rules. But the same results can be achieved by applying rules, noting the result, and applying other rules based on the new situation.

In the latter method, known as forward chaining, a certain true situation triggers the action or consequent part of a rule. This action may change the state of the knowledge base. It may also subsequently change the environment, where it may, for example, turn some hardware or software switch on or off. The new program situation may cause another rule to be invoked and triggered and another reaction to occur, until an end situation is reached that satisfies a particular goal.

Difficulties with a forward-chaining, reactive paradigm occur particularly if a rule base is large, because there is only one goal but many unproductive ways to produce irrelevant reactions. Under these conditions, a knowledge-based system that reacts without having some goal in mind easily goes off in unfocused ways and may not provide its answers efficiently.

Advantages of a forward-chaining system include the ability to react to data or conditions and not only come up with conclusions but also generate goals. In contrast, a backward-chaining system must decide on possible goals to work toward in advance. Although there are goals to work toward in a forward-chaining system, they are far more general—so general, in fact, that many experts argue that forward-chaining systems merely react without having any goal in mind.

For example, the goal in a chess game is simply to get the opponent's king in checkmate. A forward-chaining system could react to the chessboard data and come up with (plan) several strategies of its own to satisfy the general goal. In a backward-chaining system, each strategy for getting the opponent's king in checkmate would have to be determined in advance—a pretty impossible task considering the number of possible strategies.

Actually, AI is still a long way from having general methods to narrow the search space of possible solutions in order to develop either forward- or backward-chaining programs to solve many problems. However, several control strategies have been devised to minimize the search through possible solutions and produce efficient forward-chaining systems that perform computer configuration, diagnosis, design, and planning tasks. As will be shown, these control strategies limit the choice of rules based on several schemes. These include indexing structures, how specialized the rules are for a particular situation, how relevant they are to a particular subtask, time tags attached to items when they are added to memory, and assignment of priorities. Some of these control strategies work similarly to the way in which human beings perform tasks.

SETTING UP PERSONAL COMPUTERS

XCON, DEC's computer configuration program, and several knowledge systems integrated with XCON are well-known forward-chaining systems. Similar techniques can be used to configure a personal computer.

Personal computers are not necessarily turnkey systems. PC buyers may also buy a variety of boards, peripherals, and different amounts of memory. To set up these components to form a working computer system requires that the user connect, install, and arrange the various components and then set certain switches so that both the system and the components know what components are present.

A program that uses forward-chaining techniques to configure a personal computer starts out with both a database and a knowledge base. The database contains the components in the system and some information about them. The knowledge base contains rules that embody the knowledge and constraints about PC configuration.

A typical database for configuring a PC might include, among other facts, the following items and information:

Computer	Number of slots: five
	Boards contained: System board
	Maximum system board memory: 256K
	Amount of system board memory filled: 256K
Mouse board	Type of mouse: mechanical
Disk controller board	Type of disks: floppy
Memory board	Maximum amount of memory: 256K
	Amount of memory filled: 256K
Communications board	Number of ports: two
Printer board	Type of connection: parallel
Expansion interface	Number of slots: nine
Display board	Type of display: monochrome

This is not necessarily an optimal way to buy personal computer boards because more than one of these features might be contained on one board. This simple database, however, serves to illustrate the fundamentals of forward chaining.

The rules in the knowledge base know how to put together these components to form a full-fledged PC setup. Since the rules are also known as productions, they are contained in a section of memory known as "production memory" (rule memory). The section of memory where the forward-chaining knowledge-based system does its work and keeps track of what partial configurations it has already formed is appropriately known as "working memory" (Figure 6-7).

Clearly, unless the knowledge system is physically connected to a robot, it cannot physically configure the computer. Instead, it conceptually configures it and generates a set of configuration instructions to a human configurer.

To begin the configuration process, the knowledge system loads into working memory an initial set of items from the database, as well as descriptions of the starting situation. The initial items might be the computer, the expansion interface, and the six boards. The starting situation description approximates the situation that human beings might face after having received delivery of their PCs and accompanying boards.

The PC expert configurer then examines all the rules to see if one contains an IF

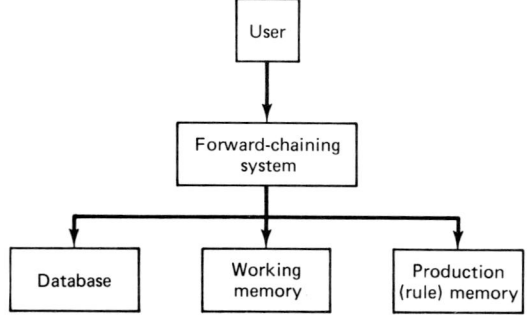

Figure 6-7 Components in a forward chaining system

Setting Up Personal Computers

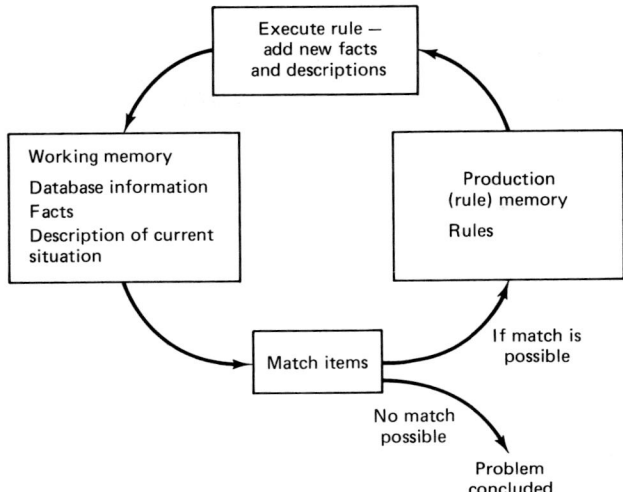

Figure 6-8 Recognize-Act cycle in forward chaining processing.

part, "all" of whose conditions match the items that happen to be in working memory at that instant. The knowledge system regards the items in rule memory and working memory simply as patterns. If the system finds a rule whose patterns match those in working memory, it performs the action indicated by the THEN part of that rule.

The THEN part of the rule that is matched might direct the knowledge system to add a new item or situation to working memory. The expert system then cycles through all the rules again to find another matching rule based on the changed state of working memory (Figure 6-8). This cycle is known as the Recognize-Act cycle.

However, the rule base might contain a very large number of rules. Examining all of them, especially on a constant basis, is a very time-consuming process. Therefore, one control strategy that typical forward-chaining systems use is to partition the task into steps.

Human beings would also likely partition a program, such as the PC-configuration task, into several different steps (called contexts). One step might be to decide where in the PC to install the boards. The next step might be to set the switches to indicate the amount of memory installed. The next step might be to insert the boards; another step might test the system, and so on.

In similar fashion, the rules in a forward-chaining PC-configuration system would be divided into steps and each step given a name. One group of rules might be called STEP ASSIGN-BOARDS. Another might be called STEP CONFIGURE-MEMORY, while still another group of rules might be STEP TEST-SYSTEM. Figure 6-9 shows a rather loose English translation figure of some typical PC-configuration rules.

When the expert PC configurer loads up working memory to start, it loads the starting components and a description of the starting situation. The starting situation description includes the name of the starting step. In this program, the starting step loaded into working memory might be STEP ASSIGN-BOARDS. So when the knowledge system

PC-RULE-1
IF: THE CURRENT STEP IS ASSIGN-BOARDS
        AND THERE ARE 5 SLOTS IN A COMPUTER
        AND THERE IS AN AVAILABLE SLOT IN THE COMPUTER
        AND THERE IS AN AVAILABLE MONOCHROME DISPLAY BOARD
THEN: PUT THE DISPLAY BOARD IN THE COMPUTER IN AN AVAILABLE SLOT
        AND SUBTRACT ONE FROM THE NUMBER OF AVAILABLE SLOTS

PC-RULE-2
IF: THE CURRENT STEP IS ASSIGN-BOARDS
        AND THERE ARE 5 SLOTS IN A COMPUTER
        AND THERE IS AN AVAILABLE SLOT IN THE COMPUTER
        AND THERE IS AN AVAILABLE PRINTER BOARD
THEN: PUT THE PRINTER BOARD IN THE COMPUTER IN AN AVAILABLE SLOT
        AND SUBTRACT ONE FROM THE NUMBER OF AVAILABLE SLOTS

PC-RULE-3   disk-controller-board rule

PC-RULE-4   memory-board-rule

PC-RULE-5   communication-board rule

PC-RULE-6   color-display-board rule
                   (not applicable to this system database)

PC-RULE-7
IF: THE CURRENT STEP IS ASSIGN-BOARDS
        AND THERE ARE 5 SLOTS IN A COMPUTER
        AND THERE IS AN AVAILABLE SLOT IN THE COMPUTER
        AND THERE IS AN AVAILABLE MOUSE BOARD
THEN: PUT THE MOUSE BOARD IN THE COMPUTER IN AN AVAILABLE SLOT
        AND SUBTRACT ONE FROM THE NUMBER OF AVAILABLE SLOTS

PC-RULE-8
IF: THE CURRENT STEP IS ASSIGN-BOARDS
        AND THERE ARE 5 SLOTS IN A COMPUTER
        AND THERE IS A MOUSE BOARD AVAILABLE
        AND THERE IS NO AVAILABLE SLOT FOR A MOUSE BOARD
THEN: FIND AN EXPANSION INTERFACE AND CONNECT IT TO THE PC

PC-RULE-9
IF: THE CURRENT STEP IS ASSIGN-BOARDS
        AND THERE IS AN EXPANSION INTERFACE
        AND THERE ARE 5 SLOTS IN THE EXPANSION INTERFACE
        AND THERE IS AN AVAILABLE SLOT IN THE EXPANSION INTERFACE
        AND THERE IS A MOUSE BOARD AVAILABLE
THEN: PUT THE MOUSE BOARD IN THE EXPANSION INTERFACE
        AND SUBTRACT ONE FROM THE NUMBER OF AVAILABLE SLOTS

PC-RULE-10
IF: THE STEP IS ASSIGN-BOARDS
THEN: END THE ASSIGN-BOARDS STEP
        BEGIN THE CONFIGURE-MEMORY STEP

PC-RULE-11
IF: THE STEP IS CONFIGURE-MEMORY
        AND THERE IS A 256K BOARD AVAILABLE
        AND THE 256K BOARD IS POPULATED WITH THE MAXIMUM AMOUNT OF MEMORY CHIPS
        AND THE SYSTEM BOARD IS POPULATED WITH THE MAXIMUM AMOUNT OF
            MEMORY CHIPS
THEN: SET THE SWITCHES ON SWITCH-1 ON THE ADD-ON BOARD TO TELL IT
        HOW MUCH MEMORY IS ON THE ADD-ON BOARD (settings listed here)
        AND SET THE SWITCHES ON SWITCH-2 ON THE ADD-ON BOARD TO TELL IT
        HOW MUCH MEMORY IT IS BEING ADDED TO (settings listed)

Figure 6-9 English translation of PC-configuration rules.

```
PC-RULE-12
IF:     THE STEP IS CONFIGURE-MEMORY
        AND THERE IS A 265K BOARD AVAILABLE
        AND THE 256K BOARD IS POPULATED WITH THE MAXIMUM AMOUNT OF MEMORY CHIPS
        AND THE SYSTEM BOARD IS POPULATED WITH THE MAXIMUM AMOUNT OF
            MEMORY CHIPS
        AND THE SYSTEM BOARD REQUIRES A KNOWLEDGE OF HOW MUCH ADDITIONAL
            MEMORY WILL BE ADDED
THEN:   SET THE SWITCHES ON THE SYSTEM BOARD TO INDICATE HOW MUCH MEMORY
            WILL BE ADDED (settings listed here)

PC-RULE-13
IF:     THE STEP IS CONFIGURE-MEMORY
        AND THERE IS A 256K BOARD AVAILABLE
        AND THE 256K BOARD IS POPULATED WITH THE MAXIMUM AMOUNT OF MEMORY CHIPS
        AND THE SYSTEM BOARD HAS AVAILABLE SPACE FOR MORE MEMORY CHIPS
THEN:   FILL THE SYSTEM BOARD COMPLETELY WITH MEMORY CHIPS
```

Figure 6-9 (Cont.)

tries to match its rules against the items in working memory, it tests component items, but also tests the step names.

The effect of testing the step names is that the step names act as a kind of indexing structure. The knowledge system only has to examine fully the rules that are suited to each step. Generally, the problem is partitioned so that the rules for each step constitute a fairly small number and the knowledge system does not have to waste too much time fully examining and testing irrelevant rules.

In this PC-configuration example illustrated here, the first configuration step that the knowledge system attends to is to assign the various boards to slots; in another step, it sets the switches on the boards.* A full configuration example will be far more complicated, with many more steps. It is possible that two different configurers will perform some of the steps in a different order.

As the expert PC configurer begins its configuration task, it notices that all the conditions in RULE-1 correspond to items in working memory. In other words, both the IF parts of RULE-1 and working memory contain the items "current step is install-boards," "computer with five slots," "an available slot in the computer," and "an available display board." Therefore, PC-RULE-1 fires and working memory is modified to indicate that the display board has been installed in one of the computer slots. Working memory is also changed to indicate that only four slots are now available instead of five. The instruction sheets to the human operator will direct him or her to install the display board in that particular slot.

In like manner, the expert PC configurer adds the disk controller board, memory board, communications board, and printer board to the slots in the PC and indicates the modifications to working memory. The rules for adding these four boards to the PC resemble the display board rule. In fact, all the conditions in all these rules match patterns in working memory just as well as the display board rule. Therefore, the knowledge system gathers all the rules that match working memory and could therefore fire, into a set of rules known, in the OPS5 rule language, as the "conflict set" (Figure 6-10).

*The PC-configuration example is based on techniques and a translation of the OPS5 rule language, developed at Carnegie–Mellon University by Charles Forgy.

To choose one rule to fire, the knowledge system might use "time tags." With this technique, every item in working memory has an associated time tag. It indicates when the item was last created or modified.

Given a choice of rules, as happens during conflict resolution, the knowledge system chooses the rule that matches the item with the most recent time tag. The assumption here is that the most recent item is part of the process being worked on most recently and is therefore the most relevant.

Of all the boards that could be matched in this example problem, the display board was chosen first intentionally. The order in which the boards are listed is the order in which they were physically added to working memory. The display board was the last board whose description was added to working memory and therefore has the most recent time tag. Although the time tag in this problem is trivial, the principle is a general one and has far far more meaning in many other examples.

If five boards have already been added, when the expert PC configurer finally comes to PC-RULE-7, about the mouse board, it cannot apply it. Since there are no more available slots, the one-rule condition about "an available slot" does not match anything in working memory. PC-RULE-9, however, matches and causes the knowledge system to find an expansion interface (in the store or stock) and connect it to the PC.

As mentioned, a full-fledged configuration is far more complex and must take into account several chunks of constraint knowledge, not included here for simplicity. For instance, in a real example, if an expansion interface were needed, a slot in the PC would have to be reserved for the expansion interface board.

At this point, there are no boards to be installed and it is time to go on to the next step. PC-RULE-10 is the rule that gets the knowledge system out of the step it has been working on and into the next step, which is CONFIGURE-MEMORY. At first glance, it seems that rule 10 could have fired at any time when the system was working on the ASSIGN-BOARDS step. Not so. Another conflict resolution strategy states that given a choice of rules whose conditions match those in working memory, if one rule is longer or contains more data items than the other, the longer rule should be selected. The rationale is that the rule with the greater number of data items is more specialized for the particular situation at hand. Therefore, it should be the rule of choice.

The value of this specialization strategy is demonstrated by seeing what the expert PC configurer does when it gets to the CONFIGURE-MEMORY steps. Two rules can generate a conflict in this step: PC-RULE-11, which assumes a fully populated 256K memory board and system board, and PC-RULE-12, which assumes a fully populated 256K memory board and system board but has the additional condition wherein the system board requires knowledge of how much additional memory will be added. In any situation where PC-RULE-12 matches working memory, PC-RULE-11 will also apply because it is a subset of PC-RULE-12. However, it is precisely because PC-RULE-12 is a special case of PC-RULE-11 that given the choice, the expert system will choose PC-RULE-12. By this technique, the system will be able to configure the PC properly for both situations.

Based on the specialization strategy, it is clear that PC-RULE-10 is the shortest and least specialized of all the rules in the STEP ASSIGN-BOARDS. Therefore, even though all its conditions (it only has one) match items in working memory, it fires only when there is nothing else left to fire. This makes it a general rule to deactivate one step and activate the next.

A forward-chaining system repeats this match/change-working-memory/match process until it can no longer find any rules that match anything in working memory, or until some action specifically stops the processing. At that point, it is assumed that it has arrived at a solution which, in this case, is to configure a PC properly.

An advantage that can be observed in a rule system such as this is the ease of adding new rules. The rules are self-contained and independent of each other. The order of the rules does not matter since the system repeatedly cycles through all the rules. Of course, it is possible that dependencies between rules exist because a new component to be added is dependent on components already in the database or associated with rules in the rule base. However, that same situation exists also when human beings configure systems. The issue here is to get the proper information from the expert to write the rule that expresses how he or she would handle such a situation.

FORWARD OR BACKWARD?

The different chaining paradigms are appropriate for different problem domains. For example, a forward-chaining-based medical system may react to a patient's medical data by suggesting relevant diagnosis or treatments. On the other hand, many diagnostic systems, at every step of a procedure, strive to zero in on some goal. As a result, they are often suited to backward-chaining techniques.

Financial knowledge-based systems and many equipment diagnosis systems profit from a combination of backward- and forward-chaining techniques. Such systems work forward from some initial database of characteristics of a company or equipment symptoms to generate some goal, such as a possible strategy or diagnosis. At the same time, they work backward to explore or prove the details of that goal. Then they meet in the middle. This is essentially the procedure that many people follow when they make decisions.

Knowledge Representation: Frames, Rules, and Processes

CHAPTER 7

Of all the possible kinds of knowledge systems, rule-based systems win the popularity contest hands-down. They are appealing because rules are the simplest of all forms of knowledge representation to understand and to use.

A rule is just a conditional statement, such as "IF the goal is to configure an IBM PC and there is room for five boards and there are six boards to insert THEN get an expansion interface," or "IF a patient's age is less than 10 years and the patient has a fever greater than 103 degrees Farenheit and the patient's white blood count is less than 5000 and the patient has a skin rash THEN there is suggestive evidence that the patient has measles."

This situation–action or symptom–cause format of rules is particularly suitable for expressing knowledge that experts in the field have gained as a result of experience—their so-called rules of thumb. Since to make a diagnosis experts such as physicians and equipment troubleshooters use a lot of rules of thumb (based on symptoms), rules provide a convenient method of representing knowledge for their applications. Once the knowledge has been expressed in rule format, a rule interpreter applies the rules which are applicable to a variety of situations, notes the result, and then applies other rules based on the changed situation.

Alas, like anything else, rules are not perfect. They lack variation and they are unstructured. Their format is inadequate or inconvenient to represent many types of knowledge, such as underlying causal knowledge, or to model the structure of a system. Their lack of variability in expressing knowledge also limits the representation of causal knowledge. This is an unfortunate inadequacy for knowledge systems because it is causal knowledge that people fall back on to solve problems when their simple rules of thumb fail.

Worse, as the number of rules in a system grows, they become difficult to manage and modify and, consequently, large rule-based systems have been known to act in some very silly ways. Even though rule-based systems are very modular, rules are not as independent as they first appear. They are independent only in the sense that they are unstructured (what some AI experts term "disorganized") and unsequenced. However, they assume information or actions found in other rules, and they work in conjunction with other rules. In many experts' experience, rule-based system developers cannot continue to add rules indefinitely because as they do so, they build in many assumptions about other rules and implicit relationships between rules. As a result, it becomes easy to add a new rule that violates some previously established assumption or relationship.

If a violation occurs in a rule-based system, the knowledge system does not fail or degrade gracefully. Instead, as the system approaches the limits of its knowledge, it may follow a bad chain of reasoning and make a silly inference.

If, however, the knowledge system uses a more organized representation that models the real-world system about which it is reasoning, it has a better chance to know when it is at the limits of its knowledge. The inference processes of such a system reflect knowledge of its limits. Knowing its limits, it knows when it cannot make an inference, or when it is making an inference that might be based on weak evidence. Using this knowledge, the knowledge system might qualify its inferences, make partial inferences, or make an inference that could be used to reach a more helpful inference. In other words, it gracefully degrades, rather than following a bad chain of reasoning because the knowledge-system developer did not anticipate some situation.

By definition, a knowledge representation that models a real-world system contains underlying causal knowledge about that system and has the potential to use that basic underlying information to reason about a new situation. Although effective for many applications, rule-based systems are more limited for others because they require too many rules to get all the effects of a causal model.

Human experts, too, have several ways of reasoning about knowledge. Automobile mechanics diagnose a car based on rules of thumb, but may not understand the underlying principles of how a car works. Doctors do routine diagnoses based on rules. However, if an event or symptom occurs that is not covered by their rules, doctors can call on their underlying causal models that tell them how the systems of the body work. With this causal knowledge, physicians can solve problems that they have not encountered previously. Without a basic causal model, such reasoning is impossible.

FRAMES

The questions of what is the best method to use to represent knowledge and how best to design a basic causal model are still open questions in the AI community. One way to circumvent the weaknesses of rule-based systems and take a step closer to modeling real world systems with underlying causal knowledge is to represent knowledge in data structures known as "frames." Hypothesized by Marvin Minsky, frames are a kind of template (a generic pattern or mold) for holding clusters of related knowledge about a particular, narrow subject, which often is the name of the frame.

Because related knowledge is grouped together, frames, and the frame-based system that contains them, structure information in a much more organized and manageable manner than do rule-based systems. Because the organized structure contains related information, frame-based systems can come closer to modeling real-world systems than rule-based knowledge systems that are unstructured. Moreover, because related knowledge is clustered together, the frame-based organization comes closer to mimicking the way human beings remember and reason about the world.

Minsky himself, when writing about his theory of frames, says: "When one encounters a new situation (or makes a substantial change in one's view of a problem), one selects from memory a structure called a frame. This is a remembered framework to be adapted to fit reality by changing details as necessary" (Minsky, 1975).

Each frame contains a number of "slots," which are really variable-length memory areas that hold different types of information associated with the frame name. For example, a knowledge-based medical diagnosis system might contain a series of frames for specific diseases. Each disease frame contains slots that describe, for example, typical disease symptoms, treatment, and morbidity rate (Figure 7-1).

The common cold frame in Figure 7-1 is a very simple one. Its information could possibly be represented in an ordinary database. For example, like the common cold frame, a database contains data, attributes, and descriptions. However, slots in frames can contain more than attributes and descriptions. As the partial frame in Figure 7-2 shows, frame slots can also contain rules, hypotheses about a situation, questions to ask users, graphical information, explanatory information for users or programmers, debugging information, and even other frames.

In other words, frames can be very highly complex and contain, in addition to data, a variety of types of information, causal knowledge, and relationships that databases cannot handle. Frames can also be linked to other frames and, as will be explained, can "inherit" information from them. Moreover, they can be manipulated by knowledge-based systems' reasoning mechanism to infer new information—a feature that does not apply to traditional databases.

Constructing a knowledge system with knowledge represented in frames is much more complicated than a rule-based system. Rule bases are simpler to build because it is

```
Common-cold frame

Slot: SYMPTOMS value:
      (stuffed nose)
      (headache)
      (general malaise)

Slot: TREATMENT value:
      (take two aspirin)
      (bedrest)
      (call the doctor in the morning)

Slot: MORBIDITY-RATE value:
```

Figure 7-1 Typical frame

```
(OUTPUT) The ACCIDENT unit
Unit: ACCIDENT in knowledge base REACTORS
Created by KUNZ on 11-Jun-83 08:37:03
Modified by KEHLER on 20-SEP-83 00:04:40
   Parents: REACTOR, RULE-METHODS from KB: RS

Reactor accident
_____

Slot: HYPOTHESES (OVERRIDE)   From ACCIDENT Value: ((ACCIDENT TYPE IS
                                                              LOSS-OF-FEEDWATER)
  (ACCIDENT TYPE IS LOSS-OF-COOLANT)
  (ACCIDENT TYPE IS STEAM-GENERATOR-TUBE-RUPTURE)
  (ACCIDENT TYPE IS STEAM-LINE-BREAK))


Slot: TYPE         (UNIQUE)     From ACCIDENT type: LITATOM Defaulted value:
NONE
Inherited value: |{LOSS-OF-COOLANT LOSS-OF-FEEDWATER NONE
STEAM-GENERATOR-TUBE-RUPTURE STEAM-LINE-BREAK}


Slot: DESCR        (OVERRIDE)   From ACCIDENT Value:
This unit describes a nuclear accident.


Slot: RULES        (OVERRIDE)   From REACTOR Value: [(RULE 1
                                                      (IF (
PRESSURE-CONTROL-SYSTEM PRESSURE IS DECREASING)
                                                          (HPIS STATUS IS
                                                                    ON))
                                                      (THEN (
PRESSURE-CONTROL-SYSTEM INTEGRITY IS CHALLENGED)))
  (RULE 2 (IF (PRESSURE-CONTROL-SYSTEM TEMPERATURE IS INCREASING))
          (THEN (SECONDARY-COOLING-SYSTEM HEAT-TRANSFER IS INADEQUATE)))
  (RULE 3 (IF (STEAM-GENERATOR LEVEL IS DECREASING))
          (THEN (STEAM-GENERATOR INVENTORY IS INADEQUATE)))
  (RULE 4 (IF (CONTAINMENT-VESSEL RADIATION IS HIGH)
              (CONTAINMENT-VESSEL PRESSURE IS HIGH))
          (THEN (CONTAINMENT-VESSEL INTEGRITY IS CHALLENGED)))
  (RULE 5 (IF (SECONDARY-COOLING-SYSTEM HEAT-TRANSFER IS INADEQUATE)
              (FEEDWATER-PUMP FLOW IS LOW))
          (THEN (ACCIDENT TYPE IS LOSS-OF-FEEDWATER)))
  (RULE 6 (IF (STEAM-GENERATOR INVENTORY IS INADEQUATE)
              (FEEDWATER-PUMP FLOW IS LOW))
          (THEN (ACCIDENT TYPE IS LOSS-OF-FEEDWATER)))
  (RULE 7 (IF (PRESSURE-CONTROL-SYSTEM INTEGRITY IS CHALLENGED)
              (CONTAINMENT-VESSEL INTEGRITY IS CHALLENGED))
          (THEN (ACCIDENT TYPE IS LOSS-OF-COOLANT)))
  (RULE 8 (IF (PRESSURE-CONTROL-SYSTEM INTEGRITY IS CHALLENGED)
              (STEAM-GENERATOR LEVEL IS INCREASING))
          (THEN (ACCIDENT TYPE IS STEAM-GENERATOR-TUBE-RUPTURE)))
  (RULE 9 (IF (STEAM-GENERATOR INVENTORY IS INADEQUATE)
              (STEAM-GENERATOR STEAM-FLOW IS HIGH))
          (THEN (ACCIDENT TYPE IS STEAM-LINE-BREAK]


Slot: ASKED        (OVERRIDE)   From RULE-METHODS in KB: RS Value: Unknown


Slot: ASKR         (METHOD)     From RULE-METHODS in KB: RS type: METHOD Val
ue: RS>RULE-METHODS:ASKR!method


Slot: DEBUGMODE    (OVERRIDE)   From ACCIDENT Value: T


Slot: DEFINEDFNS   (OVERRIDE)   From RULE-METHODS in KB: RS Value: |{EQUAL
```

Figure 7-2 Partial frame with slots containing rules, hypotheses, user questions, graphical information, explanatory information, and debugging information (Program copyrights © 1983, 1984, by Intellicorp. All rights reserved.)

107

easier to define the less complex, IF-THEN-formatted, small-sized pieces of knowledge that are rules.

Frames are a natural, however, in some subject areas where rules, conditions, or attributes tend to cluster about a central object, concept, or event. For example, in medicine certain attributes and rules tend to cluster about particular diseases. In engineering, rules may cluster about a particular type of circuit. Such natural clustering indicates natural relationships between rules and the knowledge encoded in them.

Writing down all these interrelationships in the form of rules leads to excessive numbers of rules and the disorganization discussed earlier. So frame-based systems were developed to organize information in structures that take advantage of the natural clustering. In fact, not only is the knowledge clustered in individual frames, but many frames themselves tend to cluster because they also are related.

HIERARCHIES OF FRAMES

The most important way that frames are related is hierarchically. This relationship occurs because in a frame-based knowledge system frames can contain smaller frames, called subframes, arranged in a hierarchy. An example of how this frame hierarchy works and how it is used is illustrated by some of the design information captured with Daisy Systems' (Sunnyvale, California) Logician, Megalogician, and Gatemaster software. These are frame-based computer-aided-engineering (CAE) expert systems for VLSI, circuit, and computer design that incorporate the benefits of a frame-based hierarchy.

Users of these systems typically might design a frame that describes a new object, such as a computer to be built. This frame would describe the computer's four major functional elements: the central processor, memory, control unit, and input/output unit. Each of these four objects is captured as a slot in the first or top-level frame and also as a subframe (Figure 7-3). At the next level down in the hierarchy, each of those frames will contain more primitive objects, which are also captured as frames. Finally, at the bottom of the hierarchy, frames describe physically realizable building blocks, such as gates, transistors, and chips.

To use the Logician to design an object, say a chip or a printed circuit board, electronic design engineers sit in front of a machine and interact with it in a natural language. Natural language is a requirement for most knowledge system user interfaces. Lest it be thought, however, that natural language means only languages such as English, Italian, or Chinese, note that the natural language for electronic design engineers is logic symbols (Figure 7-4). The knowledge system translates the logic symbols which make up a schematic drawing into a form that can be understood by a computer program that verifies the engineer's design.

Frames go into action when the expert computer program scans the schematic diagrams as they are being composed. During this scan, the program automatically captures the schematic—both the graphical and electrical information—in the form of frames.

Every object in the system being designed has its entire set of attributes and characterizations stored in these frames. Users need not manually fill in any slots in the frames.

Two Types of Frames 109

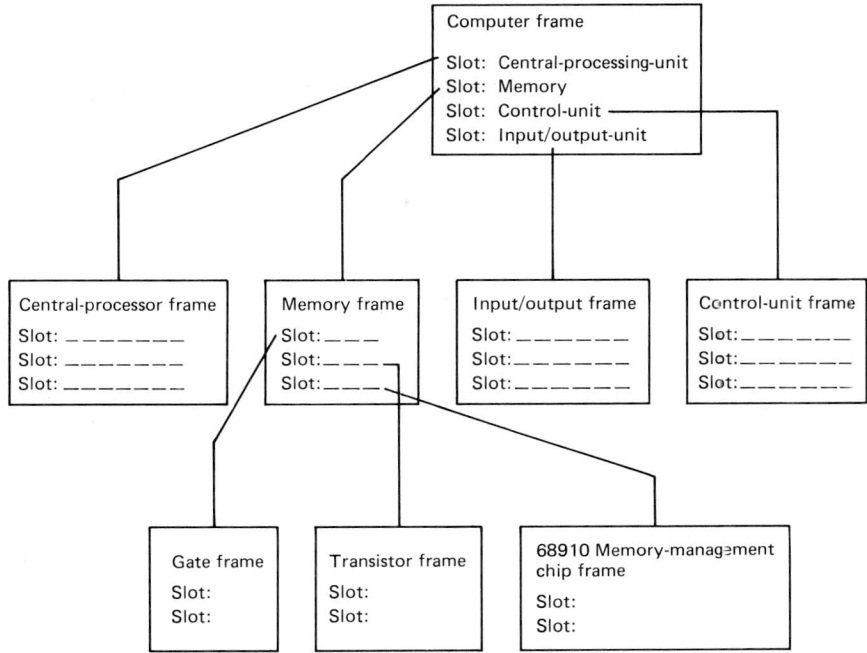

Figure 7-3 Hierarchy of frames

Instead, whenever they add information to their schematics, the Logician creates a corresponding entry in a frame. The entry describes characteristics of the system's objects, such as placement, connections, distances, data about pins, and operations that can be performed on the object. The Logician analysis programs manipulate—read, write, and modify—these frames.

TWO TYPES OF FRAMES

There are two types of frames: generic and specific. A typical generic frame in the Logician describes objects nonspecifically. This means that the slots of a generic frame list generic objects or information about locations, but never actually name the specific object or location (Figure 7-5).

In addition to the nonspecific information in generic frames, the Logician contains unique copies of a generic frame, called an "instance" frame, for each individual object. The unique copies of the frame have filled in slot values for attributes such as object type, description, electrical characteristics, connectivity rules for wire mapping, and display characteristics (Figure 7-6). Other slots might contain parameters that describe properties such as delay time through a wire, device size of a VLSI transistor, and the transistor's relationship to other components.

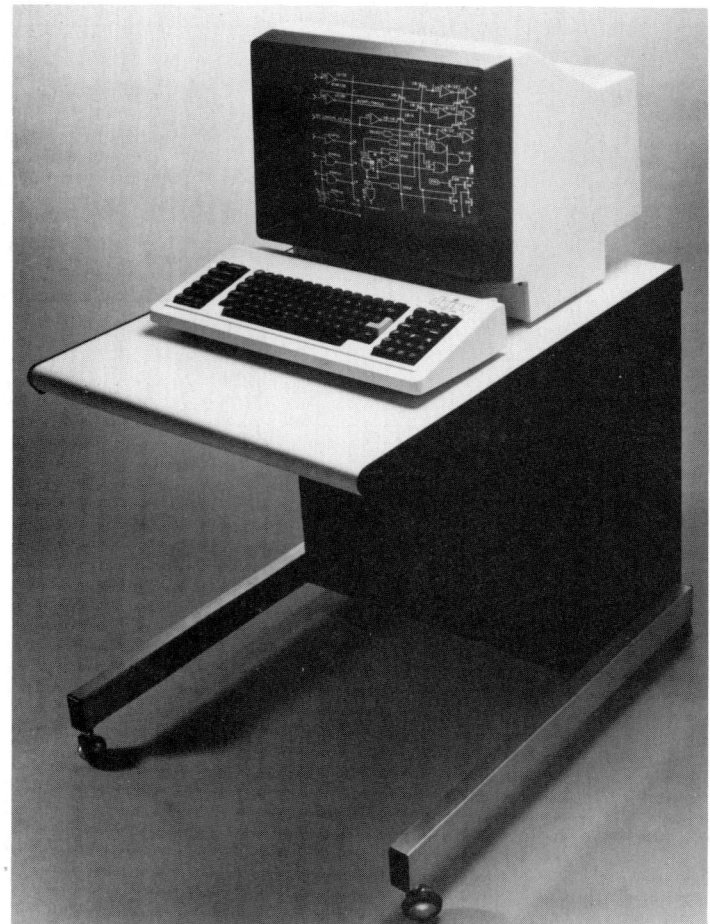

Figure 7-4 The Logician engineering work station. (Daisy Systems)

OBJECT-TYPE:	(wire, component, bus)
INSTANCE-LOCATION:	(X, Y coordinates of origin)
RECOGNITION-AREA:	(bounding box for fast selection)
INSTANCE-NAME:	(user given or default)
PARAMETER-LIST:	(type value)
REFERENCE-TO-SHARED-INVARIANT-DATA:	(component symbol description, simulation models)
CONNECTIVITY-LIST:	(wire name, component pin name)
ASSOCIATED-NOTES:	(text strings)
DISPLAY-ATTRIBUTES:	(color, brush type, highlight)

Figure 7-5 Generic frame organization (Daisy Systems)

Frame-Based Inheritance

```
OBJECT-TYPE:              component
INSTANCE-LOCATION:        (30, 40)
RECOGNITION-AREA:         (28, 38); (38, 48)
INSTANCE-NAME:            xcmp10
PARAMETER-LIST:           (DELAY-TIME 426325,
                           PART-NAME  74LS02,
                           PLACEMENT  U1)
LIBRARY-REFERENCE:        LS
                          (LEARN
CONNECTIVITY-LIST:        CLR_SCAN
                          XSIG1)
NOTE:                     "DT="
DISPLAY-ATTRIBUTES:       (COLOR      red,
                           BRUSH      medium,
                           HIGHLIGHT  blink)
```

Figure 7-6 Instance frame organization (Daisy Systems)

The generic frame in Figure 7-5 is an example of a frame that contains many types of objects that could be in a database of information about a circuit. In contrast, the instance frame in Figure 7-6 contains specific information about the switch_XY (SW_XY), shown near the far right of the schematic diagram (of a 2-for-1 multiplexer) in Figure 7-7. The frame has captured information from the schematic, such as the component names, delay-time properties, and connecting signal (wire) names.

FRAME-BASED INHERITANCE

Relationships between different frames are taxonomic, similar to the relationships between grandparents, parents, and children, or between mammals and cats. The taxonomic relationship, whether between families, biological organisms, or frames, indicates that

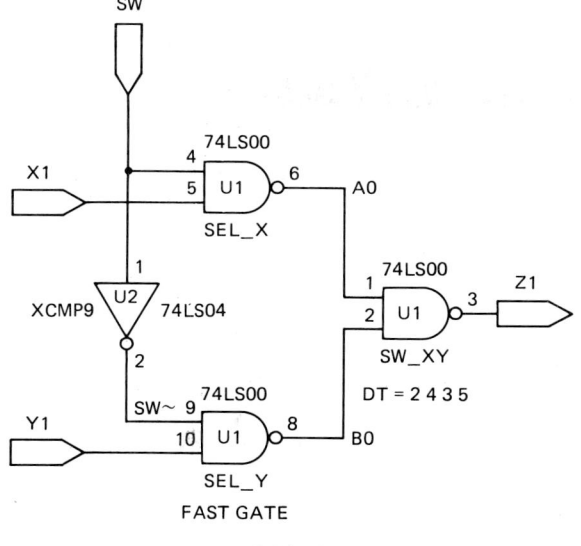

Figure 7-7 Schematic of a 2-for-1 multiplexor with component names, delay time property, and connecting signal names. (Daisy Systems)

similar characteristics exist in certain objects in a hierarchy, and these characteristics are inherited from corresponding objects (people, organisms, or frames) at a higher level in the taxonomic hierarchy. Since frames contain knowledge, a frame lower in a hierarchy automatically inherits knowledge from its parent frames.

With this inheritance mechanism, if a top-level frame for an object contains a description and programming code, for example, of how to display certain graphical characteristics, a lower-level frame inherits that description and programming code, and therefore programmers need not rewrite it. Programs that operate on frame-based information know that frames may inherit information instead of containing it directly, and they know how to get the information from the parent frames. Because the frames are hierarchically linked, if needed information is not listed in a particular frame, the program searches up the inheritance hierarchy looking for a frame that contains the applicable information.

Consequently, as a designer adds new knowledge to a frame-based knowledge system, the subframes and the objects they describe already know how they relate to other objects and how they should behave; knowledge of these relationships and behavior has been inherited. This knowledge prevents design errors from occurring. For example, as soon as a designer creates an object in a Logician frame, the object already knows that it cannot accept certain kinds of inputs.

BOTH EXPERT AND APPRENTICE

The Daisy Systems' Logician is a computer-aided engineering tool that has some unique advantages because it is AI based. Functionally, it is both a frame- and rule-based expert system that scans and captures information from schematics and performs simulation and verification of designed circuits. It then interfaces to commercially available design-automation programs such as those for circuit or logic simulation, test generation, and printed-circuit or integrated-circuit layout tools.

The Logician is actually both an expert system and a set of traditional circuit layout and design tools. When the tools play their traditional role, they perform mundane, error-prone tasks for engineers, such as placing and connecting components and routing signals and checking for mistakes in the engineer's schematics.

These types of layout and design activities are common to many design tools available today without involving artificial intelligence. Whether the tools represent design and connectivity information in frames or tables is irrelevant. What is unique and relevant is the easy modifiability of the Logician's software and its techniques, which allow engineers, who are not professional programmers, to interface to a variety of design automation tools. These features are AI based.

The Logician incorporates AI technology in two different ways. First, its software is designed to emulate knowledge system architecture and techniques. Second, it contains a user-programmable rule base that allows engineers to compose some simple rules to extract and format information to output to other design automation tools.

KNOWLEDGE SYSTEM ARCHITECTURE

The user-programmable rule-base is achievable because of the Logician's knowledge system style of architecture. The most important knowledge system architectural feature that the Logician emulates is the extremely modular design of knowledge systems compared to conventional programs. Such modularity is a hallmark of knowledge systems and one of their major contributions to software engineering.

For example, the architectural design of knowledge systems separates the component parts of the system—knowledge base, inference mechanism control mechanism, and possibly database—rather than latching and interleaving them together as do conventional programs. Moreover, within the knowledge base, individual rules and frames are modularized. This modularity allows new knowledge to be added easily. It also allows the subject area of the application to be changed by simply substituting a new knowledge base for an existing one while retaining the remainder of the knowledge program.

Daisy has gone to great lengths to duplicate this modular architecture in the design of its tools. For example, the Logician, Megalogician, and the Gatemaster contain, in the modularized fashion of knowledge systems, a database, two types of rule bases, and two rule base interpreters (inference mechanisms). Unlike conventional design automation and other programs, in the Daisy systems the database is completely decoupled from the rules that are used to manipulate it, and both are completely decoupled from the inference engine/rule interpreter. This modularity allows new information, in the form of rules that by nature are also modular, to be added without affecting other parts of the program.

The first component, the database, contains the frames, which in turn contain the schematics and the information extracted from the schematics. One rule base contains the user-programmable query rules, which, as will be seen, use AI techniques. The other rule base, used by the layout and design program, is internal to the design tools. It contains connectivity design rules for checking schematics and the different semiconductor vendors' design rules for layouts. These rules are common to many CAD tools and are not based on AI technology.

The last component in the layout and design modules in the Daisy tools are the inference engines/rule interpreters. One of these, the drawing editor connectivity engine, is the link between the modules in the layout and design program. It translates the logic symbols that the engineers enter in schematic form on the CRT screen into a frame-based representation. Then it enters the frames in the database (see Figure 7-8). In addition, it interprets the design rules and uses them to manipulate the frames and to perform the design and error-checking chores. The other inference engine, called the database query engine, accesses the same database (which contains the frames) as the layout and design program modules and interprets the user-programmable rules (Figure 7-9), which are used primarily to interface to other design automation tools.

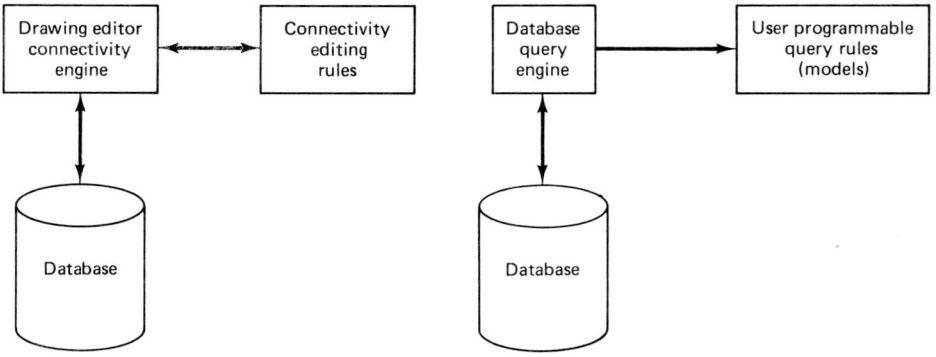

Figure 7-8 Connectivity editing assistant

Figure 7-9 Database query assistant

FROM ONE PROGRAM TO ANOTHER

The ability to interface to various design automation programs is important because different programs perform specialized tasks at different stages of the design process. For example, different design automation programs may perform or support printed-circuit layout, integrated-circuit layout, circuit simulation, logic simulation, or test generation.

The usual engineering procedure is to transmit information from a program that performs some stages of the design process into other programs that support other stages. Unfortunately, each design automation program has its own private language. Therefore, to interface to another design automation program, it is commonly necessary for a programmer to write a customized interface program. The customized program needs to extract the information from the first program, transfer it into a separate database, translate the information into the representation required by the targeted tool, and finally transmit that database to the second program.

ENTER AI

In contrast, with a modular-knowledge-system-structured tool, which can represent information to be transferred with simple IF-THEN formatted rules, customized interface programs are not necessary. Users need only compose some simple rules to extract and format information to output to each different application on each different tool.

An example of this approach is the Logician software. Its rules typically are a few lines in length and are a relatively easy task for most engineers (see Figure 7-10). They are written in a subset of Pascal called Daisy Modeling Language (DML) because Daisy refers to the rules as "models."

The user-programmable rules are used primarily for querying and extracting connectivity information to send to other design automation tools. Typically, a user rule may request the rule interpreter to search the database, collect information from the frames in the database, and compute and appropriately format arbitrary expressions for output into specific tools. For example, the user-programmed rule in Figure 7-10 (programmed in electronic engineering terminology) requests the Logician to search the schematic database, extract delay and connectivity information, and generate the necessary reporting statements in a particular format. In addition, users can write rules that request the Logician to perform CAD tasks such as checking the connectivity in a particular circuit, finding the pin information, and making sure that distances between certain components are correct.

Other design tool databases also allow database queries. However, the difference between most other systems and the Logician is the extensibility of the rule base and user-programmability capabilities. As mentioned, these capabilities are attributable to the simple rule format and to the modularity and independence of the rules and the components of the system. These are the architectural features that the Logician borrows from knowledge-based systems.

With this architecture and format, engineer-users can easily write a few to a dozen lines of a rule that requests a list of components and specifies a particular format for printout (or for transfer to another tool). After the user writes and adds the rules, the database query inference engine automatically interprets them.

For the interpretation, the inference engine searches the schematics' frames hierarchically to find the information that relates to the components named in the rule. Then, when it finds the appropriate instance (specific) frame, it executes the rule and produces the user-requested lists and formats. In contrast to this add-a-rule procedure, it is much more difficult for users to write an entire program for a conventionally designed system that interweaves program control and data of all kinds.

FRAMES ARE EDUCATIONAL

As it turns out, the Logician and Gatemaster are actually mix-and-match systems that combine both frames and rules. Mix-and-match systems are common because different types of knowledge are more easily represented in different structures.

For examaple, knowledge gained as a result of experience about the best actions to take under certain conditions is well represented by rules. In contrast, underlying causal models of structures and systems are better represented by frames. Instructions to the computer to perform straightforward procedures are most efficiently represented as conventional computer programming routines. Finally, formal mathematical logic is a concise way to represent rules and facts and gain the benefits of specific procedures that check whether the represented information is true.

To take advantage of the strengths of different knowledge representations, Daisy,

```
BEGIN
XPUT('NETLIST',%NAME||'('||%SIGNAL('O1'));      /* INSTANCE NAME WITH OUTPUT SIGNAL */
                                                /* PART TYPE WITH INPUTS, COMMA DELIMETER */
XPUT('NETLIST',') = '||%PARAM('PART_NM')||'('||%CNCT_LIST('0001',',',')');
IF %TEST_PARAM('DT') <> 0 THEN
    XPUT('NETLIST',') '||%PARAM('DT')||';'||CR)  .  /* GET DELAY INFO */
ELSE
    XPUT('NETLIST',') ///;'||CR);               /* NO DELAY SPECIFIED */
END


SEL_X(A0) = 74LS00(SW,X1) ///;
SEL_Y(B0) = 74LS00(SW~,Y1) ///;
SW_XY(Z1) = 74LS00(A0,B0) 2 4 3 5;
XCMP9(SW~) = 74LS04(SW) ///;
```

    This 4-line (not counting BEGIN and END delimiters), Pascal-like, user-programmed rule requests the Logician to search the schematic database, extract delay and connectivity information, and generate the necessary reporting statements in a particular format. Translating this rule yields the following:

    FOR EACH COMPONENT, PRINT ITS NAME, TYPE, AND CONNECTIVITY LIST. IF PARAMETER TYPE "DT" IS ENCOUNTERED, PRINT ITS VALUE. ELSE PRINT "///".

    The percent (%) signs in the rule statements, such as in %NAME, direct the Logician to get the specified information from the frame and print it in a certain format. The result of applying this rule (model) to the schematic diagram illustrated in figure 7 is shown below the rule. The results could just as well have been sent to another design tool.

    Note that while rules like this look cryptic to many readers, they are natural to electronic engineers who are their users.

Figure 7-10 Logician application rules written in the Daisy Modeling Language. (Daisy Systems)

Frames Are Educational

for example, represents the underlying structure of printed-circuit boards and chips in frames but represents user queries in a rule form. However, Steamer, an educational expert system (from Bolt Beranek and Newman) that trains Navy personnel to operate steam plants on board ships, is a different type of mix-and-match system. Steamer combines frames with symbolically represented procedures written in the Lisp programming language. It uses its frames to represent knowledge of a steam plant, steam plant components, how they fit together, how they work together, and why. The frames are coupled to procedures that simulate the actual operation of a steam plant.

A third component in Steamer, coupled to its simulation procedures, is a graphical user-interface that displays hundreds of views of a working steam plant and its components (Figure 7-11). The graphic interface animation can be controlled externally by the user, who clicks a mouse to turn pumps on and off or to open or shut valves. Or the animation may be controlled by internal simulation procedures which simulate what happens in one part of the steam plant when a change occurs elsewhere.

The changes in different parts of the steam plant are shown to trainees in a variety of ways for different objects. For example, pumps change their colors, switches change their shapes, pipes change their flow rates, and indicators on gauges change their positions.

The animated graphics screen is one of two display screens that Steamer uses to instruct its students. The other screen displays a textual tutor that contains information about steam plant procedures (Figure 7-12).

Students can use the knowledge-based system's animated display and textual tutor to learn not only how to operate the steam plant, but also to explore the maze of pipes, valves, and pumps that comprise it. The purpose of the exploration is to provide a better

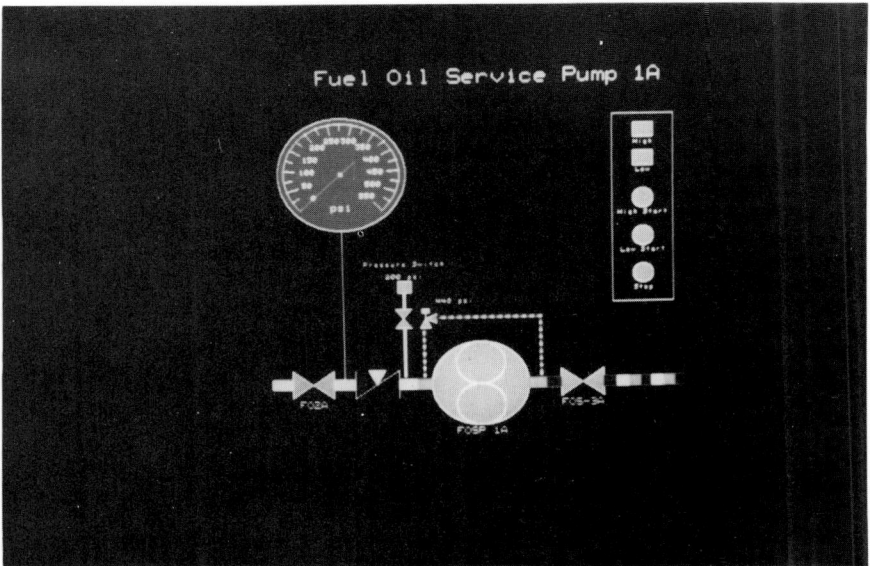

Figure 7-11 Steamer knowledge system fuel pump simulation. (Bolt Beranek and Newman, Inc.)

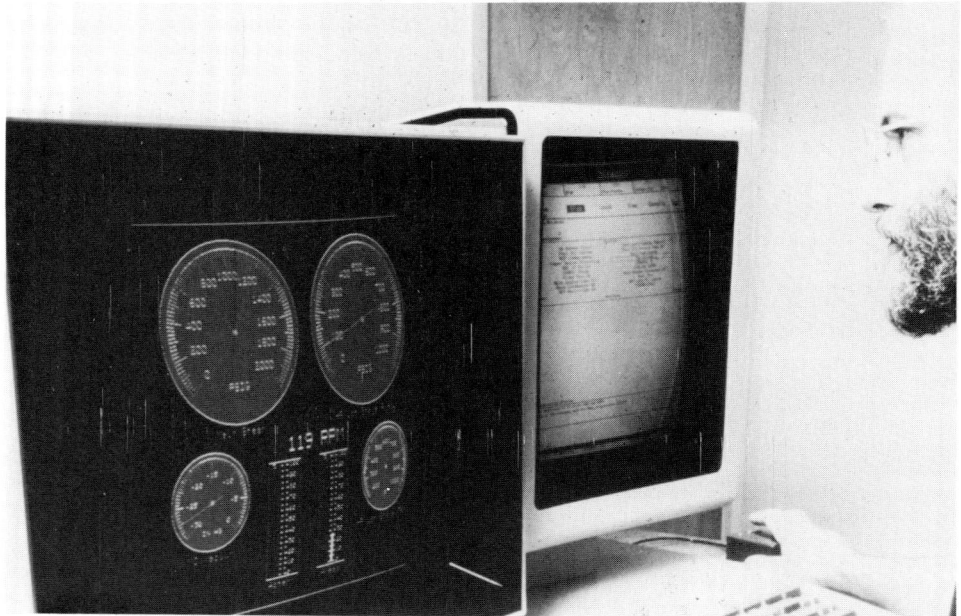

Figure 7-12 Stearmer's dual computer screens (Bolt Beranek and Newman, Inc.)

understanding of how the different parts of a steam plant interact and the principles behind a steam plant's operation.

Classically, the Navy teaches steam plant operation in a classroom with thousand-page manuals and visual aids such as pictures and equipment mock-ups. Hands-on experience is acquired by very carefully operating real equipment in a real steam plant with an instructor supervising each student. An alternative technique is for trainees and an instructor to examine a full-scale model of a working, land-based steam plant. These teaching methods can be both dangerous and expensive. Certainly, trainees have no opportunity to try out ideas. As a result, they often learn to perform procedures and to read gauges and dials, but understand little about what the information means or how different parts of the steam plant interact.

The Navy's rationale for Steamer, and its expository and exploratory teaching techniques, is simple (Figure 7-13). If a knowledge-based system could teach more Navy personnel both the concepts and operation of a steam plant (which knowledge currently only a small number of experienced Navy officer/experts possess), more personnel would be more adept at avoiding shipboard emergencies involving steam plants.*

Toward this end, steam plant operator trainees can use Steamer's frame-based

---

*Applied Artificial Intelligence as a Teaching Tool,'' Bolt Beranek and Newman, Inc. *Technology Digest,* No. 3, April 1984.

Figure 7-13 Using Steamer to teach steam plant operation. (Bolt Beranek and Newman, Inc.)

knowledge, animated displays, and textual tutor to learn about and explore the simulated steam plant in a variety of ways:

- They can use a mouse to turn pumps and valves on and off and watch the changes that occur in the animated graphical display.
- They can study a procedure presented on the screen in text form, then ask to see it execute.

- They can ask why steps in a procedure are done in a particular order and be given a textual explanation.
- They can be given a scrambled procedure in text form, unscramble it into the proper order, try it out, and be critiqued.
- They can experiment with "what-if" questions. For example, "what if this pipe were to spring a leak?" or "what if the pump were turned on before the discharge valve were opened?"

Steamer answers users' questions and teaches the steam plant operation procedures based on its encoded knowledge about steam plants, its representation of that knowledge in frames, and the coupling of the frames to a numerically oriented steam plant simulator.

The frames in the steam plant knowledge base describe both steam plant components and general concepts. For example, Figure 7-14 shows a series of Steamer frames written in the Lisp programming language. Some frames, such as "PORT," "2-PORT DEVICE," and "PUMPING-STATION" represent components. Others, such as "THERMODYNAMICS," represent concepts.

The frames contain slots, which, in turn, contain descriptions of other components or concepts. The frames may also contain subframes which represent other components and concepts. The subframes may contain still other frames, which finally contain values in the slots.

As will be seen, the frames say quite a lot about the objects they describe, both directly and indirectly. The parentheses in the frames delineate descriptions of things. The "defobject" command inside the first parenthesis of each frame is used to create or define a frame. The uppercase name (PORT, 2-DEVICE, THERMODYNAMICS, PUMPING-STATION) that follows "defobject" is the name of the frame created.

Two different sets of parenthesized information follow the frame name. The first of these is a list of slot names that are explicitly (directly) represented in that frame. For example, the 2-PORT-DEVICE frame contains two explicitly represented slots: one for inlet and one for outlet. The THERMODYNAMICS frame has a slot for pressure and another slot for temperature. Note that both of these slots describe concepts. The PUMPING-STATION frame contains three slots. These describe the pump, suction valve, and discharge-valve, all of which are components. Some frames, such as the four valve frames shown, do not contain any slots. Therefore, their parenthesized slot list is empty. Other frames may contain slots that are implicitly (indirectly) represented in that they are really slots in subframes, but the slots in the subframes also belong to the parent frames. This dual ownership of slots makes it convenient to write the code for the frame-based expert system since system developers need not rewrite slots, values, and code for every frame.

The second parenthetical quantity after the frame name houses the names of subframes that the frame contains. As Figure 7-14 indicates, the PUMPING-STATION frame contains two subframes: the 2-PORT-DEVICE shown and a STATES frame, not shown. A "states" frame contains information about the various states that an object can be in, such as "on," "off," "open," or "shut."

::: PRIMITIVE ABSTRACTIONS

```
(defobject PORT (flow) (thermodynamics)
        (  :types
           (flow (a quantity))))
```

```
(defobject 1-PORT-DEVICE (connection) ( )
        (  :types
           (connection (a port))))
```

```
(defobject 2-PORT-DEVICE (inlet outlet) ( )
        (  :types
           (inlet (a port))
           (outlet (a port))))
```

```
(defobject RESERVOIR (volume) (thermodynamics)
        (  :types
           (volume (a quantity))))
```

```
(defobject THERMODYNAMICS (pressure temperature) ( )
        (  :types
           (pressure (a quantity))
           (temperature (a quantity))))
```

```
(defobject STATE-DEVICE (states) ( )
        (  :types
           (states (a list))))
```

::: VALVES

```
(defobject VALVE ( ) (2-port-device state))
```

```
(defobject STOP-VALVE ( ) (valve open-shut-states))
```

```
(defobject CHECK-VALVE ( ) (valve))
```

```
(defobject THROTTLE-VALVE ( ) (valve continuous-open-shut-states))
```

::: PUMPS

```
(defobject PUMP (suction discharge motor) (2-port-device states)
        (  :types
           (motor (a motor)))
        (  :equalities
           ((motor attached-device) self)
           ((suction) (inlet))
           ((discharge) (outlet))))
```

```
(defobject MOTOR (attached-device controller) (states))
```

```
(defobject PUMPING-STATION (pump suction-valve discharge-valve)
                          (2-port-device states)
        (  :types
           (pump (a pump))
           (suction-valve (a stop-valve))
           discharge-valve (a stop valve)))
        (  :equalities
           ((inlet) (suction-valve inlet))
           ((suction-valve outlet) (pump suction))
           ((pump discharge) (discharge-valve inlet))
           ((discharge-valve outlet) (outlet))))
```

Figure 7-14 Generic Frames in steamer (Bolt Beranek and Newman Inc.)

FROM THE GENERIC...

Frames help to organize the knowledge related to the frame names. As in the Logician system, Steamer further organizes its frames (or subframes) as generic or unique. The idea of representing knowledge in generic and unique frames allows knowledge to be explicitly represented when needed, while making it possible to represent a generalized form of the knowledge in question. Representing knowledge at different levels of specificity and abstraction simplifies the conceptualization, design, and programming of an application because certain patterns and procedures are common across many objects, events, and actions. For example, all bank accounts belonging to individuals are unique, but in any bank, in any country, people opening an account know that certain general features will be true of that account.

Similarly, in Steamer, a generic pumping station frame describes, in a general form, all pumping stations. When a knowledge engineer enters expert system knowledge about a specific pumping station, Steamer makes a copy of that generic frame and fills in information to make it unique and specific. The unique, specific copy of the generic frame is an instance of that frame. There is only one copy of any generic frame but lots of copies of the specific ones that are instances of that generic frame.

All the frames in Figure 7-14 are generic frames for system objects. But some frames are more generic than others. How generic and specific frames are related to other frames is displayed as a hierarchy. The most generic frame is at the top of the hierarchy. The most specific is at the bottom.

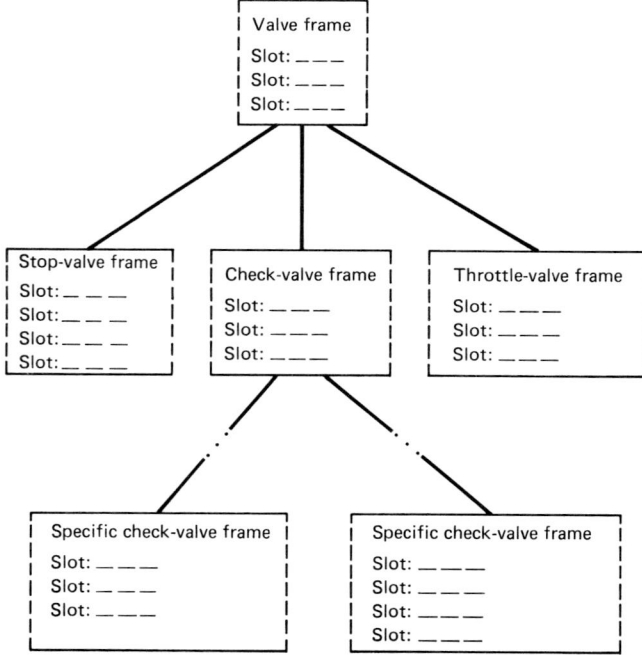

Figure 7-15 Hierarchy of generic and specific value frames.

For example, a valve is a generic component. However, there are different types of generic valves, which are more specific than just the abstract concept of a valve. So a generic frame for the valves described in Figure 7-14 would be higher in a valve hierarchy than the generic frames for stop valves, check valves, and throttle valves (Figure 7-15). There may also be frames for different types of stop valves or check valves. An instance of a frame for a particular valve would be located at the lowest level of the hierarchy.

...TO THE SPECIFIC

Figure 7-16 shows instances (occurrences) of frames that represent specific components in a steam plant, such as a particular pumping station. So specific are these frames that they identify which of several existing pumps, stop valves, or ports (and frames that describe these objects) are present in the particular pumping station represented.

For example, the specific instance of the PUMPING-STATION frame contains six slots that describe a particular PUMP, SUCTION-VALVE, DISCHARGE-VALVE, IN-LET, OUTLET, and STATES. However, the parent generic PUMPING-STATION frame contains only the first three of these slots. Where then did the two other slots come from?

```
(make-instance 'pumping-station ': (identification 'ps1))
#<PUMPING-STATION 32004124>

(describe (the ps1))
#<PUMPING-STATION 32004124>, the MSG object known as PS1,
 has variable values:
        PUMP:                   #<PUMP 32004465>
        SUCTION-VALVE:          #<STOP-VALVE 32024323>
        DISCHARGE-VALVE:        #<STOP-VALVE 32030201>
        INLET:                  #<PORT 32034057>
        OUTLET:                 #<PORT 32035630>
        STATES:                 (STOP LOW HIGH)
#<PUMPING-STATION 32004124>

(describe (the ps1 pump))
#<PUMP 32004465>, an MSG object
 has variable values:
        SUCTION:                #<PORT 32026430>
        DISCHARGE:              #<PORT 32006574>
        MOTOR:                  #<MOTOR 32010353>
        STATES:                 (STOP LOW HIGH)
        INLET:                  #<PORT 32026430>
        OUTLET:                 #<PORT 32006574>
#<PUMP 32004465>

(describe (the ps1 pump suction))
#<PORT 32026430>, an MSG object,
 has variable values:
        FLOW:                   #<QUANTITY 32026763>
        PRESSURE:               #<QUANTITY 32027315>
        TEMPERATURE:            #<QUANTITY 32027647>
#<PORT 32026430>
```

Figure 7-16 Specific frames in steamer (Bolt Beranek and Newman, Inc.)

They came from the PUMPING-STATION frame, but they came indirectly. The three slots for PUMP, SUCTION-VALVE, and DISCHARGE-VALVE that were named in the generic PUMPING-STATION frame are merely those that are explicitly represented. But the PUMPING-STATION frame also implicitly contains the slots that are contained in its subframes. The PUMPING-STATION frame contains two subframes: 2-PORT-DEVICE and STATES. INLET and OUTLET are named as slots in the 2-PORT-DEVICE frame. Therefore, they both implicitly become slots in the specific frame for PUMPING-STATION 32004124. The STATES frame has no slots, only values, such as STOP, LOW, and HIGH. These values also implicitly become part of the PUMPING-STATION frame.

Notice that the component or concept contained in a slot is treated as a variable that can take on specific values. The specific values are shown in the instance frame with their associated variables.

Similarly, the specific frame for pump 32004465 named in the PUMPING-STATION 32004124 has six slots. Three of them (SUCTION, DISCHARGE, AND MOTOR) are explicitly named. Three are implicit and are slots because in the generic PUMP frame they are subframes (STATES) or because they are slots in a subframe (INLET and OUTLET). In like manner, the PORT frame 32006430, which handles SUCTION in the PUMP 32004465 frame, gets its slots from explicit naming (FLOW) or implicitly because the slots are also slots in the PORT frame's THERMODYNAMICS subframe (PRESSURE and TEMPERATURE).

TEACHING AND EXPLAINING PROCEDURES

Slots in the lowest, most detailed level of the subframes, that describe specific components, interface to descriptions of specific steam plant procedures, and these are the procedures to which Steamer users interface indirectly in order to learn steam plant operations. Users access these procedures because procedure descriptions linked to frames are also linked to corresponding procedures in Streamer's simulation model of a steam plant. They are also linked to its graphical interface, which controls the graphical display.

Using this frame/simulation/graphical interface knowledge system, steam plant trainees can point (with a mouse) either to various components in the animated representation or to procedures in the textual tutor. These components or procedures, automatically interface both to slots in the associated frames and to the corresponding procedures in the simulation model. The pointing initiates the animated simulation.

Users can observe the simulation, experiment with procedures, or ask questions. But even with graphical AI-based educational tools, learning steam plant operation would normally be an ordeal, because of the overwhelming amount of material to learn. Learning is facilitated because Steamers designers generalized the material to be presented by the knowledge system.

For example, Steamer associates each generic and specific component frame with procedures that are correspondingly generic or specific. A procedure to start specific components such as "fuel oil service pump one alpha" might direct an operator to open a specific valve before turning on the pump. A more generic procedure for a more generic pump frame might be to start a positive displacement pump by opening the discharge valve before turning on the pump. At a higher level of abstraction, a procedure might indicate that for any system with an attached safety device, the safety device should always be aligned before the system is turned on.

The advantage of designing the frames in this manner is that a small number of generic devices and procedures cover the operation of a very large system. This often makes it easier to learn, remember, and understand the rationale for all the operational procedures without needing to go through all the pages of a thousand-page textbook. On the other hand, the detailed, specific information that is needed for learning steam plant operations is also explicitly available.

If during a Steamer instructional session, the trainee asks "why" about a procedure or concept, Steamer looks from the procedure or concept to the corresponding frame. Then it wriggles up the frame hierarchy until it finds a frame with explanatory information about the question.

Such a frame contains information about the constraints on each step of a steam plant operation procedure and the consequences of violating these constraints. For brevity, it stores such information as minimal English text (without articles and prepositions) in a slot. When the trainee asks questions about procedures or concepts, Steamer dynamically generates English text to flesh out the stored English sentence. In this way, trainees see syntactically correct and readable explanations as answers to their questions.

Steamer can briefly respond to a trainee's question about steam plant procedures, but upon further user request, elaborate on its explanations. These explanations and their elaboration are possible because Steamer has the means to inherit procedures as well as frame slots.

Figure 7-17 illustrates both Steamer's explanation and the inheritance of procedures. In response to a generic request such as "how do I start the pump," Steamer responds with a generic procedure involving aligning the pump and starting the motor. This response is too general to be of much use, so the user points to the "align the pump" statement to find out how the align procedure works.

Steamer's first response to the generic "align" question is also generic. Further probing provides more specific alignment information, such as "think of the pump as a two-port device which you align by opening a suction discharge valve."

Steamer knows the procedure for aligning the pump since it knows that the pump is an isolatable two-port device. (Isolatable means "has a valve on the inlet and outlet.") A procedure exists for aligning two-port devices and that procedure is inherited. The inheritance of procedures, as well as slot inheritance, eliminates the need to specifically encode information about how to align a pump or motor.

Every explanation given by Steamer refers to some component or concept that is represented explicitly as a frame. Therefore, users can request elaboration about any part of an explanation by pointing to it with a mouse. For example, the two steps given to align a two-port device can be made still more specific by pointing to the individual steps in the procedure. Similarly, by pointing to other subparts of Steamer explanations, such as the "start the motor" statement, users can obtain information about any part of a procedure or the entire procedure.

```
Current Object: Start a pump with motor


To start a pump with motor we:
   1. Align the pump.
   2. Start the motor.


To align a pump we:
   Think of it as an isolatable two port device and align it.

A pump can be thought as:
   An isolatable two port device.

   To align an isolatable two port device we:
      1. Open the outlet valve.
      2. Open the inlet valve.


         Open the outlet valve comes before open the inlet valve because one
         should always minimize the volume of downstream piping when aligning or
         securing a system since this minimizes the amount of energy released in
         case of an accident.

Therefore to align a pump we:
   1. Open the discharge valve.
   2. Open the suction valve.


To start a two speed motor we:
   1. Depress the motor controller designated start swich.
   2. Wait until operating condition is motor controller start speed.
   3. Release the motor controller designated start switch.


To start a pump with motor we:
   1. Open the pump discharge valve.
   2. Open the pump suction valve.
   3. Depress the motor motor controller designated start switch.
   4. Wait until operating condition is motor controller start speed.
   5. Release the motor motor controller designated start switch.




Presentation
```

Figure 7-17 Steamer answers trainees' questions and elaborates on explanations because it can inherit procedures. (Bolt Beranek and Newman, Inc.)

procedure. Similarly, by pointing to other subparts of Steamer explanations, such as the "start the motor" statement, users can obtain information about any part of a procedure or the entire procedure.

MANY WAYS TO EXPLAIN

Steamer's abbreviated-English explanations that are contained in slots of frames is one of several methods to generate explanations. A different method used by REX (Regression EXpert, developed at AT&T Bell Labs), an expert in using statistical software, is to respond to a request for an explanation by displaying an English-like version of the rules that it used to arrive at the conclusion in question.

Displaying explanations in rule form, translated into English, is the most common method used by knowledge systems to present reasoning explanations. Adherents include the CATS-1 locomotive diagnosis system, most of the oil exploration systems, and consultant systems in various domains. Another technique that knowledge-based systems use to explain their reasoning is based on a decision tree display. Some systems use combinations of these explanation techniques.

For example, to explain its chain of reasoning, one expert system prototype for nuclear power plant diagnosis (discussed in Chapter 11) displays an audit trail of rules it used, in addition to a decision tree that shows how it reached a particular conclusion (Figure 7-18). The partial audit trail and the decision tree both show how the system decided that the cause of a particular nuclear plant accident was a break in a steam line.

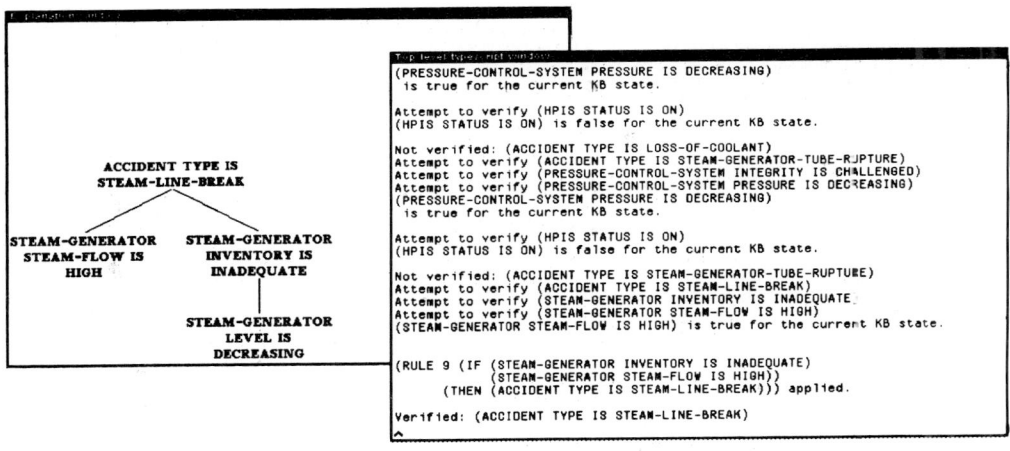

Figure 7-18 Two methods that knowledge systems use to explain their reasoning (Program copyrights © 1983, 1984 by Intellicorp. All rights reserved.)

COMBINING FRAMES AND RULES

Combination systems, whether for presenting explanations, representing knowledge, or performing reasoning, are often expedient because different people view knowledge and reasoning in different ways. In addition, systems that combine knowledge representation methods have an edge in terms of organizing and searching through the knowledge.

REX is an example. This computerized statistical knowledge-based system performs guidance, interpretation, and instruction for an AT&T Bell Labs statistical package. A mix-and-match knowledge system like Steamer and the Logician, REX combines frames with rules. REX's frames are not limited to attributes of components or concepts. Each frame also contains a slot with an average of five rules. Still another slot in the frame contains hypotheses to prove.

With this organization, REX can focus the search through its rule base more easily than can a pure rule-based system. It is easier this way because the frame structure segments the rules by placing them only in relevant frames. Thus, as the knowledge system tries to establish a hypothesis, the slot containing that hypothesis points to a restricted list of usable rules.

Logic, Semantic Networks, Inheritance, Object-Oriented Programming

CHAPTER 8

The best and most useful method to represent knowledge is an open question in the AI community. Although rules, frames, processes, and combinations of these, discussed in the last two chapters, are common ways to represent knowledge, they are by no means the only ones.

Yet another common way to represent the type of knowledge generally used in everyday language, as well as much of modern mathematics, is formal logic. Formal logic is a technique to represent information so that it is possible to check formally whether or not the information is true. For example, whether or not Roberta is a salesperson can be represented in logic as the statement (known in logic as a proposition):

```
Salesperson(Roberta)
```

Roberta is the "argument" of the statement. The statement evaluates either to true or false.

"Predicates" in logic express relations between objects. For example,

```
Worksin(Roberta, New_York)
```

uses the predicate "worksin" to represent the fact that Roberta works in New York.

The logic system used in AI systems is known as predicate calculus. Typical predicates in these systems might be "worksin," "isa," or "earns." The predicates are defined by a programmer whereas logical connectives such as "and," "not," and "if," which are also part of logic, are predefined by the logic system. It is possible to build an entire knowledge base or relational database using formal logic.

129

Basic facts about and relationships between employees, inventory, and company information are entered in a manner similar to that previously shown regarding Roberta. Unlike databases, it is not necessary to store the same amount of information or type of information for each person or item in a database based on logic.

Besides expressing basic facts and descriptions, formal logic provides a built-in method for performing deduction, or correct inference. In logic, an inference can be proved correct because a logic system guarantees that if the premises of a logical declaration (called an assertion) are true, so is the conclusion. For example, the basic facts represented in two assertions such as "Lawyer(Lew)" and "Prosecute(Lawyer Court)" means that Lew is a lawyer and lawyers prosecute in court. These facts can be used to deduce new facts, such as "if Lew is a lawyer, then he prosecutes in court." This deduction is also represented in logic:

If(Lawyer Lew) and (Prosecute(Lawyer Court))

Then(Prosecute(Lew Court))

As illustrated by this logically represented, deduced fact, which is also an example of a rule, rule-based and logic-based representations grade into one another. This gradation points up an advantage of using logic to represent information in a database. Like any conventional database, a logic-based database contains facts and relationships between the facts. Unlike conventional systems, however, a logic-based database also contains rules. The rules are knowledge-system-type IF-THENs that allow new facts to be inferred from original ones.

A LOGICAL APPLICATION

System Development Corp. has an expert system DADM (Deductively Augmented Data Management). Although written in Interlisp (not a logic-based language), DADM is designed around logic. DADM, which acts as a manager's assistant, interfaces simultaneously to multiple database systems. Not only does DADM generate intelligent database access strategies, it acts as a consultant to managers because it can deduce new information (based on data in the databases).

To allow it to perform its deduction, DADM's knowledge base contains logic-based information about selected data stored in SDC's corporate database. The data include information about costs charged to various projects, total project costs, and standard management information systems (MIS) application data. To these logic-based data representations, DADM has added logic-based rules that the expert system calls on to answer management's sophisticated questions about projects, plans, costs, and personnel.

Knowledge engineers planned the knowledge in DADM by interviewing various managers to determine what kinds of questions they are most likely to ask. Symbolic WHAT-IF questions were a popular response (Figure 8-1). These questions have the form "WHAT-IF SUCH-AND-SUCH-EVENT HAPPENED" rather than the numerically ori-

A Logical Application

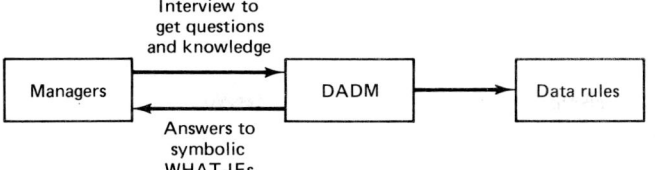

Figure 8-1 DADM answers symbolic WHAT-IF questions.

ented WHAT-IF THIS NUMBER WAS DIFFERENT, which electronic spreadsheets support. A typical symbolic WHAT-IF question might be "WHAT-IF FOX LEAVES THE COMPANY?"

DADM's response might contain information about the impact on Fox's department and the project on which he was working. DADM might even identify people with similar skills and experience levels and offer suggestions as to potential replacements.

Several features designed into DADM enable it to provide these types of responses. First, it interfaces to a database that contains the data it needs for its responses. Second, it contains rules that generate intelligent strategies to access more than one database if necessary. Third, it contains rules about the types of questions that have been identified as being of interest to managers. Fourth, DADM can generate explanations about the reasoning that it uses to come up with particular answers or suggestions. Fifth, its logic representations enable its rules to infer new knowledge included in its logically represented database.

To respond to a manager's query, DADM first chains through a series of rules that help it decide what data it needs. Then it generates a strategy to access those data. If necessary, it iterates this set of procedures until it determines the best answer to the query. Finally, it displays an audit trail or explanation of how it arrived at its answer.

As with any knowledge system, DADM's rules are modular and can be combined in many different ways. Therefore, with only several hundred rules, DADM can answer many thousands of questions that managers might generate.

There is a security aspect to a system such as DADM that potential implementers and users must consider. Security requires that sensitive information that only managers should see, such as plan information and employee salaries, must be partitioned and separated from generally available information, such as direct charges and number of people on the job per week.

To ensure company security, DADM uses two different relational database systems. The sensitive information accessible only to authorized managers resides on a Lisp machine, together with DADM's knowledge base and the deductive processor that infers information. The generally available information resides on a Britton Lee IDM 500 relational database machine (Figure 8-2).

As the DADM knowledge base and deductive processor generate multiple data access strategies to answer managers' queries, the access strategies are selectively spun off either to the Lisp machine or Britton Lee machine database systems. In many cases, DADM sends subqueries to both database systems. The partial responses that DADM receives from both machines are then combined in the Lisp machine into a final answer and explanation for that answer.

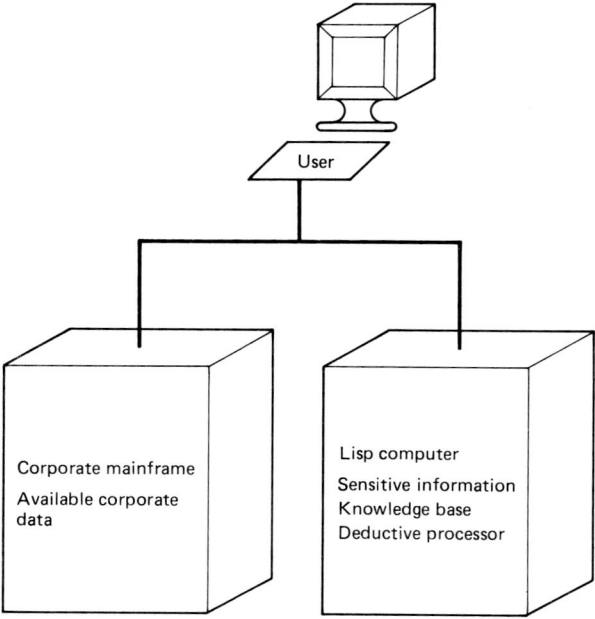

Figure 8-2 DADM security system

TWO MORE REPRESENTATIONS

Besides formal logic and the knowledge representation techniques mentioned in the last two chapters, there are two other significant knowledge representations. One, known as a "script," is a framelike structure that describes stereotypical sequences of events that occur in everyday situations. Typical scripts include eating in restaurants, playing baseball, and going to the doctor. Invented by Roger Schank of Yale University, scripts provide details that may not be included in people's natural-language sentences but nonetheless are needed to understand them. Scripts are discussed in Chapter 15.

The other symbolic knowledge representation structure commonly found in knowledge bases is semantic networks (discussed in Chapter 5). Recall that semantic networks are node-and-arc graphical notations that represent objects, actions, or events and contain built-in real-world meaning about the objects, actions, or events. Objects are illustrated in nodes. Arcs show the relationships between them. Some relationships, such as "ISA," "ON," and "MATERIAL," are commonly accepted terminology for semantic networks. Other relationships are programmer defined. Still other relationships are the result of inheritance.

INHERITANCE

Inheritance relationships are particularly important in AI because of the large size and complexity of most programs. In an inheritance relationship, some objects inherit information or attributes from others. For example, in the semantic network (Figure 8-3), since

Inheritance

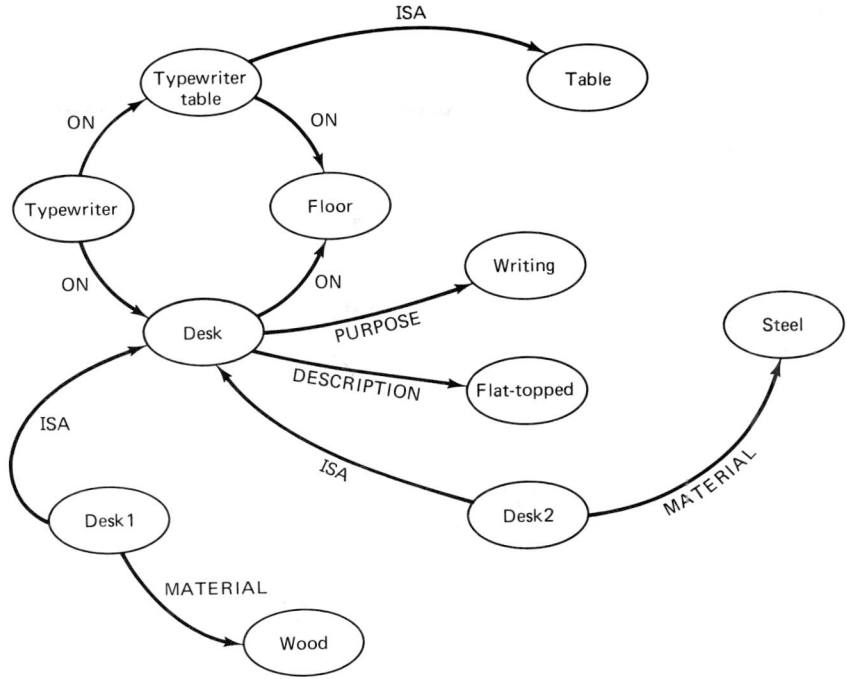

Figure 8-3 Inheritance in a semantic network

Desk1 and Desk2 are both instances of a Desk, everything true about a Desk is also true about Desk1 and Desk2. As is the case with the frame hierarchy described earlier, it is not necessary for a programmer to rewrite the attributes of a desk—to describe its flat top or its writing purpose—for Desk1 or Desk2. However, new information can be added to the data describing Desk1 and Desk2 since clearly, they each have some unique properties. For example, Desk1 is made of wood, whereas Desk2 is made of steel. Thus here, as with frames, the hierarchical relationships indicate the differences between objects at different levels.

An advantage of an inheritance hierarchy in AI systems is the ability that the hierarchy gives to new nodes, frames, or objects in a system to intuitively know information and meaning about their attributes, capabilities, and constraints as soon as they are created. The nodes, frames, or objects intuit this information in the same way that people know that a dog has hair and feeds its young milk because it is a mammal and therefore inherits the attributes of the biological class "mammal."

Most AI experts consider some type of inheritance mechanism crucial to AI programming. Such mechanisms are inherent in frame hierarchies and semantic networks. Lisp, the major AI language, does not have an embedded inheritance mechanism, but AI programmers usually extend Lisp to have that feature.

Inheritance mechanisms are found in a group of programming languages known as object-oriented languages, in addition to being incorporated in many AI development tools (discussed in Chapters 10 and 11). Two major object-oriented programming languages exist: Smalltalk and Flavors. Of these, Smalltalk was developed primarily to explore and facilitate high-quality human–machine graphics rather than for AI development. Flavors, however, has been implemented as an AI paradigm on top of Lisp in both Lisp Machine, Inc.'s Symbolics', and Texas Instruments' Lisp computers.

The value of object-oriented programming for AI development is twofold. One advantage, as mentioned, is its support of an inheritance mechanism. Its other chief advantage is its ability to support exploratory programming. As discussed in Chapter 2, this is important to AI because AI programs are often built from ill-understood specifications to solve ill-understood problems. Both the inheritance capabilities and the exploratory programming support stem from the basic style that object-oriented languages use to perform their functions. This style, which is the consequence of the concepts and technology underlying object-oriented languages, is radically different from that of conventional languages.

OBJECT-ORIENTED PROGRAMMING

Object-oriented programming languages involve a different (in fact, reversed) method of handling programs and data compared to other programming languages. As will be seen, it is this reversed program and data-handling method that lends itself to the exploratory programming necessary to develop AI programs.

In any language, programs have two components: a procedural part that operates on data, and the data on which the procedural component operates. The procedural component, known as the program, contains the instructions for an operation to be performed. Such components include procedures for "add,' "find," "read," "write," "print," and "conditional programming statements" (such as "if this condition is true, then do that"), and so on. The data on which the program operates might typically be numbers, strings of characters, graphical shapes, documents, or files.

In conventional programming, most people consider programs as primary and the data (or objects) secondary. In object-oriented programming, the reverse is true. The data, such as a graphical shape or document to be operated on, is of primary importance.

In object-oriented programming, rather than sending the program the name of an object to manipulate (which corresponds to providing the program with data in conventional programming), the programmer sends the object (or data) a message. A message is actually the name of an operation or procedure (called a method in object-oriented programming) to be performed. Typical operations on the object "document" include open and close the document, find, print, and display it. Sending the object "document" one of these messages is like the data calling a subroutine in conventional programming.

The object is able to respond appropriately to a message because an object is defined along with a group of associated procedures that it can perform. As a result, when the object, for example, "document," receives a message, such as "display," it knows how to perform that procedure because associated with the object are the procedure instructions. To perform the same task in conventional programming, the program would call a procedure called "display," which would take the document as data, execute the display instructions, and display the document.

The object-oriented style becomes important when one operation can be performed differently depending on the object to which it is applied. Under these conditions, it is very handy for each object to know how to perform its own operations. As will be seen, such knowledge avoids programming errors and allows program decisions to be made late in the program execution process. It also saves time because in object-oriented programming this knowledge of procedures is inherited.

OBJECT-ORIENTED INHERITANCE

Inheritance is possible in object-oriented programming languages such as Smalltalk or Flavors because these languages organize programs as a hierarchical arrangement of things known as classes and subclasses (Figure 8-4). Classes and subclasses are sets of the same kinds of generic objects or components. Typically, object-oriented programs might contain classes such as numbers, character strings, graphical shapes, documents, or files. Others have classes of components such as queues or frames. The highly graphical Lisp computer user interfaces are implemented with object-oriented programming techniques. These programs would likely have classes of windows, menus, and icons.

As with Steamer's PUMP frames, some descriptions of documents or graphical shapes are more generic than others. In object-oriented programming, the most generic object in a class lattice are highest in the hierarchy. The most specific objects described by a class are lowest in the hierarchy. The relationships between objects in the hierarchy and those immediately below them them are described as parent–child inheritance relationships, because some objects in the hierarchy are called "parents" and the related objects at the next lower level of the hierarchy are their children.

Associated with each class is a group of procedures (methods). Each class's sub-

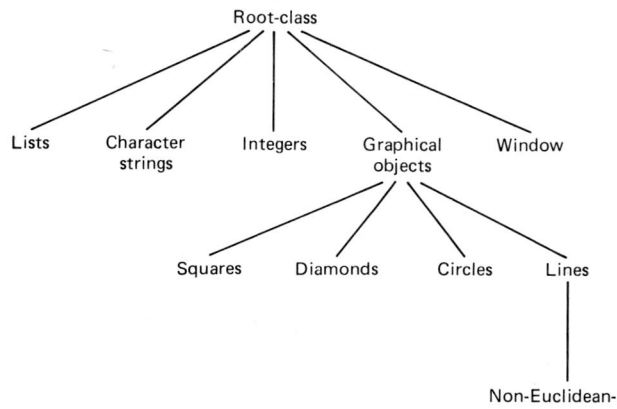

Figure 8-4 Hierarchies of classes and subclasses in object-oriented programming

classes automatically inherit these procedures from their parents unless they have their own procedures that mask out one or more particular procedures.

The highest class in a hierarchy is a single, "root" class (Figure 8-5). A particular root class—for example, for a graphics program—might, at the next lower level have classes of lists, strings, integers, graphical objects, and windows. The graphical objects class might have subclasses of squares, diamonds, circles, and lines.

Methods associated with the subclass "line" might include "clip" (which shortens a line), "new" (which creates a line), "destroy" (which destroys a line), and "length" (which computes the length of a line). To request a program to calculate the length of a line, a user or programmer sends the message "length" to the line. To determine the length, a message routine in the object-oriented program then looks at a table of methods associated with the subclass "line" and finds the method (or routine) name "length." From there, the program follows a pointer (the address of the routine's instructions in computer memory) from the table to the routine which calculates the length of the line and then executes the routine. Similar techniques are followed for the messages "create," "destroy," and "clip."

If another special subclass of "line" is added that describes lines for non-Euclidean space, a different "length" routine must be written. Now, when a user sends the message "length" to the non-Euclidean line, the newly written "length" message initiates a call to the message routine which finds and executes the new length routine.

On the other hand, if the user sends a message to the non-Euclidean line to execute the procedure "new" or "destroy," the message routine will not find such procedures in the methods table for the non-Euclidean "line" subclass because these procedures were never written there. No matter; the non-Euclidean line subclass will execute these procedures anyway because they are contained in the methods table written for a parent class higher in the hierarchy. They need not be rewritten because, in an object-oriented program, if the message routine does not find the requested procedures in a particular methods table, it will look in the methods table of the next-higher class, which is the parent class. If the method is listed there, it is automatically executed.

What really happens is that the non-Euclidean "line" class has inherited these prewritten "new" and "destroy" routines from its "parents" higher in the hierarchy. Procedures can also be inherited from grandparents or ancestor classes. In ancestral inheritance, if a message names a particular method that is not listed in the class immediately above the one in question, the message routine will continue to look up the inheritance tree until it finds the class that contains that method, and, upon finding it, will execute it.

One advantage of this inheritance hierarchy in object-oriented programming is that the programmer does not have to change or add much system code when a new class is added. He or she only need write code to specify specialized, customized functions and characteristics that make the children unique. Children inherit the rest of their attributes from their parents. Since only code that makes the children unique needs to be written, as with semantic networks, the hierarchical relationships indicate the difference between objects at different levels.

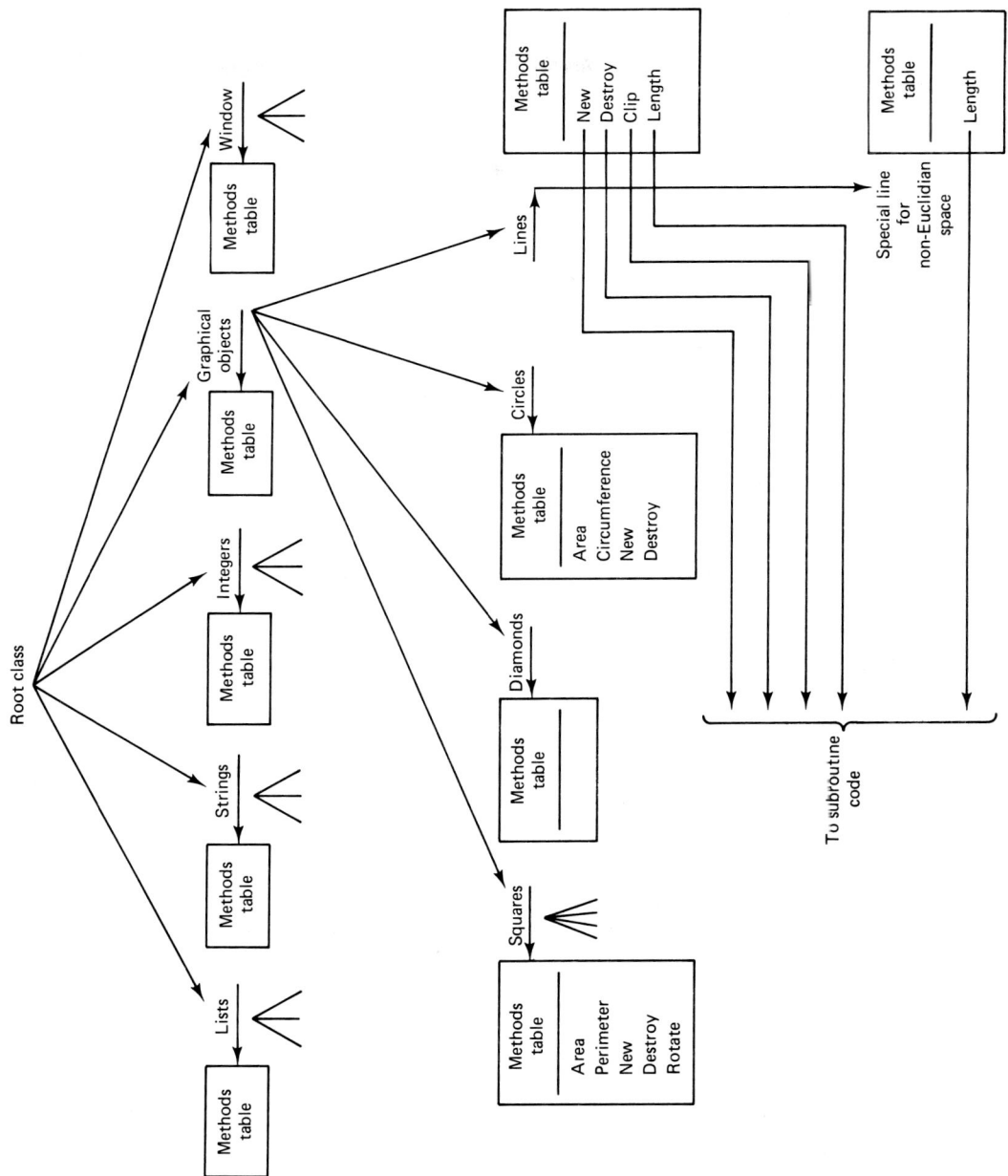

Figure 8-5 Inheritance of methods in object-oriented programming

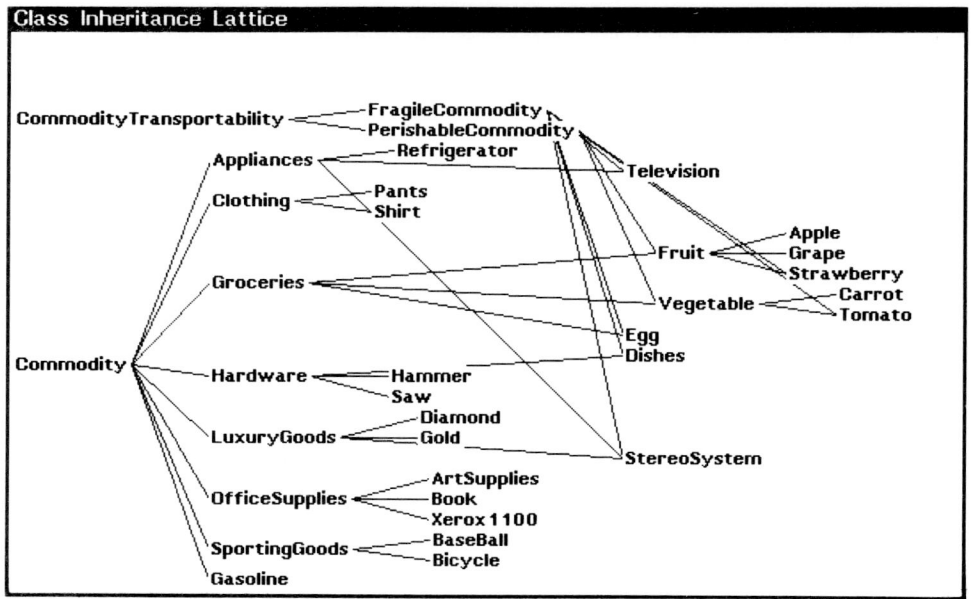

Figure 8-6 Object-oriented programming inheritance of attributes and procedures for commodity products. (Xerox Corp.)

INHERITANCE AND TRUCKING

An example of inheritance in object-oriented programming is seen in the buy-and-sell knowledge-based system developed as part of Xerox's Truckin' game used to teach knowledge system development (Chapter 3). The expert system simulates independent truckers, who buy and sell a variety of commodities for the highest profits. Clearly, procedures such as buying, selling, transporting, and storing are handled differently for commodities such as apples, grapes, gold, stereo systems, eggs, and pants.

To simplify the knowledge system programming job, as soon as the apples and grapes objects are created, the program knows from the inheritance lattice that apples and grapes have the properties of fruits (Figure 8-6). The program knows to handle fruits as groceries; the knowledge of how to do that is inherited from the parent "groceries." The inheritance hierarchy passes down a different set of rules that tell the program how to handle diamonds, gold, and stereo systems as luxury goods. For example, with no special extra software development, the program knows that diamonds and stereos are not shipped in refrigerator cars nor are apples shipped in armored cars.

Objects can have more than one parent. For example, an object "houseboat" in an inheritance lattice might inherit its characteristics from two parents: "house" and "boat."* The object "fruit" shown in the inheritance lattice in Figure 8-6 has three par-

*Example contributed by James Spoerl.

ents: Groceries, FragileCommodity, and PerishableCommodity. Therefore, "fruit" inherits from each of those parents knowledge about the characteristics and handling of groceries and fragile and perishable commodities.

This type of inheritance hierarchy would expedite the modification of object-oriented computer programs in trucking or distribution organizations as these organizations added new items to their roster of goods to be shipped. The expediting would occur because the trucking or distribution software that schedules or monitors the shipping of goods would inherit the knowledge of new goods added to the program.

So if a company undertook, for the first time, the transportation of milk, fruits, diamonds, and baseballs, and added these items to an object-oriented computer program with the class inheritance lattice shown in Figure 8-6, as soon as these items were added to the program, the program would instantly know several facts that would help prevent both programmer and human management errors. For example, the program would automatically know that diamonds do not spoil but fruits do, and thus diamonds can be dropped but not fruits. Moreover, the program could perform its chores knowing instantly, because of inheritance, that time and packaging were more important in shipping milk and fruit than in shipping baseballs. Therefore, a money-saving decision might be made by packing baseballs in cartons and shipping them in a truck making several stops and thus taking more time for delivery. However, if fruits are dropped or not crated, or the milk is transported for too long a time in a truck, the distributor is likely to lose money on the deal.

EXPLORATORY PROGRAMMING

Another significant feature of object-oriented programming is its ability to support exploratory programming for ill-understood AI systems. The key to exploratory programming techniques is deferring as many programming constraints and commitments (efficiency, typing of variables, and allocation of memory) as long as possible. To do otherwise imposes too heavy a burden on the programmer, who must spend time making and implementing programming decisions that are likely to need changing.

For example, implementing efficiency procedures too early makes the program inflexible before it works properly and requires massive programming changes to rework the program so that it works both properly and efficiently. An early choice as to typing variables and data structures requires the programmer to determine, compile, and make static some of the information about variables that may not be the best or most efficient representations for the program and are time consuming to change. Finally, allocating memory decisions early requires the programmer to spend much time to ensure that program information stored in memory is accessible when it should be and is eventually released so as not to fill up memory with information no longer needed (so-called "garbage" information). Deferring these commitments, on the other hand, allows the programmer to experiment with different program features.

The object-oriented programming languages allow these commitments to be deferred until execution time (run time). A major factor responsible for the deferment is the object-oriented view of data, or objects, as the primary components in a program, to which messages are sent to perform procedures that are associated with the objects. Commitment about a particular operation and its meaning can therefore be deferred by defining the operation generally, but having each data object provide its own definition for the operation. This technique is important because procedures often must be implemented differently depending on the object the procedure is applied to. Having each data object provide its own definition for a generic operation leads to deferred commitment because the programmer does not have to decide which specific procedure to implement. Instead, each object determines how to perform a generic procedure so that the procedure applies to the specific object. Which procedure to implement is not determined until run time.

The object-oriented technique works like this. "Print" is an operation that can be applied to many objects in a system. But there are many ways to implement "print," depending on the device associated with the procedure "print." For example, the procedure to print to a file is different from the procedure to print to a graphics screen, an ASCII terminal, or a dot-matrix printer.

For the programmer who wants a particular device to print something, it matters not which object (or device) "print" will be applied to because in object-oriented programming, "print" is a generic procedure. How to apply "print" to a particular object is determined by which object "print" is applied to. The objects determine the meaning of "print," because encapsulated within each object to which "print" can be applied (such as the file, graphics screen, ASCII terminal, and dot-matrix printer) is a procedure for "print" that is specialized for the particular object.

Consequently, during program development, a programmer who wants to print something on an ASCII terminal need only send a generic procedure message, "print," to the ASCII terminal object. How to print, and which procedure to call for the ASCII terminal to print, are not programmer concerns. It is an ASCII terminal concern because the ASCII terminal, like other objects in the system, knows how to print and also knows its own internal representation. Therefore, it has all the information necessary to apply "print" to itself.

If after some experimentation, the programmer decides that it would be better to print to a graphics screen, he or she need only send the message "print" to the graphics screen instead of to the ASCII terminal. There is no need to go into the program to fiddle with procedures and procedure calls as there is in conventional programming. This ease of change allows programmers to explore to their heart's content while depending on the objects to know how to perform their own operations.

Now suppose that the programmer wishes to add a new device to print to, such as a vocal synthesizer. Clearly, "print" applied to a vocal synthesizer is different from applying "print" to the devices named previously. In conventional programming, the programmer goes into the "print" procedure in the program where he or she is likely to find a big "case" statement. A "case" statement has the form "IF THE CASE IS PRINT AND IT IS APPLIED TO A FILE THEN PRINT LIKE THIS, BUT IF THE CASE IS PRINT AND IT IS APPLIED TO AN ASCII TERMINAL THEN PRINT LIKE THAT," and so on, sometimes for a relatively extended list of cases. To add directions to print to the vocal synthesizer, the programmer may further extend the case statement for the case of the vocal synthesizer. But if, in doing so, a mistake is made, the system may fail and nothing may print because there is a bug in "print."

In contrast, in object-oriented programming, the programmer defines both a new object to represent the vocal synthesizer and an associated routine that instructs the vocal synthesizer about the "print" procedure. As with the graphics screen, to apply "print" to the vocal synthesizer, the programmer merely sends the message "print" to the synthesizer, which knows how to execute the procedure. Unlike with conventional programs, if the "print" procedure has a bug, all the other objects in the system still print because the "print" routines are isolated from each other and instead, encapsulated with their associated objects.

The object-oriented paradigm is particularly suited for exploratory programming, AI applications, and input/output operations. In these applications, there are specialized objects, such as a file, graphics screen, and ASCII terminal, associated with a number of operations to perform for these objects. It may be necessary to implement the same procedure two different ways depending on the device to which the procedure will be applied. Object-oriented programming is convenient because its organization and structure allow the devices to be associated only with relevant procedures instead of every operation having to know about every device.

It is important to note, however, that object-oriented programming is not as suitable for other types of applications, such as Fortran-style multimode arithmetic (arithmetic that deals with different modes, such as real and integer). Its unsuitability stems first from the lack of a single designated important object. Unlike input/output operations, which are performed on a single important object such as a file, multimode arithmetic operations deal with two operands represented in different modes, neither one of which is unique. For example, it makes no difference to an additional operation if a real number is added to an integer or an integer is added to a real number.

Conventional programming languages associate the knowledge of how to perform such mixed-mode addition with the operator "plus." To perform the addition, the language decides on a common type, generally real, maps the integer into the real-number representation, and calls the real-number addition routine. In a straightforward manner, the real-number addition routine handles addition either of integer plus real or real plus integer because the knowledge is in one place associated with the operator "plus." This type of organization is a procedural organization rather than an object-oriented one.

In object-oriented organization, the real number and the integer would correspond to objects. To perform addition of these two types of numbers, it is necessary to have routines associated with integer that know how to add real numbers and also routines associated with real numbers that know how to add integers. Such a procedural problem requires information to be represented redundantly because there is no unique object associated with the "plus" operator. In this type of situation, it is more appropriate to associate the knowledge with the operators (plus) rather than the numbers (objects).

Acquiring Knowledge From an Expert

CHAPTER 9

An expert system or knowledge system acts like a real expert because it has embedded in it the factual and experiential (heuristic) knowledge of a real expert. Getting that knowledge out of the real expert and into a form that can be used by a computer is a difficult job. For one thing, it requires an expert who is both cooperative and articulate. For another, it requires a person who knows something about computers, artificial intelligence, psychology, statesmanship, and the expert's application area in order to interview the expert and convert the knowledge acquired from the interviews into a computer-usable form.

The person who interviews the expert and acquires and represents the knowledge is known as a knowledge engineer. The process of acquiring the knowledge and representing it for the computer is known as knowledge engineering. As might be expected, knowledge engineering is a labor-intensive process that takes place over a long period of time. In fact, it is one of the most difficult steps in building an expert system. Furthermore, because the acquisition of knowledge is frequently dependent on only a few people—for example one knowledge engineer and one, or maybe two, experts—the process is a bottleneck in the building of a knowledge-based system.

The knowledge engineering process is arduous and long because no matter how willing experts are to communicate their knowledge, it is impossible for the knowledge engineer to get knowledge out of experts simply by asking for it. It matters not that the experts are willing to answer all the knowledge engineer's questions because, especially at the beginning of an expert system building project, knowledge engineers do not yet know enough about the application to ask for the most useful knowledge. The fact is that it takes a certain amount of knowledge even to ask a good question. It also does not matter that the experts are willing to tell the knowledge engineers whatever they (the experts) know. Even though they know and use the knowledge, it is organized in such a way that it can only be extracted in little pieces over a fairly extensive period of time.

LIVING THROUGH ORDEALS

The length of time necessary to extract knowledge from experts can be explained by understanding what an expert really does. An expert can be thought of as a person who knows what to do in thousands of different situations. However, the mind is largely a recognition machine. Therefore, even though the experts know what to do, they cannot explain how to handle a problem unless they are immersed in the actual situation.

What knowledge engineers must do, then, is live through various situations with their experts over a long period of time. As different situations arise, the knowledge engineer systematically probes, writes, and probes again.

Although knowledge acquisition is time consuming and labor intensive, today's alternative approaches tend to be naive. Systems that learn knowledge by themselves are very rudimentary and still in the research stages. Systems that automate the knowledge acquisition process are also immature and inadequate for many applications.

One approach to easing the knowledge engineering bottleneck is to allow experts to be their own knowledge engineers. This entails the gradual elucidation by the experts of their own knowledge, either to a standard medium such as paper or tape recorders, or directly to an expert system with a natural-language interface. But even if such knowledge-acquiring expert systems were available and practical, a host of difficulties attend this approach, some of which are not related to computer technology. In particular, too often it happens that elucidating knowledge requires the presence of a second party to act as an observer, inquisitor, translator, and sounding board. These are some of the functions performed by knowledge engineers.

Howard Austin, one of Schlumberger's original knowledge engineers for its knowledge-based oil exploration system, notes some of the knowledge engineering difficulties typically encountered that require the presence of a knowledge engineer to resolve. For example, knowledge engineering experiences shows that if you just ask experts how they do something, what often happens is that they tell you what they believe is their procedure. Then if the knowledge engineer watches the experts in action, it turns out that they do something slightly differently.

Another common difficulty occurs when experts state what they believe is "one" procedure to accomplish some chore. Frequently, however, observation of the expert reveals that the one procedure is actually two or more separate procedures, all of which the expert performed without realizing it. Each of these procedures must be separated and clearly and explicitly identified for the knowledge system to work properly.

Achieving clear and explicit explanations at any point in the knowledge engineering process is no easy task. It is difficult for human experts to express their knowledge completely, accurately, and consistently under any circumstances. The ability to express this knowledge for use in a knowledge system is even more difficult because the language that is most natural for the expert to express knowledge is unnatural for the computer, and vice versa. Because of this gap, a knowledge engineer who knows how to represent knowledge for a computer is needed to pick out patterns in the expert's knowledge that can be converted to a form that is useful for a computer.

PRELIMINARY KNOWLEDGE ENGINEERING STAGES

The first thing the knowledge engineers did at Schlumberger when they designed the Dipmeter Advisor knowledge-based system (for oil exploration) was to make a commitment to become "mini-experts" so that they could talk intelligently to the experts and not slow down the expert's work. In pursuit of this goal, the knowledge engineers read the experts' papers and everything else they could find about the experts' application areas. As a result, they learned the terminology, general analysis patterns, and acquired a crude understanding of the experts' work. This allowed the knowledge engineers not only to help identify key concepts of a problem and to understand the experts' explanations, but to ask good questions.

IN THE FIELD

Unfortunately, the most significant heuristics that experts use are not generally capable of being verbally elucidated or written down. So after a time, the knowledge engineers need to inject themselves into the experts' daily job activities. To develop a knowledge-based oil exploration system for Schlumberger, knowledge engineers injected themselves into the experts' daily job activities by going with the experts out in the field, where they observed and recorded on tape recorders, video recorders, and paper (Figure 9-1). Similarly, for Bolt Beranek and Newman to develop Steamer, a knowledge-based system to teach Navy personnel how to operate a steam plant on board ship (Chapter 7), knowledge engineers participated in the traditional classroom and steam plant demonstration courses with other students. In developing Steamer, knowledge engineers found it helpful to know not only the typical problem-solving paths that an expert follows, but also the typical blunders that a student makes when first learning a subject.

Typically, knowledge engineers use a case study method as part of the knowledge acquisition process. For at least a few cases, they watch and record in detail exactly how an expert solves a particular problem. Usually, experts' problem-solving methods are not the kinds of information found in textbooks. The experts might not follow a step-by-step analysis. They know all types of analysis and decision patterns to apply when a problem develops. They know all sorts of ways to avoid searching through a very large number of possibilities and yet come up with the correct answer or appropriate action to take. And they know all kinds of conditions that will invalidate whatever answers or actions they have determined. It is this type of knowledge that a knowledge engineer must determine in order to build a knowledge base.

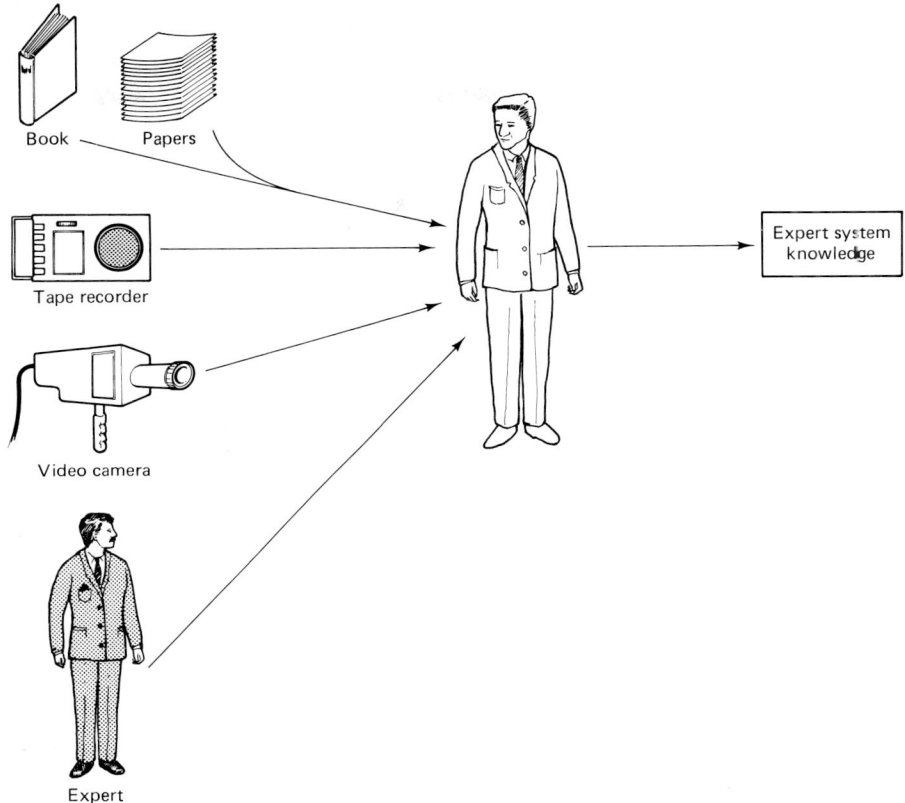

Figure 9-1 Knowledge engineering

Clearly, knowledge engineers must be diplomats. In fact, several companies building knowledge-based systems claim that for a knowledge engineer, people skills can be as important than technical skills. Knowledge engineers must be able to listen as well as ask, and to instill confidence in and draw out the expert regardless of personality differences. They must understand that because so much of the expert's knowledge is intuitive and subconscious, at times there is as much to be learned from rambling as from asking direct questions.

Knowledge engineers may discover that the information the expert has exposited is inconsistent with what was exposited yesterday, what the expert is actually doing, or what another expert says. The rule of thumb is to ask questions but never directly challenge the expert. Instead, what knowledge engineers do is compare their direct observations of the expert's work and answers to questions with written words on the subject. The knowledge engineers must watch and write long enough to confirm that what the expert says coincides with what he or she is doing. Only then are they in a position to begin transferring information to a computer. If further inconsistencies remain between the expert's explanations and procedures followed, they can be resolved later in discussions or by running a sample problem using the expert's verbalized procedure.

Above all, knowledge engineers who have become familiar with an application area must beware of thinking that they know the expert's job. Educational theory, as well as common sense, holds that there is a vast difference between learning facts so that they can be recalled, understanding them enough to teach them to a person or computer, and using the facts to solve a problem under pressure. Anyone who has watched and understood how an example mathematics problem was solved in a class, but later has not been able to do the homework problems, can attest to this.

CODING THE SYSTEM

When enough knowledge is acquired to write a rudimentary knowledge system, the knowledge engineers begin to segment all their transcribed knowledge into chunks that can be used in rules, frames, or whatever other knowledge representations will be used in the knowledge system in question.

At this point, the knowledge engineers encode the knowledge in an actual program. Or, as was done at Schlumberger, they give the marked-up, transcribed information to a different group of programmers to code. The actual knowledge base must be encoded using the same terminology that the experts use because it is the experts that will maintain the knowledge base when the program is complete.

How much knowledge is enough to begin segmenting it into knowledge representation chunks for coding depends on the system and the application. In general, the time to write the system is as soon as there is enough knowledge to write a very simple system to solve a simple problem. This may take three months or it may happen on the first day. The technique followed in building expert systems is to get something running quickly, try it out, find the problem areas, fix it, run it again, and repeat the process.

It is not necessary to have a completed knowledge base to begin writing the expert system. Furthermore, memory and time efficiency should not be considerations at this early stage of development. The issue is simply getting a prototype up and running. The prototype gives management something concrete to see, makes it easier to understand what a knowledge system can do for the organization, and provides a reason for continuing support. Equally important, it does the same things for the expert. The knowledge engineer and the expert then use the simple working prototype to discover what other knowledge needs to be added. As discussed in earlier chapters, expert system knowledge is represented in fairly independent chunks that are easy to add incrementally to an expert system.

KNOWING WHAT KNOWLEDGE LOOKS LIKE

When the knowledge engineer is ready to segment knowledge into chunks that the computer can use, clearly it is necessary for him or her to understand the different forms of representing knowledge for a computer. A knowledge of computerized knowledge representations is also necessary in the early information-gathering stages, long before the time to begin segmenting knowledge for coding.

Starting then, knowledge engineers must interview an expert in an arbitrary and complex domain and develop a symbolic representation for that expert's knowledge so that the computer can understand and use it. Unfortunately, knowledge is an elusive, abstract thing. Furthermore, as mentioned earlier, verbalizing heuristic and intuitive knowledge precisely and completely in a form that another person can use is a very difficult task. The difficulty is compounded by the gap that exists between the way the human expert expresses knowledge and what the computer, rather than a person can use.

To get the knowledge from the expert in a usable form, it is necessary to have some idea of what to look for. What to look for means much more than knowledge about an application domain or even knowing the important issues in that domain. It means, also, the ability to understand what knowledge looks like in order to recognize it, organize it, and impose a picture or structure of what general knowledge looks like on the specific knowledge that the expert is communicating.

To recognize and organize the knowledge, it is necessary to have a theory of how knowledge might be structured. How knowledge is structured is not immediately obvious. For example, an expert speaks words, and words form larger patterns such as sentences or paragraphs. But sentences and paragraphs help to organize words for people only to a limited degree. When a month, week, day, or even five minutes has passed, people are likely to have forgotten the words. One reason is organization. People remember and use knowledge more easily when it is organized around certain concepts and into certain scenarios.

Much the same is true for computers. Lots of knowledge can be stored, but the key to retrieval and proper application is organization.

TRANSLATING FROM HUMAN EXPERT TO COMPUTER

The methods for organizing knowledge in knowledge-based systems constitute the various knowledge representation techniques such as rules, frames, logic, and semantic networks, discussed earlier. But application domain experts do not talk in rule or frame languages. They know the procedures they perform, but they cannot necessarily articulate them in an organized form that is useful to a computer. Also, it is not realistic to figure on organizing reams of unorganized, transcribed information months after it has been given. In fact, knowledge systems are under development that represent, in organized knowledge-based formats, information currently contained in government and organizational documents, on the grounds that much of the partially organized information found in these documents is, in reality, inaccessible. For best results, some organization of knowledge transmitted during interviews with experts must therefore begin at the beginning of the knowledge-collecting process, at least in the mind of the knowledge engineer. Otherwise, the organization of knowledge for encoding may be an intractable problem.

Translating between an expert's and computer's understanding of knowledge is no easy task. Using the knowledge to give advice to a computer rather than to another person is a worse problem, partly because of past experiences that people may have but computers do not. Simply put, people use their past experiences and knowledge to internalize new knowledge (make it part of their mental structure). Computers generally do not, and this inability makes it much more difficult to explain knowledge so that the computer understands it. Consequently, much more knowledge must be explicitly and concretely represented than would be necessary when communicating knowledge to another person.

A person who reads about a number of companies who produced good products but are failing anyway because their prices were not competitive internalizes that information. Once the information is internalized, he or she is able to translate a single piece of advice from an expert about the need to price products appropriately into a procedure that takes into account not only cost, overhead, and profits, but also the competition, even though none of these factors were mentioned. In contrast, a price-setting policy routine in a Reveal-based expert system (developed by McDonnell Douglas, Knowledge-Engineering Products Division) must translate that piece of advice into several rules, each giving explicit advice about different requirements to satisfy when pricing a product.

So much is taking advice not a straightforward process that knowledge systems are under development for the purpose of researching automated methods on learning by taking advice. One such system (begun at Carnegie–Mellon University and continued at the University of Southern California's Information Sciences Institute) has become adept at playing Hearts by converting advice such as "avoid taking points in a trick" into explicit procedures such as "play a low card." When these advice-taking systems are further along in development, it will be easier for application experts to act as their own knowledge engineers and develop their own knowledge-based systems by using their knowledge to give advice to their computer. Until then, a knowledge engineer must be present at interviews with experts to listen to an expert's verbalized thought processes, look for patterns in these processes that can be converted to some organized knowledge representation that is usable by computers, and then organize and translate the expert's knowledge.

Which representation techniques to look for varies with the application, project, and knowledge engineer. Knowledge engineers visualize and translate some of an expert's knowledge exposited during interviews into forms such as "if this is the case, then do that" rules. They visualize and translate other types of information into logic representations such as "for all divisions such that profits are less than a certain amount, infer a particular strategy."

A great deal of knowledge is organized and coded in this manner. However, a massive amount of knowledge is collected in the building of a knowledge-based system. A lot of it must be ignored because it is not yet known how to code it.

Once a knowledge representation structure has been determined and the initial burst of information has been segmented and encoded, to some degree, automated knowledge engineering techniques are possible. For example, there are knowledge systems that, once established, prompt an application expert for new knowledge which is automatically converted to the system's knowledge representation.

CHALLENGE THE SYSTEM

As soon as some simple examples that model the way an expert solves a few problems are understood, the knowledge engineer begins building a rudimentary prototype knowledge system. Once this rudimentary system is coded, the experts identify test cases which they try out on the system.

Clearly, the system will come to a naive conclusion since it represents only the knowledge of a novice. However, using this naive conclusion as the focus for discussion, the knowledge engineer elicits more information about the problem from the expert and uses the information elicited to improve the original system. Over many iterations, the expert points out where the program went wrong, at what point different conclusions should be made, and what new chunks of knowledge should be added to the knowledge base. Once the naivete of the knowledge system is pinpointed and the expert determines exactly what he or she would have done differently, the knowledge engineer enters a new chunk of knowledge into the knowledge base.

A good example of the adding of chunks of knowledge to an evolving knowledge system is DEC's XCON, which configures VAX-11/780 orders. The first or novice version of XCON had about 250 rules that handled XCON's original database description of 100 components. However, because the rule base knowledge was rudimentary and the VAX-11/780 could support 420 components (many more than XCON's database contained), XCON could acceptably configure only the simplest standard DEC VAX computer systems.

To extend the rule base, knowledge engineers gave XCON several orders to configure. Experts then looked at the proposed configuration and pointed out where it deviated from what was considered acceptable and what knowledge it needed to avoid the unacceptable and perform the configuration task correctly. The expert's answer to the form "IF the system knew this particular item of knowledge THEN it would know enough to do the following" was added to XCON as another rule.

By 1980, XCON grew to 750 rules, its database grew also to handle the 420 components that the VAX supported, and the expert system began to configure all VAX-11 orders, including those that involved a variety of special situations. Today, XCON has more than 3500 rules. The number of components described in the database has grown commensurate with the new components supported by VAX systems. "Yet it still makes mistakes now and then," says John McDermott, XCON's principal inventor (McDermott, 1981).

Since McDermott views XCON as an expert, he expects that it will, like all experts, occasionally make mistakes. His concern is that many people view XCON (or expert systems in general) as programs and assume perfection. According to McDermott: "There is a big difference between programs and experts. Finished programs, by definition, have no bugs. When experts are finished, on the other hand, they're dead."

It is important to note that not only will knowledge systems make mistakes, they also cannot have the kind of knowledge that will obsolete the human expert. True, expert systems can acquire enough knowledge to make them very competent. But if an unusual situation arises, such as a potato in a tailpipe, no matter how good a knowledge-based automotive diagnostic system's prior performance, the system must fail and ask the human expert. The human expert will then add a rule to diagnose a potato in the tail pipe. But the next time, when the automobile turns out to have a turnip in the carburetor, it is back to the expert again.

A Guide To Building Expert/Knowledge Systems With Microcomputer-Based AI Tools

CHAPTER 10

With many companies now entering the artificial intelligence business, the question "Are there enough experts to write the programs?" has been raised. The answer is that it is no longer necessary to be a Ph.D-in-AI-type of expert to write knowledge systems, because there are several expert system development tools available to build applications.

Software engineers, programmers, and data-processing professionals should have no difficulty learning to work with these tools.. Some other types of engineers and application experts will also be up to the task. Learning to use the tools is no more difficult than learning a new programming language.

General knowledge about the basic precepts of artificial intelligence, such as expert system architecture, limitations, and knowledge representations methods, is necessary to use the development tools successfully. Often, this education is provided by the AI tool companies, in courses, seminars, and contractual consulting. History has also shown that once a subject becomes popular, educational institutions begin to offer courses, or increase their course offerings in that subject, thus providing software professionals or application experts with the background knowledge to use the tools.

The incentives for acquiring tools to build knowledge system applications transcend the scarcity of AI experts; AI tools are also intended to satisfy a company's need for confidentiality. The symbolic problems that AI can solve are important to business plans and strategies and AI solutions often gives a company an edge over its competitors. Knowledge bases, however, may contain knowledge about these plans and strategies. Consequently, many companies want application development tools to build their knowledge systems in-house, preferring not to trust outsiders with the details of their business information.

AI application development tools run on a variety of computers, from Lisp machines to microcomputers, and exhibit a range of capabilities and ease-of-use features. The application development tools that run on Lisp machines operate on top of Lisp environments, where they use the standard interactive graphics displays, editors, debuggers, and other features available there.

Another group of AI application development tools has been designed to run on microcomputers. Although microcomputer environments have less memory, processing power, graphics capabilities, and features than those of Lisp machines, microcomputer-oriented tools have the capabilities to build real-world, utilitarian knowledge systems, albeit smaller ones than those built by their more expensive, Lisp machine-oriented counterparts.

This guide to building knowledge systems will begin with microcomputer-oriented tools because they are simpler, and it is easier to understand how to use them to build a knowledge system. They tend to represent knowledge in easy-to-comprehend IF-THEN rules, use only one inference strategy, and support very limited control mechanisms. Once a fundamental understanding of knowledge system building principles, using simple knowledge representation and control techniques has been acquired, the next chapter will discuss how to use large-scale AI application tools, which contain a variety of AI-based features and capabilities, to build large-scale business, industrial, and scientific knowledge-based systems.

The large-scale AI tools often use the same techniques as those used by microcomputer-based AI tools, but they also handle frame- and logic-based representations, procedures, more reasoning strategies, object-oriented programming, hierarchical inheritance lattices, and sophisticated control structures. However, the basic steps of planning, designing, building, and testing a knowledge-based system, as well as the same pitfalls, are common to microcomputer- and Lisp machine-based AI tools, and the same precautions apply.

MICROCOMPUTER-BASED TOOLS

AI application development tools make knowledge system development accessible to AI nonexperts. Their implementation on microcomputers has great potential to bridge the technology gap between AI experts and people who would like to explore AI and determine if it can help them in their profession. Previously, AI exploration was impractical because it required not only people with AI expertise, but also the purchase of expensive AI hardware.

PC-based knowledge system tools have a variety of capabilities and techniques for building knowledge bases. Some prompt users for knowledge base information. Some represent knowledge in tabular form or combine tabular representations with block structured procedures. Others are similar to large-scale AI tools, running on Lisp machines, differing mainly in the amount of main memory available to the program (128,000 bytes instead of 140 million bytes, for example), the highly graphical environments available to programs running on Lisp machines, and the sophistication of control mechanisms that can be used.

All of the PC-based AI tools are highly interactive. Several have advanced AI capabilities, such as the ability to accept incomplete and unknown answers, uncertain information, and several values for the same expression. Some can explain the system's method of reasoning used to solve a problem. Some handle meta-rules (rules about rules), which are used most often to direct the steps of a consultation. Some even have capabilities not generally found in large-scale Lisp systems. The tool Reveal (from McDonnell Douglas), for example, handles what is known as fuzzy logic, or the ability to handle quantifiers such as almost, very, quite, high, low, few, many, and several. These quantifiers, which represent a matter of degree rather than exact quantities, are the types of quantifiers that most people use to describe most of the everyday world.

Although AI application development tools make knowledge system development accessible to nonexperts, a number of precautions apply. In particular, it is important not to be lulled into false confidence and expectations about how easy it is to build knowledge-based systems, and then be disappointed. Tools are not a panacea for learning and hard work. Much of the work occurs before the knowledge system writing begins, and entails a thorough analysis of the problem, planning of the system, gathering knowledge, and organizing it to fit the knowledge system design and structures. Testing the system to ensure that needed information is not missing, does not conflict, is understandable, and most important, gives correct answers or solutions, is an iterative, arduous task, involving intense, time-consuming effort.

These precautions apply even more to microcomputer-based AI application tools. It is easy for unsuspecting users to be fooled because AI application development tools run on easy-to-use personal computers, have easy-to-use interfaces, and are called up by a single word command. In addition, they seem simple because they require either a language midway between English and Basic, or use a menu/prompting facility to help the user write the knowledge system.

Learning to use AI tools is similar to learning a new programming language. Within a week, the learner can build a system to perform some very simple tasks. Three months of work will render the learner able to build a reasonable-sized, practical system. But at least six months is necessary to reach virtuoso levels, where the user is facile at using all or most of the capabilities of the tool.

As with developing classical software, writing the program is the easy part. The planning and design required before the writing phase of the program begins, and the testing afterward, are far more difficult. People who rush off to the keyboard and think they are going to build a knowledge system, probably will not—at least not until the preliminary planning and design work is accomplished.

THE KNOWLEDGE SYSTEM BUILDING CYCLE

In general, there are four major steps to follow in building a knowledge system with microcomputer or large-scale AI tools. The steps are: analyze the problem, design the system, build a prototype, and incrementally test the prototype. These steps are equivalent

AI practices		Software engineering practice
Analyze the problem	=	Plan
Design the system	=	Design
Build a prototype	=	Edit, code, and compile
Test the prototype	=	Test

Figure 10-1 Building an expert system

to the classical engineering phases of software development: plan, design, edit and compile, and test (Figure 10-1). Only the details are changed.

In the analysis step, the knowledge engineer, contractor, or user chooses a problem (Figure 10-2). Then he or she determines that the problem is suitable for AI solution, and figures out what type of expertise will be needed and who can effectively provide it. In a phase that overlaps the analysis and design phases, the knowledge engineer gathers the knowledge for the program.

Choose the problem
Determine the value of applying AI
Decide on the expert
Gather knowledge

Figure 10-2 Analysis stage

During the design phase, the knowledge engineer organizes the knowledge in a way that best corresponds to the expert's organization in working with it, and creates a skeletal structure for the knowledge system (Figure 10-3). A typical skeletal structure is hierarchical.

Organize knowledge
Gather more knowledge
Create skeletal structure

Figure 10-3 Design stage

For example, an investment planner expert might segregate criteria for recommendations to clients first according to their salary brackets (Figure 10-4). Recommendations for clients in each salary bracket might be further subdivided according to preferences for secure rather than speculative investments. Under secure investments might be additional criteria for recommendations for blue-chip stocks and government certificates. A different investment planner might, instead, subdivide client criteria according to preferences for short-versus long-term gains, and then further subdivide each of these categories in some way.

Automobile diagnostic experts might characterize car problems according to where the fault lies. First, they might figure out whether the fault is in the engine, transmission, cranking, charging, or some other car system (Figure 10-5). Once they pinpoint the faulty system, for example the charging system, in the next group of steps they might figure out whether the cause of the fault lies in the alternator, fan belt, battery, or other component in the charging system. If necessary, the expert, and through him or her the knowledge

The Knowledge System Building Cycle

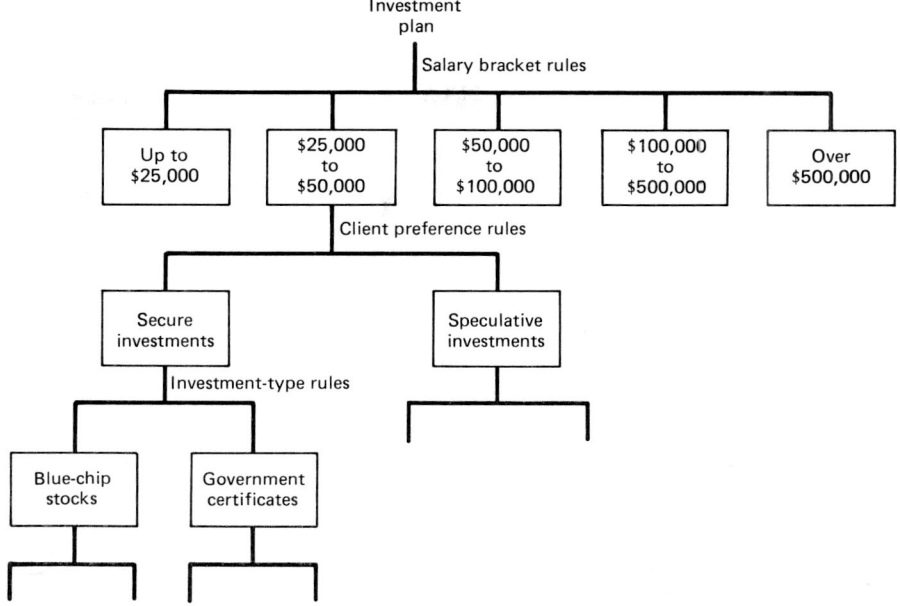

Figure 10-4 Skeletal structure for an investment advisory knowledge system.

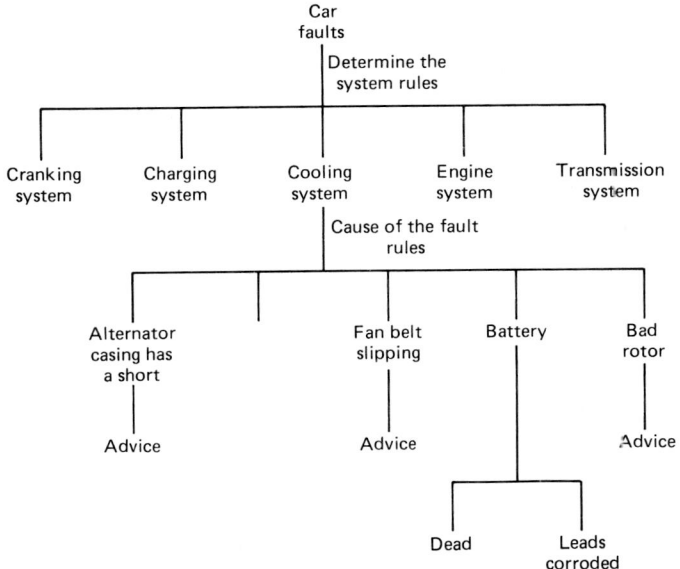

Figure 10-5 Skeletal structure for a knowledge-based automotive diagnostic system.

engineer, would further subdivide the hierarchical fault diagnostic structure until finally a sufficient level of detail is reached that supposes that the fault is that the alternator casing has a short or the battery leads are corroded.

Two types of tasks are performed during the next stage of building the prototype. In one task, the knowledge system designers fill in the detailed application information for each step of the hierarchy (Figure 10-6). Depending on the system and its knowledge representation methods, the details include diagnostic or other application rules, characteristics of physical structures, acceptable values that end users can enter, and other information necessary for the internal workings of the system. This information is written in whatever language is provided by the tool. Knowledge of these details allows the expert system to progress down the hierarchy by the reasoning strategies employed by the tool (forward chaining, backward chaining, or a combination) until it has concluded a specific diagnosis identified at the bottom of the hierarchy.

The second type of information entered during the building-the-prototype phase is control information. This is contained in rules that control an actual end-user consultation by controlling the order in which both hypotheses and different lines of reasoning should be pursued and letting the system know when the problem has been solved.

Control rules are more sophisticated and more difficult to learn to use correctly than are rules about subject application knowledge, such as "IF the car won't start, THEN check to see that it has gas." For a very small or toy system, control rules are not needed because the knowledge system can simply examine every rule to see which apply to a particular problem. As the system built grows progressively larger, this is impractical.

In the test-the-program step, the system designer challenges the knowledge system with several sample problems that it is supposed to be able to solve. The problems are identified by the expert (Figure 10-7).

If execution of any of the test cases produces erroneous results, it is necessary to go back to the expert. The expert can generally tell why the program produced the erroneous result and recommends what the knowledge system should know or do so as not to repeat the same mistake. This new knowledge is encoded in the form of new rules and added to the system, which is tested again with more sample test cases.

When enough iterative testing, and incremental modification or addition of knowledge, produces a knowledge system that consistently provides accurate answers, advice, and diagnostics for a variety of test cases, it is ready to be tried in the field. Field testing gradually uncovers new cases that the knowledge system cannot handle, and new mistakes not previously realized. To handle the new cases and mistakes requires the addition of more rules. In this way the knowledge system gradually matures to the point where it can handle much of what human experts can handle.

Identify and enter goal
Code judgemental rules
Code control rules
Write user questions and allowable answers
Add more rules, questions, and allowable answers
Expand skeletal structure
Add still more knowledge

Figure 10-6 Building a prototype

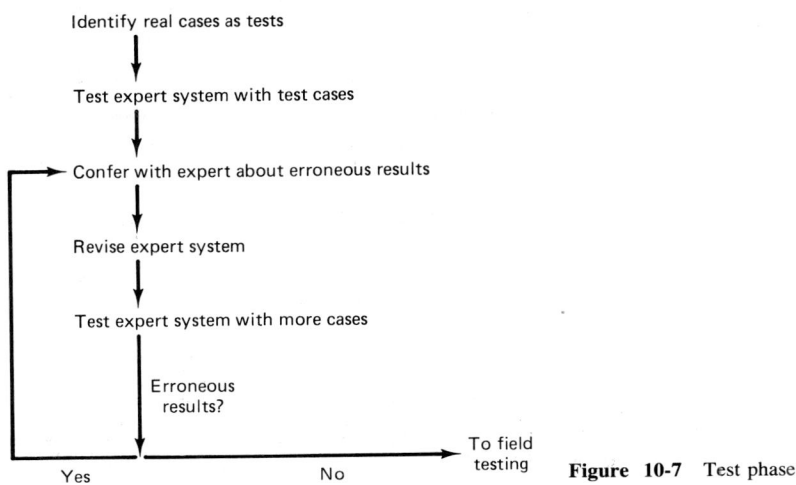

Figure 10-7 Test phase

BUILDING A PROTOTYPE

How to select and evaluate an application was discussed in Chapter 4, acquiring knowledge from experts in Chapter 9, and examples of successful or potential knowledge-based system applications are discussed in Volume II. In this chapter we therefore concentrate on how to build, test, and modify a prototype knowledge system using microcomputer-based AI application development tools.

To explain this development process, four different tools will demonstrate their methods of building four different knowledge systems. The tools are M.1 from Teknowledge, the Personal Consultant from Texas Instruments, Expert-Ease from Human Edge Software or Jeffrey Perrone & Associates, Inc., and RuleMaster from Radian Corp.

M.1

For the first demonstration example, M.1 will be used to built a simple prototype knowledge system, called system.car, to perform automotive diagnosis. The skeletal design for system.car is shown in Figure 10-5. The knowledge system built will conduct a consultation with the user and question him or her about a car's symptoms. Based on the symptoms, it will suggest the system in which the fault probably lies, and tests to perform on components in that system. Depending on the test results, it will suggest the cause of the problem with the car and offer corrective advice.

Assuming that the analysis and design for a knowledge system has been completed, the primary task the tool user must perform in building the system is building a knowledge base. With M.1 any standard text editor can be used for this purpose.

The first item needed in an M.1 knowledge base is a goal. In a backward-chaining system such as M.1, the primary or top-level goal is normally a very general one, such as to provide advice to the user. During a consultation, the knowledge system looks for every rule which concludes that the advice to the user is such-and-such. Such-and-such may be a variable that stands for advice associated with the knowledge system's diagnostic conclusion identified at the bottom of the knowledge system hierarchy and concluded by several rules.

During execution, M.1 tries the different rules that conclude hypothesized causes of a fault to see which one has preconditions that can be satisfied. The conditional parts are satisfied, depending on the test results, symptoms, and the system containing the fault. By back chaining, M.1 explores the hierarchy looking for rules that conclude the symptoms and system, until finally it back-chains to a high enough point in the hierarchy to satisfy the preconditions, and therefore the conclusions, in a hierarchical path. In this way, M.1 verifies that the hypothesized cause, and advice to the user, is correct.

For simplicity in explaining, the initial prototype automotive diagnostic system illustrated will be a very small one whose goal is just to determine the cause of a fault in the charging system. This micro knowledge system will contain one goal, one rule, two questions, and two sets of acceptable values as answers to the questions. The system will then be expanded to show how a larger, more sopohisticated system might be built.

Step one in building the system.car knowledge base is to define a goal. For this micro-system, the goal defined is the cause of the fault in the charging system. So the system designer types

```
>>add goal = cause-of-fault-in-charging-system.
```

The word "add" is M.1's command to add an entry to the knowledge base. Every entry must end with a period to signal the end of the entry to M.1.

Now that the knowledge-based system has a goal, it needs some rules to help it achieve that goal. The automotive expert providing the knowledge for system.car has found that two particular tests, known as an oscilloscope test and a field arc test, performed on the charging system help determine whether or not there is a short in the alternator casing. The system designer therefore, encodes this knowledge in the form of a rule:

```
>>add if result-of-oscilloscope-test = straight-line
    and result-of-field-arc-test = hot-yellow
    then cause-of-fault-in-charging-system =
        alternator-casing-has-a-short.
```

Upon request, M.1 will list the entries in the knowledge base developed so far (Figure 10-8). To understand how interactive knowledge-based system development tools are, how rapidly system prototypes can be built, and how easy it is to add knowledge incrementally, this automotive diagnostic knowledge system can be run right now, even though it has only two knowledge base entries. It will use its one rule to try to satisfy its goal. The M.1 tool provides a default format for asking users questions about test results,

```
M.1> list.

kb-1: goal = cause-of-fault-in-charging-system.

kb-2: if result-of-oscilloscope-test = straight-line
         and result-of-field-arc-test = hot-yellow
      then cause-of-fault-in-charging-system
         = alternator-casing-has-a-short.
```

Figure 10-8 Building a knowledge-based automotive diagnostic prototype

attributes, goals, or observations needed to satisfy conditions of a rule when the system cannot infer the information from other rules or facts. The default format is: "What is the value of (whatever is listed after the word *if*)?"

Execution of the one-rule, one-goal knowledge-based system is shown in Figure 10-9. As the system runs, M.1 conducts its user consultation in the lower half of the screen, while its interactive debugging environment displays a number of relevant facts in four windows on the upper half of the screen. The Events window shows significant events or occurrences such as results or attributes that M.1 has found or is seeking. The Reasoning window shows M.1's reasoning as it searches for a conclusion. Its reasoning consists of the rules currently being invoked or those that have already succeeded.

The Conclusions window displays the conclusions that M.1 has reached based on inference or answers from users. The Options window shows the answers that M.1 will accept from users.

The execution of the system reveals that based on the evidence at hand, the alternator casing has a short. Since knowledge base entry rule 2 did not specify a certainty factor in its conclusion, a certainty factor of 100 percent is assumed.

During the consultation, if the user had asked "why" the system was asking him or her a particular question, M.1 would have responded that it needed the answer to help

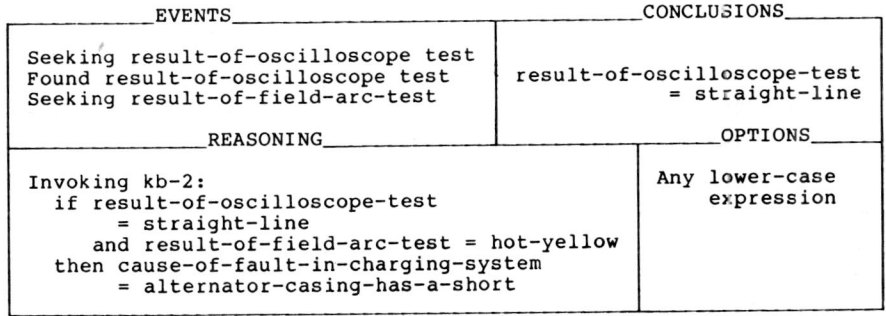

```
What is the value of: result-of-oscilloscope-test?
>> straight-line.
>>What is the value of: result-of-field-arc-test?
```

Figure 10-9 Challenging the system

determine if the rule being invoked was applicable in this consultation. In addition, as the M.1-based knowledge system executes, the Reasoning window continuously changes to keep the user apprised of what the system is doing and why.

It is helpful to phrase more informative questions than the default format provides, for the knowledge base to ask the users about the results of tests or symptoms. It is also desirable to identify to the knowledge system a restricted group of appropriate answers or "legal values" the system is allowed to accept from users. Although this is not essential to the knowledge-based system, it prevents it from failing if the user gives some silly answer or one that the program does not have a rule about. The foolproofing occurs because the system checks the user's response against the list of permissible options and will not accept any other answers. A further benefit of entering legal values for questions is that during a consultation when M.1 asks questions of the users, it shows them, on the screen, the appropriate answers from which to choose. A listing of the modified knowledge base is shown in Figure 10-10. An execution of the modified system.car knowledge-based system with the programmer-phrased questions and the restrictions on users' answers is shown in Figure 10-11.

INCREMENTALLY ADDING RULES

Clearly, there are many possible causes of faults in the charging system. Therefore, the knowledge-based system will contain many rules about the different possibilities and questions and legal values for each rule.

```
M.1> list.

    kb-1:   goal = cause-of-fault-in-charging-system.

    kb-2:   if result-of-oscilloscope-test = straight-line
               and result-of-field-arc-test = hot-yellow
            then cause-of-fault-in-charging-system
                = alternator-casing-has-a-short.

    kb-3:   question(result-of-oscilloscope-test) = '
               Please perform a standard oscilloscope test.
               What type of pattern do you see?'.

    kb-4:   legalvals(result-of-oscilloscope-test) =
               [straight-line, erratic-pattern, normal-arches,
                fluctuating-arches].

    kb-5:   question(result-of-field-arc-test) =
               Turn on the ignition and pull out the filed
               connector to the alternator.  What type of
               flash do you see?'.

    kb-6:   legalvals(result-of-field-arc-test) =
               [none, blue, hot-yellow].
```

Figure 10-10 Adding more knowledge base items

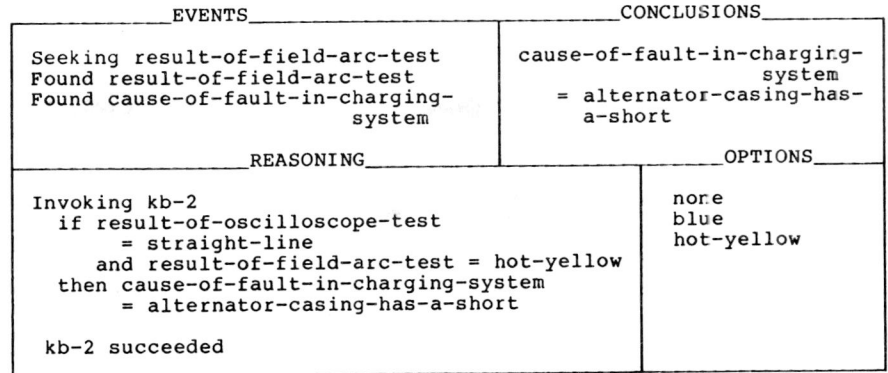

```
Please perform a standard oscilloscope test.  What type of pattern do
   you see?
>> straight-line.
Turn on the ignition and pull out the filed connector to the
   alternator.  What type of flash do you see?
>> hot-yellow.
     cause-of-fault-in-charging-system = alternator-casing-has-a-short
       (100%) because kb-2
```

Figure 10-11 Rechallenging the knowledge system

The expert providing the knowledge for system.car knows three causes of faults in the charging system: the fan belt slipping, a short in the alternator casing, and a bad rotor. He also knows from experience that he can differentiate between these causes by observing the fan belt, noting the results of some standard tests, and examining some mechanical and electrical parts and connections in the car.

The knowledge system designer encodes these causes and the mechanic's methods for differentiating between them in the three rules listed in Figure 10-12 (kb-2, 7, and 10) and formulates questions and legal values to accompany the rules. As with the questions and legal values before, the new rules and questions are simply added to the system incrementally and do not require a program redesign.

During an execution of the expanded knowledge system, M.1 checks each of the rules in numbered order. For example, it will first invoke knowledge base rule 2 and might note that the results of the oscilloscope test is a straight line but the field arc test gives no flash. Therefore, knowledge base rule 2 fails. Next, M.1 invokes knowledge base rule 7. If the user says that the fan belt does not rotate, knowledge base rule 7 fails, and knowledge base rule 10 is invoked.

The questions and legal values need not be in numbered order. Instead, once a rule is invoked and M.1 begins testing its preconditions, M.1 looks for other knowledge base entries that conclude values for the preconditions being tested or that contain the expressions in the preconditions. For example, when testing the condition "if result-of-oscilloscope-test = straight-line," M.1 will find the question asking about the result of

```
M.1> list.

kb-1:  goal = cause-of-fault-in-charging-system.

kb-2:  if result-of-oscilloscope-test = straight-line
         and result-of-field-arc-test = hot-yellow
       then cause-of-fault-in-charging-system
            = alternator-casing-has-a-short.

kb-3:  question(result-of-oscilloscope-test) = '
       Please perform a standard oscilloscope test.
       What type of pattern do you see?'.

kb-4:  legalvals(result-of-oscilloscope-test) =
       [straight-line, erratic-pattern, normal-arches,
        fluctuating-arches].

kb-5:  question(result-of-field-arc-test) = '
       Turn on the ignition and pull out the filed
       connector to the alternator. What type of
       flash do you see?'.

kb-6:  legalvals(result-of-field-arc-test) =
       [none, blue, hot-yellow].

kb-7:  if fan-belt-rotates
       then cause-of-fault-in-charging-system
            = fan-belt-slipping.

kb-8:  question(fan-belt-rotates) = '
       Try rotating the pulley attached to the alternator.
       Does it turn?'.

kb-9:  legalvals(fan-belt-rotates) =
       [yes, no].

kb-10: if result of oscilloscope-test = straight-line
         and result-of-field-arc-test = none
         and field-connector-supply-ok
         and field-connector-grounded
         and not(alternator-brushes-look-bad)
         and copper-slip-rings-connected
       then cause-of-fault-in-charging-system = bad-rotor.
```

Figure 10-12 Adding more rules and related knowledge-base items.

the oscilloscope test and the entry containing the legal values for the result of the oscilloscope test. It will also find any other rules that conclude the result of this test.

M.1 does not go on to testing the next precondition or next rule until it has obtained all the information it needs from these related knowledge base entries, either by noting facts, inferring information, or asking the user. This persistence in one subject before going on to another promotes efficiency and is similar to the way in which human beings perform diagnosis, especially in large applications that seek many possible fault causes in many subsystems. Human beings do not generally handle different systems, seek test results, and ask questions haphazardly and randomly.

CONTROLLING A CONSULTATION

As more rules are added to a knowledge base, it becomes increasingly more inefficient to test every relevant and irrelevant rule. For example, if a problem has been determined to be in a cooling system, there is little sense in cycling through all the rules to test out parts of the transmission and engine block. To avoid cycling through all the irrelevant rules, system.car first gathers initial symptoms and determines in which system the fault probably lies. Then it performs different tasks and subtasks to test out subsystems and components within the probable faulty system. Finally, it not only determines the cause of the fault, but also displays recommended corrective action.

To ensure that the diagnostic procedures are carried out in this order, users write control rules in addition to judgmental rules. Unlike judgmental rules, control rules have nothing to do with the subject matter of the consultation. Display rules that display greetings or advice to users, as well as rules that tell the knowledge system that a consultation is over, are examples of control rules.

To provide efficiency as system.car is further expanded, a new version will be written which has a single control rule that controls the consultation, in conjunction with the knowledge base system's top-level goal and subgoals generated during system execution. A top-level goal is the overall goal of a knowledge system. A top-level goal might simply be for the consultation to be over, in which case the knowledge system will perform all the diagnostic chores necessary for the consultation to be over.

The top-level goal for system.car, listed below, is to provide advice for a consumer:

```
goal = advice-for-consumer.
```

System.car's single control rule is the following rule, which concludes advice-for-consumer.

```
if system = X
    and cause-of-fault-in-X = Y
    and recommendation-for-Y = Z
then advice-for-consumer = Z.
```

Unlike the judgmental rules seen so far, this rule contains variables: X, Y, and Z. X stands for any system. Y can be replaced by any fault in the system assigned to X. Z represents a recommendation, or advice for the consumer, for the cause-of-fault represented by Y.

To conclude the appropriate advice for the consumer, system.car must satisfy the three preconditions in the control rule, in the order in which they appear. Thus the control rule determines the sequencing of the major steps in the diagnostic process.

Each of the three preconditions—determining the system, finding the cause of the fault, and making the recommendation—are actually subgoals of system.car. To satisfy these subgoals, system.car backward chains through the rules in the knowledge base that conclude the subgoals.

For example, to determine the system in which the fault lies, system.car has a set of rules. Similarly, a set of rules and knowledge base entries are used to determine the cause-of-fault in the system.

```
GOAL
    kb-1: goal = advice-for-consumer.

ADVICE-FOR-CONSUMER
    kb-2: if system = X
            and cause-of-fault-in-X = Y
            and recommendation-for-Y = Z
          then advice-for-consumer = Z.

CAUSE-OF-FAULT-IN-CHARGING-SYSTEM
    kb-3: if fan-belt-rotates
          then cause-of-fault-in-charging-system
              = fan-belt-slipping.

    kb-4: if result-of-oscilloscope-test = straight-line
            and result-of-field-arc-test = hot-yellow
          then cause-of-fault-in-charging-system
              = alternator-casing-has-a-short.

    kb-5: if result-of-oscilloscope-test = straight-line
            and result-of-field-arc-test = none
            and field-connector-supply-ok
            and field-connector-grounded
            and not(alternator-brushes-look-bad)
            and copper-slip-rings-connected
          then cause-of-fault-in-charging-system = bad rotor.

FAN-BELT-ROTATES
    kb-6: question(fan-belt-rotates) = '
            Try rotating the pulley attached to the alternator.
            Does it turn?'.

    kb-7: legalvals(fan-belt-rotates) =
            [yes, no].

RESULT-OF-CRANKING-TEST
    kb-8: question(result-of-cranking-test) = '
            Try cranking the car.  What happens?'.

    kb-9: legalvals(result-of-cranking-test) =
            [dead-silence, sluggish-cranking, vibrates,
             grinds, starter-runs, cranks-normally,
             car-starts].

RESULT-OF-FIELD-ARC-TEST
    kb-10: question(result-of-field-arc-test) = '
             Turn on the ignition and pull out the filed
             connector to the alternator.  What type of
             flash do you see?'.
```

Figure 10-13 Incrementally adding more knowledge.

```
kb-11:  legalvals(result-of-field-arc-test) =
            [none, blue, hot-yellow].
```

RESULT-OF-OSCILLOSCOPE-TEST

```
kb-12:  question(result-of-oscilloscope-test) = '
            Please perform a standard oscilloscope test.
            What type of pattern do you see?'.

kb-13:  legalvals(result-of-oscilloscope-test) =
            [straight-line, erratic-pattern, normal-arches,
             fluctuating-arches].
```

SYSTEM

```
kb-14:  if symptom = car-wont-start
           and result-of-cranking-test = grinds
           or result-of-cranking-test = vibrates
           then system = cranking-system cf 80%.

kb-15:  if symptom = battery-uses-too-much-water
           then system = cooling-system cf 80%.

kb-16:  if symptom = car-wont-start
           and result-of-cranking-test = dead-silence
           then system = charging-system cf 80%.
```

SYMPTOM

```
kb-17:  question(symptom) = '
            What is wrong with the car?'.
```

RECOMMENDATION-FOR-X

```
kb-18:  recommendation-for-alternator-casing-has-a-short = '
            The casing of the alternator is shorted out. You
            will have to replace the alternator with a new one'.

kb-19:  recommendation-for-bad-rotor = '
            The alternator rotor is bad. Please replace the
            rotor with a new one. For convenience, you may
            prefer to replace the entire alternator'.

kb-20:  recommendation-for-fan-belt-slipping = '
            The fan belt is loose and needs tightening. If the
            fan belt shows signs of wear, then it should be
            replaced'.
```

Figure 10-13 (Cont.)

Figure 10-13 shows system.car's knowledge base, which is a modified, expanded version of the original six-item knowledge base.* Using this knowledge base, system.car conducts the user consultation shown in Figure 10-14. To consult with the knowledge-based system, the user simply types in "load system.car." This causes system.car to go looking for its top-level goal, which is advice-for-consumer. It then looks for a rule that concludes advice-for-consumer, and finds its control rule.

The control rule says that the first thing that must be done during this consultation and diagnostic process is to determine the system in which the fault lies. Identification of

*Knowledge base entries 1-20 supplied by Teknowledge.

```
        What is wrong with the car?
>> car-wont-start.
        Try cranking the car.  What happens?
>> dead-silence.
        Try rotating the pulley attached to the alternator.
        Does it turn?
>> no.
        Please perform a standard oscilloscope test.
        What type of pattern do you see?
>> straight-line.
        Turn on the ignition and pull out the filed connector to the
        alternator.  What type of flash do you see?
>> hot-yellow.
System.car has reached the following conclusions about
advice-for-consumer:
        advice-for-consumer = '
        The casing of the alternator is shorted out.  You will
        have to replace the alternator with a new one'
```

Figure 10-14 Interactive automotive diagnosis consultation.

this first required step is the result of "system = X" being the first condition that must be satisfied in the control rule. Three rules, kb-14, kb-15, and kb-16, conclude system = cranking-system, cooling-system, and charging-system.

System.car will try to satisfy the conditions in these three rules to conclude which system contains the fault. The system concluded becomes the X in the control rule.

Knowledge base rules 14 and 15 fail, but kb-16, which concludes that the fault is in the charging system, succeeds. It is possible, however, that evidence might be contradictory or might indicate that the fault could be in one of several systems. If this happens, M.1 will examine each system in turn, looking for a diagnosis.

With the faulty system now identified, system.car continues with the second precondition of its control rule, equivalent to the second step of the consultation, and tries to determine the cause-of-fault-in-charging-system. Three rules conclude the cause-of-fault-in-charging-system: kb-3, kb-4, and kb-5. Of these, kb-3 fails, but since kb-4 succeeds, the cause of the fault is determined to be a short in the alternator casing and there is no need to test kb-5.

The second precondition of the control rule is now satisfied and system.car continues with the third and final consultation step. The third precondition calls for identifying an appropriate recommendation for corrective action for Y, which has been determined to

"= alternator-casing-has-a-short." The appropriate recommendation is stated in kb-18.

With all three preconditions of the control rule satisfied, the action or "then" part of the rule is executed and system.car offers the recommendation as advice to the consumer. Like mechanics, however, a full-scale knowledge system might have less than 100 percent confidence in its diagnosis. Unless it is certain of its recommendation, M.1 repeats control rule steps 1 and 2 for other implicated automotive systems and may make multiple recommendations with varying degrees of certainty.

DEBUGGING

At this point, it is important to note that although rules can easily be added, incrementally, it is not accurate to say that addition of a new rule does not affect the rest of the knowledge base. Some ways a knowledge base can be affected are illustrated by the following diagnosis of a bad battery.

Automotive mechanics know that if a car does not start, the problem may be a bad battery. Yet, during several consultations with system.car, which did not succeed in diagnosing or correcting a problem in a car that would not start, a bad battery was never suggested as a possible cause of the fault.

A sophisticated, interactive user interface and debugging tools are essential for AI environments, and M.1 is no exception. M.1's rules and other knowledge base entries are automatically indexed as they are entered in the system. Consequently, a scan of system.car's relevant knowledge base rules can be obtained by asking M.1's debugger to display on the screen all the rules which conclude that the cause of the fault is a bad battery. The display reveals that there are no rules that conclude that the cause of the fault is a bad battery. Therefore, the system designer adds the following rule:

kb-21: if level-of-charge = low
and battery-loses-charge
then cause-of-fault-in-charging-system = bad-battery.

A consultation with system.car is rerun but still does not conclude bad-battery as the cause of the fault. Therefore, the system designer reexamines the preconditions of the rule just added. The first precondition tests "if level-of-charge = low."

Upon request, M.1's debugger will show the value of any expression for a particular consultation and will also display all rules and facts in the knowledge base that contain information about or conclude a value for an expression in question. For this consultation, the system debugger shows that the expression "level-of-charge" had no value. Consequently, there are no rules or questions that pertain to level-of-charge. Therefore, another rule is needed that concludes that the level-of-charge is low, so rule kb-22 is added at the end of the knowledge base.

kb-22: if battery-voltage-when-motor-is-off = low
or battery-pH = high
then level-of-charge = low.

Still another rule, kb-23, is needed to conclude the second condition of rule kb-21:

> kb-23: if current-under-load-after-trickle-charge = low
> then battery-loses-charge.

EXPANDING THE KNOWLEDGE SYSTEM

More additions and changes must be made to the knowledge base before system.car can diagnose a bad battery. Questions are needed to ask about the battery voltage, the battery acidity (pH), and the current under load after the trickle charge. In addition, legal values are needed for each of those answers.

The addition of rules to diagnose bad batteries also affects entries already in the knowledge base. For example, the system designer must give system.car some clue about a potential battery problem and make sure it knows that the battery is part of the charging system. To provide this information, it is necessary to modify rule kb-16 that concludes that the system is the charging system.

The mechanic says that clicks heard when cranking the car is a clue to battery problems. Knowing this, the system designer asks M.1 to display rule kb-16 and modifies it to understand the relationship between clicks heard during a cranking test and a fault in the charging system. The modified rule reads as follows:

> kb-16: if symptom = car-wont-start
> and result-of-cranking-test = dead-silence
> or result-of-cranking-test = clicks
> then system = charging system (cf 80%).

A scan of the question related to the cranking test shows that the original knowledge base question is still appropriate to encompass the new information. However, the question will not accept the result, "clicks." Therefore, the system designer must modify the legal values that relate to the result of cranking so that the program accepts "clicks" as an answer and shows it as an allowable choice in the options window.

At last, system.car has a complete hierarchical path in its knowledge base structure that culminates in a diagnosis of a bad battery, as well as all the related questions and appropriate legal values to handle the responses.

ADDING EXTRA FEATURES

There are several other things that knowledge system developers ought to do to make system.car as similar as possible in its capabilities to the automobile mechanic. For example, the user might not know the answer to some of the mechanic's questions. Under these

Adding Extra Features

circumstances, if mechanics cannot easily measure or observe the requested information, they find a way to continue their diagnosis in some other manner, without it. M.1 works similarly by looking for an alternative reasoning method so that it can continue the consultation with the user without the requested information. For example, in addition to rule kb-22, system.car might have a second rule which also concludes that the level-of-charge-is-low:

```
kb-24: if current-under-load = low
       then level-of-charge = low.
```

If the user answers "unknown" to both kb-22's battery voltage and battery-pH questions, M.1 searches for and discovers kb-24. If it knows the current-under-load, it can use kb-24 instead of kb-22 to conclude the level of charge.

Alternatively, the user can provide a rule about what to do if an answer is unknown. Such a rule might provide several possible diagnoses, attaching a certainty factor to each. This certainty factor is not equivalent to a confidence factor as used in probability and statistics. It is the expert's expression of confidence in a diagnosis, based on his or her experience.

For example, during a consultation, a user might know that the battery charge is low, but might not know, or have the time to find out, whether the battery will hold a charge. Rule kb-25, shown below, can deal with the unknown case.

```
kb-25: if battery-hold-a-charge is unknown
       then cause-of-fault-in-charging-system =
                bad-battery (cf 40%)
            and cause-of-fault-in-charging-system =
                voltage-regulator-problem (cf 20%)
            and cause-of-fault-in-charging-system =
                corroded-contacts (cf 20%)
            and cause-of-fault-in-charging-system =
                not(alternator-charging-battery) (cf 20%).
```

During a consultation, if a user answers "unknown" to the question about the current-under-load-after-trickle-charge, system.car will seek kb-25 that pertains to this unknown answer. The conclusions in kb-25 will be passed to kb-23, which will provide the user with kb-25's possible causes of the car fault, together with the attached certainty factors. In some ways, this answer is equivalent to a mechanic invoking his or her own certainty factors and telling the customer that he (the mechanic) "gave the battery, which was low, a 30 minute charge," and exhorting him (the customer) to "drive the car for a while and bring it back if it shows further problems." The again-expanded, modified knowledge base is shown in Figure 10-15.

```
GOAL
    kb-1: goal = advice-for-consumer.

ADVICE-FOR-CONSUMER
    kb-2: if system = X
             and cause-of-fault-in-X = Y
             and recommendation-for-Y = Z
          then advice-for-consumer = Z.

CAUSE-OF-FAULT-IN-CHARGING-SYSTEM
    kb-3: if fan-belt-rotates
          then cause-of-fault-in-charging-system
               = fan-belt-slipping.

    kb-4: if result-of-oscilloscope-test = straight-line
             and result-of-field-arc-test = hot-yellow
          then cause-of-fault-in-charging-system
               = alternator-casing-has-a-short.

    kb-5: if result-of-oscilloscope-test = straight-line
             and result-of-field-arc-test = none
             and field-connector-supply-ok
             and field-connector-grounded
             and not(alternator-brushes-look-bad)
             and copper-slip-rings-connected
          then cause-of-fault-in-charging-system = bad/rotor.

FAN-BELT-ROTATES
    kb-6: question(fan-belt-rotates) = '
          Try rotating the pulley attached to the alternator.
          Does it turn?'.

    kb-7: legalvals(fan-belt-rotates) =
          [yes, no].

RESULT-OF-CRANKING-TEST
    kb-8: question(result-of-cranking-test) = '
          Try cranking the car.  What happens?'.

    kb-9: legalvals(result-of-cranking-test) =
          [dead-silence, clicks, sluggish-cranking,
           vibrates, grinds, starter-runs,
           cranks-normally, car-starts].

RESULT-OF-FIELD-ARC-TEST
    kb-10: question(result-of-field-arc-test) = '
           Turn on the ignition and pull out the filed
           connector to the alternator.  What type of
           flash do you see?'.

    kb-11: legalvals(result-of-field-arc-test) =
           [none, blue, hot-yellow].

RESULT-OF-OSCILLOSCOPE-TEST
    kb-12: question(result-of-oscilloscope-test) ='
           Please perform a standard oscilloscope test.
           What type of pattern do you see?'.
```

Figure 10-15 Expanding the knowledge system.

Adding Extra Features

```
    kb-13:  legalvals(result-of-oscilloscope-test) =
               [straight-line, erratic-pattern, normal-arches,
                fluctuating-arches].
```

SYSTEM

```
    kb-14:  if symptom = car-wont-start
               and result-of-cranking-test = grinds
                  or result-of-cranking-test = vibrates
            then system = cranking-system cf 80%.

    kb-15:  if symptom = battery-uses-too-much-water
            then system = cooling-system cf 80%.

    kb-16:  if symptom = car-wont-start
               and result-of-cranking-test = dead-silence
                  or result-of-cranking-test = clicks
            then system = charging-system cf 80%.
```

SYMPTOM

```
    kb-17:  question(symptom) = '
               What is wrong with the car?'.
```

RECOMMENDATION-FOR-X

```
    kb-18:  recommendation-for-alternator-casing-has-a-short = '
               The casing of the alternator is shorted out.  You
               will have to replace the alternator with a new one'.

    kb-19:  recommendation-for-bad-rotor = '
               The alternator rotor is bad.  Please replace the
               rotor with a new one.  For convenience, you may
               prefer to replace the entire alternator'.

    kb-20:  recommendation-for-fan-belt-slipping = '
               The fan belt is loose and needs tightening.  If the
               fan belt shows signs of wear, then it should be
               replaced'.
```

BAD-BATTERY

```
    kb-21:  if level-of-charge = low
               and battery-loses-charge
            then cause-of-fault-in-charging-system = bad-battery.
```

LEVEL-OF-CHARGE

```
    kb-22:  if battery-voltage-when-motor-is-off = low
               or battery-pH = high
            then level-of-charge = low.
```

BATTERY-HOLD-A-CHARGE

```
    kb-23:  if current-under-load-after-trickle-charge = low
            then battery-loses-charge.
```

LEVEL-OF-CHARGE

```
    kb-24:  if current-under-load = low
            then level-of-charge = low.
```

Figure 10-15 (Cont.)

UNCERTAIN ANSWER

```
kb-25:  if battery-hold-a-charge is unknown
        then cause-of-fault-in-charging-system =
                bad-battery (cf 40%)
            and cause-of-fault-in-charging-system =
                voltage-regulator-problem (cf 20%)
            and cause-of-fault-in-charging-system =
                corroded-contacts (cf 20%)
            and cause-of-fault-in-charging-system =
                not(alternator-charging-battery) (cf 20%).
```

BATTERY-VOLTAGE-WITH-MOTOR-OFF

```
kb-26:  question(battery-voltage-with-motor-off) = '
            Measure the voltage of the battery with the motor off.
            What is the voltage?'.

kb-27:  legalvals(battery-voltage-with-motor-off) =
            [low, okay].
```

BATTERY PH

```
kb-28:  question(battery-pH) = '
            Measure the acidity of the battery?  What is it?'.

kb-29:  legalvals(battery-pH) =
            [high, okay].
```

CURRENT-UNDER-LOAD-AFTER-TRICKLE-CHARGE

```
kb-30:  question(current-under-load-after-trickle-charge) = '
            Charge the battery for 10 hours.  Measure the current
            that it can deliver.  What is it?.

kb-31:  legalvals(current-under-load-after-trickle-charge) =
            [low, regular].
```

CURRENT-UNDER-LOAD

```
kb-32:  question(current-under-load) = '
            Measure the current the car can deliver under load?
            What is it?'.

kb-33:  legalvals(current-under-load) =
            [low, regular].
```

Figure 10-15 (Cont.)

LARGER KNOWLEDGE SYSTEMS

Building the knowledge system prototype with application development tools is not a cryptic, abstract experience. As seen, however, it entails a lot of logistics work when entries are added to the knowledge base—more as the system becomes larger because more entries are relevant. Worse, adding new knowledge base entries may require more knowledge acquisition to satisfy new rule conditions. Or it may require the system designer to act the role of automotive mechanic (or other domain expert) in order to add enough knowledge to coordinate all the new and existing rules with each other.

The large amount of logistics and knowledge coordination is one reason for partitioning the knowledge system into small, manageable blocks and then dealing with each block separately. In addition, not only do system designers find it more efficient, but so does M.1, and that enhances performance.

As a knowledge-based system becomes much larger, even partitioning the system does not make it manageable enough. The embedding of control of the program in the rules is one reason. Some rules are solely control rules such as system.car's kb-2, and specify the order of a consultation. But for large, complex systems, control embedded in rules is inadequate because it may be desirable to change the order of the consultation based on the way the consultation is proceeding. With a large knowledge system, the ability to change the order of the consultation avoids cycling through a lot of rules that the system has determined during a consultation to be irrelevant. In a large system, this avoidance makes a big difference in system efficiency and user boredom (the time required to cycle through rules is perceptible).

With M.1, control information that changes the order of a consultation midstream is interwoven in the rules. Unfortunately, this means that the rules that previously contained nicely described pieces of knowledge now also contain additional information to force control to happen in a certain way. Combining control and application information makes the rules less understandable, and maintaining the knowledge base becomes correspondingly more difficult. In addition, building control knowledge into a rule about subject matter limits the various ways and situations in which the rule might be used.

Frequently, AI programmers control their knowledge systems by escaping into the underlying language, which usually is Lisp. Lisp allows them to write code that directs the program to do this, then do that, then loop on some step and perform it iteratively a certain number of times.

Lisp has the disadvantage, however, of being a language less easily understood by nonexperts than the English-like language of AI tools. Also, setting up explanation facilities for the user to understand why some Lisp code performed a certain way requires a translation between Lisp and English, which is inefficient.

Confronting this control problem, some AI tools, among them S.1 (also from Teknowledge), have added a special procedural language for programmers to specify control for large programs in a conventional, block-structured manner. This "control block language," as it is called in S.1, contains block-structured statements such as BEGIN-END, IF-THEN, and LOOP.

M.1 had a top-level goal and a top-level control rule. S.1 has a top-level control block. Like M.1's top-level control rule, the top-level control block specifies a sequence of actions to perform. The control block, however, may invoke rules, examine facts, execute other control blocks, and modify the order of the consultation.

Similar control sequences can be performed with M.1, by coding control in rules. Experience has shown that programmers do not mind writing 10 to 20 control rules in a small- to medium-sized system such as M.1 handles. As the knowledge base grows, however, especially to 500 rules or more, many programmers perfer a more procedural programming language for control rules. In particular, the ability to write conventional loops and condition-branch statements directly saves them much time and planning.

PROMPT TOOLS: THE PERSONAL CONSULTANT

In an attempt to ensure that AI application development tools can be used by AI nonexperts, Texas Instruments has introduced a tool that prompts users for the information needed to develop a knowledge system. Dubbed the Personal Consultant, the tool is a menu- and window-oriented system that develops rule-based, backward-chaining knowledge systems on PCs under the MS-DOS operating system. Written in IQ Lisp, the Personal Consultant supports access to the graphic primitives of IQ Lisp, thus supporting graphics capabilities that can be passed on to users.

The best way to decide which professionals can use a tool such as the Personal Consultant is to have them try it. With this aim in mind, a TI-generated one-rule personal computer configuration knowledge system has been set up on the Personal Consultant to illustrate how educated users or programmers can use the tool to construct a knowledge system. It is important to note that although prompts eliminate the need for the user to memorize the commands necessary to interact with the knowledge system tool, they require the programmer to learn the prompts, especially if they involve new terminology. The prompts provide leverage, however, because the human mind acts like a recognition machine. Therefore, the programmer can easily remember the prompts once they are learned and avoid the need to memorize a lot of new commands.

The TI knowledge system prototype consults with users and, based on the software they plan to run, recommends whether they need a graphics configuration. Clearly, this is a very simple problem and does not require a knowledge system. But the technique would be the same to develop a highly complex system. In fact, as seen with M.1, the greater difficulty in developing a knowledge system is in identifying the knowledge, and the interactions between the knowledge, that are needed for PC configuration.

The first knowledge system building task is to decompose the problem into subdivisions, called "contexts," and as with M.1, to structure the contexts in a hierarachical arrangement. The hierarchical context structure allows the inference mechanism to reason efficiently about the knowledge in the program.

The choice of contexts is generally application-dependent and programmer-defined. Typical contexts for a personal computer configuration program might be hardware and software, with the hardware context further structured in subcontexts such as "assign-boards-to-slots" and "set-switches-on-the-boards" (Figure 10-16).

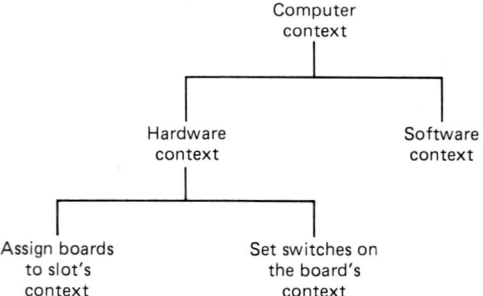

Figure 10-16 Personal computer configuration program contexts.

Each context has parameter (variable) names as well as rules to deduce new knowledge that pertains to it. Once the contexts are defined, the next procedure is to define the parameters and enter the rules for each context, one at a time. Next, the programmer executes, tests, and debugs the segment of the program under development and repeats this set of procedures to incrementally add more knowledge to the program. Throughout these procedures, the Personal Consultant prompts the system developer for all the context and parameter names, parts of the rules, and associated information.

HOW TO BUILD A SYSTEM

To develop the one-rule system, the programmer selects the command "new-knowledge-base" from a Personal Consultant computer menu. The Personal Consultant immediately displays a series of prompts, such as "Domain of consultation," "Name of root context," "Goals of COMPUTER" (context), and "Translation" (Figure 10-17). The first prompt, "Domain of consultation," is the program application, which in this case is Computer Configuration. The second prompt, "Root context," is the context located at the top of the knowledge base hierarchy designed for the program to be developed.

COMPUTER is the name assigned to the root context in this program. Its goal is CONFIGURATION. Translation, abbreviated "Trans," is the programmer-defined translation of a rule or parameter that the system understands into English that will be displayed to the user. The translation the programmer defines is particularly important because it is used to interactively debug the knowledge system with a domain expert who does not understand computer language. As Figure 10-17 shows, the translations are sentence fragments. The Personal Consultant pulls these fragments together to produce a fully translated English rule or explanation.

Other programmer prompts (not shown in the figure) ask for "Default-parameters" and "Initial data" that the knowledge system should ask for at the beginning of a consultation, if any is necessary.

CONFIGURATION is both a goal and a parameter. The user views it as a goal, but the knowledge system views it as a parameter and begins its consultation by asking about this parameter/goal and then chaining backward through other rules to satisfy the goal.

The Personal Consultant allows different types of parameters, such as single- or multivalued, those that can only have a yes or no value, those that require the system to ask for all the values of the parameter immediately, and text constants. The parameter CONFIGURATION is multivalued because this parameter (variable) may represent many values to reason about such as graphics card or graphics monitor.

Information, such as legal values, is also requested by the Personal Consultant. As in M.1, the legal values capability allows the developer to restrict the values that will be accepted by the knowledge system. Still other prompts ask the programmer to enter "User-prompt" information, which is the English-language prompt displayed to the user; "Help" information, which users can call on if they run into problems; and general information about the root text.

A prompt to specify Descendants (lower levels of the knowledge base hierarchy) of

Domain of consultation : Computer Configuration

Name of root context : COMPUTER

Goals of COMPUTER
: (CONFIGURATION)

Type of CONFIGURATION :

Valid parameter types are Yes/no, Singlevalued, Multivalued, Ask-all or Textag.

Type of CONFIGURATION : M

Premise of RULE001
: (LOTUS OR BPS)

Action of RULE001
: (CONFIGURATION = GRAPHICS)

Type of LOTUS :

Valid parameter types are Yes/no, Singlevalued, Multivalued, Ask-all or Textag.

Type of LOTUS : Y

Trans of LOTUS
: (you will be using Lotus 1-2-3)

Prompt of LOTUS
: (Will you want to use Lotus 1-2-3?)

Askfirst of LOTUS : T

Figure 10-17 Personal consultant prompts for building a knowledge system. (Texas Instruments)

the COMPUTER context directs the user to begin defining the hierarchical knowledge base structure. Because this demonstration PC-configuration program has only one rule, the context COMPUTER has no decedents. The root context is now fully defined. It has one parameter, CONFIGURATION; the next step is to begin defining rules.

A menu selection called "Rules" invokes the Personal Consultant's rule-development tool, which automatically prompts the programmer for all the "Premises" (IF parts) and "Actions" (THEN) parts of rules, beginning with rule 1. A rule premise for the PC-configuration program might be "IF YOU ARE USING EITHER LOTUS OR BPS" (Lotus and BPS are computer programs that handle graphics). The associated action would be "THEN THE CONFIGURATION = GRAPHICS." The Personal Consultant regards both Lotus and BPS as parameters and therefore asks the programmer the same questions about these parameters as it did for the configuration parameter.

For example, the "Type" of Lotus (or BPS) is a "yes/no" type (either yes or no) because the user is either using it or not using it. Based on the rule just formed, which pertains to a person using Lotus or BPS, the Type of Lotus is "YES." The programmer is prompted for a translation of the parameter Lotus to be used if the rule is translated into English. A typical English version of the rule might be "YOU WILL BE USING LOTUS 1-2-3." An associated end-user prompt might be "WILL YOU WANT TO USE LOTUS 1-2-3?"

The prompt, "Askfirst of LOTUS" is information needed by the Personal Consultant rather than the user. A "T" for "true" response to an "Askfirst of LOTUS" prompt first directs the knowledge system to ask end users if they will be using Lotus, instead of first trying to infer the information from the rules (the usual step performed first). Clearly, questioning the user first is more efficient in this case.

A few other questions about the properties of the parameters and valid rule subjects concludes the development of rule 1. Programmers can then request a listing of the rule in Lisp or an English translation of the rule. For the English translation, the Personal Consultant coordinates all the user's sentence fragments, entered as responses, in order to produce the following rule:

IF: 1) you will be using Lotus 1-2-3, or
        2) you will be using BPS Graphics package
THEN: It is definite that (1000) the following
        is one of the recommended configurations:
        GRAPHICS

The number 1000 in the THEN part of the rule is a certainty factor that indicates 100 percent certainty. Unlike conventional computer programs, the Personal Consultant can use uncertain information in analyzing a situation and making recommendations. It can assign uncertainty factors to entered information, such as "I am 80 percent certain that this is correct." When it uses these uncertain data, the Personal Consultant applies certainty factors to its recommendations.

```
            Knowledge Base : :  (Computer Configuration)

     Will you want to use Lotus 1 -2 -3 ?
     Select ONE of the followng:
            YES

          ┌──────┐
          │  NO  │
          └──────┘

     Will you be using BPS Graphics package ?
     Select ONE of the following:
          ┌──────┐
          │ YES  │
          └──────┘
            NO

     The recommended configuration is: GRAPHICS


               ... end      press RETURN.
```

Figure 10-18 Interactive computer configuration consultation (Texas Instruments)

RUNNING THE SYSTEM

An execution of the one-rule knowledge system uses the rule and other programmer-entered information to engage end users in a question-and-answer dialogue and produce the consultation shown in Figure 10-18. From here on, more complex systems can be created by adding and refining more rules that encode more knowledge about the problem. The Personal Consultant can handle the building of a knowledge system with as many as 400 rules on a PC. However, if the systems are developed on larger, higher-capacity computers, the PC can run systems with more rules.

HOW IT SOLVES PROBLEMS

The Personal Consultant solves problems using a backward-chaining, goal-oriented strategy. In the one-rule system, the goal was to determine a computer's configuration. To achieve this goal, the system looks for any rules that will deduce configuration. If it finds any rules that conclude "configuration = something," it looks to see if the premise is true. If so, the configuration has been determined. If a premise is unknown, the knowledge system sets up a subgoal to conclude that premise. If it finds a subgoal, the configuration is determined.

   Fortunately, for efficiency, the knowledge system does not need to look through every rule to find one that concludes a goal. Instead, it has an indexing system that records which rules update all its parameters. For example, one notation in the Personal

Consultant indexing system indicates that the goal (or parameter) configuration is updated by rule 1.

Similar information about how to update all other parameters—whether rules or user-entered prompts—is maintained in the index. Consequently, at run time, it is not necessary to perform exhaustive searches to find which rule may be appropriate. Instead, which rules to try is precomputed.

TABLE-BASED AI TOOLS

In knowledge systems, regardless of the inference and knowledge representation technologies employed, the accuracy and completeness of the knowledge base determine how well the system performs. In many business and industrial knowledge systems, not only the cost but also the timeliness of acquiring the knowledge base dominates other knowledge system building factors.

The AI application development tools discussed so far require a person to act as a knowledge engineer and, over an extended period of time, to interview experts, iteratively extract knowledge, organize it, and code it. The knowledge acquisition process is human-intensive, time-consuming, and in some fields where the knowledge or underlying data change rapidly, the knowledge base may be partially obsolete before the knowledge system is completed.

The problem is that the traditional knowledge acquisition process constitutes a bottleneck. Regardless, the process is often necessary to create a knowledge system with sufficient human heuristics to produce accurate system performance. But several companies are working on improving the efficiency of knowledge acquisition by characterizing various aspects of knowledge in spreadsheet-like tables from which the knowledge system induces its own rules.

There are several advantages to the spreadsheet table format. People are familiar with it. It is easy to use and consequently, nonprogrammers, rather than knowledge engineers, can rapidly build or modify the knowledge base instead of extracting knowledge over time. The system that is produced from the tables does not use a spreadsheet format, nor does it provide a single answer like a spreadsheet. Instead, it produces a dialogue system which, like other expert consultative systems, conducts a dialogue with the user and suggests advice based on the questions.

To develop a knowledge system with a table-based tool, users enter the straightforward facts and resulting decisions that come up in their routine work. For example, an investment planner recommends tax-free municipal bonds to a client who has two working members in the family, two dependent children, a total annual income of $60,000, no outstanding debt except for an $80,000 mortgage, $200,000 life insurance, no investments, and is interested in steady, tax-exempt dividends. These data and the recommendation are entered in a table (Figure 10-19). In another example, a gas turbine engine troubleshooter expert whose observations show that an engine will not start, but the fuel flow is okay and the power level is zero, suggests checking the ignition system. The engine start, fuel flow, and power-level values, together with the possible ignition system

Number of working members in family	Number of dependent children	Total annual income	Outstanding debt	Life insurance	Investments	Investment preference	Recommendation
2	2	$60,000	$80,000 Mortgage	$200,000	None	Steady tax-exempt dividend	Tax-free municipal bonds

⎵ Decision-making criteria ⎵   ⎵ consequent action ⎵

Figure 10-19 Each table row contains the same information as in a knowledge-based investment planning system rule.

Table-Based AI Tools

Start	No
Fuel flow	OK
Power level	Zero
Recommended action	Ignition

Figure 10-20 Partial table of observations and recommendations for a gas turbine engine troubleshooter.

diagnosis, are entered into tables (Figure 10-20). In still another example, a real-estate agent recommends that a client buy a four-bedroom, colonial-style house located in the Beverly Hills section of California and costs $500,000. The agent then enters the number of bedrooms, style of house, location, and price of that house, together with the buy recommendation, into a table (Figure 10-21).

These investment planning, troubleshooting, and real-estate applications are examples of decision-making situations based on certain criteria. In the tables, all the cell headings except the last represent the criteria, equivalent to the conditional parts of a knowledge system rule. The last cell heading represents the action, recommendation, or diagnosis part of a rule. Thus, each row of the table has the same information as a knowledge system (production) rule.

Every time another situation arises and the investment planner, troubleshooter, or real-estate agent makes another decision, the facts of the situation and the resulting decision are entered in the table. After a time, the table contains a large record of situations and consequent decisions.

A person new to the business might regard these facts and decisions as examples to learn from, especially if experience shows the decisions to have been successful. Often, there is a pattern contained within the examples that, if recognized, could provide **a** clue or suggestion for the less experienced person's action.

The idea behind the table-driven AI tools is to find that pattern and transform it into a rule, with a decision tree format. The decision tree then guides the questioning of the user and the eventual suggested decision.

The examples given above are real examples, developed with table-based AI application tools. The investment planning system was developed with the tool K:Base (from

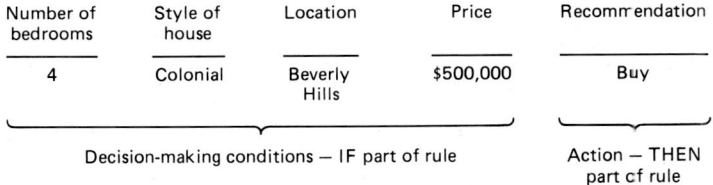

Figure 10-21 Partial table for real-estate knowledge system.

Gold Hill Computers, Inc.). K:Base was designed by a former senior vice president at Lehman Brothers/Shearson/American Express for interest-rate swapping, investment planning, and stocks and bonds trading applications at Lehman Brothers. The gas turbine troubleshooting application was developed with the AI tool GEN-X, designed by General Electric Co. So far, GEN-X has been targeted at development of knowledge-based diagnostic and troubleshooting systems for circuit boards through fighter-plane engines. Unlike K:Base and the tool Expert-Ease, which run on PCs, GEN-X runs on Digital Equipment Corp.'s PDP-11/23 computers. K:Base and GEN-X are discussed in Volume II. The real-estate application was developed with Expert-Ease (from Human Edge Software or Jeffrey Perrone & Associates, Inc.). It is a general-purpose AI tool that will be used, in the next section, to illustrate the use and limitations of table-driven AI application tools.

EXPERT-EASE

Since Expert-Ease, like other table-based AI tools, works by finding a pattern in the examples provided to the system, clearly it will only work for a problem or decision where there is such a pattern. Since it uses past examples as a guide to what action to suggest for a problem, the examples must be representative of the problem and decisions, and must be as complete a set of examples as possible. The developed system is only as good as the examples from which it is built. How many examples are enough depends on the user's desired accuracy. The greater number of examples, the more accurate the results are likely to be.

If past examples do not serve as a precedent for future actions, a table-based tool may not be suitable. For example, a table system used to choose submitted articles for acceptance in a magazine might have columns for subject of article, size and market impact of company submitting the article, and how fast to publish it. Examples entered during a six-month period might show that all articles on operating systems, submitted by large companies, were published immediately. Based on these examples, a knowledge system developed with a table-based AI tool might advise a magazine editor to immediately publish a newly submitted article on operating systems. A human editor might view the situation differently and decide that just because the magazine has published so many articles on operating systems recently, it should avoid them for a while. Expert-Ease does not support such heuristic rules.

More examples encompassing a longer period of time, or better planning of the tables that Expert-Ease uses, might indicate that other knowledge system criteria, such as saturation point, are a way around the problem. This example points out a precaution in the use of systems such as Expert-Ease, and it is the same precaution that has previously been applied to all other knowledge system tools. Users should not be fooled into expecting unreal simplicity because no special expertise or prior programming experience is necessary to use Expert-Ease. As in the case with other AI tools, writing the system is much easier than planning the system beforehand.

```
EXPERT-EASE Attribute Listing, Problem: FED.EXP  Date: 1-oct-84
         weight        type          time          service
         logical       logical       logical       logical

   1     heavy         package       today         priority
   2     normal        document      am.next       standard
   3     light                       pm.next       letter
   4     overweight                  second.day    zap.mail
   5                                               too.heavy
   6                                               bstandard
   7                                               not.avail.
```

Figure 10-22 Attributes for an Expert-Ease table-based Federal Express services advisory system.

BUILDING A SYSTEM WITH A TABLE-BASED TOOL

There are four steps to creating a knowledge system application with Expert-Ease. First, the user defines the cell headings, called attributes, for an application. Second, the user enters examples of real or hypothetical situations and the consequent action or decision. Third, the user asks Expert-Ease to "induce" a rule from the examples entered. Fourth, the system developed is tested by running a dialogue and test case.

In step one of Expert-Ease system development, users analyze their problem and identify a set of attributes (column headings) that pertain to the problem. These attributes and their values define the criteria or conditions for a decision, as well as the decision. For example, in one partially completed system that advises about types of Federal Express services, weight of parcel to be delivered, type of parcel, desired time of delivery, and recommended service are attributes (Figure 10-22).*

Attributes can have many possible values, and the values are either logical or integer. Logical values are specified as names containing up to 10 letters, such as heavy, package, second.day, or priority. Integer values are integers between 32,766 and -32,766.

The values for the weight, type of parcel, and time for delivery attributes are the conditions used to make the decision about the recommended type of service. These conditions correspond to the IF parts of knowledge system rules. The last column of the table is called the result column. It contains the recommended service attribute whose values—priority, standard, zap.mail—are the possible decisions or actions that result from the conditions in the other columns. The result column values correspond to the action or THEN part of a rule.

Neither all the attributes nor values must be planned and entered during initial system development, and new ones can easily be entered at any time.

Once the attributes and values have been entered, system developers enter values for actual or hypothetical examples of situations that pertain to the application in question. The examples are entered in another table that has the attribute headings defined previously. Figure 10-23, for instance, shows in tabular form 16 examples where Federal Ex-

*Example supplied by Jeffrey Perrone.

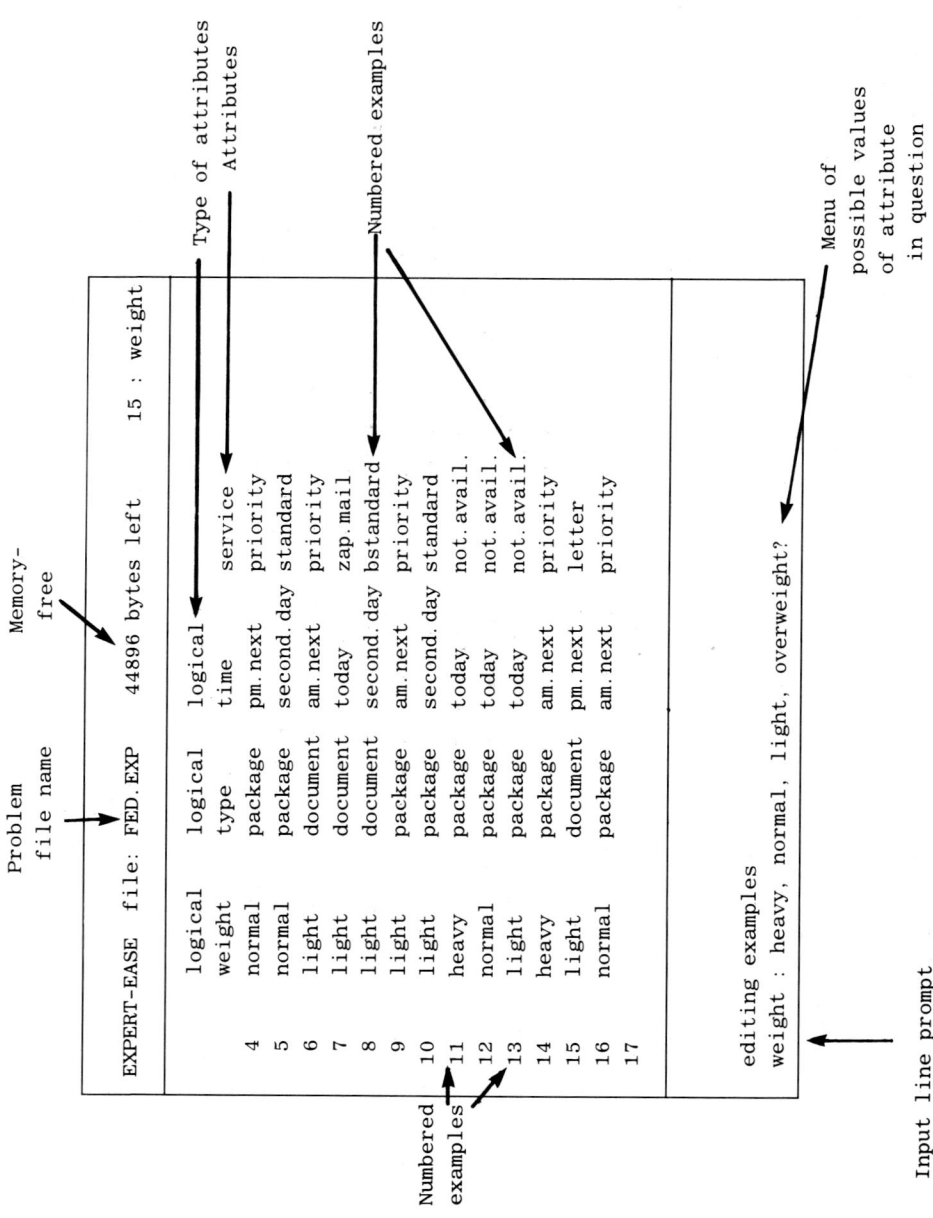

Figure 10-23 Examples for Federal Express Services advisory system.

press customers sent packages or documents of varying weights with different delivery-time requirements. The first three columns consist of the customer-specified requirements, or else an asterisk (wild-card symbol) which indicates that the value in that column does not matter because it does not affect the final result. The last column is the recommended service associated with the first three attribute values.

The examples can be added or modified at any time, even by untrained users. A simple text command allows system developers to define both questions to ask users and synonyms for the cryptic, maximum 10-character attributes in the tables (Figure 10-24).

Expert-Ease prompts the users for the values of the attributes in every new example, and displays, in an input panel, the value choices that were previously defined. Users have the option, however, of typing a choice that is not on the menu and adding it to the list of attribute values simply by replying ''yes'' to a query that asks if he or she wishes to do so.

```
EXPERT-EASE Attribute Listing, Problem: FED.EXP    Date:   1-oct-84

weight     : What is the approximate weight of your parcel?
    heavy       :
    normal      :
    light       :
    overweight  :


type       : What type of parcel do  you want to send?
    package     :
    document    :


time       : How soon do you want your parcel delivered?
    today       :
    am.next     :      Tomorrow morning.  ←――――――――――― Synonyms
    pm.next     :      Tomorrow afternoon.←
    second.day  :


service    : The service we would recommend for you is . . .
    priority    :
    standard    :
    letter      :
    zap.mail    :
    too.heavy   :
    bstandard   : . . .Put the item in a box and ship it standard.
    not.avail.  : . . .No such service available
```

Figure 10-24 Synonyms can be defined for cryptic attributes.

INDUCING RULES

After sufficient examples have been given, the user can command Expert-Ease to induce a rule by typing the ! key. Expert-Ease examines the examples, searches for an underlying pattern, and produces a rule, or "decision tree," which corresponds to this pattern. (Rule induction is based on Donald Michie's ACLS inference system using a published algorithm, Quinlan's ID3.) Expert-Ease then uses this rule to guide the questioning of users and to predict results, suggest decisions, diagnoses, and actions.

The decision tree, which can be displayed and inspected with Expert-Ease's "rule" command, consists of a nested, branchy group of nodes containing attributes and values (Figure 10-25). All the values of attributes, such as heavy, normal, and light (which are values of weight) form branches of the decision tree; their branches may be other attributes, and so on. The values at the leaf nodes, or ends of each branch, are drawn from the results column, so that any path through the tree produces an answer.

Sometimes, instead of containing a recommendation, a branch of the decision tree may be marked "null." For example, Figure 10-26 shows a decision tree based on attribute values used by automobile-insurance agents to determine what type of insurance company and plan to assign to clients. A null recommendation is given next to the insurance company rule node that handles cases where a potential client had two accidents in which he (or she) was at fault (at.fault.2). Such a recommendation means that Expert-Ease has

```
EXPERT-EASE Rule Listing, Problem: FED.EXP    Date:    1-oct-84

weight
    heavy : time
            today : not.avail.
          am.next : priority
          pm.next : priority
       second.day : standard
    normal : time
            today : not.avail.
          am.next : priority
          pm.next : priority
       second.day : standard
    light : time
            today : type
                    package  : not.avail.
                    document : zap.mail
          am.next : priority
          pm.next : letter
       second.day : type
                    package  : standard
                    document : bstandard
    overweight : too.heavy
```

Figure 10-25 Decision tree induced from Federal Express examples.

EXPERT-EASE Rule Listing, Problem: INSURANCE   Date: 5-oct-84

```
age
        <28 : company.1
        >=28 : whycalling
          dropped : company.1
          rateshopng : supprt.bus
                        none : age
                                <48 : company.2
                                >=48 : company.1
                        life : company.3
                        business : null
                        health : null
                        homeowners : company.5
                        two.or.mor : company.1
          recommend : car.type
            conservtiv : accidents
                        none : car.age
                                <8 : company.4
                                >=8 : company.2
                        at.fault.1 : company.3
                        at.fault.2 : null
                        at.fault.3 : null
                        notfault.1 : company.3
                        notfault.2 : company.2
                        notfault.3 : null
            high.perf : null
            sports : company.1
            luxury : age
                        <46 : company.2
                        >=46 : age
                                <49 : company.3
                                >=49 : company.2
          brok.retir : age
                        <35 : company.1
                        >=35 : supprt.bus
                          none : company.3
                          life : null
                          business : null
                          health : null
                          homeowners : company.4
                          two.or.mor : null
```

Figure 10-26 Decision tree induced from examples in automobile insurance advisory system.

not been given an example that covers this case. For Expert-Ease to produce an answer that handles the case marked null, it is necessary to generate a new example to provide the knowledge of how to make the decision.

If two given examples contradict one another, for example two identical sets of attributes values have different result values, the system will be unable to induce a consistent rule that covers all examples. The rule inducer flags the situation and informs the user which examples are contradictory and prevents Expert-Ease from deciding between result values. The user can delete the contradictory examples or put them in reserve store, where they will be remembered for some possible future use, but ignored when the rule is induced. If the user wants the contradictory example to be included in the decision system, he or she must add new attributes or change some values to show the system how to make decisions between the contradictory examples.

If an attribute is type "integer," Expert-Ease produces a tree that branches on conditional tests of the value. For example, nodes in Figure 10-26 contain values of ≥ 35 and < 46, indicating clients 35 years of age or older or less than 46 years old.

The decision tree in Figure 10-26 was induced from examples of insured clients; their personal and driving records, which contain the attribute values used to assign insurance plans and companies; and the assignments made.* A partial table of possible attribute values is shown in Figure 10-27.

The result attribute in the figure is insurance company (ins.cmpany), which can be one of five types of insurance companies/plans referred to by numbers. They are (1) assigned risk plan distributed among many companies, (2) highest rate substandard company, (3) standard company, (4) preferred, and (5) super preferred. The types of companies, which are correlated with different insurance rates, are assigned based on approximately 30 criteria. Among them are why the client is calling for insurance (whycalling), age, marital status, age of car, number of minor violations within four years (minor.viol), number of accidents within four years where the client is at fault (at.fault.1, at.fault.2), number of accidents within four years where the client is not at fault (notfault.1), number of major violations within 10 years (d wi = driving while intoxicated, leave.acc = leaving the scene of an accident, and veh.homcid = vehicular homicide), and supporting business with the insurance company.

Examples of clients having these attributes and values are shown in Figure 10-28, which was used to induce the decision tree. The decision tree determines the order in which questions will be asked, in addition to the recommended company assignment. The queries not only query the user during a consultation, but also test the system, with various cases, to check that it is making the right decisions.

The decisions made by this sample insurance knowledge system are limited because the number of attributes and examples that fit in Figures 10-27 and 10-28 are limited. In the real world, insurance plan and company assignments are based on many more attributes, such as residential stability, employment stability, type of occupation, and interest of the insurance company and agent in obtaining new clients. In addition, assignments and rates are determined by statistically large numbers of cases rather than the 26 exam-

*Insurance examples supplied by Joseph Mione.

EXPERT-EASE Attribute Listing, Problem: INSURANCE   Date: 5-oct-84

| whycalling | age | marital.st | car.age | car.type | accidents | minor.viol | maj.viol | supprt.bus | ins.cmpany |
logical	integer	logical	integer	logical	logical	logical	logical	logical	logical
1 dropped		single		conservtiv	none	none	none	none	company.1
2 rateshopng		married		high.perf	at.fault.1	one	leave.acc	life	company.2
3 recommend				sports	at.fault.2	two	veh.homcid	busines	company.3
4 brok.retir				luxury	at.fault.3	three	dwi.lt5yrs	health	company.4
5					notfault.1		dwi.gt5yrs	homeowners	company.5
6					notfault.2		dwi.gt8yrs	two.or.mor	
7					notfault.3		dwi.10yrs		

Figure 10-27 Table of some possible attribute values for an automobile insurance advisory system.

189

```
EXPERT-EASE Attribute Listing, Problem: INSURANCE     Date:  5-oct-84
```

	whycalling logical	age integer	marital.st logical	car.age integer	car.type logical	accidents logical	minor.viol logical	maj.viol logical	supprt.bus logical	ins.cmpany logical
1	rateshopng	28	married	6	conservtiv	none	one	none	life	company.3
2	dropped	*	*	*	*	*	*	*	*	company.1
3	*	17	*	*	*	*	*	*	*	company.1
4	rateshopng	30	married	3	conservtiv	none	none	none	homeowners	company.5
5	recommend	40	married	5	conservtiv	none	one	none	homeowners	company.4
6	recommend	42	married	5	conservtiv	at.fault.1	none	none	homeowners	company.3
7	recommend	36	single	12	conservtiv	none	none	none	none	company.2
8	*	18	*	*	*	*	*	*	*	company.1
9	rateshopng	45	married	2	conservtiv	none	none	dwi.gt8yrs	two.or.mor	company.1
10	brok.retir	50	married	1	luxury	notfault.1	none	none	homeowners	company.4
11	recommend	50	married	1	luxury	notfault.1	one	none	homeowners	company.2
12	recommend	30	single	10	conservtiv	none	none	none	none	company.2
13	recommend	30	single	2	conservtiv	none	none	none	none	company.4
14	rateshopng	60	married	5	conservtiv	none	two	none	none	company.1
15	rateshopng	70	married	5	conservtiv	none	none	none	none	company.1
16	recommend	40	married	2	sports	*	*	*	none	company.1
17	brok.retir	31	married	3	sports	*	*	*	*	company.1
18	recommend	27	married	5	conservtiv	none	one	dwi.10yrs	none	company.1
19	rateshopng	35	single	3	conservtiv	none	one	none	none	company.2
20	recommend	44	married	2	luxury	none	two	none	none	company.2
21	recommend	46	married	4	conservtiv	notfault.2	none	none	none	company.2
22	recommend	25	single	4	conservtiv	notfault.2	one	none	none	company.1
23	recommend	47	married	1	luxury	none	one	none	none	company.3
24	brok.retir	38	married	2	luxury	none	one	none	homeowners	company.4
25	brok.retir	40	married	2	luxury	none	one	none	none	company.3
26	recommend	41	married	3	conservtiv	notfault.1	none	none	none	company.3

Figure 10-28 Partial table of examples used to develop an automobile insurance advisory system.

ples shown. Setting up this insurance system with appropriate numbers of attributes and examples of their values ensures better decisions and covers the null decision in the decision tree.

The complexity of a multiple-attribute with a multiple-value system is very great. Expert-Ease often finds a rule that restricts this complexity and produces an answer by asking only a few of the questions implied in the attribute sheet. Thus, if the first question in the insurance knowledge system is "why calling" and the answer is "being dropped by current insurance company," neither a human being nor the Expert-Ease system need ask any further questions to conclude that the client will be recommended for the assigned risk plan. Unfortunately, the major place where Expert-Ease falls slightly short of knowledge system expectations is seen in the query facility. It cannot give explanations of how it reached its conclusion or why it is asking a question.

Testing of an Expert-Ease system is similar to testing any other knowledge system. If incorrect results are found, it is necessary to add more knowledge, in the form of new attributes, values, or examples, after which the system is tested again. This cycle is repeated until a desired level of performance is reached.

The table-based tools have been criticized by some members of the AI community as not producing true knowledge systems. It is fair to say at this point, however, that there is not yet a definition of what AI is. Certainly, the table-based tools produce models of processes that require specialized knowledge, normally associated with intelligence. Certainly, they can be used by people with the least expertise or training. Certainly, also, they have many limitations which their larger-scale cousins do not have. Yet the ability to produce models of processes requiring specialized knowledge and the ability to be used by nonprogrammers gives them a niche of their own.

PROCEDURE AND TABLE TOOLS

Greater capabilities and resulting benefits can be gained if table-based knowledge representation facilities are combined with other programming techniques. An example of such a combination tool is RuleMaster, an integrated table-based knowledge tool and a block-structured procedural tool. The tool has two components. One is Radial, an English-like, structured, recursive programming language with constructs of finite state machines. The other is RuleMaker, which induces rules and decision trees from examples of cases represented as knowledge in tables. Written in C, RuleMaster runs under Unix on machines such as Sun Microsystems, Apollo, Gould, IBM's PC AT, AT&T's Unix PC, Perkin-Elmer, and VAX computers.

A Radial program is a collection of related modules which can call one another. Each module defines one or more states which change to another state either in the same or another module. The modules also contain either an action which can be an executable procedure, advice, or a piece of data.

The RuleMaker table-based component allows users to enter rules from examples. An example of this capability is seen in Titan, an expert system that trains and aids Radian Corp.'s service technicians in troubleshooting faults in the TI 990 minicomputer system.

A diagnostic feature of the computer's WD500 disk drives is a set of six LED indicator lights, each of which has three possible states: on, off, or blinking. Different combinations of lights and states indicate the probable cause of a failure. A fifteen page troubleshooting flowchart for the disk drive, which deals mostly with the information contained in the LED indicators, normally provides the procedural knowledge and advice for troubleshooters to follow. Some of this procedural advice is shown in Figure 10-29.

With RuleMaster, however, the various LED indicators, probable cause of the failure they indicate, and the appropriate action to take is entered in a table (Figure 10-30). Such tabular knowledge is an example of declarative knowledge. Generally it is easier for experts, technicians, and knowledge engineers to work with declarative than procedural knowledge. RuleMaster allows them to do so and then converts the declarative knowledge into the more difficult-to-work-with procedural knowledge represented in the form of rules or a decision tree (Figure 10-31).

```
                        - Troubleshooting Chart
-------------------------------------------------------------------------------
                            WD 500 SELF-TEST ANALYSIS

    LED INDICATION      |       PROBABLE CAUSE           |       ACTION
------------------------|--------------------------------|-----------------------
 6 On or 6 Blinking or  | 1) Formatter Failure           | 1) Replace
 All On or 2-5 On with  |                                |
 6 Blinking             |                                |
------------------------|--------------------------------|-----------------------
 2-6 Blinking           | 1) P-BUS ID Incorrectly        | 1) Reset ID Switch
                        |    Set                         |
                        | 2) Formatter Fault             | 2) Replace Formatter
------------------------|--------------------------------|-----------------------
 2,6 On or 1,2,6 On     | 1) WIN #1 Faulty               | 1) Replace Faulty Part
                        | 2) WIN #1 Cables Bad           | 2) Replace Faulty Cable(s)
                        | 3) Formatter Faulty            | 3) Replace Formatter
------------------------|--------------------------------|-----------------------
 3,6 On or 1,3,6 On     | 1) WIN #2 Faulty               | 1) Replace Faulty Part
                        | 2) WIN #2 Cables Bad           | 2) Replace Faulty Cable(s)
                        | 3) Formatter Faulty            | 3) Replace Formatter
------------------------|--------------------------------|-----------------------
 2,3,6 On               | 1) Formatter and/or            | 1) Replace Faulty Part(s)
                        |    WIN#1 and/or WIN #2         |
                        |    and/or Terminators(s)       |
------------------------|--------------------------------|-----------------------
 4,6 On or 1,4,6 On     | 1) Flexible Drive Faulty       | 1) Replace Flexible Drive
                        | 2) Flexible Cable(s) Bad       | 2) Replace Faulty Cable(s)
                        | 3) Formatter Faulty            | 3) Replace Formatter
------------------------|--------------------------------|-----------------------
 5,6 On or 1,5,6 On     | 1) P-BUS Loopback Test         | 1) Replace or Repair Cable
                        |    Failed (PBIF Connector      |
                        |    pins bent at Controller     |
                        |    or WD 500)                  |
                        | 2) Formatter Failure           | 2) Replace Formatter
------------------------|--------------------------------|-----------------------
 No LEDs On             | 1) Blown Fuse                  | 1) Replace Fuse
                        | 2) Faulty Internal Power       | 2) Repair or Replace Cables
                        |    Connections                 |
                        | 3) EMI Filter Faulty           | 3) Replace EMI Filter
                        | 4) Bad Front Panel Cable       | 4) Replace Cable
                        | 5) Faulty Front Panel PWB      | 5) Replace Front Panel PWB
                        | 6) Faulty Power Supply         | 6) Replace Power Supply
-------------------------------------------------------------------------------
```

Figure 10-29 A partial troubleshooting chart for Texas Instruments minicomputer disk drives. (Radian Corp.)

Procedure and Table Tools

```
/* The purpose of this module is to determine the status of the WD500
   disk drive based on a combination of indicator lights. First, the
   user is given directions to power up the unit, then questioned about
   the state of the indicator lights. The rule that is generated from
   these examples is structured in such a way that the problem can be
   determined with the fewest number of questions asked about the lights. */

module: ti.device.disk_drive.wd500
declarations:
[ intent: "\the WD500 disk problem\"
    child: power_up         win_term
           formatter        flex
           p_bus_id         p_bus_loop
           win_1            no_lights
           win_2
]
state: directions
  [( power_up, check )]

state: check
actions:
    formatter    [ formatter ]    /* problem with disk formatter */
    p_bus_id     [ p_bus_id ]     /* peripheral bus id problem   */
    win_1        [ win_1 ]        /* problem with winchester disk # 1 */
    win_2        [ win_2 ]        /* problem with winchester disk # 2 */
    win_term     [ win_term ]     /* problem with winchester terminators */
    flex         [ flex ]         /* flexible drive or cable problem */
    p_bus_loop   [ p_bus_loop ]   /* peripheral bus loopback test failure */
    no_lights    [ no_lights ]    /* fuse, power, connections, cable, etc. */

conditions:
    light_1 [ ask2 "What is the status of LED indicator 1?" "on,blinking,not_on"
             "LED indicator 1" "on,blink,off" ] {on,blink,off}
    light_2 [ ask2 "What is the status of LED indicator 2?" "on,blinking,not_on"
             "LED indicator 2" "on,blink,off" ] {on,blink,off}
    light_3 [ ask2 "What is the status of LED indicator 3?" "on,not_on"
             "LED indicator 3" "on,off" ] {on,off}
    light_4 [ ask2 "What is the status of LED indicator 4?" "on,not_on"
             "LED indicator 4" "on,off" ] {on,off}
    light_5 [ ask2 "What is the status of LED indicator 5?" "on,not_on"
             "LED indicator 5" "on,off" ] {on,off}
    light_6 [ ask2 "What is the status of LED indicator 6?" "on,blinking,not_on"
             "LED indicator 6" "on,blink,off" ] {on,blink,off}

examples:
/*   1       2       3       4       5       6                              */
    off     off     off     off     off     on     => (formatter,goal)
    off     off     off     off     off     blink  => (formatter,goal)
    on      on      on      on      on      on     => (formatter,goal)
    off     on      on      on      on      blink  => (formatter,goal)
    off     blink   off     off     off     blink  => (p_bus_id,goal)
    off     on      off     off     off     on     => (win_1,goal)
    on      on      off     off     off     on     => (win_1,goal)
    off     off     on      off     off     on     => (win_2,goal)
    on      off     on      off     off     on     => (win_2,goal)
    off     on      on      off     off     on     => (win_term,goal)
    off     off     off     on      off     on     => (flex,goal)
    on      off     off     on      off     on     => (flex,goal)
    off     off     off     off     on      on     => (p_bus_loop,goal)
    on      off     off     off     on      on     => (p_bus_loop,goal)
    off     off     off     off     off     off    => (no_lights,goal)
```

Figure 10-30 A RuleMaster knowledge system module containing states, actions, user-questions, and a table of example criteria and consequent actions, in this or other modules, from which a decision tree is induced. (Radian Corp.)

-- RuleMaker™ Generated Rule

```
The induced rule for state check is:
[light_2]
            on : [light_3]
                on : [light_4]
                    on :   => ( formatter, goal )
                    off :  => ( win_term, goal )
                off :   => ( win_1, goal )
            blink :   => ( p_bus_id, goal )
            off : [light_3]
                on :   => ( win_2, goal )
                off : [light_4]
                    on :   => ( flex, goal )
                    off : [light_5]
                        on :   => ( p_bus_loop, goal )
                        off : [light_6]
                            on :    => ( formatter, goal )
                            blink : => ( formatter, goal )
                            off :   => ( no_lights, goal )
```

The induced rule has 7 test nodes and 10 leaf nodes.

The following meaning should be assigned to the symbols in Figure 4 :

```
[ ]   -  IF
  :   -  AND
  : => -  THEN
```

Figure 10-31 A RuleMaker generated rule (Radian Corp.)

Although a table-based tool, RuleMaster differs from the Expert-Ease type of tools in several respects, some of which stem from the integration of knowledge-based and procedural-based components. In Expert-Ease, an action is only advice; in RuleMaster, it can be advice or executable code.

Furthermore, RuleMaster's knowledge-based advice can be based on partial certainty using multi-valued logic, Zadeh's fuzzy set operators, or heuristic uncertainty defined by the expert. Unlike Expert-Ease, RuleMaster has a "next_state" capability and also can explain its reasoning. In addition, programs in other languages, such as Pascal, C, and Fortran are callable from RuleMaster. In fact, because RuleMaster runs under Unix, it can interface to other Unix-based languages through the Unix "pipes" facility (which allows the output of one program to directly be the input to another). Finally, using its procedural component capabilities, RuleMaster allows users to define their own compound data types (like Pascal records) or abstract data types, and supports consistency, completeness, and data type checking.

A Guide To Building Expert/Knowledge Systems With Large-Scale Application Development Tools

CHAPTER 11

The microcomputer-based AI tools discussed in Chapter 10 are useful for many knowledge system applications. Moreover, they promote AI exploration and take a giant step toward bridging the AI technology gap because of their low price and the fact that they run on microcomputers. But large-scale knowledge systems often need integrated development environments and special AI capabilities that may be had only from large-scale tools that run mostly on Lisp machines. Microcomputer-oriented AI tools are more limited in their knowledge representation, reasoning and control strategies, and graphical techniques for working with an expert program's design and framework.

Rules alone, for example, may not be adequate to describe the variety of physical and abstract objects, structures, and concepts in a large, complex program. Nor may they be sufficient to model the interrelationships, events, and situations involving these objects, structures, and concepts.

In addition, although possible, it may not be practical to represent all types of knowledge in a large knowledge system in rules (the dominant knowledge representation on micros), and then reason with the knowledge by searching through large numbers of rules. Even where practical, different knowledge engineers more naturally think of various kinds of knowledge differently, and thus prefer an assortment of knowledge representations, which large-scale AI tools provide.

Large-scale AI tools that operate on Lisp machines can access the integrated, interactive graphics featured in Lisp environments. These graphics environments make it easy to visually show the different structures of the knowledge system and the relationships between them, which, in turn, makes it easier to understand the developing knowledge system. In addition, large-scale AI tools accommodate different ways of thinking about, formulating, and solving complex problems.

MULTIPLE PARADIGMS

Many of the Lisp computer-oriented tools incorporate, within one tool, multiple AI paradigms such as object-oriented programming, different knowledge representation methods, and different reasoning strategies. Several tools can represent knowledge with frames, rules, and logic. They can reason by backward chaining and forward chaining, or a combination of these. Some support gaugelike images, on the terminal screen, that access and monitor changes to data during program execution. For efficiency and familiarity reasons, several tools also incorporate conventional programming procedures. Sometimes these control a consultation for a large system—a tiresome task to accomplish exclusively with rules—and, other times, they implement algorithms.

Typical of the multiple paradigm tools, for example, is Xerox's Loops, which features four programming paradigms: object-oriented, procedure-oriented, rule-oriented, and data-oriented. The object-oriented paradigm lets users view programs as collections of objects with associated (encapsulated) procedures that send and receive messages to execute these procedures. The objects are organized in a class hierarchy where each class describes one or more similar objects, such as gauges (Figure 11-1). Traveling down the hierarchy, the classes are subdivided into subclasses such as instruments and LCDs, which may be further subdivided until a specific object is reached. Subclasses and instances lower down in the hierarchy inherit both attributes and procedures from those higher in the hierarchy.

The rule-oriented paradigm is specialized for specifying knowledge in the form of condition–action rules. The procedure-oriented paradigm allows users to build classical procedures in Interlisp.

Data-oriented programming is supported by most large-scale tools under a variety of names such as access-oriented programming, active values, and procedural attachments. With procedural attachments, procedures can be attached to variables or frame slots designated as active. Whenever these designated variables or slots are accessed or changed, the program automatically invokes attached specified procedures. In this way, data-driven control of these procedures is supported.

Although the attached procedures may be used for a variety of purposes, often users of data-driven programming tools attach variables or slots to graphically represented physical devices and measuring instruments, such as gauges and meters. Associated with the attached devices and instruments are the routines to handle them. The procedural attachments supported by Loops, and as will be seen IntelliCorp's KEE (Knowledge Engineering Environment) tool, are unusual because Loops and KEE also supply knowledge bases of prewritten graphical devices and corresponding, straightforward-to-use, handling routines.

In Loops, for example, variables can be designated to be active. Whenever an active variable is accessed or changed, a procedure invoked drives the attached gauge, meter, or other graphics icons to display the new values (Figure 11-1). This allows users to monitor programs during program development and debugging, as well as during application execution.

Whether a tool with a single or a variety of knowledge representation methods and

Multiple Paradigms

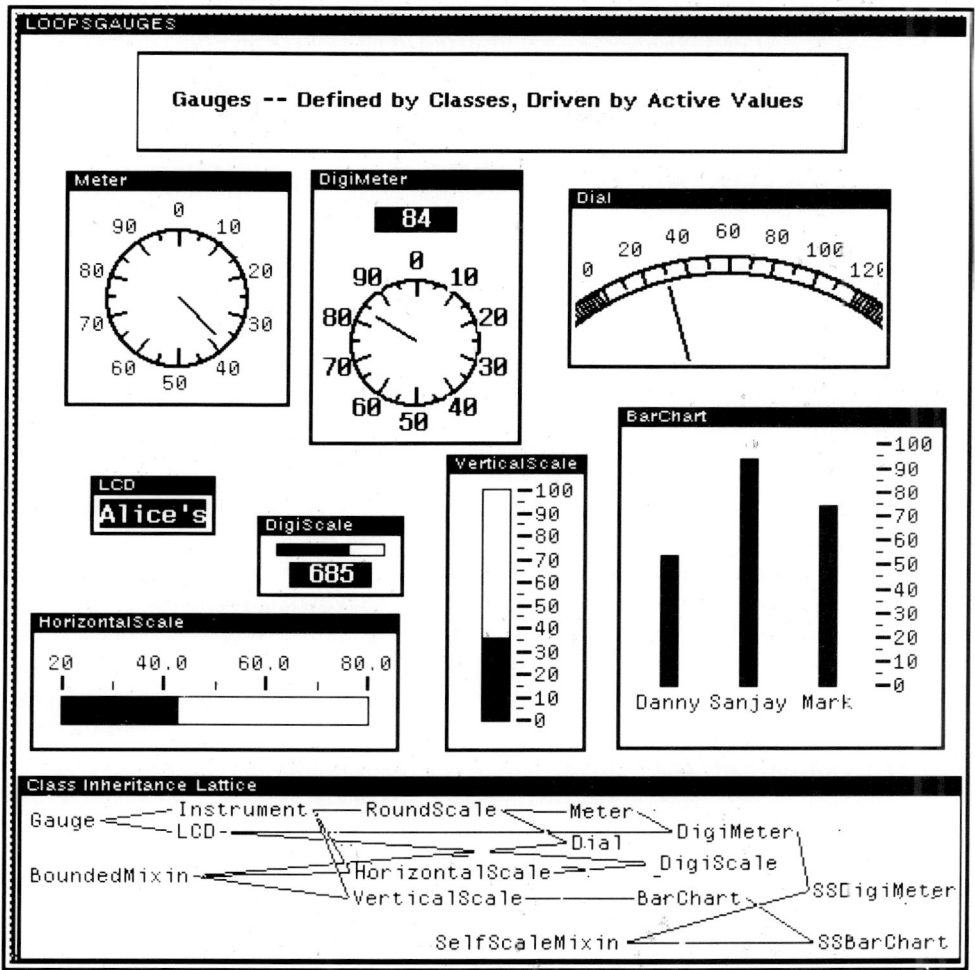

Figure 11-1 Loops' gauges attached to program variables are responsive to changes in these variables (Xerox Corp.)

reasoning strategies is more beneficial is an open question. Proponents of multiple-paradigm tools believe that from a company's point of view in making an investment, it is important to have a flexible tool that handles as many knowledge representations and reasoning strategies as possible. They claim that it is not always clear at the beginning of knowledge system development which paradigm will have the most payoff. Even if that is determined, another company application may have different characteristics and be more suited to development with different paradigms. Then, if knowledge system designers need to switch to a different-paradigm tool, they must go through a new learning period. Worse, changes or enhancements that the designer made to the environment when working on the original project may not be applicable to a new project. These drawbacks may have a serious economic impact on a company that is interested in AI for the long term.

There is another school of thought. Advocates of a single-paradigm tool claim that a tool that incorporates multiple knowledge representation methods and reasoning strategies is a general-purpose tool and is not sufficiently optimized to efficiently perform individual applications as a tool that is specialized for the job.

ENVIRONMENTS FOR TOOLS

Several vendors of the AI application development tools that run on dedicated Lisp computers plan to rewrite them to run on conventional computers, such as the DEC VAX and the IBM 43XX and 30XX series. These computers are less flashy than the highly graphically oriented Lisp machine–based systems. But they have several very practical advantages. They already exist in corporate environments. Corporate data and programs reside on these machines. Personnel are accustomed to working on these conventional machines. And the per user cost for conventional machines is less than that for a dedicated Lisp machine.

Lisp machines also have several important advantages. The integrated AI and graphical environments found on Lisp computers make program development easier, especially for less sophisticated users. The graphical environments allow AI application developers to move about within the framework of the program under development, view the structures they have built, and simultaneously, in another window on the computer screen, graphically display and manipulate the relationships between them. This increases the chances of knowledge system success.

To accommodate both the AI development environment and traditional computing world, some tool companies have developed tools that allow programmers to develop an application on a dedicated Lisp computer, but transport the completed knowledge system to run on a conventional computer. This allows companies to justify smaller numbers of higher-cost Lisp machines for program development, but to use standard, less expensive computers for the execution environment. The execution version of the knowledge system can be interfaced to routinely used financial, database, or computer-aided-design software.

WHO USES THE TOOLS?

A new question arises: "If large-scale tools have so many sophisticated capabilities, how easy are they and their accompanying documentation to use?" Some insight into the ease of use of these application development tools can be gleaned from a knowledge of what kind of people are using the tools. For example, with basic knowledge and training provided by AI tool vendors, some application experts at companies such as Arthur D. Little, Inc. (ADL), a management consulting firm, have been using IntelliCorp's KEE to help provide AI systems and services for its clients (Volume II, Chapter 7). Some Lawrence Livermore Laboratory chemists have used KEE to develop intelligent interfaces that help tune Triple Quadrapole Mass Spectrometers (Volume II, Chapter 8).

Ohio State University and its medical school use Xerox's Loops to develop medical applications. Battelle Memorial Institute, Inc., a contract research firm, uses Loops to develop knowledge system applications that, in conjunction with computer vision system, detect flaws in welds. Applied Expert Systems (APEX) uses Loops to help develop commercial AI applications for the financial industry. APEX has trained financial and data-processing personnel to perform AI development work. These examples support the notion that AI n onexperts can successfully build knowledge systems with the help of AI application development tools.

Further insight into the training needed to use these commercial AI application development tools can be gained by looking at two end-user companies who built operational AI systems with large-scale tools. One application is a knowledge-based design system, developed with a VAX-based version of S.1 and operational at Delco Products, Division of General Motors. It provides an idea of tool use and required training. (S.1 is discussed in Chap. 10.) Built by project engineers with mechanical and electrical engineering backgrounds, the Delco system consults with designers of brushes (for motors), and specifies the information sent to a computer-aided-design system to make the production drawing for these brushes.

As preparation for this project, one engineer enrolled in a Teknowledge two-week training course and then trained other Delco engineers in basic AI concepts and the use of the tool. It required about four months development to make the brush design system operational. Delco is now developing a knowledge system to design the spring that holds the brushes against the commutator.

The second system, a Babcock & Wilcox (B&W) knowledge-based weld scheduler developed with KEE on a Symbolics machine, illustrates tool use and required training, and also points out a major hardware concern in commercial AI deployment. KEE is a very graphically-oriented tool. B&W admits that the graphical interfaces supported both by KEE and B&W's Symbolics machine were a productivity aid during knowledge system development, and that they are also an adjunct to run-time versions of many graphically-oriented programs (knowledge-based simulation systems and intelligent interfaces to scientific instruments or complex control panels). But, the input (a matrix of engineering design data) and output (a schedule) for B&W's run- time system is alphanumeric text and seldom requires expensive graphics. Consequently, B&W, as well as several other commercial companies, are looking for a more economic deployment vehicle.

The B&W weld scheduler automates the generation of weld schedule information being done manually. At present, B&W welding engineers generate weld schedule information, such as selection of the proper weld procedure and determination of specific preheat, post-heat, and NDE (non-destructive examination) requirements. The schedule information generated is based on engineering data, the detailed industry code requirements, and heuristic rules developed over years of welders' experience. The AI program incorporates these different kinds of knowledge into an automated weld scheduler that will free experienced welding engineers from a tedious and sometimes schedule-intensive task.

B&W designers used a mixture of frames, rules, object-oriented programming, and KEE's forward chaining mechanism to build the system (Figure 11-2). They received a week of on-site training and consultation after KEE was delivered (Feb. 1985). During the initial week, the application designers put together a first cut of the weld-scheduler project; thereafter, they worked independently.

By June 1985, the weld scheduler was functional at B&W's Lynchburg Research Center and initial system deployment was scheduled for the next year. But how to deploy the system was an issue that first had to be resolved.

Because graphics capabilities were not critical to B&W's run-time system, B&W considered two options: a centralized Symbolics machine with remote access via

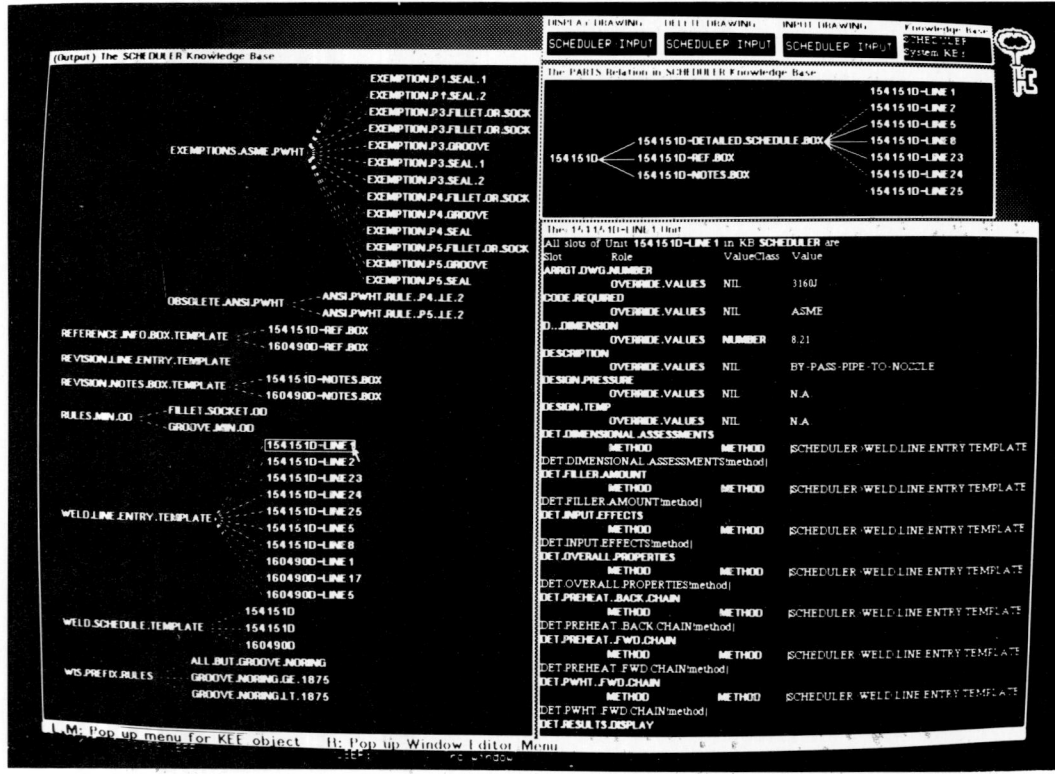

Figure 11-2 The left window displays part of the Weld Scheduler knowledge base, using KEE's graphical format for objects associated by either a class-subclass or class-member relationship. The objects in the knowledge base range from conceptual objects used as templates for creating new objects, specific objects instantiated from these templates, as well as numerous rules (both industry code standards as well as heuristic rules-of-thumb) organized into appropriate rule classes.

The upper right window displays a typical instantiated weld schedule using KEE's graphical format for whole-part object relationships.

The lower right window displays details of relevant slot information associated with one of the objects in the knowledge base. (Babock & Wilcox)

modems, and programs on less-expensive computers in the company's field offices. Pending its deployment decision, B&W was clear about its desire for hardware and software vendors to provide run-time support of AI software on hardware costing between $25,000 and $35,000, without requiring users to perform any code translation.

Both hardware and software vendors have responded to users' run-time needs. Run-time hardware solutions include low-cost Lisp machines, in addition to PCs, engineering workstations, and minicomputers that run knowledge systems developed on Lisp machines. Soon there will also be Lisp processor boards that plug into PCs and programmable logic controllers (discussed in Volume II, Chapter 14).

Several companies also are providing run-time software solutions. IntelliCorp, for example, has developed a non-graphics version of KEE for conventional, time-shared computers that do not support extensive graphics capabilities. In addition, it has designed a run-time version of KEE, with capabilities distributed across a large-scale host computer and a PC. The goal of the run-time system is to allow a KEE-based application to be developed on a Lisp machine, but transferred to, and executed on, any conventional computer that supports Common Lisp. Conversion to a traditional programming language is not necessary.

Typical hosts (available or planned) for the KEE run-time system include minicomputers like the DEC VAX and MicroVAX II, some engineering workstations, and some Lisp machines. PCs include computers like the IBM PC and the Apple Macintosh.

The PC supports a bit-mapped, high resolution, KEE-type graphics interface. Such graphics capabilities are built into the Macintosh. They are provided by Digital Research Inc.'s graphics environment program, GEM, for MS-DOS-based PCs.

More than a dumb user interface, KEE's PC-based run-time component allows users to downline-load the local knowledge base, browse through it, modify values, and delete or add members to the knowledge base structure (such as CENTRIFUGAL PUMP2) to a defined class of CENTRIFUGAL PUMPS. Users are not allowed, however, to make changes to the knowledge base architecture.

The host computer provides high performance knowledge system execution, large memory capacities, and access to company databases. The core of KEE, such as the rule system, inheritance mechanism, inference mechanisms, object-oriented programming capabilities, and the full knowledge base reside on the host computer.

To use the run-time version of KEE, a user's knowledge system is first transferred from a development to a conventional host computer via tape, disk, or network. A KEE filter program then scans the system and flags differences between Common Lisp on the run-time and development machines, Zetalisp (a version of Lisp that runs on several Lisp machines), and the KEE-language code. Users fix syntax differences; however, reimplementation of the user's program is not needed because most of the knowledge program is generally written in KEE code which is common both to the development and run-time machines. Reimplementation because an application uses a Lisp machine's object-oriented programming features and graphics interface also is not necessary. The object-oriented programming facility is part of KEE rather than a separate Lisp machine facility. The graphics interface is part of KEE on the host computer and supported by GEM on the PC.

There are hardware differences that must be resolved, particularly those involving size and color of graphical images. One way that the KEE run-time system handles these differences is through an "active image editor" that allows users to reconfigure images for the PC.

The PC-to-host computer link permits the integration of knowledge systems and PC- or host-based conventional programs. Knowledge system developers will be able to design programs that send traditionally collected, accessed, and processed data to a knowledge system. The knowledge system will perform a knowledge analysis and send its data back to the traditional program for further processing or for storage in a database.

But learning from secondhand stories of other company's experiences is limited. To really understand what can be done with knowledge system development tools, the potential user needs to take a close look at an AI application development tool and how it works, both from the knowledge system end user and the developer points of view. KEE, and a KEE-developed knowledge system called Reactors, which interfaces to the controlling instrumentation for a nuclear power plant, provides a good example of both a tool and application, with information transferable to other applications.

The control panels that normally interface to the controlling instrumentation of nuclear power plants, as well as to many types of equipment, industrial processes, and so on, are extremely complex. Their fifty to several hundred meters, gauges, digital readouts, and various kinds of alarms produce an information overload under the best of conditions and can cause total confusion on the part of the system operators during a crisis. Reactors performs status and monitoring functions for a nuclear power plant, analyzes the plant's behavior, indicates its status, reports when unusual events have occurred, and provides maintenance and diagnostic advice in routine and crisis situations. Although few people have nuclear reactors, the application illustrates the different steps, design, knowledge-base organization, and defining of related and interacting details to build a large-scale knowledge system with a knowledge system development tool.

Before understanding how to build a knowledge system using KEE, it is necessary to understand the basic components from which a KEE-based knowledge system is built. These components are KEE's frames, rules, hierarchies, and inheritance mechanisms. System builders must understand what is in a frame, how to write and modify a rule, how a hierarchical structure is organized, why it is important, and how system components inherit knowledge from others. Once these fundamentals are understood, the frames, rules, and hierarchies can be combined to build the knowledge system that accomplishes specific goals and performs "intelligent-like" tasks. Like most knowledge system development tools, KEE handles the reasoning and control strategies for the users.

FRAMES

KEE organizes knowledge in knowledge bases. Each knowledge base contains frames. In KEE, frames are called units. They may contain knowledge about components, rules, or combinations of the two.

The partial frame, or unit, shown in Figure 11-3 is named PUMP1 and contains knowledge about a particular component. It is located in the REACTORS2 knowledge base. This is one of several knowledge bases on a KEE system, some of which are supplied with KEE for tasks such as building gauges or interpreting rules, and some of

```
(OUTPUT) The PUMP1 unit
Unit: PUMP1 in knowledge base REACTORS2
Created by   on 28-Mar-84 11:35:44
Modified by FARRAH on 23-Aug-84 15:04:36
 Member of: CENTRIFUGAL.PUMPS, FEEDWATER.PUMPS

A centrifugal feedwater pump

OwnSlot: DETERMINE.FLOW from FEEDWATER.PUMPS
    Inheritance: METHOD in KB KEEROLES
    ValueClass: (METHOD in KB KEEDATATYPES)
    Value: REACTORS2>FEEDWATER.PUMPS:DETERMINE.FLOW!method

OwnSlot: FLOW from PUMP1
    Inheritance: OVERRIDE
    ValueClass: ((ONE.OF LOW NORMAL HIGH))
    Cardinality: |[1 1]
    Value: LOW

OwnSlot: NET.POSITIVE.SUCTION.HEAD from PUMP1
    Inheritance: OVERRIDE
    ValueClass: (NUMBER)
    Cardinality: |[1 1]
    Value: 36

OwnSlot: RADIUS from CENTRIFUGAL.PUMPS
    Inheritance: OVERRIDE
    ValueClass: (NUMBER)
    Cardinality: |[1 1]
    UNITS: Meters
    Value: 1.4

OwnSlot: REACTOR from PUMP1
    Inheritance: OVERRIDE
    ValueClass: (REACTORS)
    Cardinality: |[1 1]
    Value: R1

OwnSlot: VOLUME from PUMP1
    Inheritance: OVERRIDE
    ValueClass: (NUMBER)
    Cardinality: |[1 1]
```

Figure 11-3 Partial PUMP1 unit in KEE-based Reactors system. (Program copyrights © 1983, 1984, by IntelliCorp. All rights reserved).

which are built by application designers. The unit shown in Figure 11-4, called RULE4, contains knowledge about a rule and is also located in the REACTORS2 knowledge base.

Each unit is composed of slots. Slots may contain, among other things, descriptive attributes, rules, methods (operations that execute when they receive a "message"), textual information, logical assertions, and other units. The PUMP1 unit contains more slots than Figure 11-3 shows. In fact, units in a completed system often contain dozens of slots.

In the PUMP1 unit, which is typical of component units, some slots contain observable or measurable characteristics of the component. Other slots contain general information or knowledge of how to obtain needed information. For example, the slot named FLOW describes PUMP1's flow, which can be low, normal, or high. NET.POSITIVE.SUCTION.HEAD and RADIUS are measurable quantities. The slot

```
The RULE4 unit
Unit: RULE4 in knowledge base REACTORS2
Created by   on 4-Feb-84 14:56:22
Modified by FARRAH on 21-Aug-84 16:23:51
 Member of: REACTOR.TESTERS

OwnSlot: ACTION from RULES
   Inheritance: APPEND
   Value: Unknown

OwnSlot: ASSERTION from RULE4
   Inheritance: APPEND
   AVUNITS: (WFFINDEX)
   Value: (|Wff:(AN INTEGRITY OF ?A.VESSEL IS CHALLENGED))

OwnSlot: BACKCHAINER.BREAK from RULES
   Inheritance: OVERRIDE
   ValueClass: ((ONE.OF T))
   Cardinality: |[0 1]
   Value: Unknown

OwnSlot: EXTERNAL.FORM from RULE4
   Inheritance: SAME
   ValueClass: (LIST)
   Value: (IF ((?A.VESSEL IS IN CLASS CONTAINMENT.VESSELS)
              AND
              (THE RADIATION OF ?A.VESSEL IS HIGH)
              AND
              (THE PRESSURE OF ?A.VESSEL IS HIGH))
           THEN
              (THE INTEGRITY OF ?A.VESSEL IS CHALLENGED))

OwnSlot: PARSE from RULES
   Inheritance: METHOD in KB KEEROLES
   ValueClass: (METHOD in KB KEEDATATYPES)
   Value: DEFAULT.RULE.PARSER

OwnSlot: PREMISE from RULE4
   Inheritance: APPEND
   AVUNITS: (WFFINDEX)
   Value: (|Wff:(?A.VESSEL IS IN CLASS CONTAINMENT.VESSELS)
           |Wff:(A RADIATION OF ?A.VESSEL IS HIGH)

           |Wff:(A PRESSURE OF ?A.VESSEL IS HIGH))
```

Figure 11-4   KEE Unit containing rule-based knowledge. (Program copyrights © 1983, 1984 by IntelliCorp. All rights reserved.)

named VOLUME contains the volume of fluid flow per unit time of PUMP1. Slot DETERMINE.FLOW contains a Lisp function that calculates what the flow of this pump will be, depending on parameters contained in other slots in this and other units. Slot REACTOR points to the particular reactor unit—R1 or R2—that PUMP1 belongs to.

  Slots in the RULE4 unit contain various versions of a particular rule, mechanisms for debugging the rule, and the means for manipulating and reasoning about parts of the rule. One RULE4 slot, named EXTERNAL.FORM, contains an IF-THEN version of the rule. For KEE's internal purposes, however, and also to allow knowledge system designers as great an ability as possible to reason about, manipulate, and restrict parts of the rule, the rule is broken down into structural parts. These structural parts, the parser which breaks down the rule into its parts or puts them back together again, and the rule debugger, are identified in individual slots.

For example, the slot named PREMISE contains the IF part of the rule. The ASSERTION slot contains a statement, or assertion, which happens to be the THEN part of the rule. The ACTION slot is a trap door to the Lisp system and enables the programmers to write Lisp procedures to execute some action other than those indicated by simple assertions. The BACKCHAINER.BREAK slot controls a program debugging mechanism. If the programmer defines the value in the slot to be T (or True), then whenever rule 4 fires, the program breaks (stops) and prints out values that are in the system at that time. This allows the programmer to uncover errors by tracing what happens as the system executes.

A question mark in front of a character or string of characters, as shown in some rule slots, indicates a variable. For example, one condition clause of the rule (shown in the EXTERNAL.FORM slot) states that "THE RADIATION OF ?A.VESSEL IS HIGH." The term "?A.VESSEL" represents some variable vessel in the system.

The term "wff" contained in the assertion and premise slots stands for "well-formed formula." A wff is a legal sentence in the language of predicate calculus. Most commonly, programmers or users enter rules into the knowledge system in the external (IF-THEN) rather than the wff form. The parser decomposes the rule, translates it into the logical form, and stuffs the appropriate wffs into the premise, assertion, and action slots for the knowledge system internals to execute. Programmers can, however, if they wish, enter, edit, and manipulate rules in logical form. Upon request, the parser can translate the wff structures into an IF-THEN rule form for display to the user.

HIERARCHIES

Different units in a KEE knowledge base are related hierarchically (Figure 11-5). The most conceptually abstract or general frame, such as REACTOR.COMPONENTS, is at the top of the hierarchy. Units that describe specific objects, such as CV1 and CV2 (Containment Vessels 1 and 2), PCS1 (Primary Cooling System 1), HPIS1 (High Pressure Injection System 1), and PUMP1 are at the bottom of the hierarchy.

A unit that is connected to another unit one level down in the hierarchy is said to be the parent of that unit, and the lower unit is called the child of the parent. Children, in turn, are also parents.

A KEE-created knowledge system is organized into not one, but several different hierarchies. For example, the Reactors system shows four hierarchies. They are the Pumps hierarchy, the Reactor components hierarchy, the Reactor testers hierarchy, and the Reactors hierarchy.

Frames within any one hierarchy are interconnected by two different types of

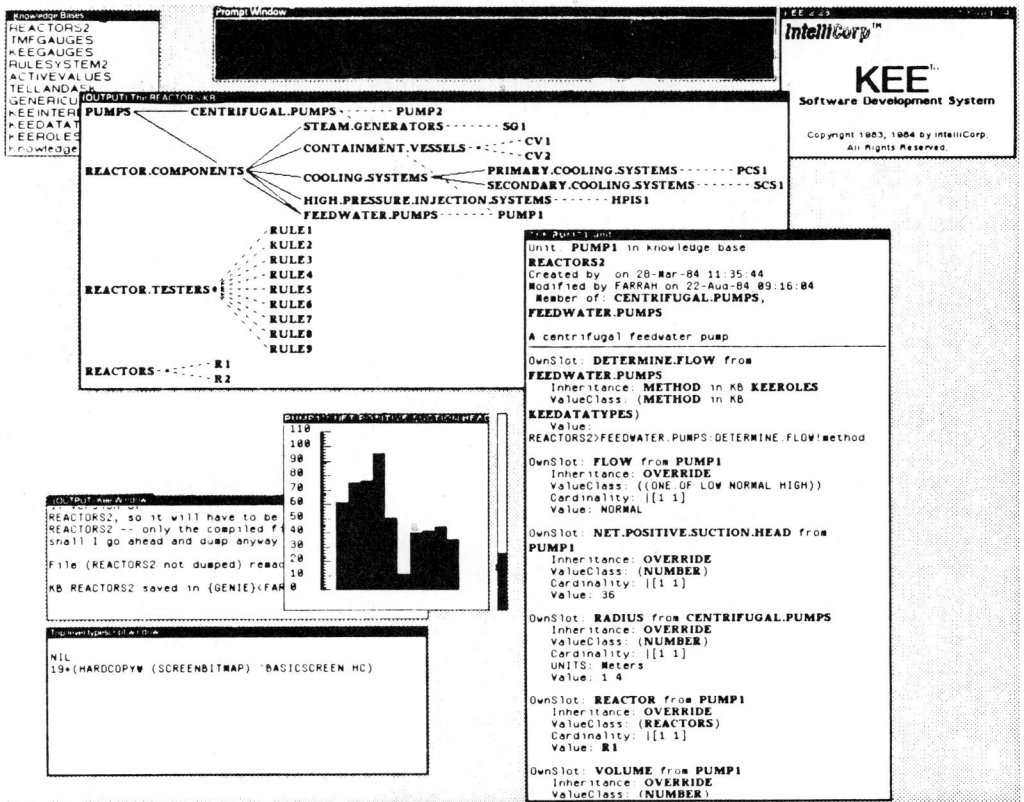

Figure 11-5 Hierarchical relationships between units in the Reactors system. (Program copyrights © 1983, 1984 by IntelliCorp. All rights reserved.)

parent–child links: class–subclass links and member links. Class–subclass links, shown by solid lines in the diagram, connect a parent and child, where the parent represents a general group or category of objects called a "class" and the children represent different types of the parent objects that are similar enough to be members of the parent class.

For example, in Figure 11-5, PUMPS is a general class of objects, while its children CENTRIFUGAL.PUMPS and FEEDWATER.PUMPS are types of pumps that form subclasses of the class of pumps. Similarly, five types of reactor components which are subclasses of REACTOR.COMPONENTS are shown: STEAM.GENERATORS, CONTAINMENT.VESSELS, COOLING.SYSTEMS, HIGH.PRESSURE.INJECTION.SYSTEMS, and FEEDWATER.PUMPS. Actually, all the subclasses also represent classes of objects. But subclasses, such as COOLING.SYSTEMS or FEEDWATER.PUMPS are a more restricted class than REACTOR.COMPONENTS, while REACTOR.COMPONENTS are a superclass of COOLING.SYSTEMS or FEEDWATER.PUMPS.

Inheritance

The other kind of parent–child link is a member link, shown by a dashed line. It connects parents and children, where the child is the same type of object as the parent, but is a particular instance (or occurrence) of the parent. Thus, in the nuclear power plant to which the Reactors knowledge system interfaces, there are two centrifugal pumps, two containment vessels, nine rules, and two reactors. PUMP1 and PUMP2 are each specific instances of centrifugal pumps. CV1 and CV2 are instances of containment vessels. R1 and R2 are instances of reactors. Rules 1 through 9 are instances of REACTOR.TESTERS, which is a knowledge-based structure that contains expert system rules. R1 and R2 are instances of reactors.

The different hierarchies can be related. As the hierarchy diagram shows, PUMP1 is an instance in both the PUMPS and REACTOR.COMPONENTS hierarchies.

INHERITANCE

There are two major advantages to arranging objects in a knowledge system hierarchically. For one, a display of this hierarchy allows knowledge system designers to determine how to move from unit to unit within the knowledge system and see, at a glance, how the various units are related.

The second advantage is the inheritance capabilities made possible by the hierarchical links. Attributes and procedures associated with units that represent classes of objects are inherited by the subclasses and members of these units. This makes it unnecessary for programmers to rewrite already written characteristics and procedures. Instead, they can concentrate on specifying changes and additions that make children unique, letting them inherit the rest of their attributes and procedures from their parents.

Inheritance in KEE takes place according to certain rules. Children may inherit all attributes (such as structure of the slot, characteristics, values, and procedures), override some attributes with their own values, append values from multiple parents to get an object with behaviors of all the parents, or they may be unique and take no values from parents. There are other inheritance mechanisms and, in addition, users can write their own.

For example, the PUMP1 unit inherits some slots from FEEDWATER.PUMPS and others from CENTRIFUGAL.PUMPS, which makes PUMP1 a centrifugal-feedwater pump. The BACKCHAINER.BREAK and PARSE slots are inherited from units in a knowledge base that contains knowledge about processing and debugging rules. If the programmer desires, however, the slots could override inherited information with their own. The external form of the rule in the RULE4 unit has been created at the RULE4 level of the hierarchy, and therefore it does not take information from its parent. Similarly, the CURRENT.STATE slot in the R1 unit in Figure 11-4, and the ASSERTION, PREMISE, and ACTION slots in the RULE4 unit, use knowledge created for their own units, but such slots could append knowledge from other units.

As Figures 11-3 and 11-4 show, slots themselves contain attributes that describe their behavior. These attributes are called "facets." Rules for inheritance are determined by an Inheritance Role facet. Another facet, ValueClass, places programmer-defined restrictions on the types of values that a slot may contain. For example, the NET.POSITIVE.SUCTION.HEAD, RADIUS, and VOLUME slots in the PUMP1 unit have a ValueClass of NUMBER. This means that the value of this slot must be a number. The REACTOR slot has a ValueClass of REACTORS. This specifies that the value of this slot must be a member of the class REACTORS. With this value restriction capability, a KEE-created knowledge system will check input values and reject unacceptable ones, whether the values are explicitly input by end users or implicitly obtained during program execution.

The Cardinality facet determines the number of values that a slot may contain. Cardinality is specified as a range. The REACTOR slot in the PUMP1 unit has a Cardinality of [1 1]. This means that there must be between 1 and 1 (i.e., exactly 1) values in this slot. This makes sense, since a particular pump should be a component of only one reactor. If a user entered two reactors for PUMP1, KEE would flag it as an error.

There are other system-defined facets besides Inheritance Role, ValueClass, and Cardinality, and the user may define still other facets. For instance, the UNITS facet of the RADIUS slot is a user-defined facet that describes the units of measurement for the pump radius.

BUILDING A KNOWLEDGE SYSTEM

Building any knowledge system involves a certain amount of planning before rushing to the keyboard—and the larger the knowledge system to be built, the greater the amount of planning necessary. System designers must know, first, the expected behavior of their system and the types of objects it will contain. They must be able to draw at least a minimal hierarchical diagram showing the relationships between these objects. The hierarchy can be expanded incrementally as the system evolves.

System designers also need to know some details about the knowledge system objects in order to begin defining both their attributes and behavior. These details are acquired from interviews with experts. More details are added, also incrementally, as the system evolves. And the knowledge system designers must know the knowledge bases available to them so that they know what slots, procedures, and features they can inherit from these knowledge bases.

When the planning stage is completed and enough knowledge of details has been acquired to build a minimal working system, the programmer is ready to begin constructing his or her knowledge system prototype. To build a knowledge system prototype using the KEE tool, in step 1, system builders use a mouse to move a pointer into a window in their display (not shown in the figures) that contains various KEE options (Figure 11-6). Pointing to the option "CreateKnowledgeBase" causes KEE to respond by creating a blank knowledge base.

In step two of the procedure, the system builder selects a "CreateUnit" option that asks KEE to create a frame or unit in the knowledge base. Selection of the "CreateUnit" option causes KEE to query the user about the information necessary to create the unit, such as name of the unit and who its parents are. Based on the answers, KEE hooks up the

Building A Knowledge System

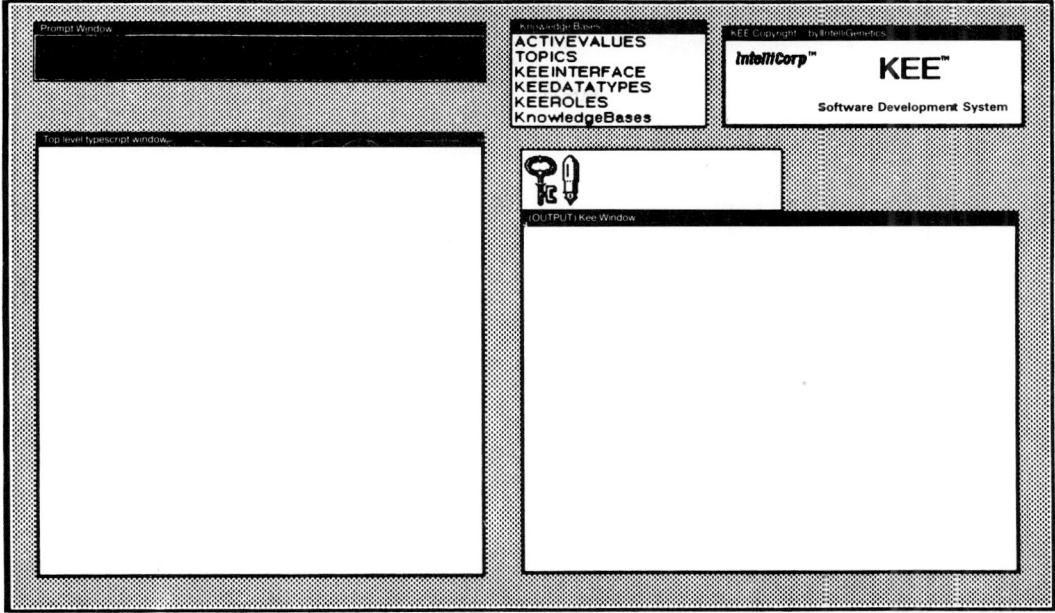

Figure 11-6 Pointing to a KEE options display causes KEE to create an empty knowledge base. (Program copyrights © 1983, 1984 by IntelliCorp. All rights reserved).

unit created in its proper place in the knowledge base hierarchy so that it will inherit the values and procedures due it.

If the knowledge system will contain rules, according to KEE's designers, the desirable first unit to create should be a subclass of the unit RULES and a member of the unit RULE.CLASSES. Both RULES and RULE.CLASSES are located in the RULESYSTEM2 knowledge base. A subclass of RULES automatically inherits its "rule methods." System builders can then specialize the new unit for their own purposes.

The specialized unit that the system builder creates is a "rule class" and its member units are individual rules. In the Reactors knowledge system in Figure 11-5, REACTORS.TESTERS is an example of a rule class. It has nine members, each of which represents a single rule. The rules are written in an English-like language. A set of rules being modified in the unit editor is shown in Figure 11-7.

The first specialization steps require the addition of knowledge system rules to the rule class, REACTOR.TESTERS. Once there are enough rules to make the system look like a knowledge system (albeit a novice one), the designer creates other units to represent the object referred to in the rules, and fills in their slots.

KEE's designers recommend that "novice" system builders develop a knowledge system in this order, because the rules already written guide the user in deciding what units and slots to create. For example, RULE4 concludes "THE INTEGRITY OF ?A.VESSEL IS CHALLENGED." This statement suggests that vessels should be units

```
(DEFINE.UNIT REACTOR.TESTERS
  (MemberOf (RULE.CLASSES RULESYSTEM2))
  (Comment "Rules for determining the current state of a reactor.")
  (Rules (RULE1 (IF ((?A.PRIMARY.COOLING.SYSTEM IS IN CLASS PRIMARY.COOLING.SYSTEMS)
                     AND (THE PRESSURE OF ?A.PRIMARY.COOLING.SYSTEM IS DECREASING)
                     AND (THE STATUS OF (THE HIGH.PRESSURE.INJECTION.SYSTEM OF (THE REACTOR OF
                                                                               ?A.PRIMARY.COOLING.SYSTEM))
                          IS ON))
                  THEN (THE INTEGRITY OF ?A.PRIMARY.COOLING.SYSTEM IS CHALLENGED)))
         (RULE2 (IF ((?A.SECONDARY.COOLING.SYSTEM IS IN CLASS SECONDARY.COOLING.SYSTEMS)
                     AND (THE TEMPERATURE OF (THE PRIMARY.COOLING.SYSTEM OF (THE REACTOR OF
                                                                            ?A.SECONDARY.COOLING.SYSTEM))
                          IS INCREASING))
                  THEN (THE HEAT.TRANSFER OF ?A.SECONDARY.COOLING.SYSTEM IS INADEQUATE)))
         (RULE3 (IF ((?A.GENERATOR IS IN CLASS STEAM.GENERATORS) AND (THE LEVEL OF ?A.GENERATOR IS DECREASING))
                  THEN (THE INVENTORY OF ?A.GENERATOR IS INADEQUATE)))
         (RULE4 (IF ((?A.VESSEL IS IN CLASS CONTAINMENT.VESSELS) AND (THE RADIATION OF ?A.VESSEL IS HIGH)
                     AND (THE PRESSURE OF ?A.VESSEL IS HIGH))
                  THEN (THE INTEGRITY OF ?A.VESSEL IS CHALLENGED)))
         (RULE5 (IF ((?A.REACTOR IS IN CLASS REACTORS) AND (THE HEAT.TRANSFER OF (THE SECONDARY.COOLING.SYSTEM OF
                                                                                 ?A.REACTOR)
                                                            IS INADEQUATE)
                     AND (THE FLOW OF (THE FEEDWATER.PUMP OF ?A.REACTOR)
                          IS LOW))
                  THEN (A CURRENT.STATE OF ?A.REACTOR IS "Loss of Feedwater Accident")))
         (RULE6 (IF ((?A.REACTOR IS IN CLASS REACTORS) AND (THE INVENTORY OF (THE STEAM.GENERATOR OF ?A.REACTOR)
                                                            IS INADEQUATE)
                     AND (THE FLOW OF (THE FEEDWATER.PUMP OF ?A.REACTOR)
                          IS LOW))
                  THEN (A CURRENT.STATE OF ?A.REACTOR IS "Loss of Feedwater Accident")))
         (RULE7 (IF ((?A.REACTOR IS IN CLASS REACTORS) AND (THE INTEGRITY OF (THE PRIMARY.COOLING.SYSTEM OF
                                                                              ?A.REACTOR)
                                                            IS CHALLENGED)
                     AND (THE INTEGRITY OF (THE CONTAINMENT.VESSEL OF ?A.REACTOR)
                          IS CHALLENGED))
                  THEN (A CURRENT.STATE OF ?A.REACTOR IS "Loss of Coolant Accident")))
         (RULE8 (IF ((?A.REACTOR IS IN CLASS REACTORS) AND (THE INTEGRITY OF (THE PRIMARY.COOLING.SYSTEM OF
                                                                              ?A.REACTOR)
                                                            IS CHALLENGED)
                     AND (THE LEVEL OF (THE STEAM.GENERATOR OF ?A.REACTOR)
                          IS INCREASING))
                  THEN (A CURRENT.STATE OF ?A.REACTOR IS "Steam Generator Tube Rupture")))
         (RULE9 (IF ((?A.REACTOR IS IN CLASS REACTORS) AND (THE INVENTORY OF (THE STEAM.GENERATOR OF ?A.REACTOR)
                                                            IS INADEQUATE)
                     AND (THE STEAM.FLOW OF (THE STEAM.GENERATOR OF ?A.REACTOR)
                          IS HIGH))
                  THEN (A CURRENT.STATE OF ?A.REACTOR IS "Steam Line Break")))))
```

Figure 11-7 Reactors system rules. (Program copyrights © 1983, 1984 by IntelliCorp. All rights reserved).

and added to the system hierarchy if they are not already there, that INTEGRITY is a slot name, and that CHALLENGED is a possible value for the slot.

KEE's rule system is logic-oriented. Premises make use of a full set of logical and set operators, such as AND, OR, NOT, ONE.OF, and SUBCLASS.OF. Rules can contain variables, which allow a single rule to apply in more than one situation. For example, RULE4 contains the variable ?A.VESSEL. This variable can be replaced with the name of any unit that has the slots RADIATION, PRESSURE, and INTEGRITY (slots indicated by the rule) and that is in the class CONTAINMENT.VESSELS. In the REACTORS2 knowledge base, the units CV1 and CV2 qualify for replacement.

ATTACHING GRAPHICAL IMAGES

Values that are of particular interest can be displayed and manipulated graphically using a set of predefined images, such as plots, pie charts, thermometers, pipes, and valves. For example, in Figure 11-5, a graphic image of a histogram has been attached to the NET.POSITIVE.SUCTION.HEAD slot of PUMP1. This particular histogram, which

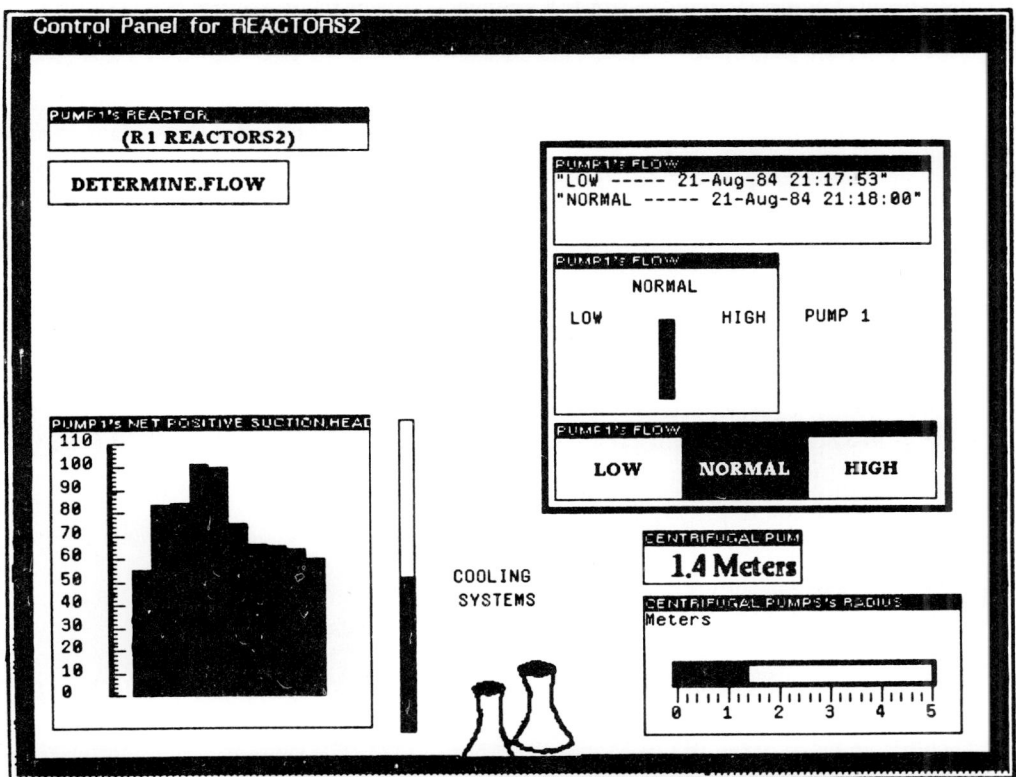

Figure 11-8 KEE images, attached to frame slots, form a miniature control panel to monitor pump activity. (Program copyrights © 1983, 1984 by IntelliCorp. All rights reserved).

simulates the monitoring of the pressure on the inlet side of the pump over time, changes as the value of the NET.POSITIVE.SUCTION.HEAD slot changes. Conversely, the user can change the value of the slot by pointing to the histogram image with the mouse.

This histogram is one of many graphical images that are predefined in the ACTIVEIMAGES AND KEEGAUGES knowledge bases. Programmers select and place graphical images on the screen via menu choices, attach the images to particular slots by pointing with a mouse, and then edit or specialize the image for their own purposes.

Collections of images can be created for different applications, as illustrated in Figure 11-8. Here the knowledge system designer built a miniature control panel just to monitor pump activity. The control panel contains the NET.POSITIVE.SUCTION.HEAD histogram, a meter resembling a metric ruler, digital readouts, two cooling towers, and a levelometer.

Within the control panel, the programmer has also designed a composite gauge, with its own border. The composite gauge consists of a group of gauges that display flow measures determined according to a method gauge button called DETERMINE.FLOW. When pointed at this button carries out a specified action. DETERMINE.FLOW is a slot in the PUMP1 unit. The FLOW that it determines is also a slot in that unit. Because of the restricted flow values indicated in that slot, the meter readings can be only LOW, MEDIUM, or HIGH.

With the initial objects, hierarchies, units, and rules created, KEE users can use the unit editor to add or modify units, their slots, values, or children in the inheritance hierarchy. Much like all knowledge system designers, they will engage in short, tight, repetitive cycles of modify and test—in other words, exploratory programming and rapid prototyping. This REACTORS2 knowledge base is an example of what a knowledge system designer might construct in a day or two as the first development cycle of a large system.

USING THE KEE-CREATED KNOWLEDGE SYSTEM

To use the KEE-developed expert diagnostic or maintenance system, end users may respond to knowledge system prompts for symptoms. Or they may use an English-like assertion/retrieval language either to make statements or to ask questions about the system.

For example, to enter into the system the fact that the flow of the feedwater pump of reactor R1 is low, the user can enter the assertion

```
(ASSERT (THE FLOW OF (THE FEEDWATER.PUMP OF R1) IS LOW))
```

The system will figure out that the value of the slot FEEDWATER.PUMP of the unit R1, shown in Figure 11-9, is FP1 (feedwater pump 1). It will then respond to the assertion by setting the value of the FLOW slot of PUMP1 to LOW. The same assertion/retrieval language can also be used, together with the unit editor, to build the system's frame structure during the knowledge system's development phases.

Using the KEE-Created Knowledge System

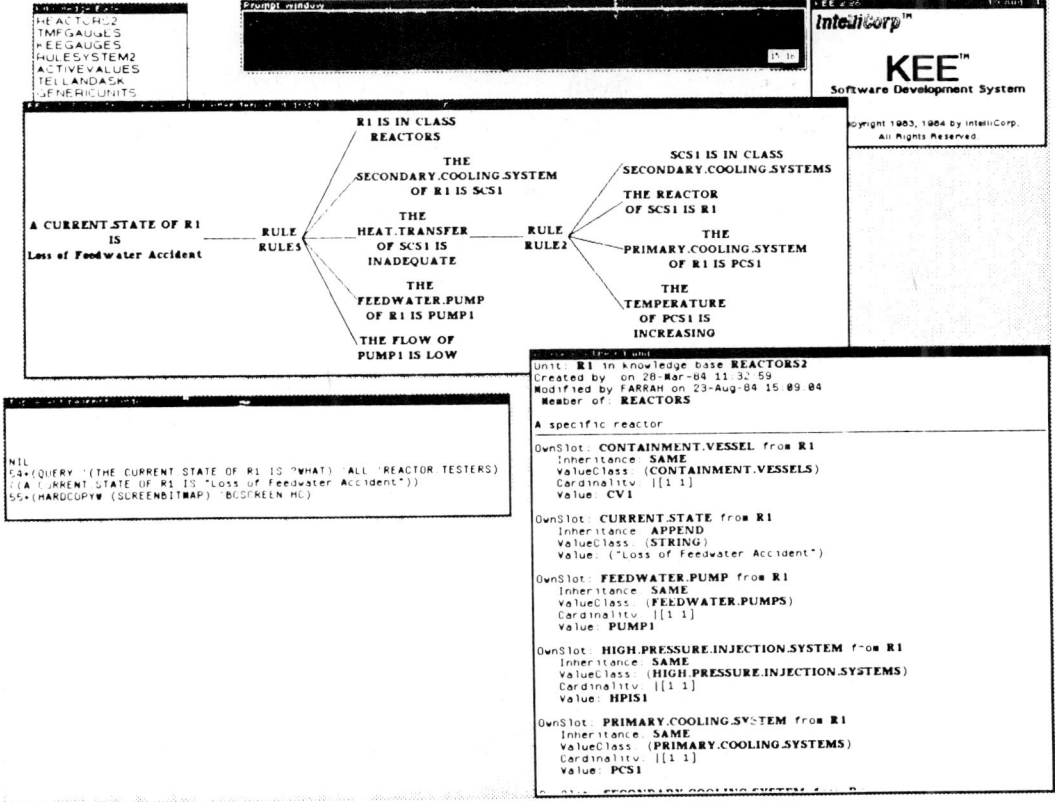

Figure 11-9 The Reactors knowledge system solves a problem and explains its reasoning. (Programs copyright © 1983, 1984, by IntelliCorp. All rights reserved.)

After a system parameter has been altered, the user might want to know the current state of the reactor. Using the assertion/retrieval language, the user enters

(QUERY (THE CURRENT.STATE OF R1 IS ?WHAT) 'ALL 'REACTOR.TESTERS)

This query is shown in the Top Level Typescript window (bottom left window) of Figure 11-9. The hypothesis in this query contains a variable, ?WHAT KEE's rule system will backward-chain through all rules with conclusions that match this hypothesis, allowing arbitrary substitutions for the variable ?WHAT. The argument 'ALL tells the rule system to test all the hypotheses that conclude THE CURRENT.STATE OF R1 IS ?WHAT, continuing even after one has been found to be true. The argument 'REACTOR.TESTERS tells which rule class to use.

Rules 5 through 9 in Figure 11-7 have conclusions that make statements about the current state of a reactor. KEE concludes, however, that the CURRENT.STATE OF R1 IS LOSS OF FEEDWATER ACCIDENT. The decision tree in Figure 11-9 is KEE's explanation of how it arrived at this conclusion.

KEE hypothesizes first that the current state is Loss of Feedwater Accident. It then attempts to verify this hypothesis. Rule 5, which concludes this hypothesis, has five clauses that must be satisfied. KEE tries to satisfy each of the clauses in several ways. It scans the list of facts in the units contained in the knowledge base to verify whether the clauses are already known to be true or false. It also scans the list of facts that have already been concluded by other rules to see whether the clauses in question are known to be true or false. Failing these clause verification techniques, KEE scans the conclusion of each rule to determine whether the clause in question can be inferred by at least one other rule.

To conclude a rule, it is sometimes necessary to back-chain recursively. In such a case, KEE evaluates a clause in the premise of one rule to use that rule's conclusion to satisfy a premise of a second rule to use the second rule's conclusion to satisfy the premise of a third rule, and so on, until the desired conclusion is inferred. Finally, when a necessary fact is not listed in a unit and cannot be directly inferred by a rule, KEE requests information from either the user or a sensor.

The first clause in rule 5 hypothesizes that ?A.REACTOR IS IN CLASS REACTORS. ?A.REACTOR is a variable, and therefore KEE looks through its knowledge base for reactors. It finds two, R1 and R2. The unit R1 states that R1 is a member of REACTORS, and therefore the first clause of rule 5 is satisfied.

The rule listing shows the next two clauses on the explanation graph written as a nested statement. The clause THE SECONDARY.COOLING.SYSTEM OF R1 IS SCS1 is a known fact, because a slot in the R1 unit indicates that the value of SECONDARY.COOLING.SYSTEM is SCS1. This slot is scrolled off the portion of the R1 unit shown in Figure 11-9 and therefore is not visible.

The third clause, THE HEAT.TRANSFER OF SCS1 IS INADEQUATE, is not a fact but a conclusion of rule 2. So to conclude inadequate heat transfer, KEE chains back to rule 2 and tries to satisfy rule 2's conditions. The first three clauses in rule 2 are facts found in the SCS1 and R1 units. That the fourth clause, TEMPERATURE OF PCS1 IS INCREASING, is true is known because the value in a slot of the PCS1 unit says so. The information in the PCS1 slot comes from sensor readings.

Having concluded the conditions of rule 2, KEE can now conclude the third clause of rule 5 about the heat transfer of SCS1 being inadequate. Rule 5's fourth clause is satisfied because the value of the FEEDWATER.PUMP slot from the R1 unit is PUMP1. The PUMP1 unit in Figure 11-3, whose readings correspond to the explanation graph, shows the value of the FLOW OF PUMP1 IS LOW.

After backward chaining in this way, KEE responds with

```
THE CURRENT.STATE OF R1 IS LOSS OF FEEDWATER ACCIDENT
```

KEE automatically enters this fact into the knowledge base by adding LOSS OF

FEEDWATER ACCIDENT to the list of values for the slot CURRENT.STATE in R1. There it is accessible for further reasoning and decision making on the part of either KEE or the user.

MANY VIEWPOINTS

A range of capabilities and features characterize the various knowledge system application tools. Inference Corp.'s ART (Advanced Reasoning Tool) is unusual in its use of a mechanism known as "viewpoints" in its reasoning processes. In database terms, viewpoints are analogous to a logical user view—the view that different users have of a database. The personnel manager, department manager, and accounting manager may have different views of the same database, which allow each of the people mentioned to view different data depending on their needs and applications.

Similarly, in ART, a viewpoint is a view that rules have of the knowledge. In other words, when a viewpoint is created, rules may view only those facts that have been created or asserted for that viewpoint, or are inherited; other information is excluded.

Like objects in object-oriented programming, and frames in frame-based tools, the viewpoints are organized into an inheritance hierarchy. The viewpoints lower in this hierarchy inherit facts and conceptual information from the higher-level viewpoints.

A major advantage to ART's viewpoint mechanism is that knowledge system developers using ART can create, in one knowledge system, different viewpoints that may represent different situations, one situation at different times, hypothetical situations, or alternative courses of action. This segregation of knowledge into viewpoints allows knowledge systems to reason along independent paths using the different viewpoints and to explore various solutions or the consequences of several possible decisions in parallel.

For example, financial analysts reason about highly uncertain information, such as estimates of market conditions. Analysts must also entertain competing explanations for observations made about a business. ART allows various viewpoints to be created for analysts' different estimates of a market, or their competing explanations. The analysts then use the viewpoints to reason about and compare competing explanations and choose one that best fits a situation or observation. The same viewpoint mechanism could just as well apply to the signal-processing domain, where there are input data with a lot of uncertainties, noise, and conflicting interpretations of what is occurring.

Another benefit of having a viewpoint mechanism is its ability to reason in parallel about different partial solutions instead of committing to one solution until it is proved wrong. More commonly, knowledge systems do not reason in parallel, but approach problem solving through a mechanism called backtracking. With backtracking, a program selects a rule, applies the rule that changes the database, applies another rule against the new database, and so on, until a problem solution is reached.

Alas, it may happen that a solution is not reached and the program must backtrack to some decision point to begin again the process of selecting and applying rules in a new decision path. Needless to say, a large search space can result in an exponentially large computation.

The viewpoint mechanism reduces the amount of backtracking necessary by creating several viewpoints representing alternative reasoning paths. As the program reasons, it proceeds along different reasoning paths in parallel. Since one of the parallel paths generally leads to a solution or decision, while others may lead to a dead end along the way, parallel reasoning about viewpoints avoids the need for sequential, exhaustive consideration of all options.

Geese can be used to illustrate the benefits of viewpoints. In a signal-processing application, incoming data may suggest either bombers approaching a country's borders or a flock of geese. With a viewpoints mechanism, a knowledge system need not assume bombers and travel all the way down the path of reasoning until it uncovers a contradiction, and then backtrack and try out the flock-of-geese hypothesis. Instead, the viewpoints-based system can assume the bombers in one viewpoint, the flock of geese in the other, and explore in parallel the ramifications of each.

One knowledge system, developed with ART, schedules helicopters (but could be designed to schedule any vehicle or machine) in response to reservation requests and route availability information. The ART-based scheduling system contains two different levels of viewpoints: a hypothetical level which contains hypotheses to satisfy routing requests and, within it, a state level which contains vehicle-related state information. During the scheduling process, new hypothetical and state viewpoints are created. For example, it may not be possible to satisfy a reservation request in a single (non-stop) step. Therefore, during system execution, a hierarchical chain of hypothetical viewpoints may be created to represent possible ways to satisfy reservations at different legs of a journey while hierarchical chains of state viewpoints may represent reservations satisfied during the legs of the journey. Children in these multiple (but separate) chains of hypothetical and state viewpoints inherit information from their parent viewpoints.

To design a scheduling system using viewpoints, global scheduling and routing information are placed in the root viewpoint at the hypothetical level. Initial system information that indicates what vehicle routings are desired, the current location of each vehicle in the system, and logistics about possible reservations that have not yet been satisfied are placed in the root viewpoint at the state level.

When a vehicle reservation requires movement of the vehicle from its current location to another, one or more children of the root viewpoint at the hypothetical level are created. Each of these represents possible reservations and each contains inherited information about routing and previous reservations.

Rules reason about each of the hypothetical viewpoints created, in parallel where applicable. As route and reservation viewpoints are explored, bad ones are rejected. Rules then update the state viewpoint by creating either a single child or a hierarchical chain of viewpoints. The child viewpoint indicates the state, or partial schedule, that results after the first reservation has been satisfied. ART then repeats these procedures and reasons about partial schedule viewpoints until it satisfies all reservations and produces a completed schedule.

A KNOWLEDGE BASE TOOL WITH DATABASE FEATURES

Another knowledge system tool, Knowledge Craft (from Carnegie Group, Inc.), has distinguished itself not only by its knowledge engineering features, but also because it implements some features normally associated with database management systems. Its knowledge engineering features include multiple, embedded knowledge representation languages to represent knowledge in whatever way is best for a problem at hand, an "agenda" mechanism that keeps track of queues of events, and a viewpoint mechanism. Its database features are important because they give to knowledge-based systems some of the database management capabilities taken for granted in database applications.

Unlike databases, most knowledge bases are limited in size and performance because they require the complete program and knowledge base to be contained in main memory during program operation. Knowledge-based systems have gotten by, until now, with these main memory requirements because most knowledge systems have been small enough to be able to rely on virtual memory techniques. With virtual memory, program parts that do not fit in main memory remain temporarily on a disk but are swapped with program parts already in main memory in order to be used. It goes without saying that as a program becomes very large, the increasing number of disk accesses required to page material into main memory cause performance to suffer. This, in turn, limits the size of programs. In addition, the handling of virtual memory by the operating system environment interferes with knowledge base control over such functions as buffering and transaction handling. Removal of this control, in favor of the operating system, further limits performance as well as the ability to ensure data integrity.

Databases do not encounter these problems because they come equipped with a disk storage management system which allows them to store, access, and manipulate large amounts of data on a disk without first needing to load it into main memory. Handling data directly on disk permits further increases in performance through sophisticated indexing of the disk data and fine tuning of the layout of the databases on the disk.

Knowledge Craft provides such disk storage management capabilities for its knowledge bases, with all the attendant benefits. With a knowledge-based management system (the knowledge system counterpart of a database management system), gone is the time wasted waiting while hundreds of frames are loaded into main memory in order to start knowledge system operation. Gone also is the time that programmers spend waiting while no longer useful or accessible frames are garbage-collected (a technique used to remove useless information, called "garbage," from main memory) to make room for other frames needed by the program. Performance is gained because the inefficiencies of virtual memory are eliminated. Also, the knowledge bases can be tuned for optimized performance. Since knowledge-based management systems manage and manipulate knowledge on disk, they can support very large knowledge-based applications without requiring huge amounts of memory.

The Knowledge Craft system is not new, nor are its undertakings in building large knowledge-based systems. Developed at Carnegie–Mellon University, in its precommercial days the system was named SRL (Schema Representation Language) and was used in a number of large-scale, knowledge-based manufacturing projects. Subsequently, SRL was enhanced and renamed.

SRL was designed to model organizations at different levels of abstraction. At a concrete level, it models machines, tools, materials, and people. At a more abstract level, it models departments, tasks, goals, events, communications, authority interactions, and time. The organization models developed are used by assorted knowledge system processes to perform analyses and make decisions.

Three design goals influenced Knowledge Craft's model-building decisions. First, the system should be able to model many types of organizations (continuous and discrete). Second, managers and engineers, who are the prime users of such systems, should be able to easily learn, peruse, modify, and understand the model, preferably because it uses the same terms that people use to think about the organization and its problems. Third, all objects, system features, and program capabilities must be integrated. Since no single problem-solving or knowledge representation technique has yet proven adequate, Knowledge Craft's designers endowed the system with several integrated problem-solving and knowledge representation techniques, which may be combined in a single application.

For example, the system contains three embedded AI languages: OPS5, Prolog, and SRL. OPS5 is the rule-based language used to build commercial applications such as XCON, DEC's knowledge-based computer configuration system, and XSEL, the sales representative's version of the application. Prolog is a logic-based language which has rule-based and inference capabilities in addition to relational database characteristics. SRL (Schema Representation Language) is a frame-based language (a frame in the CMU systems is called a "schema"). It was used to build ISIS, a CMU/Westinghouse factory scheduling system, and a variety of other planning, factory management, and monitoring systems developed for DEC, Westinghouse, and the U.S. Air Force.

These languages, and their associated knowledge representation techniques (rules, logic, and frames), allow knowledge system designers to describe different types of organizations in whatever manner is most natural for that organization, for different users, and preferred by the designer. Further flexibility, and functionality, in problem solving is provided because ordinary programs may be associated with slots in frames.

The agenda mechanism keeps track of multiple queues of events and manages the scheduling of the events for execution. Such a mechanism helps adapt Knowledge Craft for applications such as simulation and scheduling systems. In simulation systems, the agenda mechanism is instrumental in tracking and simulating events. In scheduling systems, the agenda mechanism manages and schedules events for execution on a critical or specified time basis.

Coupled with the rule-based mechanism, the agenda mechanism can provide a viewpoint mechanism. This is accomplished because the rules can sprout new contexts (subdivisions of a problem). The agenda mechanism then keeps track of the multiple contexts. The result is a viewpoint mechanism that can explore alternative problem-solving paths, simultaneously.

Further details on the use of Knowledge Craft's features for factory planning and scheduling, simulation, cost analysis, project management, and other operations are discussed in Volume II, Chapters 1 to 4, in the context of the manufacturing systems it was used to develop.

MORE ABOUT DATABASES

Even though knowledge system development tools are essential elements in commercializing knowledge systems, it is the practical issues that will pace their penetration into industry. Only as the knowledge systems developed become compatible with existing computers and software applications, and the knowledge base size and performance constraints are overcome, can AI technology really catch on.

Carnegie Group, Inc. addressed some of these problems via Knowledge Craft's database management capabilities and ability to run on a variety of time-sharing systems, in addition to AI workstations. To varying degrees, Teknowledge, Inference Corp., and IntelliCorp are transporting their knowledge-based tools to conventional computers so that knowledge systems developed with these tools can execute on relatively inexpensive computers and be integrated with conventional applications.

Silogic, Inc. is in agreement with this kind of thinking, and putting its money where its mouth is, it designed its Logic Workbench with database capabilities and standard computer compatibility. The logic Workbench is a Prolog application development system that addresses several issues important to commercial knowledge system acceptance. Available on 68000-based Unix machines, which are relatively inexpensive and common in standard operational environments, the Logic Workbench stores and manages its knowledge bases on disk rather than in main (or virtual) memory. As a result, like Knowledge Craft, the Logic Workbench's knowledge-based management system supports enhanced performance and very large knowledge-based applications.

The Logic Workbench carries its database and compatibility capabilities even further in that it interfaces not only to its knowledge bases, but also to ordinary Unix databases. Consequently, programmers and users need not rekey information already present in their corporate databases in order to gain AI capabilities. Because Prolog has many characteristics of relational databases, including query and database representation capabilities, they can use the same Prolog commands to access and manipulate both database and knowledge base information. The queried database information has the same representation in the relational database and the Prolog-based knowledge system. This single, consistent interface across the database and knowledge base contributes to ease of use of knowledge systems developed with such a dual access tool.

MENU-DRIVEN TOOLS FOR VERTICAL MARKETS

Most large-scale tools discussed have been general purpose tools. However, there is a developing trend toward specialized tools, with generic knowledge applicable to a particular application domain. For example, Escort, a shell developed by London, England's

220 A Guide to Building Expert/Knowledge Systems

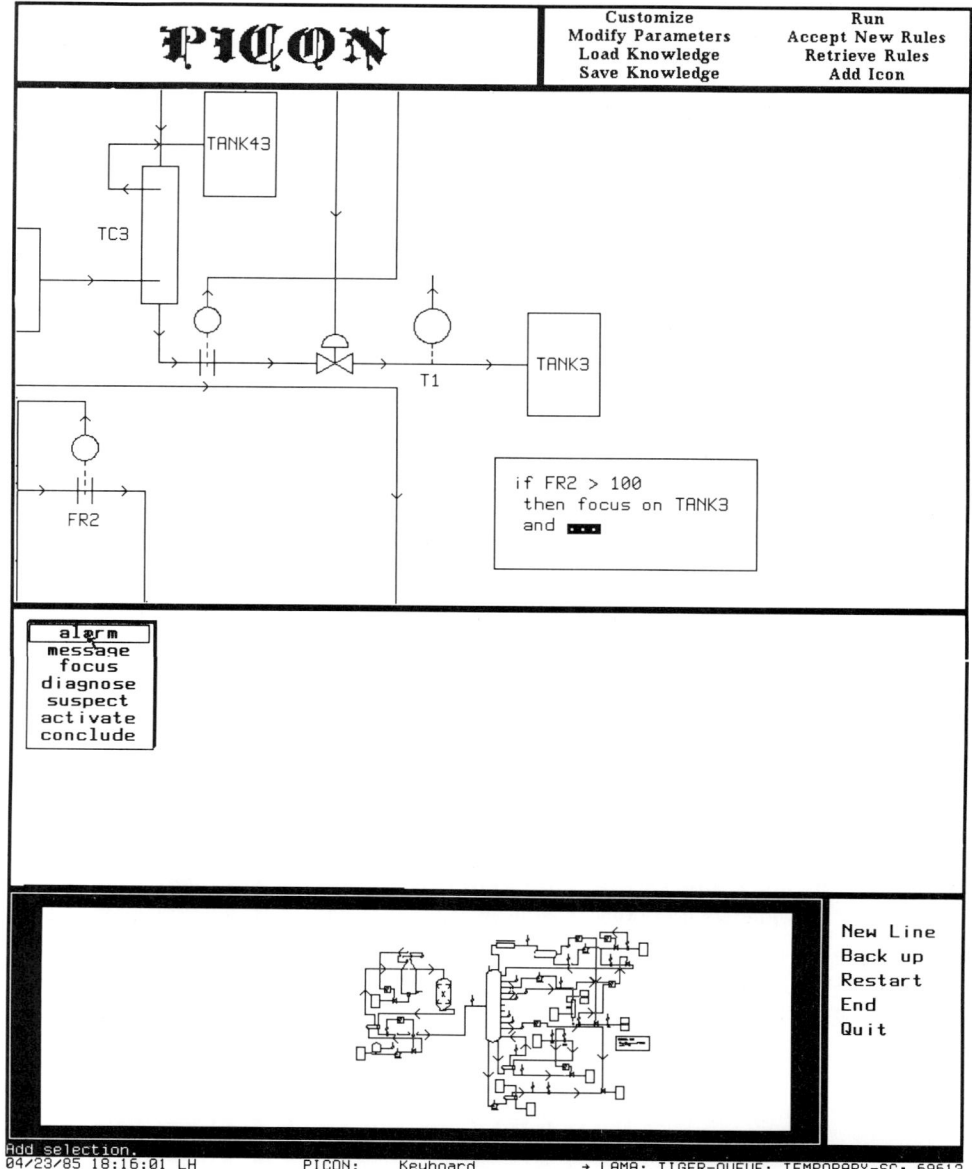

Figure 11-10 Picon's knowledge system development tools provides both icons for users to construct schematics of their process control plants and menus from which users select words and phrases to build rules. (Lisp Machine, Inc.)

PA Computers and Telecommunications for machine fault diagnosis (as part of an interface to process plant instrumentation), knows about process plant things like stop valves, control loops, and sensor switches. This kind of knowledge forms part of a precanned, generic knowledge base, applicable to any process plant. Users need add only specific company process-plant knowledge.

The trend toward vertical market tools is also illustrated by Picon. Picon is LMI's knowledge-based, real-time process control system. It has two communicating components, residing within one LMI Lisp machine. One, a knowledge-based program, running on a Lisp processor, reasons, analyzes, provides advice, and dynamically reprograms a Motorola 68010 microprocessor. The other integrated component is a conventional process control program and real-time operating system, which is written in C and runs on the 68010 either in standalone mode or under Unix. It performs real-time monitoring, data acquisition, and control operations. Picon is discussed in detail in Volume II, Chapter 8.

Picon incorporates a knowledge system development tool to develop expert process control applications. The Picon tool supports knowledge entry by process engineers through a natural language, menu driven, interactive graphics system and a schematic capture system. Process engineers combine plant component icons to construct a schematic that represents their plant. Picon captures the component/icon information, its type, connections, and relationship to the process control plant. The tool also displays menus, containing words and phrases, that users can select and combine to form conditional clauses and consequences of a rule (Figure 11-10). These menus are connected to Picon's underlying grammar for understanding rules in natural language. Consequently, the tool knows the legal grammar for the knowledge system rules. It presents to users only those words and phrases which are permissible to use to continue constructing a grammatical sentence-rule (although it does not recognize nonsensical physical constants). In Figure 11-9, a user has partially built a rule and is about to select the next word in the rule from the menu in the middle window.

Knowledge engineers can modify some of the menus themselves through a facility that prompts them for additional attributes. To modify or design other menus, however, it is necessary to use a text editor and augment the grammar.

IKE (Integrated Knowledge Evnironment) (from LMI), is a similar but general-purpose version of the Picon tool for building rule-based, backward chaining systems. Like Picon, IKE provides menus that allow users to build knowledge systems by entering syntactically correct rule elements in natural language. It differs from Picon in its lack of a schematic capture system specific to process control plants and in its general-purpose nature.

As users construct rules, a graphical interface displays the selected menu words and phrases in parse trees to verify IKE's understanding of these rules (Figure 11-11). As the rule is constructed, IKE keeps track of undefined terms and prompts users for necessary information if they attempt to define a rule using incompletely defined terms.

Knowledge engineers/application experts can augment both the menu vocabulary and the rule grammar with application-specific vocabulary and knowledge. The basic IKE consists of a generic grammar that handles rules containing objects, attributes, and values;

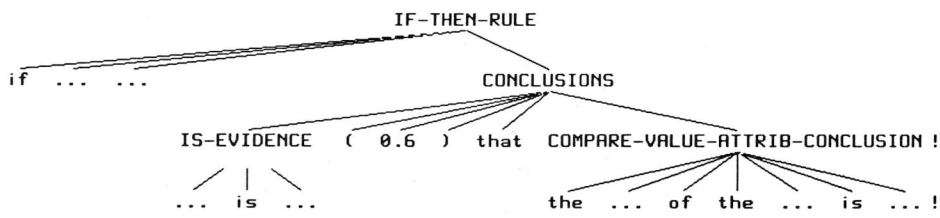

Figure 11-11 As users construct rules with the IKE knowledge system development tool, IKE displays the user's selected menu words and phrases in a parse tree and displays the rule in Lisp and in English (The . . . in the parse tree indicate truncated parts that do not fit on the screen.) (Lisp Machine, Inc.)

menus that contain basic domain-independent terms such as "is," "greater than," "above," and "is below," and terms like "IF;" and empty menus for objects, attributes, and values. To help application experts design or add to end-user menus, IKE prompts them for objects (such as a Lambda machine), their attributes (such as problem symptoms and resolution), and their values (such as boot-failure during microcode or reformatting the bad partition). This information is automatically captured in a frame. From this frame, IKE builds everything it needs to drive the end-user display. Beyond this menu design technique, knowledgeable system builders can modify the grammar or use Lisp to augment predicate functions.

All in all, solutions to many problems limiting widespread acceptance of knowledge systems are evolving. Tools are alleviating the problems caused by scarcity of AI experts by allowing AI non-experts to develop knowledge systems. Disk storage management systems are being incorporated in the tools to support large knowledge programs and fast performance. Interfaces to standard databases are being built to avoid wasting time rekeying information already existing in databases. Some tools are being installed on conventional computers. In the future, many large-scale applications are expected to be developed on special-purpose AI computers and then reimplemented on conventional computers installed in corporate environments for delivery and execution. A major problem that remains can be solved only with time; users must have experience in building and running a variety of applications.

Natural Language

CHAPTER 12

Natural language is the communications medium of people everywhere in the world, and exclusively of people. In an attempt to change that exclusivity, in the 1970s a number of experiments were performed to teach natural language to chimpanzees. Of course, the chimps could not speak. But they could understand American Sign Language (the language developed for the deaf) and they could understand felt material symbols for words on a felt board.

One chimp, named Sarah, had a vocabulary of 130 word symbols. Another chimp, named Washoe, could sign 130 words with her fingers and hands. These vocabularies were less than that of a small schoolchild. Nonetheless, Sarah's trainer could, for example, say "Sarah insert apple pail banana dish" in symbols and Sarah would respond by putting the apple in the pail and the banana in the dish (Figure 12-1). As another example of what the chimps could do, Washoe could put together the words and sign "Roger you tickle" and "come hug" and Roger would respond by tickling or hugging Washoe.

Despite these and similar communications examples, the success of the natural language and chimpanzee experiments were always controversial. Proponents said that clearly Sarah understood the trainer because she gave the appropriate response, which was to put the apple in the pail and the banana in the dish. As further proof of natural-language communications, they said, Washoe was able to map her needs and desires into the trainer's natural language. That natural-language communications occurred was evidenced by the fact that Washoe elicited the appropriate response from her trainer, who responded by tickling or hugging her.

Since we do not know how or why people understand natural language, the appropriate response or action is the usual measure of natural-language understanding and often the only point of interest. For example, we know that students have understood a teacher's

Natural Language

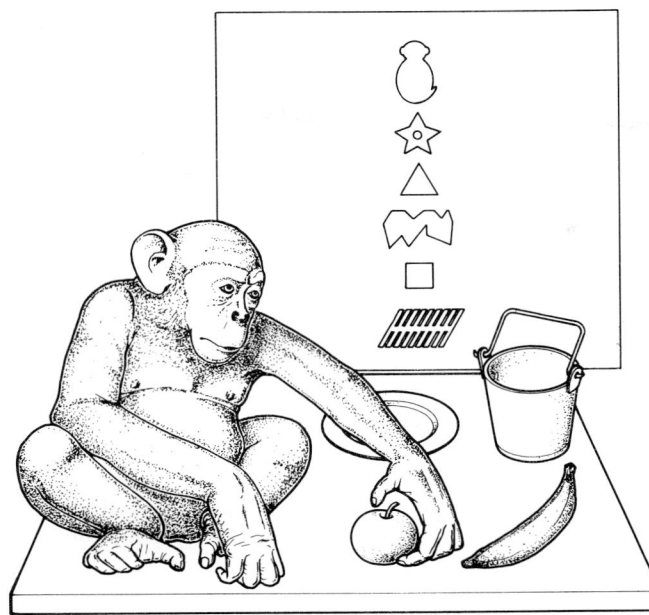

Figure 12-1 Sarah, the talking chimp? (Scientific American)

natural-language communications if they give the appropriate responses on a test. We also know that a toddler has developed to the point where the toddler understands language when that toddler can respond to a request such as "show me the new car" by producing a toy (Figure 12-2). On the other hand, if we said the same thing to an automobile salesperson, the salesperson will have understood if he or she goes into a sales pitch.

By this appropriate response and action measure, Sarah and Washoe understood natural language. Critics of the natural-language experiments argue, however, that Sarah's and Washoe's responses were nothing more than conditioning of the same type that causes a dog to respond to human language.

With the success of the chimp language experiments still undetermined, natural language remains the communications medium solely of human beings. Recently, however, a new candidate—the computer—has emerged that appears to be able to communicate in natural language. Consider, as evidence, the following office scenario that took place on one of those days when nothing seems to go right.

On that day, Joe NewManager, very concerned with rising to the responsibilities of his new position, arrived at the office late because of traffic, only to be informed that an emergency marketing meeting had been called for 20 minutes hence. Losing no time, Joe turned to his assistant and said, "We need to find where the money's going. Get me a list of the last two months' total expenses for each department and a piechart of total salaries in each department."

Ten minutes later, Joe had his figures and graphs and was off to the meeting. His assistant stayed behind on the desk. Yes, on the desk, because Joe's assistant was a com-

Figure 12-2 Toddler indicates understanding of natural language by her response. (Photo courtesy Erik Keller)

puter, not a person. Nonetheless, his nonhuman assistant understood his humanoid, ungrammatical, natural-language requests.

How do we know the computer understood him? We know because it performed the appropriate actions; it fetched the data from the database and made up Joe's graphs for him.

The nice thing about Joe (or anyone else) being able to speak natural language to a computer is that natural language is so natural to human beings. It stands in marked contrast to formal computer languages, such as Basic, Fortran, and Cobol. Such formal languages are ideal for expressing algorithms and data structures so that they are easily understood by computers. Unfortunately, because they are complex and highly structured, they are not as easily understood by noncomputing professionals who require or desire access to computers.

For this reason there is a rapidly growing movement to put natural-language systems on computers. Such systems make computer capabilities and data stored in databases more accessible to users because they allow users to communicate with their machines in a language as close as possible to the one they use to communicate with each other (Figure 12-3).

In keeping with this movement, several firms have either introduced or are developing commercial natural-language systems. These firms run the gamut from Fortune

Figure 12-3 Natural language communications with computer databases.

1000 computer and database companies to artificial intelligence company startups. The most popular of the natural-language systems, which address the most immediate need, are database front ends that understand database queries phrased in unconstrained English (or other native language) rather than formal query languages. Other natural-language systems solve problems based on users' English language requests or act as advisory and consulting systems that converse with the user.

The most primitive natural-language systems merely recognize key words and patterns. More commonly, natural-language systems employ a mixture of knowledge of grammar (syntax) and meaning (semantics) to understand human requests for data or instructions to perform simple chores. However, to carry on human-type dialogues, natural-language systems need a knowledge base containing information and rules about the real world they converse about.

Typically, natural-language systems can handle a range of queries, phrased differently. They can understand sentences with missing parts and they can deal with users who do not speak correct English.

Despite this flexibility, natural-language systems have several limitations. Most important, they are inherently limited to handling queries about a specifically designed narrow domain of knowledge. For example, they can answer questions that pertain only to their own database or database application. But the system with information about personnel cannot handle queries about sales even though there is some overlapping information.

Similarly, most commercial natural-language systems can only recognize vocabulary that is encoded in their dictionaries. Some of the natural-language companies are alleviating this problem by automating the acquisition-of-knowledge process so that users can easily extend the dictionary and some of the database definitions themselves. Adding vocabulary of different databases by moving the natural-language interface from one database to another is a more difficult problem that requires knowledge of both natural language and databases.

Computer programs that understand natural language must also be able to resolve the problems associated with ambiguous sentences. Most natural-language systems handle ambiguities by using sentences structure, grammatical and dictionary knowledge, and sometimes, also, a knowledge of what is in the database. But these are only partially adequate solutions. Human beings typically resolve ambiguity by understanding sentences in the context of their knowledge of the real world. Only a few sophisticated natural-language systems can imitate this method, and then, only to some degree.

For example, consider the classified ad

DOG FOR SALE. VERY FRIENDLY. NOT FEROCIOUS. WILL EAT ANYTHING. ESPECIALLY FOND OF CHILDREN.

Although amusing, this ad points out a real problem. Few people would misinterpret this ad as describing the dog's preferred diet. Most natural-language systems would probably be misled.

Similarly, human beings interpret the newspaper headline "AIR FORCE CONSIDERS DROPPING SOME NEW WEAPONS" (*New Orleans Times-Picayune,* 5/23/83) in light of whether the country is in a wartime situation and what type of announcements the government usually makes to the populace. But, although possible, representing the knowledge of the context of the headline on a computer is a difficult task.

Motivation analysis is a difficult capability to computerize, but it is necessary to fully understand and interpret natural language. Motivation analysis is the reason that telephone callers who say "HELLO, CAN I SPEAK TO SONIA" or even "HELLO, IS SONIA THERE," are not generally given a simple yes-or-no answer (Figure 12-4). Similarly, an ideal natural-language-based tax assistant advisory system that helps a client fill out tax forms could use motivation analysis to respond to a question such as "What is a 1040?" Instead of a dictionary-definition response, a more valuable answer (based on the probable motivation for the question) is "It is the form that says 1040 in block letters at the top."

Finally, pronouns, and determining what they refer to, often cause natural-language-system developers grave woes. For example, human beings interpret sentences such as "STEVE WENT TO THE STORE, FOUND A BASEBALL GLOVE ON THE SHELF, PAID FOR IT AND LEFT" in light of common sense knowledge of real-world

Figure 12-4 Result of lack of motivation analysis

Figure 12-5 The problem with determining pronoun referents

situations (Figure 12-5). Unfortunately, the average natural-language system does not have much common sense. It relies on more mundane techniques. For example, if the sentence represents information contained in an interfacing database, the natural-language system commonly determines the referent by interrogating the database to see whether the glove or the shelf has an associated price. Otherwise, it determines the referent with the help of grammatical rules. These rules commonly associate the pronoun with the closest noun, which, in this case, is clearly incorrect.

Despite these limitations, several successful natural-language systems, particularly natural-language interfaces to databases, have been built, and driven by demand, more are coming. In fact, a number of database companies and analysts contend that because of the marketing and competitive pressures, every serious database company will have to provide natural-language front ends to all its operations.

There is another school of thought. Some firms will not plan a natural-language interface for their databases because there are still too many limitations and problems left to solve. They point out that natural-language interfaces to databases are not general-purpose interfaces. Instead, they are suitable for specific database applications. They also claim that it is still too difficult for end-user companies to set up a lexicon (dictionary) for new applications.

NATURAL-LANGUAGE-SYSTEM INNARDS

As mentioned, there are three basic natural-language techniques: pattern and keyword matching, syntax and (some) semantics directed, and knowledge-based systems containing representations of real-world information and scenarios. One of the earliest natural-language programs, ELIZA, which simulates the behavior of a psychologist (Rogerian therapist) and a patient, is a pattern-matching system. Considered a very primitive system today, ELIZA carries on a doctor–patient dialogue but does not really understand the meaning of any input sentences (Figure 12-6). Instead, the ELIZA system tests

```
P.  I FEEL UNHAPPY LATELY.

D.  Do you often feel unhappy lately?
P.  YES.

D.  Is there something bothering you?
P.  MY MOTHER HATES MY SCIENTIFIC STUDIES.

D.  Is it important to you that your mother hates your scientific studies?
P.  I WANT HER TO APPROVE OF ME.

D.  What would it mean to you if you got her to approve of you?
P.  I WOULD FEEL PLEASED.

D.  You say you would feel pleased?
P.  YES, IT IS NICE WHEN PEOPLE ADMIRE YOU.

D.  Is there any other time?
P.
```

Figure 12-6 An Eliza dialog

for keywords and phrases. But it fools users into thinking that it is intelligent because it responds to the user–patient input with associated canned responses and because it echoes the user's sentence but substitutes personal pronouns such as "your" for "my" and "you" for "I."

Most of the current natural-language programs are more useful than ELIZA and employ more intelligent techniques. The dominant technique (although not the most flexible) is to use a formal grammar that contains rules of the English language to help understand a user's sentence. These rules describe the structure of English sentences. Typical rules state that a sentence is made up of a noun phrase followed by a verb phrase, and a verb phrase is a verb followed by a noun phrase (Figure 12-7). No system, however, can be totally syntax-based because such a system would understand only whether the structure of a sentence is legal. Clearly, this capability would not satisfy users' needs.

For a natural-language system to be useful, it must also be able to deal with semantic information. In the most common type of natural-language system, semantic as well as syntactic information is contained in a lexicon (dictionary). The natural-language system then uses the information in the formal grammar and the lexicon to generate some representation or translation for the input sentence. The representation or translation is necessary to map the natural language of the user to the unnatural language of the computer. For a user's natural-language database query that asks for, say, "the numbers and names of the employees that make more than $300 per week," the representation or translation may be a formal database query, such as, "SELECT EMPNO, LASTNAME FROM DSN8.TEMPL WHERE (SALARY /52) > 300". For a story-reading program, the representation or translation of a UPI newspaper article might be a paraphrase of an input paragraph. If the users' goal is to trigger some action or response, the users' input might be represented as computer instructions to perform a task.

SENTENCE ⟶ <noun phrase> <verb phrase>

Figure 12-7 A formal grammar contains rules that describe English sentence structure.

RECOGNIZING WORDS

The most common way to represent the rules of grammar is to use what is known as an "augmented transition network." To understand an augmented transition network, it is first necessary to understand simpler transition networks. A transition network (also called a finite-state automaton) is a node-and-arc graph. The nodes represent "states" of some system, such as "starting state" or the "state of having recognized a noun phrase or a verb phrase." The arcs represent rules to apply, or operations or tests to perform, to get to those states.

For example, the transition network in Figure 12-8a is a graphical way of showing that a sentence is composed of a noun phrase followed by a verb phrase. The starting state of the transition network is S1. The arc that leads out of S1 indicates that to get from "state 1" to "state 2" it is necessary to find a noun phrase. To get from "state 2" to "state 3" it is necessary to find a verb phrase.

Other transition networks show the structure of other speech constructs, such as noun phrases, verb phrases, and prepositional phrases. As seen, Figure 12-8b shows that a noun phrase is composed of either a determiner (such as "the" or "an") or a proper noun or an adjective, followed by any number of adjectives (or no adjectives), followed by a noun, and possibly followed by a prepositional phrase. The arc labeled "jump" indicates

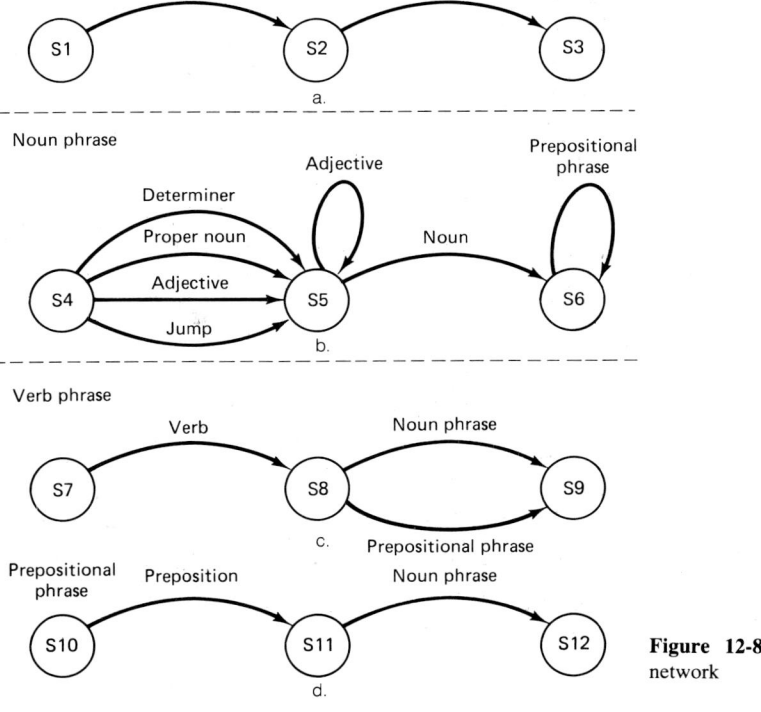

Figure 12-8 Augmented transition network

that it is possible to jump over this arc without satisfying any rules or matching any words or phrases. Using the jump arc, a noun phrase can also be just a single noun.

These transition network rules can be used to string together words to produce several types of sentences. For example, according to these rules, the phrase "the opera" is a noun phrase because it is composed of a determiner followed by a noun. The phrase "the good opera," which contains a determiner followed by an adjective and then a noun, is also a legal noun phrase, as is the phrase "the magnificently great opera," which is made of a determiner followed by two adjectives followed by a noun. Similarly, "the opera in the park" is a noun phrase because it is composed of a determiner followed by a noun followed by a prepositional phrase. The single noun "opera" also fits the noun phrase definition because jumping from state 4 to state 5 shows that a single noun is allowed.

By the same reasoning, Figure 12-8c shows that a verb phrase is composed of a verb followed by either a noun phrase or a prepositional phrase. Figure 12-8d shows that a prepositional phrase is composed of a preposition followed by a noun phrase.

A "parser" is a natural-language mechanism that takes a sentence apart word by word. It can use transition networks to recognize sentences. To recognize a sentence, the parser goes from one node to another by finding the construct specified by the arc. Thus when the parser has found a noun phrase followed by a verb phrase, it knows that it has found a sentence.

The parser's goal is to get from one end of a transition network to another. When it has done that, it has succeeded in recognizing a sentence. However, to get from end to end, rules must be able to call other transition networks as subroutines. For example, in Figure 12-8a, to get from state 1 to state 2, the transition network that specializes in sentences must be able to call the noun-phrase specialist. This ability to call different transition networks, like a computer program calls subroutines, is one way that simple transition networks have been augmented. Hence the name "augmented transition network," usually abbreviated to ATN.

ANALYZING SENTENCES

For a parser to parse a sentence and get through a transition network, it must obtain syntactical (grammatical) information about the words in the sentence. Such information is stored in the natural-language system's lexicon.

Typically, the lexicon contains not only information about parts of speech, but also semantic information (Figure 12-9). The semantic information includes the meaning of a word, whether it is a name or a cardinal or ordinal number, an interrogative word, and whether it is contained in a database. Irregular nouns and verbs have separate entries for singular, plural, and irregular forms. Otherwise, plurals and various verb forms are usually generated from the corresponding root entries.

If a word is contained in an interfacing database, the lexicon contains a pointer to (a computer address for) that word's entry in the database. On the other hand, if the word has a representation in some semantic network, the lexicon contains a pointer to the relevant node in that semantic network.

Word	Category	Features
A	Determiner	Number: singular
Banana	Noun	
Be	Verb	Transitivity: intransitive
Been	Verb	Form: past participle; Type: be
Cat	Noun	
Caught	Verb	Form: past, past participle
Crate	Noun	
Fish	Noun	Number: singular, plural
	Verb	Transitivity: intransitive
Fly	Noun	
	Verb	Transitivity: intransitive
Forty	Adjective	
Fruit	Noun, Adjective	
Like	Verb	Transitivity: transitive
	Preposition	
	Conjunction	
Orange	Adjective, Noun	
Purchase	Noun	
	Verb	Transitivity: transitive
Sparkle	Proper noun	
	Verb	Transitivity: intransitive
Store	Noun	
	Verb	Transitivity: transitive
That	Complementizer	
	Determiner	
	Pronoun	
	Relative	
The	Determiner	
To	Complementizer	
	Preposition	
We	Pronoun	Number: plural; Person: first; Case: subjective
Which	Determiner	Question: yes
	Relative	
Whom	Pronoun	Case: objective; Question: yes
	Relative	
With	Preposition	

Figure 12-9   Some dictionary entries

To analyze the sentence "Sparkle fruit stores purchase 40 orange crates," the parser begins with the sentence transition network and looks for a noun phrase. To determine if it has found one, the parser must call the noun phrase network.

There are four possible paths in the noun phrase network: determiner, proper noun, adjective, and jump. The parser examines the first word of the sentence to see if it corresponds to its list of determiners, such as the, a, one, and each. Since the lexicon shows that it does not, the parser proceeds to check the next, or proper noun, path.

Since "Sparkle" is both a proper noun and a verb, the parser now has two different choices. At this point, however, the transition network will accept only a determiner, proper noun, adjective, or noun if the jump path is used. Therefore, the parser rules out the possibility that Sparkle is a verb and there is no ambiguity involved in the first noun phrase. The parser takes the proper noun definition of Sparkle and continues.

However, when the parser comes to the next word, "fruit", a temporarily ambiguous situation occurs. "Fruit" is both an adjective and a noun, and the transition network node coming up accepts both an adjective and a noun.

In situations like this where the natural-language system does not specify how to choose, many systems generate two sentences, one based on each possible choice. They then proceed to examine the rest of the phrase and defer their final decision until they find some information that allows them to make a choice.

In the "Sparkle fruit" noun phrase under consideration, only one choice (fruit as an adjective) leads to eventual success in getting through the network. Thus the system resolves the ambiguity by waiting before it chooses, and choosing when it discovers that there is only one possible successful choice. Sometimes, however, a system may need to wend its way through several transition networks before it can finally make a choice.

This type of scheme, where the natural-language system does not choose until it is certain, but instead tries all the arcs at a particular network node and generates and tests all possible sentences, is called a "nondeterministic" scheme.

PARSE TREES

It is not enough to merely recognize sentences by traversing arcs of transition networks. A natural-language system also must represent the syntactic structure of a sentence in a way that shows how words and phrases in a sentence relate to one another. This syntactic structure and word and phrase relationships are usually represented in a form known as a "parse tree" (Figure 12-10).

The parse tree for the sentence "the cat caught a fish" looks like an upside-down tree with its single root at the top. Like the ATN discussed previously, this parse tree begins with a sentence at its root. The first level of branches decompose the sentence into a noun phrase and a verb phrase. The next level of branches decompose the noun and verb phrases into their component parts. The final level of branches, called the "terminal branches" or just plain "terminals" or "leaves," contain the results of repeatedly decomposing sentence parts until only single words in the sentence remain.

The syntactic structure, so conveniently displayed in a parse tree, acts as a guide to merging the small chunks and phrases that comprise a sentence into a meaningful representation of the complete sentence. The syntactic-structured parse tree can provide information necessary for a meaningful representation because, for one thing, when it is built, it incorporates knowledge about which words modify others. In addition, syntactic parsing and semantic processing occur in parallel. As a result, to generate the parse tree, the parser identifies the sentence as an active rather than a passive one. Therefore, the parse tree shows facts such as the cat caught the fish instead of the fish catching the cat.

It is possible to generate a parse tree because a notation known as a "context-free"

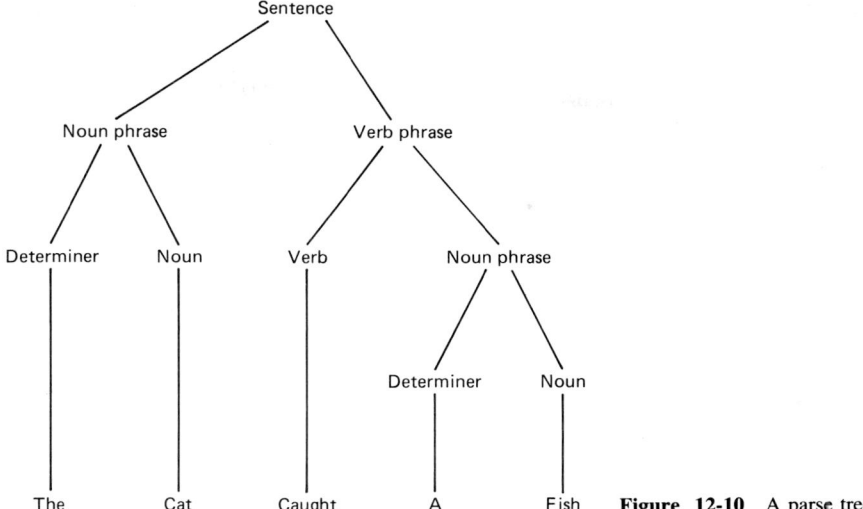

Figure 12-10 A parse tree

grammar is used to represent English-language syntax, A context-free grammar is one of four types of grammars defined by Noam Chomsky (at MIT) in the 1950s. The grammars range from very general to highly restricted in terms of the rules that allow sentence components (such as "prepositional phrase") to be replaced by other sentence components (such as "preposition followed by a noun phrase") in order to generate well-formed sentences in a language.

Basically, Chomsky's grammars consist of a series of rewrite rules (also called production rules) to rewrite a sentence in terms of the sentence parts of which it is made. A typical production rule states that a sentence can be rewritten as (or produces) a noun phrase and a verb phrase. (Figure 12-11)

Production rules replace parts of a sentence with their component parts, down to the terminal branch level, where replacement is no longer possible. For example, the second production rule in Figure 12-11 states that "a noun phrase can be rewritten as a determiner

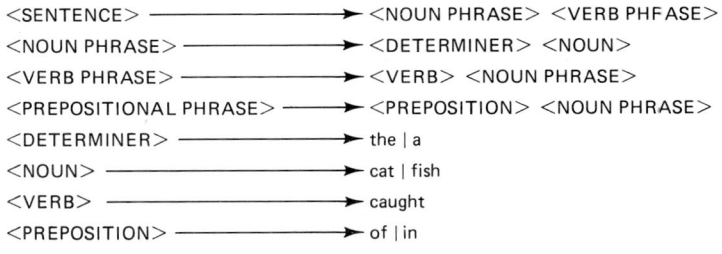

(*Note*: | means "or". For example, a determiner can be "the" or "a.")

Figure 12-11 Production rules for a small subset of a context-free English grammar.

followed by a noun." This rule allows a noun phrase in a sentence to be replaced by a determiner and noun. Determiner and noun can be further decomposed. As other production rules in the figure show, "a determiner can be rewritten as either the words 'the' or 'a' " and "a noun can be rewritten as either 'cat' or 'fish'." The words "the," "a," "cat," and "fish" cannot be further decomposed. To indicate that the decomposition process is at an end, terminal symbols are written in lower case letters.

To generate a parse tree, it is necessary to follow this process and replace the left side of each rule with the appropriate symbols on the right side. What makes a context-free grammar suitable for generating parse trees is that the left side of each rule consists of only one symbol to be replaced. Clearly, if there were more than one symbol on the left side of the rule, as there are in some other grammars, it would be much more difficult to generate a parse tree.

The production rules in the figure, which are used to generate the parse tree in the previous figure, are an example of a context-free grammar. However, because graphical representations are convenient to read, production rules are frequently written in the form of an ATN.

PARSE TREES ARE NOT A BED OF ROSES

ATNs and production rule grammars fail their users when they verify a sentence to be legal and parse it correctly, but the sentence turns out to be illogical. For example, the statement "IT'S 24 PARTLY CLOUDY DEGREES TODAY" is a syntactically correct statement. Yet the statement is meaningless.

Worse, grammars can encounter ambiguity difficulties when there is more than one way to build a parse tree with the same sequence of leaf nodes. One of the best known examples is the sentence "FRUIT FLIES LIKE A BANANA," which clearly has two successful parses (Figure 12-12). The two successful parses occur because "fruit" functions as both a noun and an adjective, while "flies" is a noun as well as a verb, and "like" functions as a verb, preposition, and conjunction. Based on the same sequence of words, in the same order, the parser can traverse the ATN taking the path either of noun-verb-prepositional phrase, or adjective-noun-verb-noun phrase. In cases of true ambiguity, such as this one, in order to clarify meaning, a natural-language system usually must ask the user which choice is the intended one. Although this example is meant to be amusing and educational, similar types of ambiguities occur in newspapers, textbooks, advertisements, and everyday language (Figure 12-13). There are existing natural-language systems (discussed in Chapter 15) that can read newspaper stories and decide which of two successful parses is really meant. Based on their parse decision, they paraphrase the stories or infer other information from them. Because of ambiguity difficulties, these natural-language systems have, at least partially, abandoned syntactical parsing methods. Instead, they deal, as best as possible, with ambiguous headlines and newspaper stories by incorporating real-world knowledge in their systems.

A system containing such real-world knowledge could probably interpret Barnum's original ad that read "PAY 25 CENTS AND SEE A MAN EATING CHICKEN" be-

Parse Trees Are Not A Bed of Roses

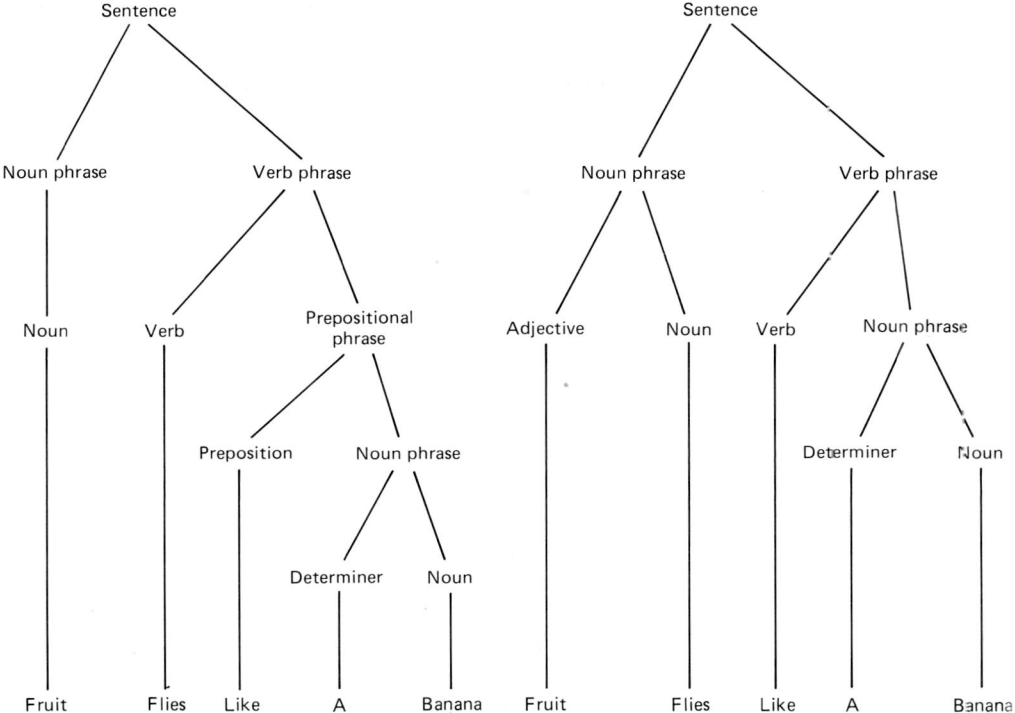

Figure 12-12 Two successful parses of a sentence result in ambiguity.

```
Commuter Tax
On New Yorkers
Killed in Jersey
```
The New York Times 6/9/81

```
3 Arrested in Slaying
Of Economist for FTC
```
The Washington Post 1/12/83

```
2 Teen-Agers Indicted
For Drowning in Lake
```
The New York Times 10/10/82

Figure 12-13 Everyday ambiguities are resolved by using knowledge of what makes sense.

cause it would know that few people would pay to see a man chomping on a chicken but people might pay money to see a chicken eating a man. But even a system with real-world knowledge could not decipher the grammatically correct sentence, "FLYING PLANES CAN BE DANGEROUS." This sentence has two correct parses with the same sequence of leaf nodes, and unfortunately, both of them make sense.

UNDERSTANDING WHAT IS SAID

If there were no correlation between the structure of a sentence and its social and functional meaning, the sentence analyses discussed until now would be of interest only to a linguist. Clearly, this is not the case. In the end, the structure of a sentence is correlated with meaning, by identifying the roles that component words and phrases play in a sentence and the relationships between these roles. For example, the sentence "Reynold jumped over the moon" contains information about the action "jumped," who jumped, and where Reynold jumped. Similarly, to respond to the statememt "List the employees who work in Chicago," it is necessary to know how "employees" and "Chicago" relate to the verb "work" and how all these words relate to the verb "list."

Most commonly, a system of "grammatical cases," which denote relationships between agents of an action, the action, and states, is used to identify these roles. Researchers have proposed a number of different cases to identify roles and relationships in English. In various theories, these identify, for example, the causal agent of an action, the coagent, counteragent, instrument or means by which an action is performed, location, source, destination, theme, object of the action, experiencer, and result of the action.

Natural-language systems use syntax as an aid to determining the roles of words and phrases in a sentence. For example, the agent is almost always the subject of the sentence, as in "Tony ate green cheese." However, the logical subject may be an entire noun phrase, as in "Sparkle fruit stores ordered 40 orange crates." Similarly, the instrument is likely to be an indirect object, as in "Tony ate green cheese with a fork."

EXCEPTIONS ABOUND

Because English is a large and difficult language, there are more rules that provide for exceptions than rules that determine the probable cases. One major exception occurs if the sentence in question is a passive rather than an active one. In a passive sentence, the subject, and therefore the agent, is usually the word in the "by" phrase instead of the first noun phrase. Consequently, in "Green cheese was eaten by Tony," Tony remains the agent.

But even here there are exceptions, depending on the verb. Some verbs, for example, allow an instrument in the subject position. Thus, in the sentences "Richard broke the window with a brick" and "A brick broke the window," "brick" is the instrument and not the agent.

As these examples show, it is dangerous to make automatic assumptions about roles of sentence parts in order to understand underlying meaning. Attempts to do so lead to misconceptions about scenarios such as "Juana is cooking" and "The meat is cooking." Pointing up the same difficulties are "He made Robert a soda" and "He made Robert the engineering director." Similarly, different cases are required to understand the differences in meaning between "I am warm, the weather is warm, the coat is warm, Tahiti is warm, and the day is warm."

Neither case grammars nor ATNs nor parsing oriented systems can differentiate between the meaning and serving methods of two simple sentences such as "Helen ordered a frankfurter with mustard" and "Helen ordered a frankfurter with soda." Since Helen is not likely to want the soda on her frankfurter, a different type of natural-language system that contains a knowledge-based mechanism is necessary to determine what is likely and plausible in the real world. Finally, even such a knowledge-based mechanism fails for a legitimate legal sentence such as "the duck is ready to eat." Only examination of the sentence in the context of a larger story, which reveals whether the sentence in question is about a dinner or a farm, may indicate whether the duck is performing the action of eating or is being acted upon and thus eaten.

Natural Language Goes Commercial for Mainframes Through Micros

CHAPTER 13

The office worker, manager, and scientist scurrying between file cabinets and copying figures with a pen and pad is fast becoming an anachronism in this computer age. Increasing numbers of people are discovering that computers can find the figures faster and at the same time relieve their work loads and drudgery.

That is the good news. Now for the bad. People speak natural language. But computers speak a cryptic, formal language, which most people find difficult to understand and to use. So with the aid of AI experts and linguists, computers are gradually learning to communicate with their users in natural language.

The ability to speak the user's language makes the computer far more accessible to noncomputing professionals. Boeing Computer Services calls these noncomputing professionals "appliance" users because they want to use the power of the computer like they use the power of a car, washing machine, copying machine, or any other appliance—that is, as a means to get their jobs done without having to learn the inner workings, underlying theory, or special language of these appliances. Because so many of these appliance users exist, commercial computer systems that communicate in natural language are fast becoming more than just talk.

Most of the present natural-language systems are interfaces to databases. They allow users to issue randomly phrased requests to get data out of the database. An example is

```
"HOW MANY COOKS WORK AT THE COMPANY? HOW MANY BAKERS?
HOW MANY COOKS ARE BAKERS?"
```

Besides functioning as a database query language, some natural-language systems can also be used as programming languages. One such natural-language programming system (from Excalibur Technologies Corp.) allows users to write English-language programs to solve problems such as "WHAT IS A PORCUPINE WORTH" depending on how many quills it has (Figure 13-1).

Because natural language is not yet well understood, and because the nature, interpretation, and representation of meaning is far from an exact science, computerized natural-language systems are subject to the ever-present danger of misinterpretation. For example, the query "HOW MANY COOKS WORK AT THE COMPANY?" might have a different meaning if the company is a restaurant or law firm. Even if the company is a restaurant, misinterpretation is still possible because several cooks, named Cook, could work for a restaurant. Clearly, cooks could also be bakers, and people named Cook could be bakers.

Despite the dangers of misinterpretation, several vendors have created fairly robust

```
What would you like me to do now?           The user types this,
What is a porcupine worth?                   and Savvy-PC executes this task

Enter quill count  9
Enter size  3
Buying power is 729

What would you like me to do now?


What is a porcupine worth?  (a Task)         This line of code executes this
1  Ask for the porcupine's quill count and size
2  Compute a porcupine's buying power with the same quill count
   but next smaller size          This line of code executes this
3  SHOW the buying power
4  END   (Task is 32 bytes.)


Compute a porcupine's <1> with the same <2> but next smaller <3>   (a Function)

1  IF the size .. IS NOT .. 0 then
2     Decrement the size by 1
3     Increase the buying power by quill count
4     Compute a porcupine's buying power with the same quill
      count but next smaller size
5     END of test
6  END   (Task is 55 bytes.)


Ask for the porcupine's <1> and <2>   (a Function)

1  PROMPT for <1>
2  PROMPT for <2>
3  Set the buying power to 1
4  END   (Task is 21 bytes.)


What would you like me to do now?
```

Figure 13-1 Natural language system supports the writing of programs in English. (Excalibur Technologies)

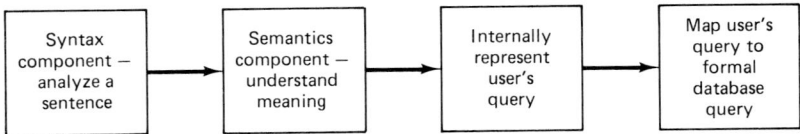

Figure 13-2 Natural-language database interface components.

natural-language interfaces to databases. The greatest number of these systems use variations on the syntactic/semantic type of language analysis, described in Chapter 12, as their underlying technology.

Most commercial natural-language systems have four components (Figure 13-2). One component contains knowledge about syntax (grammar) to tell the natural-language system how to put together, take apart, and analyze a user's sentence. A second component has knowledge of the meaning of words (semantics) and their roles and relationships to each other in a sentence. The third component of a natural-language system internally represents the user's natural-language input in some language form that the computer can understand. The fourth component, which is common to all types of natural-language systems, maps the user's natural query into some formal database query, programming language instruction, or sentence paraphrase.

Although natural-language systems based on a syntactic/semantic type of analysis are the most common ones, they are by no means the only type. For example, another type of natural-language system interprets users' words and phrases using pattern-recognition techniques (not keywords) similar to those that biological organisms use to interpret speech and visual signals (Chapter 14). Still another type uses expert system-like rules and heuristics, in conjuction with syntactic and semantic components, to interpret users' queries (Chapter 14).

A very different type of natural-language system seeks to understand users' input sentences almost exclusively through meaning. To achieve this goal, the system contains encoded knowledge about particular subject areas of interest that correspond to people's stored-up past experiences. Like human beings, the natural-language system can refer to this stored subject knowledge to help understand, interpret, and anticipate new situations (Chapter 15).

CHOOSING A NATURAL-LANGUAGE SYSTEM

Larry Harris, president of Artificial Intelligence Corp. and designer of the natural-language system called Intellect, defines four key issues that natural-language interfaces to databases must handle (Figure 13-3). The issues are density of language coverage, ambiguity, navigation of a database, and references to database fields with long descriptive

To evaluate natural-language system, check:
— Density of coverage
— Handling of ambiguity
— Database navigation
— Series information (multiword field names)

Figure 13-3 Key issues for natural language interfaces to databases.

names (particularly containing time-related information) (Harris, 1984). Users must understand these issues to evaluate natural-language systems.

DENSITY OF COVERAGE

Contrary to many people's first impressions, density of coverage does not refer to how large a subset of a natural language a system can cover. Instead, it means how densely a natural-language system covers the portion of the language it is designed to handle.

This definition is actually another way of saying that a system with dense coverage is tolerant to minor alterations or rewording of a request. In contrast, a system with sparse coverage may keel over if the user drops an article or a preposition.

Unfortunately, it is difficult to determine whether or not a system provides dense coverage just from viewing a demonstration. By choosing the right examples, a system with sparse coverage can be made to look good. Then when the users get the system back in their home office, they discover that it behaves erratically.

Users will swear that the same query that the system understood yesterday, is no longer understood today. In reality, the system is not behaving erratically. It only seems so because yesterday's query is not phrased exactly the same as today's. Today's query may be reasonably similar, except that it is lacking, say, the article "a" or the preposition "of." Although this lack is not significant to users, some natural-language systems may cover the language too sparsely to understand the many different ways of wording a request.

Users can gain some clues to the density of coverage characteristics of a natural-language system by taking note of a demonstrator's sample queries. Harris advises users to be suspicious if the samples chosen consistently show a stylized form of English. For example, the query (Harris, 1984)

SHOW TOTAL SALES FOR EACH STATE FOR EACH CITY

is clearly stylized because repeated use of "FOR EACH" is not very natural. Systems that require such stylized queries have sparse coverage. In contrast, a natural-language system with dense coverage would understand each of the following wordings (Harris, 1984):

SHOW THE TOTAL SALES IN EACH STATE AND CITY.
WHAT ARE THE SALES OR TOTALS FOR EACH CITY WITHIN EACH STATE.

AMBIGUITY

The second key issue that natural-language systems must handle is ambiguity, because natural languages are ambiguous. Formal computer languages, in contrast, do not have an ambiguity problem because they are carefully designed to be unambiguous.

As Chapter 12 indicated, the ambiguity in natural languages stems from several sources. For example, natural-language systems often find it difficult to determine which noun a pronoun refers to. Consider the following set of queries (Harris, 1984):

```
"LIST THE TOP 10 COMPANIES IN THE UNITED STATES"
"WHICH OF THEM ARE LOCATED IN THE WESTERN UNITED STATES?"
"WHICH OF THEM ARE LOCATED IN THE EASTERN UNITED STATES?"
"WHICH OF THESE ARE HIGH-TECHNOLOGY FIRMS?"
```

The problem with this sequence is that clearly the pronoun "them" in the second and third queries refers to the "top 10 companies" mentioned in the first query. It is not clear, however, whether the pronoun "these" in the fourth query refers to the original top 10 companies or only the companies in the eastern region.

Ambiguity in natural language also occurs because words have different meanings when they are used in different contexts. The *New York Times* headline in Figure 13-4 illustrates the problem with different meanings in different contexts. A natural-language interface to a newspaper-story database might receive a query that refers to this article. The query might ask for the date that Cuomo, governor of New York State at the time of this story, froze New York's hospital building. The natural-language system might become perplexed, however, trying to determine whether to search the index for newspaper-story subjects pertaining to cryogenics, disasters, or building preservation programs.

Still another source for ambiguity is conjunctions. For example, determination of

(From New York Times, Jan. 6, 1983)

```
CUOMO TO FREEZE
HOSPITAL BUILDING
```

Possible subheads:

```
Lack of volunteers for cryogenic
experiments cited by officials
```

```
Governor criticized for not
emptying the building first
```

```
Part of new program to stem
decay of aging city buildings
```

Figure 13-4 Ambiguity can result from words that have different meanings in different contexts. (Subheads courtesy Ronald Schneiderman)

meaning is difficult in the following query because the conjunction "and" has four different meanings (Harris, 1984):

> FOR OHIO AND IOWA, PRINT THE NAME AND AGE OF ANYONE WHO EARNS BETWEEN $30,000 AND $50,000 AND IS MARRIED.

In its first occurrence, "AND" implies search union. Search union means that the final printout will contain the names of everyone who lives in Ohio as well as (AND) everyone who lives in Iowa, as long as they meet the stated conditions.

The second occurrence of "AND" specifies a list of fields to be retrieved. The two fields, which are equivalent to lines to be filled out on a paper form in a file cabinet, are "name" AND "age."

The third occurrence of "AND" specifies a range search. In other words, the user wants information about people who earn salaries between the range $30,000 AND $50,000.

The fourth occurrence of "AND" implies what is known as search intersection. This query calls for information about people who meet two conditions. They must earn between $30,000 and $50,000 AND they must be married.

NAVIGATING THE DATABASE

The third key issue, the ability to navigate through the database, clearly is necessary because the purpose of most natural-language systems is to allow users to retrieve database information without knowing anything about database structure or database access languages. Since users are permitted to be naive about database structure and access, the natural-language system must be knowledgeable in these areas and assume the responsibilities of the sophisticated database user.

To perform accordingly, natural-language systems must know how to map the user's natural-language requests into a formal database query. They also need knowledge of the underlying database architecture. With these kinds of knowledge, natural-language interfaces interpret and translate user queries into formal database queries. In addition, they know how to instruct the formal database system to relate or join files. This knowledge permits the handling of complex queries which require the retrieval of requested data scattered in several files.

SERIES INFORMATION

The fourth issue that a natural-language system must handle successfully is the understanding of randomly phrased queries that refer to a database field name. This is not a problem when database fields are named with a single word such as NAME or ADDRESS. Difficulties in fluency of expression may be encountered in this area, however, when database fields are named by a series of words, such as "ACTUAL YEAR TO DATE SALES."

The difficulties arise if the database field name is directly coupled to lexicon words and phrases via a 1:1 association. Under this condition, a user query about a database field must contain the name of that database field exactly as it appears in the database. A multiple-word database field name such as NEW YORK will not generally cause trouble because few people are likely to refer to "YORK NEW." But a field name such as "1985 ACTUAL YEAR TO DATE SALES" may present a problem because the probability of users always typing these words in that order is slim. Words such as "actual" and "year to date" are concepts in the users' heads and they are therefore likely to refer to them in random orders. To allow fluency of natural-language expression, a natural-language system must contain definitions for each word in a database field name and be able to put these words together linguistically, rather than in the database field name order, and retrieve the data items referred to.

It turns out that this issue of series data is particularly pertinent to time-related information. The ability to handle time-related information is an important issue because so many types of database information have minimal usefulness unless compared with the same or similar information in a previous or estimated future time period. Consequently, the areas of time-related information are so replete with long descriptive field names such as ACTUAL YEAR TO DATE SALES or ESTIMATED YEAR TO DATE SALES that the term "time series" has been coined to refer to the coupling (or decoupling) of these fields with lexicons.

Second only to the problem of word order in trying to achieve natural-language fluency is the problem of awkward, repetitious qualifiers and modifiers. It is unlikely that people would use their native language to ask questions such as "SHOW ME THE 1985 ACTUAL YEAR TO DATE SALES AND THE 1985 ESTIMATED YEAR TO DATE SALES" without being taught to do so. It is more natural to ask for "THE ACTUAL AND ESTIMATED YEAR TO DATE SALES." Therefore, to be maximally useful, a natural-language analyzer must be able to determine that "year-to-date" sales has been factored out of the names of the two fields. It must also recognize if a particular year (often different for the actual and estimated information) has been defaulted.

COMMERCIAL SYSTEMS

Mainframes, minicomputers, and micros can all boast of hosting natural-language interfaces to databases. Some of these natural-language interfaces allow users to input free-form queries, phrased any way they want. The system then attempts to figure out what the user really meant.

Other natural-language systems operate more like multiple-choice questionnaires. They allow the users to string together selected words and phrases from choices that the system presents on a screen.

Finally, some natural-language database interfaces are extensions of fourth-generation database languages. These are English-like languages that are too stylized and structured to be considered natural. Because their structure and style are oriented toward computer capabilities, it is often easier for knowledgeable users to express complex formatting directions and some database update requests in the fourth-generation language than in a natural-language. However, fourth-generation languages with natural-language extensions allow users to switch between the two language applications, depending on the functions they wish to perform.

These commercialized natural-language systems can be bought as off-the-shelf packages. However, they generally contain some means to allow users to customize the system for their own company's applications and to accommodate their own personal or company terminology.

To avoid misinterpretation and ensure robustness, after analyzing user's queries, most natural-language systems check their interpretations for correctness by paraphrasing the query back to the user. Users view the paraphrase to check that the computer's understanding of a query corresponds to what they meant to say.

A good example of a natural-language interface is Intellect from Artificial Intelligence Corp. The grand-daddy of commercial natural-language systems (marketed since 1980), Intellect uses classic natural-language syntactic and semantic techniques, described in Chapter 12. It interfaces to major databases, graphics systems, and statistical analysis tools to allow computer operators to use natural language to request not only data but graphic and statistical analyses.

Licensed by IBM, Cullinet (who markets Intellect under the name On-line English), and Information Builders, Inc., Intellect draws on five different sources of information to help analyze users' queries. The sources are two types of lexicons, a grammar, knowledge both of database structure and the information in the database, and as a last resort, the user.

Intellect's knowledge of English words comes from three of these sources: the root lexicon that is built into the system, the application-specific lexicon that is constructed at the site by the users, and the database system itself (Figure 13-5).

The root lexicon, which is delivered with Intellect, contains syntactic and semantic information about generic English words (such as who, is, friend, and but) that can be used in any subject domain.

In contrast to the root lexicon, the application-specific lexicon is created locally by a person who is building an application. This person is typically a data-processing person who knows the application and is trained to work with the lexicon. He or she defines the words that are unique to the application that will interface to Intellect. Rather than being linguistic in nature, the definitions in the application-specific lexicon map between the way the user views the data (user's conceptual schema) and how the database views it (logical database schema).

Some of the information in the application-specific dictionary is either contained in or related to information in the database system's data dictionary. The data dictionary is an organized listing of specifications and descriptions of data in database fields. Because its information overlaps that contained in the application-specific lexicon, Intellect can automatically generate parts of the application-specific lexicon from a user-company's data dictionary.

The database system, the last source for English word knowledge, includes the database schema information and all the indexed fields within the database. Armed with

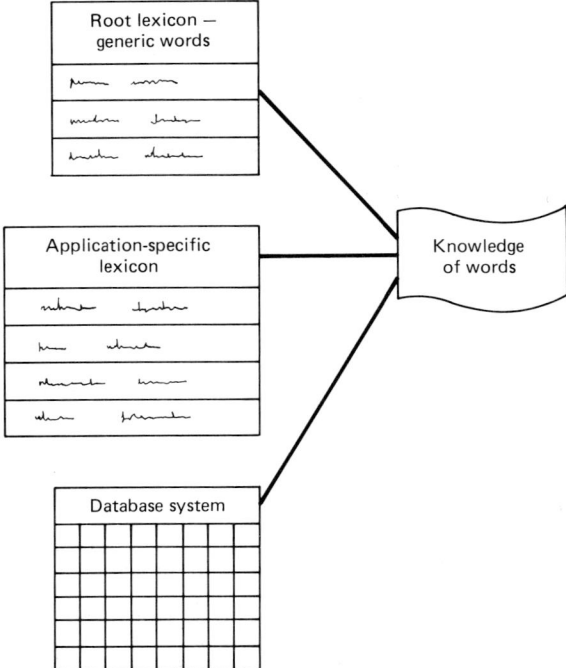

Figure 13-5 Intellect's sources of English word knowledge.

this information, Intellect can correlate the type of information in the database and the names of the database fields with the data requested by a user's query.

But Intellect does not require a one-to-one relationship between its field names and user phrases. Instead, it handles a user request that refers to the field named "ACTUAL YEAR TO DATE SALES" by providing separate definitions for the field name components, such as "ACTUAL" or "YEAR TO DATE."

These individual definitions, combined with knowledge of the context in which the words are used, allow Intellect to understand more naturally worded references to database fields. For example, Intellect responds to the request to "COMPARE THE ACTUAL SALES FOR JUNE TO THE ESTIMATES" by printing the current year's ACTUAL JUNE SALES, the current year's ESTIMATED JUNE SALES, and the absolute and relative differences between them.

Intellect's second source for natural-language analysis is its ATN-based English-language grammar (Figure 13-6). This grammar contains the mechanism to build up parse tree–level information from input words (described in Chapter 12) and eventually map this information into database queries.

Actually, to provide density of coverage, Intellect has more than one ATN. It uses its primary ATN to parse requests that it assumes are phrased in proper grammar. If the primary ATN fails to understand the user's request, Intellect calls a second ATN that

Commercial Systems

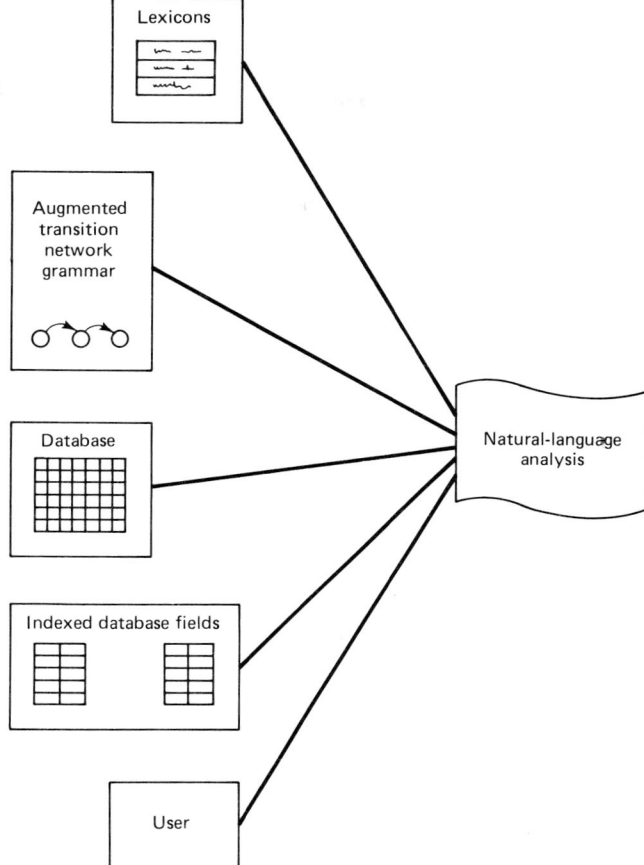

Figure 13-6 Intellect's sources for natural language analysis.

helps understand sentence fragments and ungrammatical requests. The two ATN's help provide additional coverage of user requests.

Intellect's third source of query analysis is knowledge about how the data are structured in the database. This knowledge is necessary because unlike queries posed by data-processing professionals, typical natural-language users' queries are not phrased in any way that indicates the data's location. Therefore, the natural-language system must know how the data are organized in order to project a high-level English representation onto a particular database structure and to navigate that database. The fourth query analysis source is knowledge of the indexed fields of the database. Intellect uses this information to minimize the likelihood of errors that stem from ambiguity.

To resolve ambiguity using the database, if more than one interpretation of a query is possible, Intellect's parser, which is nondeterministic, generates multiple interpretations. It then assigns a preference rating to each interpretation. The preference ratings are based on how easily the query fit the grammar rules or whether the grammar rules had to be stretched to fit the query.

If the preference ratings are different and one interpretation has a high rating, Intellect chooses the high-preference interpretation. However, if the preference ratings are approximately equal, Intellect looks in the database to see which interpretation makes more sense.

If one interpretation makes more sense in light of the database information, Intellect will prefer that interpretation. However, it checks with the user anyway. If the preferred interpretation is not the user's intended one, Intellect prints out all the other possible interpretations. Thus the database is actually a heuristic rather than an absolute deciding factor.

If the database system treats both interpretations equally because it has answers to both, Intellect goes to its fifth source of query analysis information, which is the user (Figure 13-7a). For example, in the query "HOW MANY COOKS ARE IN THE COMPANY?", Intellect will first use its ATNs to determine that the query makes equal sense whether "cooks" refers to a person's name or a job title. Since both queries are valid, Intellect will check the database for clues to the user's meaning. If the database indicates that the company has no job title of "cook" but several people by that name work there, it will assume that the user wants to know about people of that name. However, it will warn the user by asking "Is this the meaning you intended?" If the database indicates that the company has people named "Cook," as well as people with the job title of "cook," it will confront the user with both interpretations and ask the user to choose the intended one.

Natural-language database interfaces are not limited to database query systems. As Figure 13-7b and c show, Intellect users can use English to count the number of employees or to request a spreadsheet or graph. The system will first echo back its understanding of the user's directions to make sure that its interpretation is correct; second, it performs the task.

Intellect is written in the PL/1 programming language rather than Lisp, the language

```
User:      How many cooks are in the company?

Computer:  YOUR REQUEST IS AMBIGUOUS TO ME.  DO YOU WANT:
              1): CURRENT JOB TITLE = COOK.

              2): LAST NAME = COOK.

           PLEASE ENTER THE NUMBER OF THE INTERPRETATION YOU INTENDED
User:         .2

Computer
Paraphrase: COUNT THE EMPLOYEES WITH LAST NAME = COOK.

Computer   ANSWER:   1                                              (A)

Computer:  NEXT REQUEST.
```

Figure 13-7 (a) Intellect's final source for resolving ambiguity is the user. (b) Natural language systems can be used in spreadsheet work. (c) Natural language system can handle graphic requests. (Artificial Intelligence Corp.)

Commercial Systems

User: .Give me a spreadsheet of the percent of total salary in each department.

Computer: PRINT A CALC PERCENTAGE OF THE TOTAL ANNUAL SALARY IN EACH DEPARTMENT OF ALL EMPLOYEES.
GIVE ME A SPREADSHEET OF THE PERCENT OF TOTAL SALARY IN EACH DEPARTMENT

DEPARTMENT	ANNUAL SALARY	PERCENT
ACCOUNTING	360201.24	3.88
ADMINISTRATION	730210.2	7.87
CUSTOMER SERVICE	786917.88	8.49
DATA PROCESSING	1646756.88	17.76
ENGINEERING	907770.12	9.79
FINANCIAL PLANNING	133623.96	1.44
HUMAN RESOURCES	291225.48	3.14
MAIL	26460	.29
MANUFACTURING	45000	.49
PLANT OPERATIONS	1377403.68	14.85
PURCHASING	98527.92	1.06
Q & A	30000	.32
RESEARCH	398051.04	4.29
SALES & MARKETING	1164240	12.56
SHIPPING	44052	.48
STORES	78600	.85
TRAINING	1153551	12.44
	9272591.4	100.00 (B)

User: Show it in a piechart

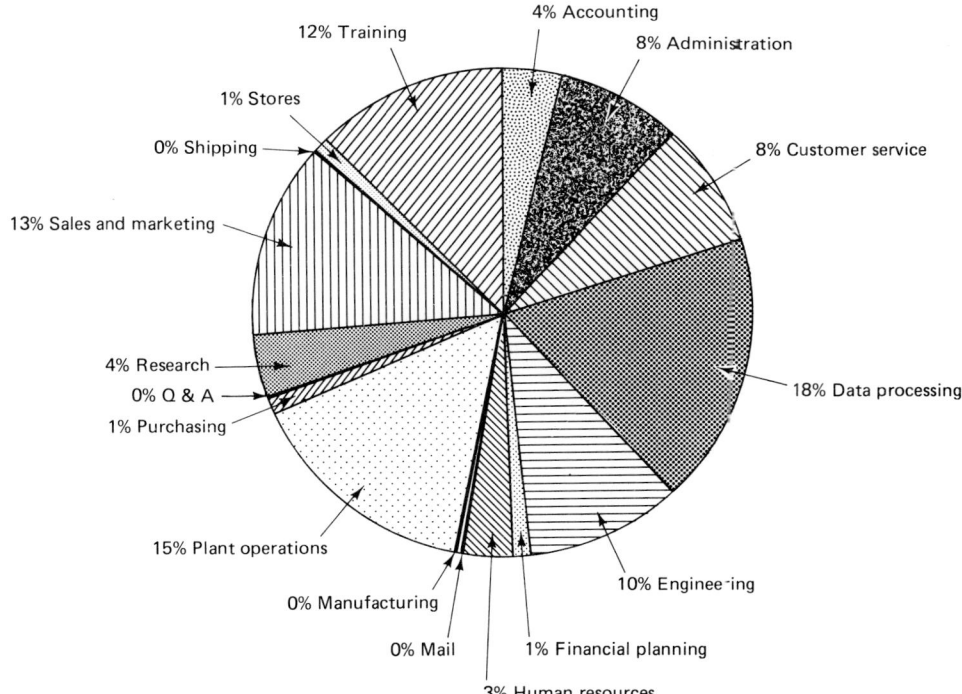

Figure 13-7 (cont.)

most commonly used for AI, for a very practical reason. Most commercial databases support Cobol, PL/1, and Fortran interfaces, but not Lisp. However, there are so many Lisp capabilities important to AI but lacking in PL/1 that in designing Intellect, it was necessary first to build up some of the Lisp environment under PL/1.

TEACHING NATURAL-LANGUAGE SYSTEMS NEW WORDS

Themis, a minicomputer-based natural-language system from Frey Associates, provides a typical example of how a natural-language database interface interactively learns English from its users. When Themis encounters a word it does not know, it first informs the user that it does not know that word. Then it originates a prompted dialogue with the user to learn the new word (Figure 13-8).

```
User:      which company has the highest dollar amount

Computer:  In the last request, I couldn't understand AMOUNT
           In your query, I understand DOLLAR to be a reference to
             a unit of measure or duration, but I can't relate this
             unit with anything else in the query.

Computer:  Enter your request:

User:      dollar amount means number of shares times price per share

Computer:  Should I consider 'DOLLAR AMOUNT' to be a noun phrase,
             which would mean that 'THE DOLLAR AMOUNT' is meaningful?

User:      y

Computer:  Should I consider 'AMOUNT' to be a noun, which would mean
             that 'THE AMOUNT' is meaningful?

User:      yes

Computer:  Should I consider 'DOLLAR' to be an adjective?

User:      yes

Computer:  Should I make this definition a part of your personal
             permanent definition?

User:      yes


Computer:  WHICH COMPANY HAS THE HIGHEST DOLLAR AMOUNT


Computer:                  COMPANY NAME              DOLLAR AMOUNT

           Systems & Comp. Tech Corporation           42570000.00
```

Figure 13-8 Natural language systems can learn new words through interactive dialogues with users. (Frey Associates)

During this dialogue, users may teach Themis either ordinary words applicable to all subject areas, synonyms, or words that are dependent on information in the database. For example, in Figure 13-8, the definition for the phrase "dollar amount" as "number of shares times price per share" is defined based on database information.

Themis prompts the user both for syntactic and semantic information. This includes information such as parts of speech (as shown), and singular and plurals of nouns and verb forms.

Themis employs a mixture of classical syntax analysis with knowledge-based and thematic understanding techniques to analyze and interpret users' queries in light of general knowledge. But it always begins its query analysis with syntax analysis techniques. If the syntax analysis runs into difficulties, the natural-language system tries to make sense out of a query by switching to a thematic understanding mode (Figure 13-9).

In this new mode, Themis gathers information not from production rules or ATNs, but from structures that represent more general knowledge about what is reasonable in the real world. If the thematic procedure is successful, it will feedback information that the syntax analyzer will be able to use to continue its job.

With such a knowledge base, Themis can process a query that asks about a $20,000 salary even though its database tables list only monthly salaries—which clearly are not in a $20,000 price range. Normally, such a query would not make sense because it does not refer to any salary range listed in the database. However, Themis tries to rationalize that salary by checking for any time period for which $20,000 is reasonable.

To rationalize the $20,000 salary, Themis searches its knowledge base for general salary knowledge. From this knowledge, Themis infers that $20,000 is a good yearly salary. Also, it knows that a year is 12 months, and $20,000 is in the range of its monthly salaries multiplied by 12. Therefore, Themis assumes that the user was thinking of yearly salaries, adjusts the figures accordingly, and responds with the anticipated type of answer. Similarly, if the user asks about a salary between $12 and $18, Themis would employ a similar piece of logic and convert its data to hourly salaries.

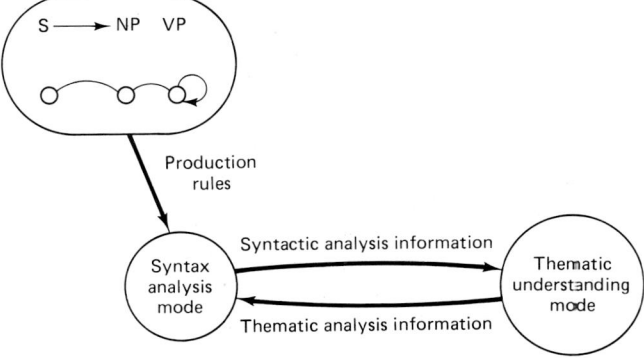

Figure 13-9 Themis uses two techniques to understand user queries.

TRUST THE USER

It has often been said that we learn from our mistakes. However, it is a good thing that we do not learn only from our mistakes because Texas Instruments has gone to great lengths to design a natural-language database query system which ensures that database end users, and even the systems analysts who define specific database interfaces, do not make any.

Called NaturalLink, the TI natural-language query system guarantees correct user queries because at every step in the query-building process it offers users a choice of all the valid words and phrases they can select. Since users can select only from the choices that NaturalLink offers, they are never given the opportunity to make an invalid selection.

NaturalLink runs on PCs and interfaces to company databases on mainframes and minicomputers. It differs from other natural-language systems because they usually require users to generate a natural-language query and the computer to understand it. NaturalLink works in reverse. The computer, under guidance from the user, creates the natural-language query. The user understands it.

To create a query, NaturalLink offers the user a screen divided into windows. Each window contains a different type of word, phrase, or other query element (Figure 13-10).

For example, one window may contain generic nouns from a database, such as parts, shipments, or suppliers. Other windows may contain attributes, qualifiers, connectors (and, or), comparison operators (greater than, equal to), and database operations (find).

Words and phrases from the different windows can be strung together to make up just about any kind of query that is valid for a particular database. Normally, they can also be strung together to make up a number of invalid queries. For this reason, natural-language query systems that allow users to key in free-form words and phrases can produce invalid queries.

COMMANDS:	Find		Find the		Find all	
FEATURES: part number part name quantity supplier name supplier address supplier number color weight	CONNECTORS: and or of the average		QUALIFIERS: which are supplied by whose colors are whose weight is whose shipment number is whose name is whose address is who supply		COMPARISONS: between >= = < > <= <>	
	NOUNS: parts shipments suppliers				ATTRIBUTES: <part number> <quantity> <supplier> <weight> <color>	
QUERY OPERATIONS: BUILD RECALL SAVE DELETE EDIT SHOW EXECUTE						

Figure 13-10 NaturalLink offers the user a screen of windows, each containing a different type of word, phrase, or other query element. (Texas Instruments)

The difference between NaturalLink and other natural-language query systems is that while covering all valid database items and allowable operations, NaturalLink restricts user choices of elements that formulate a query to only valid ones.

Users can make their choices only from certain windows which NaturalLink terms "active" windows. The choice of an item from a window may cause that window to become inactive and determines which windows will become active next. Thus NaturalLink enforces the stringing together of valid choices in a valid order. This guarantees that every query that users ask is valid in the context of the referenced database (Figure 13-11).

The guarantee of correct queries, however, is only as good as the choices that are offered to the user. These choices depend on both the content of the database that NaturalLink interfaces to and the formal database query language. As with other natural-language database interface vocabularies, the database interface choices are defined not by a linguist or natural-language developer, but by a person knowledgeable about the database and its contents. Such a person could be an end user, a data-processing professional, or a system analyst.

To eliminate as many mistakes as possible in defining the choices, as well as to simplify the process of defining a database interface, TI provides a toolkit of interface definition tools. The tools prompt the system analyst or user for database items, phrasing

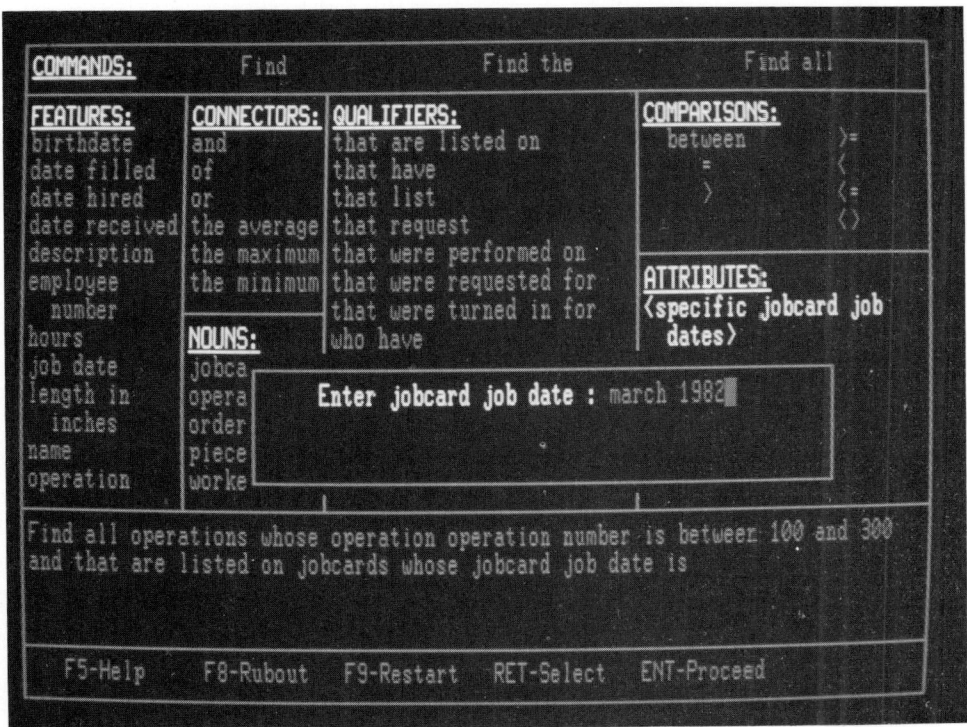

Figure 13-11 NaturalLink users build a query by selecting words and phrases only from allowable windows. (Texas Instruments)

of choices that are offered to users, and database access rights. They also check the analyst's entered information for completeness and errors. Finally, the interface definition tools manage NaturalLink's windows. This window management function is a particularly important function because, as will be seen, NaturalLink's windows perform query building as well as display functions. Thus, if the wrong window is made active, the user will build an incorrect query.

INTERFACING A NATURAL LANGUAGE TO A DATABASE

To guarantee that the user can make only valid selections, the natural-language query system needs at any time to know two things: which windows should be active and what data should be displayed in each active window. To determine the active windows and their data requires three types of input: a grammar, a lexicon, and a screen description (Figure 13-12).

The first component, the grammar, contains the formal rules that specify how words and phrases can be combined correctly. It also contains some information that affects how these words and phrases map into a target database query language. The second, or lexicon, component contains the rest of the information necessary to translate a natural-language query into a target database query language. It also defines the text to be displayed in the screen windows. The third component is the screen description that specifies the placement and content of all windows that are presented to the user.

Information from these components are input to a parser and translator (Figure

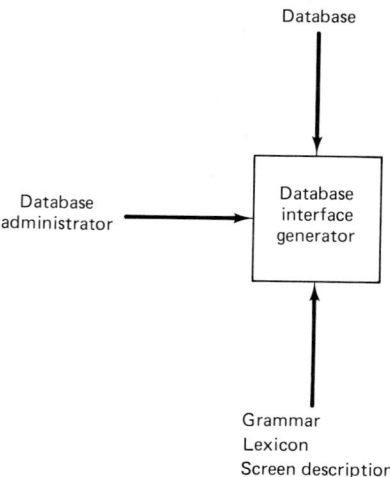

Figure 13-12 To build a NaturalLink database interface, a database administrator determines the active windows and allowable data with the help of a grammar, a lexicon, and a screen description. (Texas Instruments)

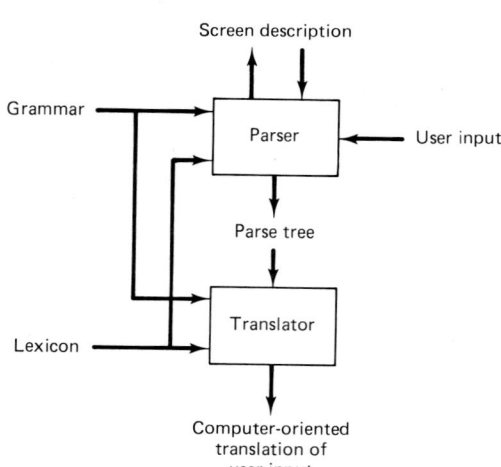

Figure 13-13 NaturalLink's parser and translator accepts inputs from the grammar, lexicon, screen description, and user and generates a query translation for a target database query language. (Texas Instruments)

13-13). The parser and translator parse a sentence into its grammatical elements and perform the translation into the target database query language.

The translation from user query to database query proceeds as follows. First the user selects an item from an active window. Every time the user selects an item, the parser continues to resolve the input into grammatical elements.

WRITING A GRAMMAR

To resolve the sentence into grammatical parts, the parser uses formal rules defined in the natural-language grammar. The grammar rules describe the structure of sentences. Specifically, they describe all the grammatical sentence components, such as noun, verb, and prepositional phrase, down to ordinary words that can be put together in a certain order to form a legitimate sentence. The systems analyst who knows the database and application defines this grammar by determining the sentences that best fit a particular application.

For example, a partial grammar (often called a semantic grammar) shown in Figure 13-14 is defined for the database interface language shown in Figure 13–10. This grammar may be read as follows:

- A sentence may consist of the terminal symbol ''find'' followed by NP (Noun Phrase).
- NP may consist of SHIPMENTS_NP OR PARTS_NP.
- SHIPMENT_NP may consist of an optional element of the SHIPMENT_ATTRIBUTE followed by SHIPMENTS_NOUN.
- SHIPMENT_ATTRIBUTE may consist of the terminal symbol ''supplier.''
- SHIPMENTS_NOUN consists of the terminal symbol ''shipments.''
- And so on.

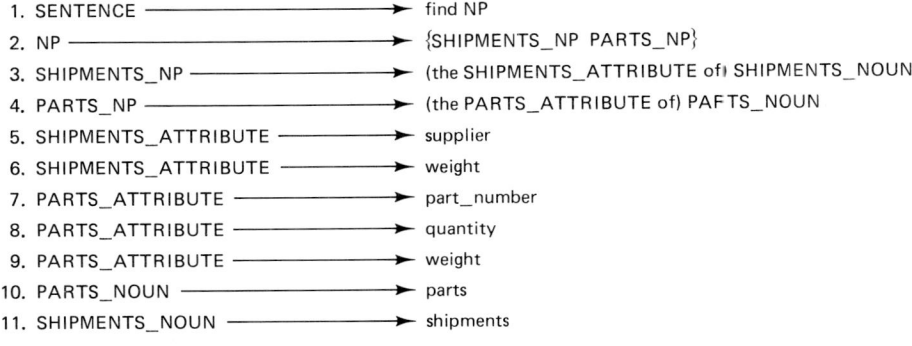

1. SENTENCE ⟶ find NP
2. NP ⟶ {SHIPMENTS_NP PARTS_NP}
3. SHIPMENTS_NP ⟶ (the SHIPMENTS_ATTRIBUTE of) SHIPMENTS_NOUN
4. PARTS_NP ⟶ (the PARTS_ATTRIBUTE of) PAFTS_NOUN
5. SHIPMENTS_ATTRIBUTE ⟶ supplier
6. SHIPMENTS_ATTRIBUTE ⟶ weight
7. PARTS_ATTRIBUTE ⟶ part_number
8. PARTS_ATTRIBUTE ⟶ quantity
9. PARTS_ATTRIBUTE ⟶ weight
10. PARTS_NOUN ⟶ parts
11. SHIPMENTS_NOUN ⟶ shipments

Note: NP means Noun Phrase

Figure 13-14 A partial grammar for a database interface

The left side of each of these rules, called production rules, consists of only one component. Each rule can be rewritten by replacing the left-hand element by the right side of the rule. Therefore, production rules are also called "rewrite" rules or "replacement" rules.

The uppercase symbols shown indicate that those symbols are compound symbols and can be replaced by more fundamental symbols. The lowercase symbols, called terminals, are the most fundamental symbols and cannot be decomposed any further. By performing the replacements indicated by these production rules, the partial grammar shown in the figure can generate and recognize legal sentences such as "Find the suppliers of shipments" and "Find the quantity of parts."

For example, to generate the first sentence, it is necessary first to use rule 1, which says that a sentence can be replaced by "find" followed by a NOUN PHRASE. Rule 2 says that a NOUN PHRASE can be replaced by something called "SHIPMENTS_NP" (shipments noun-phrase). Rule 3 says SHIPMENTS_NP can be replaced by (the SHIPMENTS_ATTRIBUTE of) followed by SHIPMENTS_NOUN. Applying these three rules gives us, at this point, a partial sentence which reads

"Find the SHIPMENTS_ATTRIBUTE OF SHIPMENTS_NOUN."

To generate more of the sentence, it is necessary to apply rule 5, which states that SHIPMENTS_ATTRIBUTE can be replaced by the word "supplier." The sentence now reads

"Find the supplier of SHIPMENTS_NOUN."

One sentence component, SHIPMENTS_NOUN yet needs to be resolved. Rule 11 tells us that SHIPMENTS_NOUN can be replaced by the single word "shipments." With SHIPMENTS_NOUN resolved, the sentence "Find the supplier of shipments" is complete.

When the user issues a natural-language database query, NaturalLink follows a similar procedure to the manual one above. Every time the user selects a word or phrase from an active window, NaturalLink uses its production rules to resolve the query into its grammatical components. From these grammatical components, NaturalLink builds a query sentence which it displays to the user. Ultimately, NaturalLink parses this sentence, analyzes it, and maps it into a formal query which it submits to the underlying database system.

THE GRAMMARIAN

There is nothing particularly difficult about writing a grammar, but the process is error prone. It is easy to overlook errors that range from missing parentheses and leaving out some rules that represent allowable sentences to inconsistencies with the query system lexicon.

To avoid mistakes, the TI natural-language toolkit contains a Grammarian which assists the system analyst by checking a grammar for several kinds of errors. First, it checks for formal errors such as use of proper syntax to form rules, balanced braces, and the inclusion of only valid characters.

Second, the Grammarian checks to see if the grammar contains any hanging parts that are not reachable. For example, a rule in the Figure 13-14 grammar such as "ORDER_ATTRIBUTE→quantity" cannot be reached from any sentence generated by this grammar. It is unreachable because although the word "quantity" is part of the grammar, "ORDER_ATTRIBUTE" is not.

A third check tests whether or not two or more rules have a common replacement. Such a situation would create an ambiguous situation. The fourth check, for inconsistent translation, tests each grammar rule for wellformedness of the translation information. Finally, the fifth check makes sure that the grammar does not contain a sequence of rules that permit an infinite number of parses.

LEXICONS...

The NaturalLink parser plays a number of nontraditional as well as traditional roles. On the traditional side, it uses the grammar and user input to build a tree structure (called a parse tree) that describes the syntactical relationships of the user input.

The parser passes this parse tree to the translator. The translator examines the tree to identify the newest grammatical component. It then uses the lexicon to get the text needed to map the new grammatical component to a database query language. Since the lexicon contains the translation text for the terminal symbols that reside in the grammar, information in the grammar and lexicon must be consistent.

The parser also requires other, less traditional information that is generally stored in the lexicon, such as information about NaturalLink's windows. For example, the information in the grammar and the lexicon, as well as the progression of phrases selected by the user from active windows, constrains which windows and contents of windows the users can choose from to construct a query. Based on the system grammar, lexicon, and previous user selections, the parser modifies the presentation of active and inactive windows, and decides which window contents should appear or be removed.

To control these windows and therefore ensure correct user queries, the parser must know both the window and the location within the window of each "terminal" component of the user language. This information is contained in the lexicon.

...AND THE LEXICOGRAPHER

As can be seen, the creation of a lexicon can be a messy task. It normally requires the system analyst or programmer to understand, and remember, the details of the internal structure of the lexicon and manually format the data using a text editor.

The Lexicographer that the natural-language toolkit provides eliminates much of the mess and detail by either simplifying or actually performing some of the normal user tasks. For example, the Lexicographer prompts the analyst for information about the data items contained in the database that the interface will reference, the target language phrases that the English selections map to, and the screen description.

System analysts can input this information in a format convenient for them. The Lexicographer then reformats the analysts' input into the form required by the internal structure of the lexicon.

The Lexicographer also checks the lexicon against the grammar to make sure that the complete set of "terminal" grammatical components are matched by translation text in the lexicon. This frees the analyst from the burden of checking the lexicon for completeness by inspection.

THE SCREENBUILDER

Since screens containing groupings of windows that each hold various kinds of information influence NaturalLink's query understanding process, the screens and windows need more careful specification than a system that uses them solely for display purposes. So the TI natural-language toolkit contains a ScreenBuilder tool which helps the analyst specify window descriptions.

The window descriptions include window characteristics such as display coordinates, size, and contents of each window. To facilitate quick and easy changes to a window, ScreenBuilder keeps the window descriptions in a file rather than embedded in program code. This allows system analysts to easily add new window descriptions to the file and modify and delete existing windows.

PUT IT TOGETHER

For a natural-language interface to work correctly, its components must be coordinated and compatible with one another. A NaturalLink toolkit utility called the Coordinator helps the analyst to coordinate the various functional parts of the interface.

Coordination is necessary because the various functional parts of the interface—grammar, lexicon, and window—depend on each other. For example, the contents of the lexicon is a function of the grammar. Both the grammar and the lexicon determine the contents of windows.

In addition, the set of currently active windows and the set of selectable items within the windows are a function of the grammatical components currently selected by the user. If the parser determines from the grammar that a specific window is to be made inactive at a stage of a parse, and if that window is not defined, an error will result.

Among its functions, the Coordinator ensures that if changes are made in one component, all possible affected components will be checked and the corresponding changes also made. It also checks the specification of the grammar and lexicon and notifies the analyst if any windows are referenced but not defined, or defined but not referenced.

Finally, the Coordinator can, from a completed grammar, construct a set of statements that can be used to test all grammatical paths.

NATURAL LANGUAGES AND FOURTH-GENERATION LANGUAGES

The natural-language database front ends described so far are limited to retrieval capabilities only. Martin Marietta Data Systems has partially circumvented this limitation by adding "English," its natural-language interface, to Ramis II, its fourth-generation programming and database language.

Both languages are very high level English or English-like languages. Fourth-generation languages, however, require much more stylized and constrained English than natural-language systems. For example, a typical "English" (the natural-language extension) query is "TELL ME HOW MANY SALESPERSONS ARE IN THE NORTHEAST." English might respond with "17." The user can then say "LIST THEM." The system will remember the previous query, flesh out the missing sentence parts, and list those 17 salespersons. Moreover, users can specify their queries in various ways, including Ramis II, that will all be understood by "English" (Figure 13-15). The more constrained English of Ramis II requires a user to phrase the same query as "PRINT NAME IF REGION IS NORTHEAST AND IF JOB TITLE IS SALESPERSON."

It is important at this point to note that although fourth-generation languages are more stylized and constrained than natural languages, they are, as mentioned, English-like. True, they require more training to use than natural language. However, they bear no resemblance to the more cryptic, difficult-to-learn, formal programming languages such as Cobol, Fortran, or PL/1.

Which system—natural language or fourth-generation language—is most effective depends on the type of user. Applied Data Research (ADR) has identified three classes of users: expert, frequent, and infrequent or naive. According to Kenneth Sloan, product manager at ADR, for the expert or frequent user, the more structured systems are the most efficient. Whatever the user types in has been explicitly specified by the language. There is no need for structured language systems to try to interpret what the user really meant. Consequently, they provide the least ambiguity and the most reliable results.

To make the computer accessible to the infrequent or naive user, however, Sloan points out the necessity to provide natural-language facilities, even though it provides more ambiguity, costs more to provide the service, and sometimes is less reliable.

The advantage of combining Ramis II and "English" into one system, or for that matter extending any fourth-generation database language with a natural language, is the ability to switch between the two. It is not only that users can switch to the more stylized Ramis to update the database and to the more natural "English" to query it. Users can also switch between the languages to avoid problems that may arise when users try to use natural language for detailed operations such as complex printouts of reports. In addition, novices can use "English" as a start-up query language and as an aid to the gradual learning of Ramis since, upon request, the combination system will display the Ramis II equivalent of an English language query.

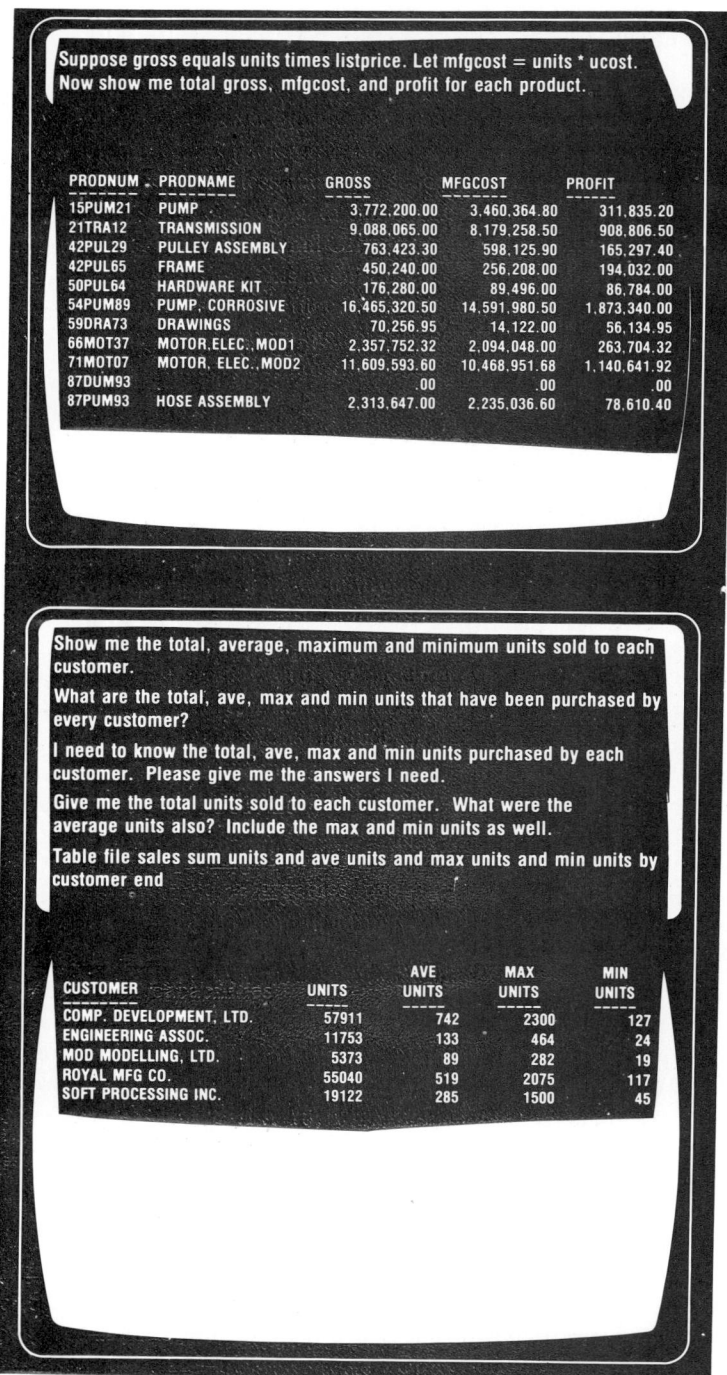

Figure 13-15 Ramis can specify database queries in various ways, using natural language or a fourth generation language. The first four queries are equivalent English language versions. The fifth, also equivalent, query is written in Ramis II. (Martin Marietta Data Systems)

It turns out that while natural languages are easily understandable by people, unnatural computer languages are more natural to computers because they are oriented toward computer rather than human functions. The result is that it is frequently difficult to use natural language to request a complex printout with specific headings, organization of data, and a visually pleasing look. It may actually be easier to specify such reports in the more compact Ramis II. For that reason, some users and analysts interchange "English" and Ramis, depending on the queries and reports they want.

Unconventional Natural-Language Technologies for Micros

CHAPTER 14

Years ago, only computing professionals used database management systems to manage and access data stored in computers. But it is human nature to rapidly get used to new developments. So, soon, noncomputing professionals also wanted to manage and access their data on a computer.

Natural-language database interfaces provided the opportunity for them to do so. Economics, however, dictates that noncomputing professionals are more likely to store their data on microcomputers rather than on larger mainframes or minicomputers. And while some natural-language systems designed for large-scale computers have been shoehorned into micros, many natural-language system developers feel that different techniques are needed for personal computers in order to maximize natural-language understanding in a scaled-down environment.

NaturalLink, discussed in Chapter 13, had micros in mind when its designers required users to select query words and phrases only from those offered in computer windows, instead of allowing free-form queries. This multiple-choice technique has two goals. One, relevant to both micros and large-scale machines, is to prevent users from asking invalid questions. A further goal and advantage to restricting the users' choices of words and phrases is the elimination of the need for the natural-language system to interpret the same question asked many different ways. As a result, the system requires less memory to interpret users' queries accurately and unambiguously. This makes it easier to implement the natural-language interface on personal computers.

Although NaturalLink runs on micros, its basic technology for understanding users' queries is a variant of the classical combination of syntactic and semantic analysis (Chapters 12 and 13), originally targeted at large-scale machines. Despite its advantages, clearly some users will prefer systems that permit them to issue free-form queries.

This preference creates problems for many micros becausse classical syntactic/semantic systems require large amounts of memory and processing power to parse, accurately interpret, and clarify the many variants of legitimate sentences, as well as ambiguous, poorly phrased, and incomplete free-form queries. Syntactic/semantic analysis is one of the two major approaches to natural language and is the technique that underlies most existing natural languages today. The second major natural-language technology relies on encoding knowledge about a subject area in a type of frame called a "script." (This is a state-of-the-art technique that is discussed in detail in Chapter 15.) A scripts-based approach to natural language also requires a large amount of processing and memory for its operation. It has still another characteristic that may make it unsuitable for microcomputer databases. Database interfaces that contain encoded subject knowledge, require a priori knowledge of what subject users will ask about. But microcomputer databases are frequently geared to mass markets. Therefore, they must be general-purpose systems, whose strength is the ability to contain information about a variety of unanticipated subjects.

With microcomputer users pushing for easy access to their databases, and considering the limitations that existing natural-language systems pose for small-scale machines, designers of natural-language systems for micros are looking for more drastically different natural-language technologies adapted to microcomputer characteristics. Two new microcomputer-oriented commercial approaches to natural language are emerging. One approach uses knowledge-based system heuristic techniques to interpret user queries. The other employs pattern-recognition techniques that are similar to those that biological organisms use to intetpret speech and visual signals.

These approaches have not eliminated the traditional syntactic/semantic approach to natural-language, even on micros. The traditional approach is particularly effective for certain tasks, such as resolving ambiguities and handling conditions in queries (limitations placed on data to be selected such as "sales between $10,000 and $17,000" or "last name begins with Mc"). So borrowing the best of different worlds, designers of microcomputer-oriented natural-language systems are integrating traditional natural-language approaches with techniques borrowed from knowledge system and pattern-recognition fields. This integrated approach provides greater microcomputer language-understanding power with less memory.

INTEGRATING KNOWLEDGE SYSTEMS WITH SYNTAX ANALYSIS

Typical of a microcomputer-oriented approach to natural-language is Clout (from Microrim). A natural-language program, Clout uses a combination syntactic/semantic and rule-based knowledge system approach to interface to Microrim's R:Base series of general-purpose relational database management systems. A relational database management system is a database system that views its data as a collection of tables or files, called relations (Figure 14-1). Rows in a relation correspond to individual records in a file. Columns are analogous to fields in a file or individual types of information on a file card.

Because the table format of relational databases is one that people are accustomed to working with, relational databases are the easiest to learn and the most popular kind of

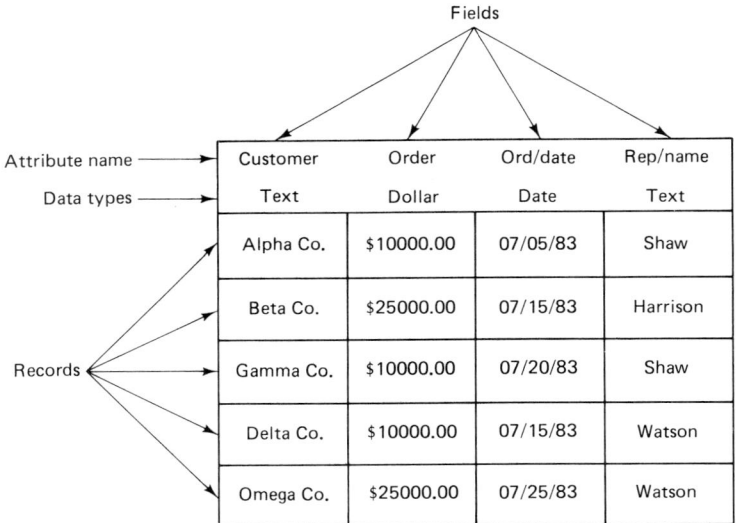

Figure 14-1 A single relation

microcomputer databases. However, when requested information is stored not in one relation (table) but is scattered in three or more, relational queries can become complex. Hence there is a motivation for developing natural-language interfaces to relational databases.

Like many natural-language database interfaces, Clout accepts users' unconstrained English-language queries. Queries need not all be stand-alone, complete sentences. As in human conversation, Clout can understand query fragments in the context of previous queries (Figure 14-2). With such queries, pronouns provide one clue to the possibility that a query refers to a previous request. So does the determination of whether the query makes sense as a stand-alone query. Finally, if Clout encounters an unfamiliar term in a user's query, it interrupts its dialogue with the user and asks for a temporary or permanent dictionary definition (Figure 14-3).

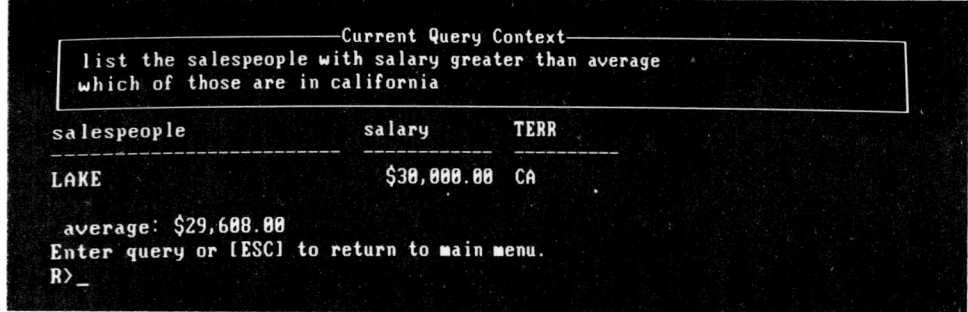

Figure 14-2 Clout understands query fragments in the context of previous queries. (Microrim, Inc.)

```
                    ─Current Query Context─
    list the salespeople with salary greater than average
    which of those are in california
    are there any poor performers


  Did not understand: poor performers
  Please enter a synonym or change spelling.
  R>salespeople with sales less than plan

  Do you want to make this a permanent definition? (Y/N)..............
```

Figure 14-3 Clout asks the user for definitions of unknown words. (Microrim Inc.)

Interactive definition capabilities are not only useful but are necessary in natural-language applications where computer professionals are not on-hand to define new lexicon words. Such situations are particularly relevant to microcomputer users. In departments of large organizations, the overburdened data-processing department frequently prefers microcomputer users to attend to this task independently. Small businesses may not have a data-processing department, in which case microcomputer users are on their own.

However, the interactive definition capability can have an annoying side. Although words such as "LIST," "GIVE ME," and "HOW MANY" are standard database vocabulary words, many other words are peculiar to individual users. Consequently, the first few weeks of working with a natural-language system can turn into a guessing game where the language system seems to understand nothing and prompts the user to define everything. The situation is similar to translating a foreign-language document where the meaning of almost every word must be looked up.

A recommended procedure for new natural-language system users, which avoids this guess-what-I-mean situation, is to inaugurate the dictionary by defining as many synonyms and definitions as they can think of the first time they use the system. Such a procedure takes about 30 minutes in a system like Clout, which walks new users through the database and prompts them for synonyms for database attribute (field) names. The procedure results in the system instantly knowing a large percentage of the user's vocabulary. After this, it is a matter of convenience to be able to interactively define other new words as they occur.

MICROCOMPUTER PROCESSING

Three design features of Clout help make up for the scaled-down environment of micros (Figure 14-4). Clout sparingly uses syntactic/semantic techniques which are processing-intensive. It parses sentences into components such as database attributes (names of fields or records in a relation, such as "employee" or "address"), comparison operators (greater than, equal to), and values (in the database fields), rather than into grammatical components. It uses knowledge system rules and heuristics (rules of thumb) to understand bad grammar, and queries worded in different ways, to navigate through the database, and to limit the searching of databases for information.

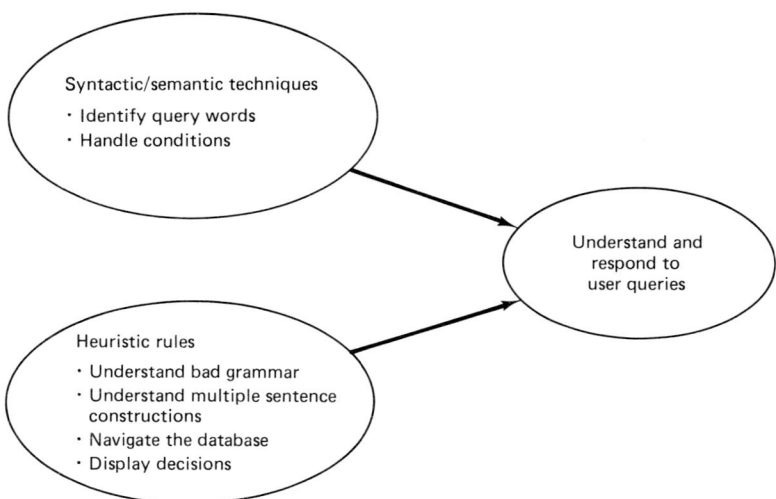

Figure 14-4 Clout's language understanding techniques

NONGRAMMATICAL ATNs

Clout uses augmented transition networks (ATNs) to parse a user's request into possible interpretations (Chapter 12). ATNs are groups of node and arc graphs, called transition networks. The arcs are labeled with sentence components that must be found to get to the next sentence parsing state, represented by nodes (Figure 14-5). These transition networks are augmented with registers that give the natural-language program the ability to store and remember information aobut the components it has found. The program uses the stored information to construct phrases from individual components, sentences from phrases, and to make decisions about the grammatical role of a new component, based on previous components found and the partial sentence already constructed. (Without registers, once the program used a component to move to a new node, it would forget the component, and when it reached the end of the transition network, it would be able to say only that it parsed the input sentence successfully and therefore the sentence was legal.)

ATNs in Clout differ from classical ATNs in that Clout's arcs do not specify grammatical components. Instead, they specify database information such as attributes, comparison operators, and values (Figure 14-6).

Using these arc labels to parse and interpret the query "SHOW ME THE EM-

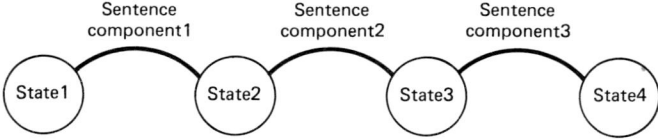

Figure 14-5 Clout's augmented transition networks

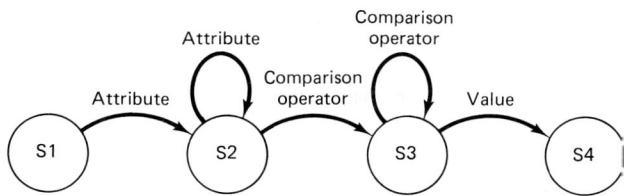

Figure 14-6 Localized augmented transition network to handle a simple comparison. This net catches comparisons such as, salaries greater than 40K, and names beginning with Mc. (Microrim Inc.)

PLOYEES WITH SALARIES GREATER THAN $40,000,'' Clout first identifies the word SHOW from its lexicon as equivalent to a command to list something.* To find out what to list, Clout examines the rest of the query and looks for database attributes. Finding two of them consecutively, it moves first from state 1 to state 2 on the attribute ''EMPLOYEES,'' and from state 2 again to state 2 on the attribute ''SALARY.'' The next arc in the transition network specifies a comparison operator, and thus Clout moves to state 3 based on the requested comparison ''GREATER THAN.'' The sentence parse and the transition network traversal are both complete as Clout moves to state 4 when it finds the value of $40,000.

In the case of a compound sentence, such as ''SHOW ME THE EMPLOYEES WITH SALARIES GREATER THAN $40,000 AND LAST NAMES THAT BEGIN WITH A,'' Clout parses the first segment of the query that ends with $40,000 and stores the information from that ATN in table form. Then it takes a similar pass through the lexicon and other (or same) ATN to parse the second segment of the query. With the query parsing complete, Clout combines the information obtained from its lexicon and ATNs in order to translate a complete query into a formal database request.

LIMITS OF ATNs

Neither the database query translation, nor the full query parsing necessary for the translation, are wholy accomplished by ATNs in Clout. Knowledge-based heuristic rules also play a large role in these tasks because they reduce the amount of time and processing needed to analyze the complex structures of natural-language.

Some of the difficulties in an exclusively ATN-based approach to natural-language on microcomputers become clear by pointing out the large number of ATNs needed to fully interpret queries. Multiple ATNs are needed to translate each of the many different grammatical constructions that express the same query. Multiple ATNs are also needed to handle incomplete or badly phrased queries.

For example, ''LIST THE SECRETARIES IN CHICAGO'' and ''LIST THE CHICAGO SECRETARIES'' both translate to the same formal database inquiry. Yet they each require different transition networks for their translation.

Even the existence of multiple ATNs to handle all legitimately phrased queries is

*Clout examples supplied by Geoffrey von Limbach.

inadequate to provide full natural-language understanding because people's queries are not always grammatically correct or stated in complete sentences. There are two ATN-based approaches to handling bad grammar and incomplete sentences. With one, the natural-language system tries to parse a query with the normal ATN rules. If that proves impossible, it relaxes the rules and tries again.

With the second approach, the natural-language system has two types of ATNs. One type includes the full set of ATNs for parsing legitimately phrased sentences. The other includes ATNs for parsing sentence fragments and grammatically poor constructions.

Clout's approach is comparable to human beings who instinctively recognize the various proper and improper sentence constructions that express the same query. Clout has encoded some of these instinctive recognition methods in knowledge system rules. The system's developers admit that the rules are not perfect but say they work often enough to be useful. In addition, the modularity of knowledge system rules allows them to be continuously refined and new rules added to cover exceptions. Finally, incorporation of knowledge system rules eliminates much of the time needed to analyze syntax. This rule-based approach makes the natural-language system more efficient for microcomputer applications.

A KNOWLEDGE SYSTEM APPROACH

A typical Clout heuristic rule that avoids much syntax analysis states that

IF: A QUERY HAS A DATABASE ENTRY
AND IT IS NOT NEXT TO SOME SORT OF CONDITION (SUCH AS SALARIES GREATER THAN $12,000)
THEN: INSTEAD OF PARSING THE SENTENCE WITH AN ATN, PICK OUT THE ROWS IN THE DATABASE THAT CONTAIN THE REQUESTED VALUE.

Clout uses this heuristic to process the queries "LIST THE SECRETARIES IN CHICAGO" and "LIST THE CHICAGO SECRETARIES." It does not matter whether SECRETARIES and CHICAGO are nouns, adjectives, or parts of prepositional phrases because they are both database entries. Therefore, following the direction in the rule, Clout discontinues its ATN processing and heads for the database. There it notes that "SECRETARIES" is found in the database job title field, and "CHICAGO" is in the city field, and the requested values are available for the asking.

A more difficult-to-handle example occurs in the analysis of the similar queries "SHOW ME THE PARTS OF THE PUMP THAT WERE FIXED BY JOE" versus "SHOW ME THE PARTS OF THE PUMP THAT WAS FIXED BY JOE." The first of these sentences (parts that were) refers to the parts that Joe fixed. The second (pump that was) refers to the pump that Joe fixed.

An ATN-based approach requires much syntax analysis to resolve the agreement between the verb (fixed) and the referent (which could be parts or pumps) in order to translate this sentence to the intended formal database inquiry. A heuristic rule might direct Clout to bypass the ATNs if it finds that the referenced database contains fields either for parts or for pumps. This would eliminate the need to resolve the verb and referent agreement issue, thus saving time and processing.

The ATN approach, however, has proven the most useful method of parsing queries with conditions because it requires a relatively simple set of ATNs. The ATN in Figure 14-6 is typical. Similar simple ATNs suffice for complex conditions involving expressions, lists of attributes, and sorting of information into unusual orders. In contrast, a heuristic approach to identifying conditions usually results in a system with a lot of heuristics. Therefore, Clout uses ATNs for identifying conditions, selecting lists for output, and sorting. It reserves heuristics for resolution of ambiguities, database searches, joining parsed sentence segments, and translation of user queries into formal database inquiries.

DATABASE SEARCHES

Clout employs heuristics to limit database searches because the heuristics guide it first to the most likely relations (tables) that contain the requested information. This reduction of processing becomes increasingly important in cases where the data that users requested are scattered in many relations.

A request for data that are contained in one relation, such as "LIST THE PRODUCTION WORKERS IN THE NEW YORK CITY DIVISION," is a simple matter. However, a personnel manager might want a one-time answer to the question "WHICH PRODUCTION WORKERS HAD LESS THAN 20 TOTAL TRAINING HOURS IN 1985?" The training records and department information might be in two separate relations or files. Other requests might require data that span, for example, five relations.

The process of retrieving data located in multiple relations involves finding the data requested in two relations with a common field. The two tables are then joined, using the common field, to form a new relation that contains the desired data and the common field from each of the original tables (Figure 14-7). Other tables containing other desired data are similarly joined with each other, and with the newly formed relation, until finally a relation is formed that contains all the desired data. The user's data are retrieved from this relation. Unfortunately, the searching and linking of multiple relations in this way is time consuming. Heuristics in Clout optimize and speed this process.

For example, Clout heuristics may direct Clout to look in relations where some things mentioned in the user query are already known. Another heuristic may guide Clout to count how many facts are known about various relations and first examine the relations about which the most information is known. Still other heuristics may favor looking in short relations first or in relations that were involved in the previous question that the user asked.

These heuristics are some of the instinctive techniques of human beings that are encoded in the program. Most people, for example, would find the salespeople that work for the IBM Corp. in a Hong Kong office by first accessing the files of the Hong Kong office and then searching for salespeople. The alternative, examining the files of all IBM salespeople, then determining which ones work out of Hong Kong, is likely to result in a search of far more voluminous files.

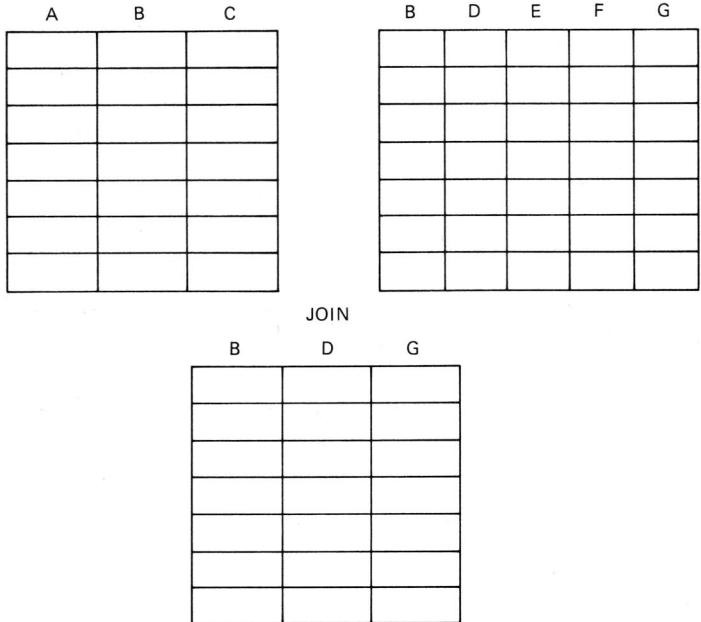

Figure 14-7 Retrieving data from two relations via a "join" operation.

DISPLAYING THE APPROPRIATE DATA

To a computer, a request for the top three salespeople in Hong Kong could refer to an alphabetical listing, or a listing by sales, salary, or other criteria. Deciding how to display the requested data to the user entails deciding how to handle the conditions imposed, how to sort the data and by what, and whether to group the data together and by what. This is a complex problem that human beings handle through common sense and experience and which is driven by Clout's heuristic, rather than syntactic, techniques.

How heuristics handle data display is too involved a subject to discuss here in great detail. Typically, however, a rule-based natural-language system might perform some tasks and use the following heuristics to decide on ranking criteria (von Limbach and Taylor, 1984). For example, the request

```
SHOW ME THE TOP 3 SALARIES
```

implies ranking the output by some criterion. An appropriate heuristic might be

```
Heuristic 1: THE RANKING CRITERION FOLLOWS THE "TOP N"
             PHRASE.
```

This heuristic directs the natural-language system to rank the requested database values by salaries, because in the query, the attribute SALARY follows TOP N (top 3). However, the request

```
                SHOW ME THE TOP 3 SALESPEOPLE RANKED BY SALES
```

requires a modification of the original heuristic. The modification is necessary because SALESPEOPLE follows the TOP N phrase. There are many ways to rank salespeople, but in this query, the ranking criterion is specifically mentioned in the query. A possible refinement might be

```
            Heuristic 2:  THE RANKING CRITERION FOLLOWS THE
                          TOP N PHRASE UNLESS THE CRITERIA
                          IS SPECIFICALLY MENTIONED ELSEWHERE.
```

Further refinement, or a new heuristic, is needed for the query that asks

```
                    SHOW ME THE TOP 3 SALESPEOPLE.
```

From experience we know that the user probably does not want the people whose last name begins with an "A" (alphabetical ranking). In the real world, people have a greater tendency to rank by numerics. Therefore, a heuristic might say the following:

```
            Heuristic 3:  UNLESS PEOPLE EXPLICITLY STATE IN THEIR
                          QUERY, "RANKED BY SALESPEOPLE," THEN ASK
                          THE USER "RANKED BY WHAT?"
```

FROM QUERY TO RESPONSE

Heuristic 3 points up one method that Clout employs to cope with unknown information necessary to respond to a user's query—it asks the user. However, the user is only one source of information toward understanding natural-language queries and building a formal database request (Figure 14-8).

Clout begins its natural-language processing tasks by matching query words and phrases with those in its application dictionary and then in its internal dictionary (lexicon). The application dictionary contains user-defined words such as synonyms for database attributes, user definitions (including arithmetic expressions) such as profits equals sales minus expenses, and general vocabulary, for example to initiate standard reports. In contrast, the internal dictionary is factory defined, shipped with the natural-language system, and contains standard database request words. These include prepositions, articles, pronouns, arithmetic operators, comparison operators, and subtotal phrases. Other generic lexicon vocabulary includes request words such as "list," phrases that indicate sorts such as "by" or "for each," and conjunctions such as "and," "or," and "not." Synonyms

274 Unconventional Natural-Language Technologies for Micros

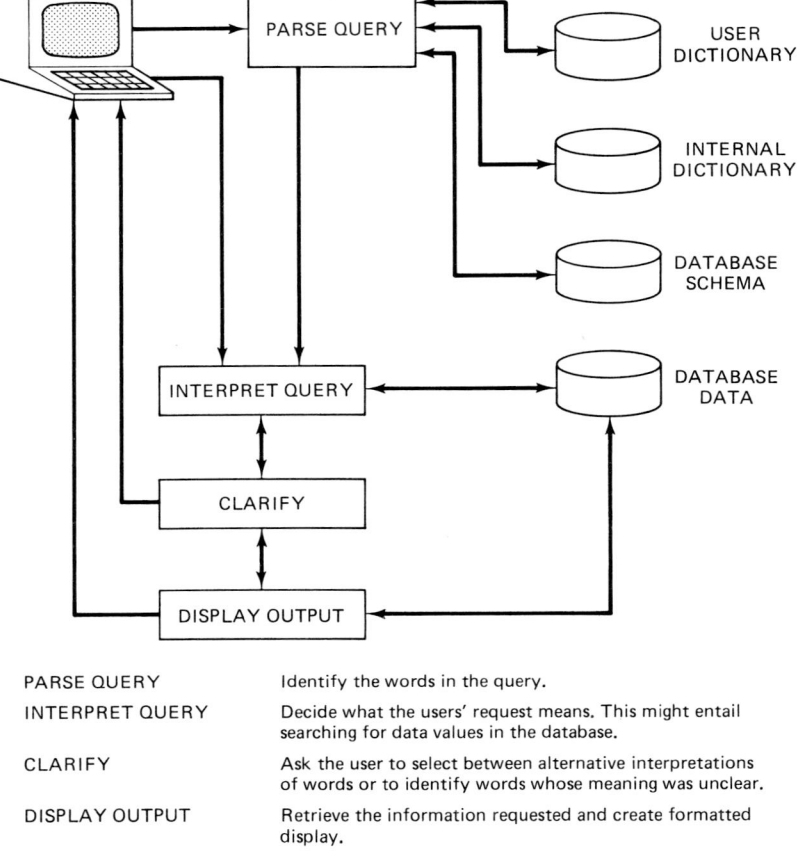

PARSE QUERY	Identify the words in the query.
INTERPRET QUERY	Decide what the users' request means. This might entail searching for data values in the database.
CLARIFY	Ask the user to select between alternative interpretations of words or to identify words whose meaning was unclear.
DISPLAY OUTPUT	Retrieve the information requested and create formatted display.

Figure 14-8 Clout's sources for language understanding. (Microrim Inc.)

for these words may be defined in the application dictionary. When matching query with dictionary words, if a choice exists, Clout selects the longest expressions first. For example, given the choice of "west coast" and "west coast salespeople," Clout replaces the longer phrase with its dictionary meaning. Although Clout expands users' queries by replacing words with longer definitions, it still retains knowledge of the original query words. For example, if Clout replaces the term "profits" with "sales minus expenses," it can still handle queries that refer to profits. In addition, unlike most spelling checkers, Clout understands various tenses and inflections of words such as plurals and present and past participles.

With matching of query and dictionary words complete, Clout seeks out information it needs from both the database schema and the database. The schema refers to the structure and organization of the database, the types of information contained, and the relationships between the data. The database is the set of tables that contains the actual data.

Both types of knowledge are necessary to select and process database fields and retrieve the specifically requested data. As explained, for this type of processing, Clout uses both parsing and heuristic techniques. Parsing, for example, is the choice to identify conditions. Clout uses heuristic rules to bypass the parser and resolve ambiguity with database help or to efficiently search the database.

When all else fails, Clout assumes that the user request is a legitimate one that happens to include a new word or phrase. Therefore, it asks the user to identify unrecognized words or phrases as data from the database, retype the word or phrase, omit the word or phrase from the request, or define the word to the language program.

Once the terminology and context is resolved, the user's request must be converted into a formal database inquiry, the requested data retrieved from the database, and the retrieved data displayed for the user. Conversion to a formal database inquiry is an internal mapping procedure. The task of displaying data in listed, grouped, sorted, totaled, or subsetted formats, however, is performed mostly by heuristic rules that in many ways parallel human styles of understanding natural language queries and returning the requested information.

TALK LIKE THE ANIMALS

No one knows how human beings understand natural language. Nonetheless, it is clear that certain observed human styles of operating, thinking, and interpreting the environment can be used to build useful computerized systems that understand natural language. An example of human styles of doing things that have been incorporated into a natural-language system is Clout's heuristic rules. Many of these rules contain or imply knowledge of what makes sense in the world.

Like Clout, the Savvy natural-language database interface and programming language (from Excalibur Technologies, Inc.) also borrows techniques from biological organisms to help understand natural-language queries. Like Clout, Savvy combines its biologically based techniques with the classical syntactic and semantic techniques. Like Clout, Savvy is microcomputer-oriented. But except for these similarities, the two systems employ drastically different underlying technologies.

To understand natural-language queries, Savvy uses pattern-recognition techniques similar to those used by biological organisms, together with the syntactic and semantic techniques used in classical natural-language systems (Figure 14-9). The two techniques work cooperatively with each other. The combination of technologies allows Savvy to fit into only 24 kilobytes of memory. At the same time, the Savvy technologies require less computer processing than other natural-language systems to understand queries. The small memory and processing requirements allow Savvy to operate on a range of very small to large microcomputers.

Small, however, does not mean limited. Because of its underlying technologies, Savvy can often handle a broader range of common street-language wording than is possible with larger-scale natural-language query systems and programming languages.

Savvy's technique (Excalibur calls it adaptive pattern recognition processing) is to

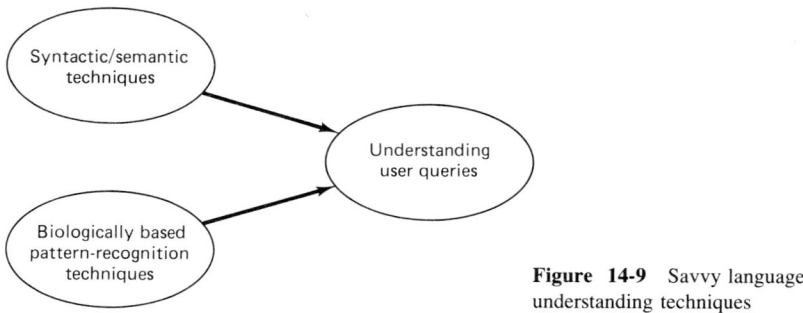

Figure 14-9 Savvy language understanding techniques

start out with a number of built-in programs and associated names. For example, "LIST THE ACCOUNTS RECEIVABLE BALANCES" might be the name of a program that does just that.

To determine the memory address of this program, Savvy performs a number of mathematical transformations on the string (group) of characters that comprises the database query. The transformations are based on a general-purpose pattern-recognition algorithm that operates on many types of data, such as voice or video. The final result of that transformation is the actual memory address (Figure 14-10). Thus the name of the program determines the address of the program in computer memory.

This address generation technique provides flexibility that allows for misspelling or inexact wording of queries. For example, if a user keys in a slightly dissimilar command, such as "LIST THE ACCOUNTS RECEIVABLE BALANCES FOR ME," Savvy performs its transformation on the slightly different string, generates a new address, but finds

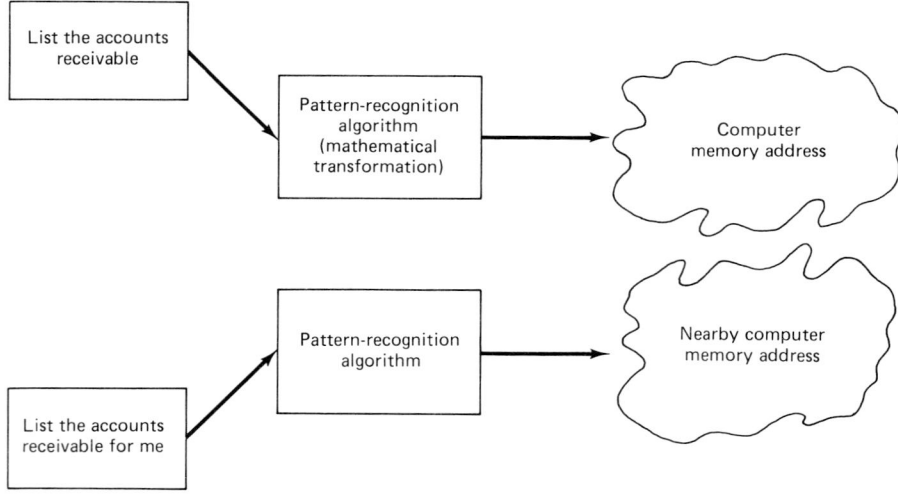

Figure 14-10 The name of a program or query determines its computer address.

nothing there. However, it does find that the original program, with a similar name, resides nearby in memory. Therefore, it concludes that this is what the user means and responds accordingly. If, however, the address turns out to be equidistant from a number of programs, it presents the user with the list of programs and asks which one is the desired one.

Savvy is extendible—a necessary feature for dealing with all kinds of human language. Users who decide that "LIST THE ACCOUNTS RECEIVABLE BALANCES" is too formal can teach Savvy to recognize, as a synonym, "WHO OWES ME MONEY?" (in any language). The user need only type the instruction "ASSOCIATE," the original command "LIST THE ACCOUNTS RECEIVABLE BALANCES," and the synonym "WHO OWES ME MONEY?" Savvy then performs its transformation. However, at the computer address generated by "WHO OWES ME MONEY?" it inserts a pointer to the address (stores the address) generated by "LIST THE ACCOUNTS RECEIVABLE BALANCES" (Figure 14-11). Subsequent user queries that request of Savvy "WHO OWES ME MONEY?" follow that pointer to the original program and print out a list of the accounts receivable balances.

Although simple, and fairly flexible, if this technique were used exclusively it would limit Savvy in terms of recognizing ambiguities. For example, "WHICH DOG BIT A MAN?" and "WHICH MAN BIT A DOG?" both generate the same address. The inability to discriminate between such address-equivalent queries is the reason that Excalibur added limited syntactic/semantic techniques to the system. With these combinations of techniques, Savvy can understand ambiguities that caused the original, solely-pattern-recognition-based version to fail. For example, the original version collapsed when a user taught it the phrase "FIRST ONE," and later "ONE FIRST," and then typed in "GIVE ME THE FIRST ONE FIRST." To avoid such a collapse, the integrated version passes the ambiguous query to the syntactic/semantic component, which parses and analyzes it using classical techniques.

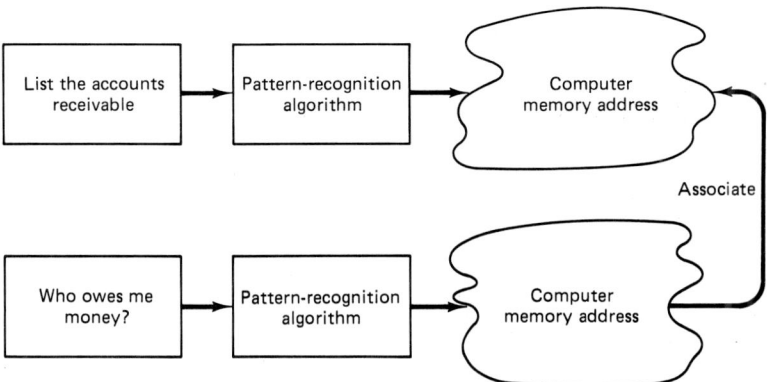

Figure 14-11 Extending Savvy

THE BIOLOGY ANGLE IN NATURAL-LANGUAGE PROCESSING

Pattern-recognition techniques such as Savvy's are well known in the areas of acoustic and optical recognition. However pattern recognition was invented not by man, but by nature. Evidence has it that as part of the brain's process of understanding the outside world, receptors in the ears and eyes receive acoustic and optical signals, convey them randomly to scattered areas of the brain to form various patterns, and then attach meaning to the patterns formed.

It is not known why biological organisms randomize the incoming signals before interpreting them. However, it turns out that this technique greatly reduces the size of the processing area and amount of processing necessary to understand complex speech and visual patterns and differentiate patterns from one another.

Biological evidence strongly indicates, however, that there is a blending of pattern recognition and rule-based systems in nature. For example, a rule that pertains to visual images in frogs—viewed most often as a pattern-recognition activity—states that certain neurons in the eye of a frog will fire an impulse if and only if an object is black and moves across the frog's eye from left to right.

Similarly, Savvy's syntactic and semantic techniques, combined with Savvy's pattern recognizer, are also examples of a rule-based pattern-recognition system. Instead of visual imagery, the rules pertain to how to put together words and phrases to make legal, meaningful sentences.

INSIDE A LANGUAGE/SPEECH RECOGNITION SYSTEM

Savvy's developers latched on to pattern-recognition techniques as the technology underlying their natural-language query system because the query system evolved out of the work that they were doing in speech recognition. (In fact, Savvy still performs speech recognition as well as text understanding).

The switchover to a natural-language query system and programming language began because a large amount of capital is required to commercialize speech-recognition implementations and the marketplace is currently small. At the same time, Savvy's developers realized that their biologically oriented speech-pattern-recognition techniques could be applied to text understanding and provide similar benefits and new capabilities.

For example, speech recognition requires the ability to distinguish different sounds, accents, and slurred words—all of which entails the recognition and processing of a large number and variety of signals and patterns.

In a manner which can be viewed as analogous to that used for speech recognition, Savvy treats input letters, that make up words and phrases, as just another incoming signal. Normally, the receptors for different sound or optical signals sense different frequencies or energy intensities. For Savvy, which is the receptor for keyed-in characters such as letters or digits, the number of bits (1s and 0s) turned on in a computer to represent each keyed-in character can be viewed as the quantity corresponding to frequency or energy intensity.

Scrambling the Bits

The number of bits turned on for any particular keyed-in character is equal to the numerical values of the ASCII representation for that character. ASCII representations are numerical computer codes for all characters that computers recognize. An ASCII number exists for every upper- and lowercase letter, digit, printable character such as ;, *, and ?, and unprintable characters such as carriage return and line feeds (Chapter 1, Figure 7). As an example of how Savvy uses the ASCII codes, since the ASCII value of uppercase "Z" is 90, 90 bits are turned on; the ASCII for 5 is 53, so 53 bits are turned on to represent the number 5.

A graph that shows the number of bits turned on for each letter versus the keyed-in letters corresponds to the graphs of frequency versus time that are often used to illustrate speech patterns. Thus a graph of the query "GIVE ME THE NAMES OF ALL THOSE MALE EMPLOYEES WHO MAKE MORE THAN $5000 AND WHOSE WIFE'S NAME IS ROSE AND WHO LIVE IN SAN FRANCISCO" would show 130 different characters (including spaces), for a total of 8983 bits turned on in a Savvy bit buffer (Figure 14-12).

The reason that Savvy turns on the ASCII number of bits is to ensure that as little information as possible is lost during a symbol's processing. For example, the dropping of just one ASCII bit from an ASCII representation of a character (say "Z," ASCII value 90) results in a different character. On the other hand, with Savvy's approach, 90 bits must be turned on to represent the letter "Z." One lost bit is only 1/90 of the information which makes little difference to the overall pattern created by the characters.

SCRAMBLING THE BITS

Savvy's next step in understanding this query is to randomize (actually pseudorandomize) the bits in this Original bit buffer and move the randomized bits to another area, called the Randomized bit buffer (Figure 14-13). To randomize the bits, Savvy generates a random number between 1 and the total number of bits that represent the keyed-in characters.

For the query discussed here, a random number would be generated between 1 and 8983. That random number determines an address in the new Randomized bit buffer. The first bit in the Original bit buffer is then moved to that address.

This process is now iterated. Savvy generates another random number. This time, however, the random number generated is one less in its range than the first time. In other words, the second random number (call it "R") must fall between 1 and 8982 because one location in the Randomized bit buffer was already used. Based on counting, beginning with the first unused address, the second bit in the Original bit buffer is then moved to the Rth unused address in the Randomized bit buffer.

In this manner, the 8983 bits in the Original bit buffer are mapped to 8983 addresses in the Randomized bit buffer by generating random numbers between 1 and 8983 minus the number of bits already used. A graph of the Randomized bit buffer, analogous to that for the Original bit buffer, looks like a diagram of scattered points.

A key point necessary to understand how the Savvy system works is the idea that

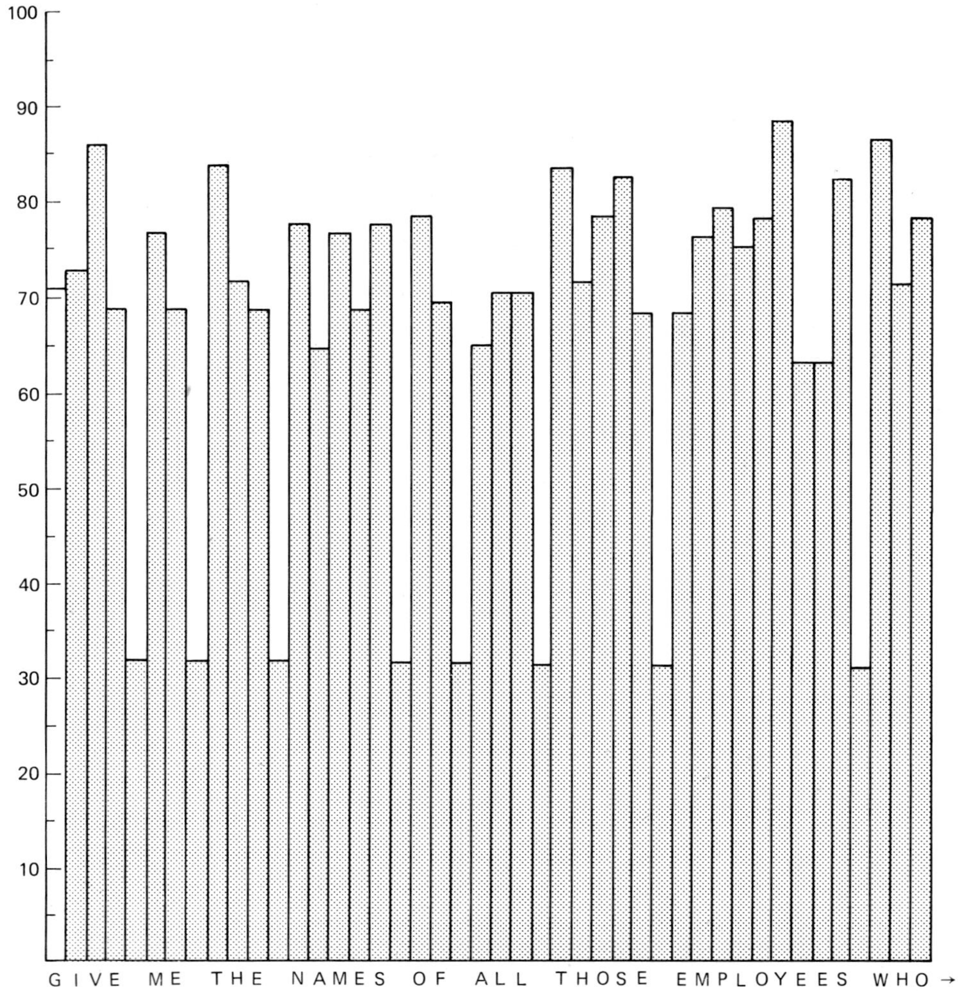

280 Unconventional Natural-Language Technologies for Micros

Figure 14-12 The bits turned on for each character keyed in is equal to the numerical value of the ASCII representation for that character.

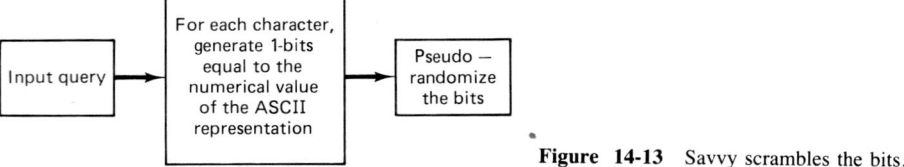

Figure 14-13 Savvy scrambles the bits.

these randomized numbers are actually pseudorandomized. In other words, they are truly random only the first time they are generated.

However, the seeds (starting points) for the random number generator are known and stored with the queries. As a result, Savvy can repeat this pseudorandomizing process anytime and find the same address for the same query and a close-by address for a similar query.

Savvy's pseudorandom mapping from the Original bit buffer to the Randomized bit buffer to a large extent works the way information is mapped from the sensor (ear or eye) into the processing areas of the brain. As long as each pattern of signals conveyed to the brain is always randomized the same way, once the brain (or Savvy) learns the meaning of a particular signal input pattern, it always attaches the same meaning to that pattern when it recurs.

As will be seen, it can be a short step from recognizing a pattern with a certain meaning to recognizing and then attaching the same meaning to similar patterns. This pattern-recognition capability applied to speech and visual understanding may account for some of the human abilities to understand and fill in missing information, multiple speech accents, incorrectly written English, and complicated, ill-illuminated scenes. This understanding of blurred or slurred information is more difficult for human beings or computers to accomplish if objects, sounds, and works are recognized only according to explicit rules.

SHRINKING THE LANGUAGE SYSTEM

The next steps in Savvy's query analysis include the dividing of the Randomized bits into subgroups, performing a proprietary mathematical transformation on the subgroups to compute other coordinates that represent a query or lexicon word, performing this transformation for many word and query samples, and finally performing a cluster analysis on these coordinates (Figure 14-14). The goal of these first three steps is to get these coordinates necessary to perform the cluster analysis in the last step. During the cluster analysis, Savvy determines that similar patterns cluster close together, assumes that closely clustered patterns therefore have similar meanings, and associates meaning with these patterns. It is during the subgrouping, transformation, and cluster analysis steps that the amount of space needed to represent the input queries is sharply reduced.

For Savvy on the IBM PC, the coordinates computed for the cluster analysis are points in a 200-dimensional space. The cluster analysis is performed on the Savvy-computed coordinates rather than the scattered data because, as Jim Dowe, developer of Savvy's underlying technology explains, the proprietary transformation better separates the real pattern from the presupposed patterns that could exist.

For speech recognition, Savvy performs the randomization and cluster analysis for a word or phrase spoken by many different people. In its natural-language query and programming system, these steps are performed for variants on a query or command such as "give me," "gimme," and "giv me," or "list employees" and "lust employees."

Whether speech or natural language, Savvy's purpose is the same. The cluster anal-

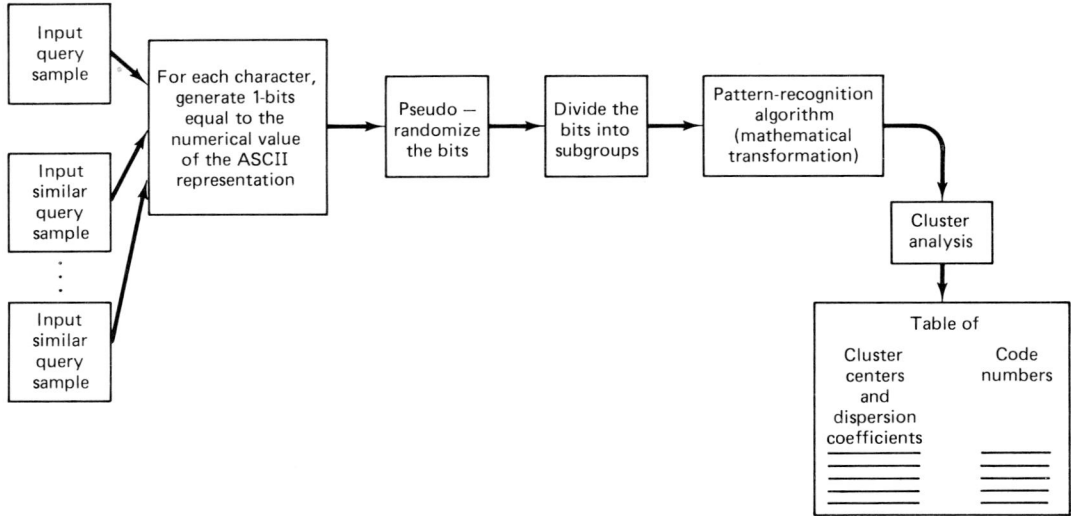

Figure 14-14 Savvy performs a mathematical transformation and cluster analysis.

ysis indicates that variants on the spoken word or the typewritten query cluster closely. Unless taught differently, to Savvy each cluster then represents a word or query and several variants or misspellings.

The cluster patterns that Savvy discovers as a result of the randomization through cluster analysis steps can be printed for human observation. For example, the graph in Figure 14-15 shows how the word "Apple" spoken by many people appears to Savvy. The x-axis represents the natural logarithm of the frequency. The y-axis represents signal intensity in decibels. The z-axis represents signal duration measured in milliseconds.

TRAINING THE LANGUAGE SYSTEM

It turns out that there is enough similarity between correct, mistaken, and variant forms of languages that after the cluster patterns are obtained, it is no longer necessary to save the entire pattern of points that represent a query. Only the center of the cluster and a coefficient that indicates the dispersion around that center need to be saved. This greatly shrinks the amount of space necessary to represent information.

To train Savvy to understand natural-language queries and commands, Savvy's engineers perform the randomization, grouping, and mathematical transformation of the words, phrases, and commands to execute tasks that will be shipped with Savvy. Code numbers for these words and phrases are then stored with the shrunken cluster information, now represented only by a center and dispersion coefficient.

During the recognition phase, Savvy looks to see if the point that results from the transformation of user input information falls within any of the clusters (Figure 14-16).

If "GIMME ALL THE WHOOPDOODLES" falls into one of its clusters, Savvy

Training the Language System

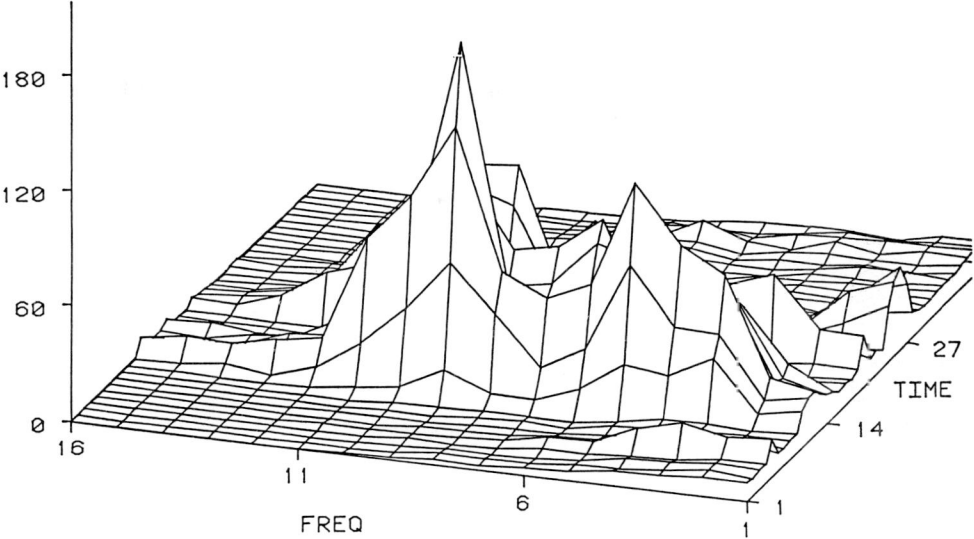

Figure 14-15 Savvy's cluster patterns can be printed for human observation. (Excalibur Technologies)

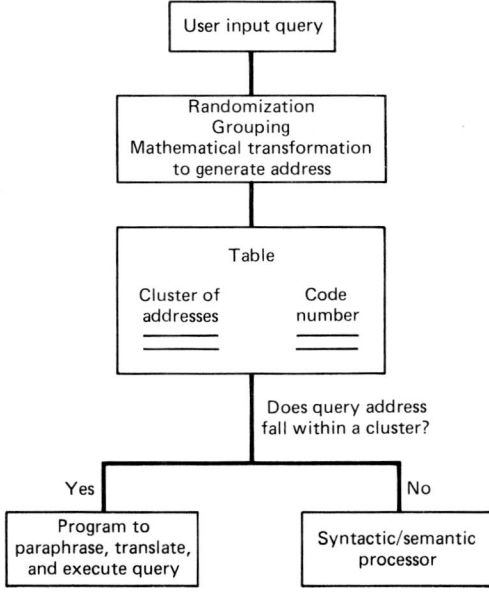

Figure 14-16 The Savvy language recognition phase.

pulls out a code number for that cluster, looks up the code number in a table, and finds that the query really is the letters

"GIVE ME ALL THE WHOOPDOODLES."

It then displays the properly spelled query on the screen, translates it into a database query, or executes a particular task.

If Savvy does not recognize "GIMME ALL THE WHOOPDOODLES" as one of its clusters, rather than coming back with an error message to the user, it looks to its syntactic/semantic processor for help. The syntactic/semantic processor might parse the sentence and examine its lexicon or the database for the entry, "WHOOPDOODLES." If the syntactic/semantic processor cannot find it, it backs up and passes off its previous state of information (after "GIMME ALL THE") in the parsing process to the pattern recognizer (Figure 14-17).

The pattern recognizer then looks for a WHOOPDOODLE. It may find that WHOOPDOODLE falls within the cluster for "HULA HOOP." If so, it asks the user whether HULA HOOP was really the word meant. If the answer is yes, the recognition machine locates the WHOOPDOODLE problem word in the partially parsed query and passes off its newly discovered information.

It is important to note at this point that Savvy's pattern recognizer is recursive, which means that it will call itself and work with patterns of patterns. This feature allows the pattern recognizer, as well as the syntactic/semantic processor, to discriminate words with different meanings in different contexts.

It may happen that neither Savvy's pattern recognizer nor its syntactic/semantic processor are able to find a WHOOPDOODLE. In that case, Savvy will ask the user if WHOOPDOODLE is a new item that it should learn.

Savvy learns new items in such a way that both the pattern recognizer and the syntactic/semantic processor will understand them afterward. For example, the pattern recognizer randomizes, groups, and performs the transformation on WHOOPDOODLE to get its coordinates in the cluster space. It then stores WHOOPDOODLE together with a code number which it assigns to the newly computed coordinate.

Although it would enhance the quality of the pattern recognition, Savvy does not perform any cluster analysis in the user environment because the process is too computationally intensive. Subsequent user queries are randomized, grouped, transformed, and checked for the proximity to the newly determined WHOOPDOODLE point.

For its part, the syntactic/semantic processor prompts the user for new information for its lexicon. Savvy seeks information for its lexicon, such as whether the new word is an action, something acted upon, a qualifier, or a word that integrates or interrelates any of the other three categories of words.

Finally, if users find the word WHOOPDOODLE too weird to remember, they may give it a synonym, perhaps "FLOX." To teach the new word FLOX, as mentioned earlier, users employ the command ASSOCIATE, the original word WHOOPDOODLE, and the new word FLOX.

Training the Language System

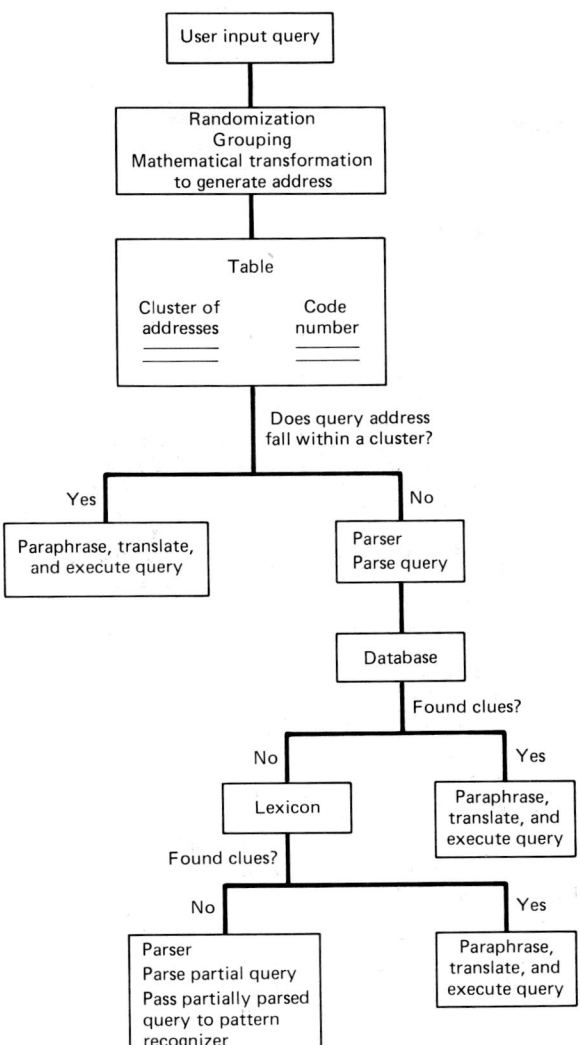

Figure 14-17 Savvy switches between its pattern recognizer and syntactic/semantic processor.

Savvy then performs its randomization procedures to generate an address, for the pattern "FLOX," which will contain a pointer to the WHOOPDOODLE address. Subsequently, when Savvy sees queries that contain the word FLOX, it follows that pointer to the original WHOOPDOODLE and continues its processing as before.

Natural Language Through Meaning

CHAPTER 15

Compared to human beings, most natural-language systems underachieve. True, they can parse an English-language query and respond to it. They can even understand a partial query, such as "List them," if "them" is related to a prior query such as "How many clerical employees work here?" And to some degree, they can resolve ambiguities using such techniques as nondeterministic parsing, dictionary definitions, and database information.

Yet natural-language systems cannot demonstrate even a fraction of the natural-language competence of three-year-old children. Average three-year-olds not only understand their native language but know that differently phrased sentences can have identical meanings. In addition, they can translate one meaning or concept into several differently phrased sentences. By five years of age, children can recognize long sequences of sentences, comprehend them, fill in gaps with information that was implied but not spoken, draw inferences, and generalize some things. In addition, they can perform actions or paraphrase information based on their realization of analogies between a language sequence and some previous event or observation.

Many of these capabilities are possible because children approach language through meaning, not structure. To help decipher meaning, they rely on a broad range of experiences, observations, and general knowledge which they can refer to and apply whenever necessary. For example, as soon as children are told that a book's name is *The Three Bears,* they instantly anticipate some of the material in the book because they already know a lot about bears. They know that bears are living creatures, big, furry, and either brown or black. They know that the bears like honey, live in woods, and sleep in caves. Part of the book's appeal stems from the children's knowledge that bears do not live in houses, sit on chairs, sleep in beds, and cook porridge.

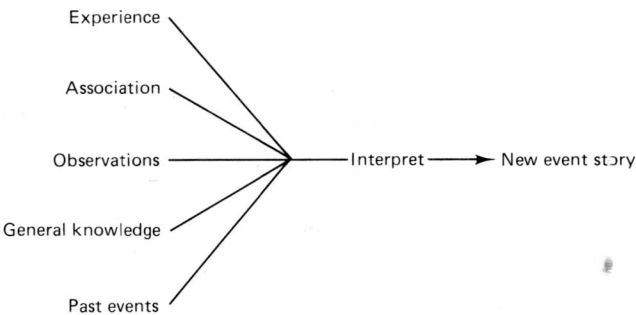

Figure 15-1 Sources that people use to help understand stories.

The fact is that children stand a better chance of understanding and answering questions about stories than computers do, because the children can retrieve a variety of associations from past experiences and reconstruct the general context of knowledge in which some event occurred. This past and reconstructed knowledge is available to help interpret meaning for a specific story or conversation (Figure 15-1). When grandma says "I'm cold," children know that it means "You put on a sweater." Similarly, children are not misled by a phrase such as "With the passage of time, the jacket grew too small to fit." Children invariably know that "the jacket didn't grow small; the child grew bigger."

UNDERSTANDING MEANING

Unlike children, most modern natural-language systems cannot reconstruct and bring to bear past experiences. Instead, they generally use a combination of syntax, language structure mechanisms, and semantics to interpret natural language. Much is known about the syntactical and structural components of natural-language systems. Unfortunately, little is known about the semantic components and methods for interpreting meaning. Consequently, greater emphasis in most natural-language systems is placed on syntax and structure.

For Roger Schank, computer science department chairman at Yale University, however, to have even a small child's understanding of natural language, it is necessary to approach natural language in the same way that human beings do—through meaning. Taking this approach, Schank has built not only natural-language interfaces to databases, but conversational advisory systems and systems that can comprehend and paraphrase stories and newspaper articles. Schank's systems differ from previous natural-language systems in that their internal techniques emphasize, almost exclusively, the representation of meaning.

Another approach to language through meaning, taken by Carnegie Group, Inc., emphasizes meaning less exclusively and focuses on different sorts of meanings than Schank's systems. Positioned in-between Schank's exclusive emphasis on meaning and more limited syntactic analysis techniques, Carnegie Group's approach has been used to build interfaces to knowledge acquisition systems so that programmers can use their natural language to enter knowledge in knowledge-based systems.

With either approach, the emphasis on meaning gives natural-language systems the humanlike ability to infer varying amounts of information that is implied but not said. For example, Schank's systems realize that a simple statement such as "Harvey went to Burger King and bought a hamburger" implies eating. Yet nowhere in this statement is eating mentioned.

Furthermore, Schank's language systems can check that the facts in a series of sentences and the inferences drawn from them are consistent. So it would interpret a simple statement such as "Andrea took the train" in terms of cities and time schedules. However, the system would reinterpret the statement about Andrea in terms of the more consistent domain of children and toys if the next statement in a sequence turned out to be "Eric grabbed it back."

STEREOTYPES AND SCRIPTS

Schank's natural-language systems recognize both ambiguous and implied information because, like human beings, they contain internal representations of stereotypical situations and events. The stereotypical situations are represented in framelike templates called scripts. This stereotypical knowledge helps the programs interpret new situations because the stored stereotypical situation tells them what to expect.

A stereotypical situation might be a story of a prince who saves a princess after a two-hour fight with a dragon. A Schank script represents a generalized form of this stereotypical story, including the anticipated ending wherein the prince marries the princess and lives happily ever after (Figure 15-2). Like human beings, the natural-language system that uses scripts is able to answer a variety of questions, which require information both specifically stated and implied, based on what is stereotypical.

UNDERNEATH SCRIPTS

Scripts are made of fundamental unambiguous representations of meaning called "conceptual dependencies." These conceptual dependencies consist of 11 primitive acts (defined by Schank) to represent actions and state changes (such as who has, owns, or transfers something) that languages handle (Figure 15-3). They include primitives for physically or mentally transferring objects or ideas. There are also primitives for move-

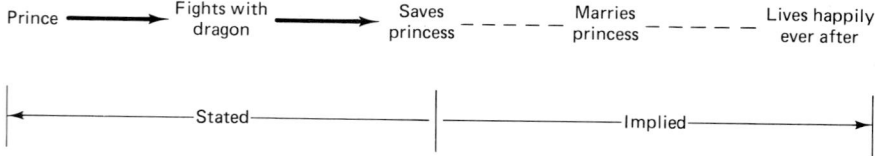

Figure 15-2 Script-like stereotypical situation.

PTRANS:		The transfer of location of a physical object, such as Manny PTRANSed the book to Trudy, or to "go" is to PTRANS oneself to a place
ATRANS:		The transfer of an abstract relationship, such as possession, ownership, or control. For example, "buy" is made of two conceptualizations that cause each other. One is an ATRANS of money. The other is an ATRANS of the object being bought.
PROPEL:		The application of physical force to an object.
MOVE:		Movement of a body part.
GRASP:		The grasping of an object by an actor.
INGEST:		The taking in of an object by an animal to the inside of that animal. This includes food, liquid, and gas.
EXPEL:		The expulsion of an object from the body of an animal into the physical world. This includes sweat, spit, and cry.
MTRANS:		Memory or mental transfer between animals or within an animal. This includes "tell," which is MTRANS between people; "see," which is MTRANS between eyes and consciousness; and think, remember, forget, and learn.
MBUILD:		The construction by an animal of new information from old information. This includes decide, conclude, imagine, and consider.
SPEAK:		The actions of producing sounds. This includes say, purr, play music, and scream.
ATTEND:		The action of attending or focusing a sense organ toward a stimulus. For example, ATTEND ear is listen. ATTEND eye is see. But "see" is treated as MTRANS to consciousness by instrument of ATTEND eye to object.

Figure 15-3 The primitive acts of conceptual dependency. (Roger Schank, Yale University)

ment, grasping, and applying force. Still other primitives pertain to sense organs, ingestion by animals, and thinking types of acts such as "decide" and "imagine."

Like human beings, conceptual dependency primitives can translate the many different sentences that have the same meaning into one unique representation. For example, PTRANS is an action that means the transfer of the location of a physical object. Thus, whether a sentence is written "Manny gave Trudy a book," "Trudy got a book from Manny," or "Manny put a book in Trudy's hand," a conceptual dependency template in a computer represents the sentence as "Manny PRTANSed the book to Trudy."

This ability to translate the many different sentence constructs that can express one conceptual idea into one unique conceptual dependency representation allows Schank's natural-language systems to understand, translate, and paraphrase text independently of language. At execution time, the conceptual dependency-based system translates the user's input sentences into a conceptual dependency representation (Figure 15-4). Then a generator, which is a set of instructions for mapping a conceptual dependency representation into a given language, generates a paraphrased text or otherwise translated output from the conceptual dependency representation.

Since the generator is modular and separate from the rest of the conceptual dependency system, it can be written to produce its output in any language. The task of synthesizing output once the input has been properly analyzed, understood, and represented is one of the easier chores of a conceptual dependency-based natural-language system. Once the system can understand or summarize a text in one language, it can readily translate it into another by passing through the conceptual dependency representation. As a result, the Yale conceptual dependency system generators already knows several languages, including English, French, Chinese, and Spanish.

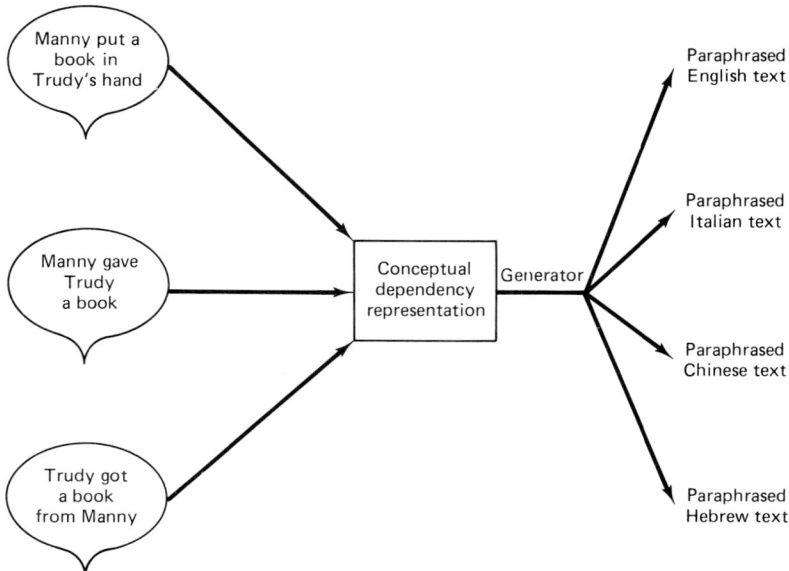

Figure 15-4 A unique conceptual dependency that represents different sentence constructs can be translated into many languages.

Conceptual dependency primitives can, to some degree, infer information—a capability they use to help translate and interpret sentences. The inference capability is partly due to the many relationships between objects, actions, and concepts that become apparent when different sentences are translated into the same conceptual dependency representation.

For example, "Marianne likes reading" and "Marianne likes books" have the same representation. This sameness allows the natural-language system to infer that reading and books are related. Another example shows that a conceptual dependency-based language program can infer that the sentence "Ellen likes apples" is related to eating. The relationship is inferred because the conceptual dependency representation for "Ellen likes apples" requires the primitive INGEST, which involves eating (Figure 15-5). Thus the system can infer that "Ellen eats apples."

Inferences can also be made based on the actual information incorporated in the

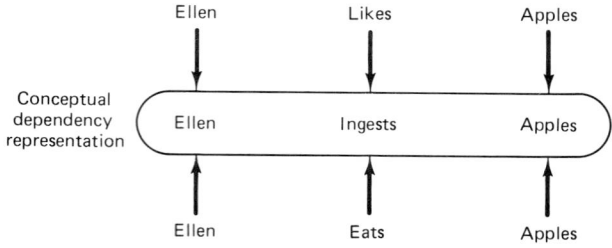

Figure 15-5 Inferring information through translation of sentences into the same conceptual dependency.

definition of some conceptual dependency primitives. For instance, in the earlier PTRANS example (Manny gave Trudy a book), the computer infers that the book is now possessed by Trudy, it is no longer in the location it was when it was possessed by Manny, and it is located wherever Trudy put it.

The slightly different sentence "Manny sold Trudy a book" still involves the physical transfer of a book. However, the sentence meaning is changed because the definition of "sold" involves not only the transfer of a book, but also the transfer of a second physical object—money. A conceptual dependency primitive called ATRANS describes this two-concept action. Although similar to PTRANS in that both primitives involve some sort of transfer, ATRANS entails a different set of inferences. For example, after Manny ATRANSed the book to Trudy, not only does Manny no longer have the book, but Trudy has less money while, unless he spent the money received, Manny is richer.

UNDERSTANDING WITH CONCEPTUAL DEPENDENCIES

Unlike the natural-language systems discussed in previous chapters, when conceptual dependency-based sentences interpret users' sentences, they do not look for syntactic sentence elements such as nouns, subjects, and verbs. Instead, they read a sentence from left to right to look for elements such as the primitive action, its actor, an object transferred, and the direction of transference. So to interpret "Manny sold Trudy a book," the natural-language program first understands "Manny" to be a human being. That information conveys little knowledge, so the language program moves to the next word. It understands the next word, "sold," to be an ATRANS. As soon as the language program recognizes the ATRANS, it realizes that Manny is probably the actor who is doing the ATRANS (Figure 15-6).

Besides creating expectations about an actor doing the ATRANS, the word "sold" also creates expectations about what else the sentence contains. For example, the computer expects to hear what was sold and to whom it was sold. However, when the computer reaches "Manny sold Trudy," it must wait for more of the sentence because the sentence could read "Manny sold Trudy to the slavedrivers."

Once the computer reads the words "a book," it makes its final inferences. It realizes that people usually sell physical objects. Moreover, they do not sell objects or people to physical objects. Therefore, the computer eliminates these possibilities and concludes that the book is the object that was sold and that it was sold to Trudy.

Manny	Sold	Trudy	A book
Actor, and receiver of money	ATRANS (transfer)	Receiver of possession and ownership relationship	Physical object
Step 1	Step 2	Step 4	Step 3

Figure 15-6 Understanding with conceptual dependencies.

UNDERSTANDING WITH SCRIPTS

Interpreting events, objects, and descriptions by literally analyzing stories or dialogues word by word or sentence by sentence is difficult at best and can result in some weird pitfalls. Human beings generally avoid the pitfalls because they bring their past experiences, observations, and general knowledge to bear on their understanding of natural-language sequences.

Consider, for example, the following two sentences from the same laboratory manual: "Take turns sanding a piece of wood with your partner" and "You will need a classmate for this experiment." Although not well written, these directions give the laboratory partner and the classmate no cause for alarm. However, the directions make sense to students only because the students can retrieve from their memories a host of experiences, observations, and knowledge about what students do in laboratories which they use to help interpret the laboratory directions as they were intended. To provide computerized language programs with these humanlike capabilities, Schank invented the concept and structure called "scripts."

Scripts, as the name suggests, are a sequence of events (stored in a computer) that illustrate a stereotypical situation. Schank has developed scripts for going to a restaurant, to a theatre, riding on a bus, and visiting the doctor.

Natural-language programs use these scripts as though they were previous experiences that can facilitate the interpretation of new situations. Like human beings, when script-based natural-language systems encounter a new situation (similar to one described in a script), they start with strong expectations about what will happen. The expectations allow the language systems to understand implied information and fill in missing information.

For example, a restaurant script describes entering the restaurant, waiting to be seated, sitting at the table, reading the menu, choosing food, ordering from the waiter or waitress, paying, tipping, and leaving (Figure 15-7). The script acts as a reference guide that can supply missing details needed to understand a dialogue and answer questions about it. Thus, in the story "Eva went to a restaurant, ordered some chicken, and left," a script-based system would assume that she was served, ate the chicken, and paid for it. In fact, it would assume that she left a tip even if the chicken was not very good. Yet nowhere in the story is there any mention of waiters, eating, or money.

USING SCRIPTS AND MOPS

To know which existing script (for example, geology, banking, airlines, fast-food establishment) is appropriate for a sentence, a Schank system scans the sentence in question from left to right. In the sentence "The sergeant ordered a lobster to go," the system gathers as much information as possible from the words, "the," "sergeant," and "ordered." The word "ordered," in this example, signifies an action that requires an actor. Although the system realizes that "the sergeant" is the actor, it does not yet know what type of script to instantiate. "Ordered" may require the restaurant script, but it could require a military script, as in "The sergeant ordered the soldier to go."

Since the sergeant clearly does not want a soldier wrapped like a lobster, the system

Script:	Restaurant		
Track:	Diner	Roles:	Customer
Props:	Tables		Waiter, waitress
	Chairs		Cook
	Menu		Cashier
	Food		Owner
	Check		
	Money		

Entry conditions:

    Customer is hungry.
    Customer has money.

Result conditions:

    Customer has less money.
    Owner has more money.
    Customer is not hungry.

Scene 1: Entering

    Enter restaurant (Customer PTRANS into restaurant)
    Wait to be seated . . . . . .
    Decide where to sit . . . . . .
    Move to table . . . . . .
    Sit down . . . . . .

Scene 2: Ordering

    Menu on table, or waiter brings menu, or customer asks for menu
    Read menu
    Choose food
    Signal waiter
    Order food
    Waiter transmits order to cook

    Cook tells waiter no food   Cook prepares food
    Waiter tells customer
    Customer rechooses food or
        customer goes to scene 4
        at the "no pay path."

Scene 3: Eating

    Cook gives food to waiter
    Waiter gives food to customer
    Customer eats food

Scene 4: Exiting

    Waiter writes check
    Waiter gives check to customer
    Customer gives tip to waiter
    Customer pays cashier
(no-pay path): Customer leaves restaurant

Figure 15-7 Translation of an abridged eat-at-restaurant script. (Roger Schank, Yale University)

must postpone its script decision until it has more information. Only after the system reads "ordered a lobster" does it guess that the story pertains to buying food. At that point it instantiates the restaurant script.

Although scripts for different domains are different, in some ways they are repetitive. For example, a visit to a doctor, dentist, or lawyer contains many similar experiences. To accommodate the similarities and make the natural-language programs more efficient, scripts with shared experiences have been structured into a hierarchy called MOPS (Memory Organization Packages). Just the organizing of information in this way facilitates faster inferencing in less memory space.

With MOPS, instead of having to handle separate scripts for every situation, a Schank system calls upon a Professional Office Visit MOP, whether it is conversing about doctor, dentist, or lawyer visits. This MOP describes the sequence of events that occurs when a person enters a professional office, waits at a reception desk, fills out forms during the first visit, waits in a waiting room, gets a service (generically), pays, and leaves (Figure 15-8). For the particular service, however, the Professional Office Visit MOP calls on the specific script.

SCRIPTS GO COMMERCIAL

Like all other natural-language systems, script-based systems apply only to a narrow domain described by the script. Yet their ability to understand implied meaning and fill in missing conversational details in these domains makes them tolerable to human beings who expect and get such capabilities in their people-to-people conversations. The potential for natural-language systems with these capabilities and advantages has led Schank to form Cognitive Systems, Inc. to commercialize and market the script-based systems for a variety of applications. Applications include not only natural-language interfaces to databases, but also advisory systems.

Typical script-based interfaces to databases are tailored to highly specialized domains of knowledge. For example, one database interface, called the Explorer, contains geological knowledge that pertains to oil-well operations. Actually, the Explorer is a natural-language interface to a graphics package that retrieves information from a database and produces maps that help determine where to drill for oil. The database con-

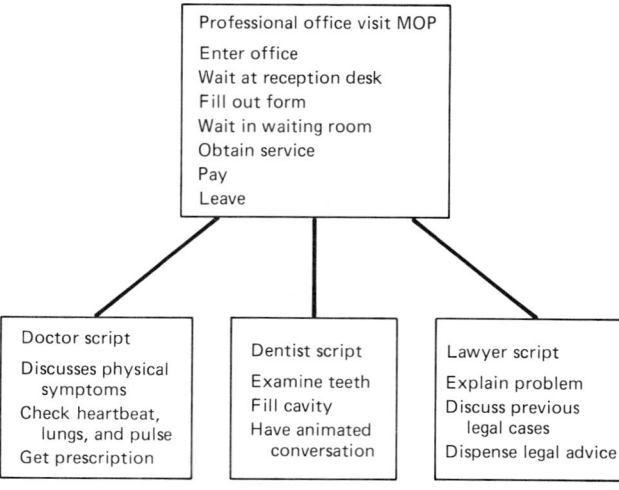

Figure 15-8 One MOP can be invoked by several scripts.

Scripts Go Commercial

tains geological data and information about thousands of oil wells. The graphics program uses these data and information to prepare maps that display both geological data and oil-well information.

The difference between the Explorer and classical natural-language interfaces to databases is the amount of geology and oil exploration information that the Explorer contains in its scripts. The Explorer is not a general-purpose interface to a general-purpose database. Its script-based knowledge allows geologists and geophysicists to converse and interact not only in ordinary unconstrained natural language, but to use geology and oil exploration jargon to specify the geological maps that they need generated. Its oil exploration knowledge base also allows the Explorer to anticipate some of the geologists' geological needs and be flexible in its understanding of their input. Consequently, the program can handle requests for the specialized maps even when the requests are incomplete or ambiguous (Figure 15-9).

Script-based language systems' ability to understand meaning and implied information also makes them suitable for advisory systems that Cognitive Systems plans for bank and company lobbies, shopping malls, and videotext applications. A typical script-based advisory system in a bank lobby will converse in unconstrained English with untrained users to advise customers about the fine points of opening bank accounts.

Normally, knowledgeable white-collar workers perform these account advice

*Map the tcg.

A map region was not specified.
Do you want the same geographic region as the last request?
*n

Do you wish to specify the map region by county or by geographic coordinates?
*c

Please input county or counties by name or number.
*Bibb

BIBB County is in the following states:
ALABAMA GEORGIA

Please input the appropriate state or a new county specification.
*make it new haven, ct.

A contour interval was not specified.
Would you like the contour interval from the previous request?
Previous CI = **100'**
*y

A scale was not specified.
Would you like the scale from the previous request?
Previous scale = **2000.0 FT-PER-IN**
*y

User requests a **STRUCTURE** map
   output medium: **PAPER**
   output device: **PHOTODOT**
   county: **NEW HAVEN, CT**
   on **TCG**
   CI = **100'**
   scale of **1" = 2000.0'**

Figure 15-9 A script-based language understanding system dialogue. (Cognitive Systems, Inc.)

chores. They explain the different types of bank accounts and their options. Based on their knowledge of customer needs, they provide suitable advice. Although not a difficult task, advice giving is time consuming. Banks claim that customers who consult with bank employees for 10 minutes and then deposit only $100 cost the bank more than the worth of their accounts.

For computers to perform this advice-giving job, they must be conversant with the task domain, be able to choose a client's intended meaning, and answer questions without requiring clients to express every last detail. A syntactically based system that misinterprets syntactically correct statements such as "DA SAYS NON-PROFIT GROUPS MAY OPERATE ILLEGAL GAMES" (*Albuquerque Journal,* 4/29/83) will not only give incorrect answers to questions, but will frustrate and exasperate users in any field. Script-based natural-language systems, however, can retrieve scripts that pertain to the subject at hand and choose the correct meaning in light of what is appropriate and makes sense in a particular situation. Thus a script-based system may instantiate a restaurant or circus script to determine the most plausible interpretation of the phrase "PAY 50 CENTS AND SEE A MAN EATING CHICKEN."

Using script-based techniques, Cognitive Systems has built advisory systems for an automated will writer and estate planner and an automated tax assistant. A personal financial planner, an insurance advisor, and several decision support systems for banking and financial applications are under development. A dialogue between users and these advisory systems in some ways resembles extended menu-prompted systems. But script-based systems are less likely to issue frustrating, noninformative responses such as "ILLEGAL SYNTAX" or "I DON'T UNDERSTAND YOUR ANSWER." Because the scripts, like human memory, contain information about the ramifications of the topics under advisement, script-based natural-language systems stand a better chance than classical syntactic systems of making sense of users' input.

BETWEEN SYNTACTIC ANALYSIS AND SCRIPTS

The script-based program developers at Cognitive Systems consider unconstrained natural-language systems to be the most important type of AI systems today, even more so than expert systems. They maintain that expert systems are geared to a small segment of the world community compared to natural languages, which are geared to the layperson in the entire world community.

Script-based natural languages, however, have their limitations. For example, some companies and research institutions consider scripts static, limited only to stereotypical situations, and inadequate for full language understanding. Script-based systems depend too much on knowledge of a domain. If a script happens to exist for a subject area, the system understands both in-depth and implied information; without this specialized information, the system understands almost nothing. Clearly, it would be impractical for a language-understanding system to contain scripts for every conceivable subject and contingency that could arise during a query or dialogue session. Even building scripts is a cumbersome process because it requires construction, from scratch, of a parser program to process the semantics for each new area of subject knowledge.

Part of the reason for these problems is simply that the script-based approach to language understanding is a state-of-the-art, still-evolving technique. But as is often the case, while the evolution is in progress, a simultaneous search is on to improve language-understanding systems by combining the best of the old with the most feasible of the new.

One such combination evolved into Language Craft (from Carnegie Group, Inc.), a language-understanding system and natural-language development environment that combines syntactic analysis with scriptlike semantics. Language Craft is a frame-based system with a general-purpose parser that works across all frames in the system.

The parser operates similarly to script-based system parsers. It sifts through the words and phrases in a sentence to discover semantic components such as actions and agents performing the action. If necessary, it can query a knowledge base to get its semantic information. It may also look for traditional grammatical components, such as noun phrases or verbs. But unlike syntactic analysis systems, it does not build a grammatical parse tree. The parser's goal, instead, is to find words or patterns that indicate which frame to instantiate (activate).

The frames, called "case frames," contain both worldly and linguistic knowledge. As will be seen, the world knowledge in case frames is more general than subject knowledge scripts. This knowledge may be represented as declarative knowledge, or embedded in rules that can infer new information while a system is running.

The linguistic knowledge, also used by case frames to help understand meaning, comes from two different sources. One source is a data structure known as a "sentence structure." It contains information about possible legal syntactic combinations of words that conform to different types of sentences, such as imperative, declarative, or interrogative. For example, the sentence structure indicates that an imperative sentence contains a central verb, usually conjugated in the present tense, has no subject field, may have a direct object, and so on.

The second source of linguistic knowledge is dictionary entries. These indicate all the words, in various forms, that signify a particular topic and therefore should activate relevant case frames.

When a user inputs a sentence, Language Craft performs a syntactic and semantic analysis simultaneously. For example, it looks up the words in the dictionary and assigns syntactic categories to them. If words fall into more than one syntactic category, the parser generates interpretations for both categories and then uses semantic information to determine the correct one. With this combination syntactic and semantic analysis, if the system semantics understand that crocodiles are not normally part of people's dietary habits, the system interprets the ambiguous phrase "man eating crocodile" to be a phrase containing a noun compound (man eating) which describes the crocodile, instead of a sentence about a man who happens to be eating a crocodile.

The dictionary entries consist of various semantic constraints which, if satisfied, indicate the appropriate case frame to instantiate. For example, in the following three sentences, the word "ordered" has different meanings: commanded, purchased, and put in a particular sequence.

The sergeant ordered the soldier to go.

The sergeant ordered a lobster to go.

The sergeant ordered the list of names alphabetically.

Separate case frames—call them A, B, and C—exist for each definition of "ordered." All point to the same syntactic structure, which defines "ordered" as the main point, warranting a direct object. But each case frame contains different semantics.

In examining these sentences, the parser ignores phrases like "the sergeant" and "to go" because the sentence structure indicates that "ordered" is the central verb and central point of the sentence. "Ordered" therefore becomes the key to decisions about which case frame to instantiate.

Case frame A, where "ordered" means "command," indicates that a human recipient of "ordered" is required, as well as an action that the human being can perform. Since the first sentence is consistent with these inputs, case frame A is instantiated.

The second sentence requires a particular food, packaged in a particular way. Since the soldier does not qualify as food, case frame A would not be instantiated. The system therefore continues looking for an appropriate case frame, and it finds case frame B, containing syntactic and semantic information about the definition "purchase." Similarly, the dictionary indicates that case frame C, containing knowledge about sequencing, should be instantiated if the direct object consists of (or refers to) a list of items.

This frame-based approach differs from Schankian scripts in that frame instantiation is not tied to a stereotypical situation. A problem with stereotypical script systems is that they may require a good deal of information to be explicitly stated in order to reliably instantiate the correct script. For example, the sentence, "the sergeant ordered a lobster to go" might incorrectly cause a restaurant script to be instantiated unless the sentence was extended to read "the sergeant went to the restaurant and ordered a lobster to go." Just the word "lobster," or any other food item, is insufficient because the next sentence could say "the fish store manager wrapped it and gave it to him."

Language Craft operates differently because "ordering to go," meaning "purchase," is not confined to a restaurant. Instead, it is tied to a particular activity that can be performed in many different places, wherever it is possible to purchase the thing ordered.

Another major difference between Language Craft's frame-based approach and Schankian scripts is that script-based systems require a separate script for every stereotypical situation rather than one for central words or points. For example, a Schankian system would have separate scripts for a military, classroom, warehouse, and hospital environment for the following four sentences:

The sergeant ordered the soldier to go to the office.

The teacher ordered Olga to do her homework.

The boss ordered Mickey to load the truck.

The doctor ordered Sara to set up an intraveneous feeding.

Yet all four sentences are built around the idea of issuing a command, and much information can be gleaned just by understanding what it means to command someone to do something. Taking a different approach from Schankian scripts, only a single Language Craft case frame is instantiated for all these sentences, and it focuses on the meaning of issuing a command rather than the stereotypical situation in which the command is issued. The case frame is created with skeletal information about a command situation. This skeletal information, represented by slots in the frame, sets up general expectations about things involved in issuing a command, such as a command giver, recipients of the command, actions to take, and a number of other ramifications of commanding not present in most syntactic analysis-based language systems. These expectations are the same for all contexts of the command definition of the word, ''order,'' or any other word synonymous with command. The meaning of a particular command situation becomes more specific as the slots are filled in with the information contained in the sentence.

If additional detailed information is needed, frames akin to Schankian scripts are required. This information does come not from Language Craft's basic language understanding system, but from knowledge representation frames found in a knowledge system development tool called Knowledge Craft (also from Carnegie Group, Inc., and discussed in Chapter 11). Since Knowledge Craft is used to build knowledge-based applications, it contains detailed information about the application domain. Language Craft interfaces to Knowledge Craft, so this detailed information is available, resulting in a specialized scriptlike language system.

Without the tie-in to Knowledge Craft, Language Craft becomes a general-purpose language understanding system, more fluent in understanding meaning than syntactic analysis systems, but less so than Schankian script programs. Unlike script-based systems, even if Language Craft does not have specialized, thorough understanding of a subject, it still can understand a good deal of immediate meaning.

This mixed paradigm approach gives Language Craft a unique niche. Like other natural-language systems, Language Craft can interface to a database or application, and it has also been used to develop interfaces to operating systems. But its method of understanding meaning also equips it to be an interface to a knowledge acquisition system. In this capacity, the language-understanding system allows programmers to build new scripts, frames, and other knowledge representations, for knowledge systems, by communicating in their native language. To achieve the level of comprehension necessary for this purpose, clearly the system needs to be able to understand the meaning of the users' input sentences without having a preexisting script (because the frames and scripts are first being built).

Language Craft interfaces to the Knowledge Craft knowledge system development tool and allows a variety of types of people to use Knowledge Craft to build knowledge-based systems. Experts entering first-time knowledge into a knowledge base use their natural language to type in rules or assertions pertaining to a particular topic. Language Craft then creates the frames corresponding to the new knowledge that has been typed in. In doing so, it builds an internal network. This network indicates relationships, as well as missing relationships, between frames and other knowledge pieces. As Language Craft spots the missing relationships, it asks the user how to connect new knowledge to previous knowledge. Once these initial relationships between pieces of knowledge are established, when the system is used, it can infer the information itself.

NATURAL-LANGUAGE SYSTEMS TELL TALES

It is often said that the United States has become an information-processing society. Certainly, the amount of information produced—reports, magazines, newspapers, transaction records, memos, documentation, this book, and just general paper work—attests to it. How handy it would be if a computer program could read, skim, summarize, highlight, or answer questions about this printed information.

Such programs exist. They generally require detailed knowledge of the subject being read, and therefore many of them are based on scripts. Although they are still in their infancy, some use knowledge not only of facts, but also about why people do things, to interpret, fill in implied information, generalize, paraphrase, and answer questions about stories. One of these script-based story-understanding programs is known as Sam (Script Applying Mechanism). In addition to processing scripts, Sam works with a program called Pam (Plan Applying Mechanism), which contains information about human goals, plans, beliefs, motivations, and how people achieve what they want.

With Pam's help, Sam can read and analyze stories such the following: "John wanted some money. John got a gun and walked into a liquor store. John told the owner he wanted some money. The owner gave John the money and he left." (Nelson, 1978).

This story does not explain what John planned to do in the store or why the owner gave him money. But using knowledge that Pam supplies about people's plans, motivations, and behavior, Sam infers that John probably did not go to the store to buy liquor since a purchase requires money but does not normally require a gun. Sam therefore switches to the knowledge structure about robbery motives. It interprets the statement "John got a gun" as part of a plan to get some money. It knows that people fear harm when confronted with a gun. From these facts and motivations, Sam deduces that the store owner gave John the money because he was afraid.

Another story-understanding program, called Frump (Fast Reading Understanding and Memory Program), funded by the Navy, reads and summarizes UPI (United Press International) stories. Unlike Sam, Frump does not read the news stories very carefully. It reads in a more sketchy fashion, similar to the way a person skims a newspaper. When skimming a newspaper, people read very quickly, catching key words and phrases that attract them. They often have preconceived ideas of what to look for, what an item of interest is, and how much they want to get out of a story. Based on these ideas, they stop to carefully read only certain articles of interest.

To skim a story as people do, Frump uses what are called "sketchy scripts." These differ from ordinary scripts in that sketchy scripts have room for far fewer conceptual dependency representations. As a result, they only represent facts, concepts, and events that the script designer considers the most important.

Newspaper-reading programs are particularly suited to a sketchy script approach to understanding because the important facts to look for in news stories, such as "who," "what," "when," "where," and "how" are easily represented by sketchy scripts. Frump uses the sketchy scripts as templates of expected facts, concepts, and events to look for when reading a story. Each type of newspaper story has its own defined list of expected facts. The collection of all the expectations for one type of story constitutes the sketchy script for that type of story and is equivalent to the preconceived ideas that people use when reading that story type.

Sketchy scripts have been defined for a number of story types. Newspaper-reading programs use these sketchy scripts to read stories, for example, about automobile accidents, earthquakes, and visiting dignitaries, international terrorism, oil spills, and heads of state.

For example, the vehicle-accident sketchy script used for the newspaper story shown in Figure 15-10 defines four types of expectations (called requests in the script) for Frump to look for (Figure 15-11). The first request is the type of vehicle involved in the accident, the object that the vehicle collided with, and the location of the accident. The second type of request is the number of people killed. The third is the number injured. The fourth is who was at fault in the accident.

But Frump is not perfect. Stephen Slade, assistant chairman of the computer science department at Yale, recalls that Frump, which also reads UPI earthquake stories, once sent out a message stating that an earthquake had occurred in the United States (O'Connor, 1981). In reporting this disaster, it left out information normally included, such as the quake's exact location, the scale of the quake, and any damages or casualties. Moreover, no other media were able to confirm an earthquake anywhere in the nation. When AI researchers checked the UPI original copy, they found the headline that Frump interpreted as an American earthquake: "DEATH OF POPE SHAKES U.S."

INPUT: A PASSENGER TRAIN CARRYING TOURISTS, INCLUDING SOME AMERICANS, COLLIDED WITH A FREIGHT TRAIN IN THE RUGGED SIERRA MADRE OF NORTHERN MEXICO, KILLING AT LEAST SEVENTEEN PERSONS AND INJURING 45, THE POLICE REPORTED TODAY.

THEY SAID THAT AT LEAST FIVE OF THE INJURED WERE AMERICANS, AND THERE WERE UNOFFICIAL REPORTS THAT ONE OF THE DEAD WAS FROM NEW YORK CITY.

SOME OF THE PASSENGERS WERE TRAVEL AGENTS, MOST FROM MEXICO CITY, MAKING THE TRIP AS PART OF A TOURISM PROMOTION, THE POLICE SAID.

THE AMERICAN SOCIETY OF TRAVEL AGENTS HAD BEEN MEETING IN GUADALAJARA, THOUGH IT WAS NOT KNOWN WHETHER ANY OF THE GROUP WERE ABOARD THE TRAIN.

ONE OBSERVATION CAR ON THE RAILROAD TO THE PACIFIC TUMBLED INTO A 45 FOOT CANYON WHEN THE PASSENGER TRAIN SMASHED INTO THE FREIGHT YESTERDAY AFTERNOON NEAR THE VILLAGE OF PITTORREAL ABOUT 20 MILES WEST OF CHIHUAHUA CITY AND 200 MILES SOUTH OF THE UNITED STATES BORDER, THE POLICE SAID.

THEY SAID THAT RESCUE WORKERS WERE STILL TRYING TO PRY APART THE CAR'S WRECKAGE TO REACH PASSENGERS TRAPPED INSIDE. THE RESCUE SQUADS COULD NOT USE CUTTING TORCHES ON THE WRECKAGE BECAUSE SPILLED DIESEL FUEL MIGHT IGNITE, THE POLICE REPORTED.

Figure 15-10 Vehicle accident newspaper story (Roger Schank, Yale University)

```
SELECTED SKETCHY SCRIPT $VEHACCIDENT
SATISFIED REQUESTS:
((SCRIPT ($VEHACCIDENT VEH $V-VEH OBJ $V-OBJ
LOC $V-LOC)))
$V-VEH
        CLASS       (PHYSOBJ)
        TYPE        (*VEHICLE*)
        SROLE       ($V-TRAIN)
        SCRIPT      ($TRAIN)
$V-OBJ
        CLASS       (PHYSOBJ)
        TYPE        (*VEHICLE*)
        SROLE       ($V-TRAIN)
        SCRIPT      ($TRAIN)
$V-LOC
        CLASS       (LOCATION)
        LOCALE      (*MEXICO*)
((ACTOR $V-HURTGRP TOWARD (*HEALTH*VAL (-LT10))))
$V-DEADGRP
        NUMBER      (17)
        CLASS       (PERSON)


((ACTOR $V-DEADGRP TOWARD (*HEALTH*VAL (-10))))
$V-HURTGRP
        NUMBER      (45)
        CLASS       (PERSON)


CPU TIME 4.504 SECONDS
SUMMARY: A TRAIN HIT A TRAIN IN MEXICO. 17 PEOPLE DIED. 45
PEOPLE WERE INJURED.
```

Figure 15-11 Facts extracted from a newspaper story to produce a summary of the story. (Roger Schank, Yale University)

Despite its overly literal interpretation (Frump makes humanlike mistakes), Frump has an action-packed history. During the Carter administration, (U.S. presidential) Frump was connected to another program called Cyrus (Computerized Yale Retrieval and Updating System). Cyrus, the given name of the Secretary of State at that time, kept tract of news events that involved the diplomatic life of Cyrus Vance. The Cyrus text-understanding program remembers the contents of the stories that it reads because it stores these contents in its equivalent of a database. It uses this remembered information as an aid in analyzing future stories.

The Secretary of State was chosen as the subject to track for two reasons (Kaarsberg, 1981). For one, such a high-ranking diplomat is likely to be in the news often. This means that Cyrus's database is continually updating itself. Since Cyrus's data processes and memory organization are modeled on the techniques that many psychologists believe is akin to human organization, storage, and retrieval of information in long-term memory, this continuous updating gives Cyrus's developers a chance to observe how Cyrus actually stores its new information. The memory organization underlying Cyrus's database is based on the reconstructive theories mentioned earlier. These reconstructive theories maintain that people do not remember actual events, but instead remember the general context of these events. For example, they recall a museum visit by remembering that it occurred in the context of a visit to a large city. Similarly, Cyrus's model of reconstructive memory organizes information and events and indexes them by their distinguishing features.

The second reason the Secretary of State was chosen as the subject for the program is that the reported activities of a diplomat are all of the same sort. Because these similarities in activities exist, it is possible to represent diplomatic activities in scripts.

As it turned out, besides summarizing news stories, Cyrus was able to make some interesting inferences. For example, it was asked whether Vance's wife had ever met the wife of the then Israeli Prime Minister Menachem Begin. Although that information was never explicitly stated in any story it had read, Cyrus discovered that Vance and Begin attended a couple of state banquets together. Since it also knew that wives were often present at such affairs, it deduced that Mrs. Vance and Mrs. Begin had met. And, indeed, they had.

A similar newspaper reader story, called IPP (Integrated Partial Parser), uses MOPs to store and organize knowledge about international terrorism (Kaarsberg, 1981). Like Cyrus, IPP remembers the contents of stories it has read and uses them to analyze future stories. It differs from Cyrus in that instead of answering questions about specific events, it uses its updating database to make generalizations.

For example, IPP read several stories about businessmen who were kidnapped and held for ransom in Italy. Based on information gleaned from these stories, IPP generalized that ''when there is a kidnapping in Italy, the victim is usually a businessman.''

Another state-of-the-art, script-based natural-language program argues. Called Abdul–Ilana, it contains subject knowledge about the Middle East and it argues about the responsibility for wars there. Abdul, in the program, represents the Arabic side. Ilana is the Israeli. Each arguer in the program tries both to understand the arguments produced by the opposing side, to refute them, and to look as good as possible at the opponent's expense. Here is a fragment from an Abdul–Ilana argument (Kaarsberg, 1981).

1. Arab: Who started the '67 war?
2. Israeli: The Arabs did, by blockading the Straits of Tiran.
3. Arab: But Israel fired first.
4. Israeli: According to international law, blockades are acts of war.
5. Arab: Were we supposed to let you import American arms through the Straits?
6. Israli: Israel was not importing arms through the Straits. The reason for the blockade was to keep Israel from importing oil from Iran.
7. Arab: But Israel was importing arms and that's because Israel is trying to take over the Middle East.

The Abdul–Ilana program, the true frontier of current research, transcends just ordinary natural-language understanding. The program deals also with understanding the opposing arguer's claims and motivation analysis for these claims and it plans rebuttals. Part of the goal of this program is to provide some insight into how our own minds work and how they handle the process of argumentation.

For example, rebuttals are not preplanned. Researchers discover that the program often finds the rebuttal it is seeking while it is trying to understand the opposing argument. According to Lawrence Birnbaum, one of Abdul–Ilana's developers at Yale, this technique "accords more with our intuition and experience that argumentation is a combination of plan and fortuitous discovery" (O'Connor, 1981).

An examination of the arguments shows that statement 1 begins the argument (Kaarsberg, 1981). Statement 2 is generated by an argument rule that assumes that the opponent in the argument is responsible for any bad events. In statements 3 and 4, both the Arab and the Israeli search their memories to find a possible cause of war that could justify their positions. In statement 5, the Arab program component changes its tactics. It calls on its knowledge of Israeli importation of arms from the United States and updates some pertinent facts in its memory to attempt to justify the blockade. However, in statement 6, the Israeli counters the argument by showing that the Arab's facts were mistaken and states the actual reason for the blockade. Backed into a corner, in statement 7, the Arab program-component shifts the focus of the argument away from the question of whether or not the blockade was justified. It mentions the factual basis for its assumption as an excuse for it and then proceeds to change the subject.

It is important to note that in this program, both arguers use the same techniques of argumentation, and both arguers share the same historical facts. Thus the program can easily take either side in an argument.

Abdul–Ilana is only one of many state-of-the-art AI programs under development. Many projects are under way in developing systems that learn, see, and hear, and that probe theories of the structure of the human mind and how it works.

These systems are part of the distant future. They promise information accessibility in the face of the deluge of paper inundating our society and the increasing difficulty of assessing so much information by manual reading techniques.

Meanwhile, language-understanding programs are available to make computer-based data and applications accessible to large numbers of noncomputing professionals. In the form of natural-language interfaces to knowledge acquisition systems, they alleviate the need to know specialized AI languages or even stylized seminatural languages or cryptic prompts in order to build knowledge-based systems. All in all, natural-language systems have the potential to provide accessibility to information and promote the widespread building of knowledge systems for all sorts of applications, users, and people.

SELECTED VENDORS OF AI HARDWARE AND SOFTWARE

Apollo Computer, Inc.
  330 Billerica Road, Chelmsford, MA 01824
  Lisp and AI environments

Applied Expert Systems, Inc. (APEX)
  5 Cambridge Center, Cambridge, MA 02142
  Expert systems for financial applications

Arity Corp.
  358 Baker Ave., Concord, MA 01742
  Prolog

ArtellIgence, Inc.
  14902 Preston Rd, Dallas, TX 75240
  OPS5 for IBM PCs

Artificial Intelligence Corp.
  200 Fifth Ave., Waltham, MA 02254
  Natural language systems

Beckman Instruments, Inc.
  1050 Page Mill Road, Palo Alto, CA 94304
  Expert ultra-centrifuge systems

Bolt Beranek & Newman, Inc.
  10 Moulton Street, Cambridge, MA 02238
  Custom expert systems

Brattle Research Corp.
  215 First St., Cambridge, MA 02142
  Expert systems

Carnegie Group, Inc.
  Commerce Court at Station Square, Pittsburgh, PA 15219
  Knowledge system development tools, natural language systems, custom and packaged expert systems

CCA Uniworks, Inc.
  20 William St., Wellesley, MA 02181
  Common Lisp,. OPS5, Prolog

Chalcedony Software
  5580 La Jolla Blvd., La Jolla, CA 92037
  Prolog

Cognitive Systems, Inc.
  234 Church St., New Haven, CT 06510
  Natural language systems, Advisory systems

Computer*Thought Corp.
  1721 W. Plano Parkway, Plano, TX 75057
  Knowledge-based computer-aided instruction

Conception et Realisation Industrielles de Logiciel
  12 Bis, Rue Jean-Jaures 92807 Puteaux, France
  Prolog

Data General Corp.
  4400 Computer Drive, Westboro, MA 01580
  Lisp, AI environments

Digital Equipment Corp,
  146 Main St., Maynard, MA 01754
  AI Environments, Languages, Workstations

Excalibur Technologies Corp.
  800 Rio Grande Blvd. N. W., 21 Mercado Plaza, Alburquerque, NM 87104
  Natural language systems

Expert Systems, Inc.
   868 West End Ave., New York, NY 10025
   Expert system development tools

ExperTelligence, Inc.
   559 San Ysidro Road, Santa Barbara, CA 93108
   Lisp and OPS5 for the Apple Macintosh

Expert Systems International
   1150 First Ave., King of Prussia, PA 19406
   Prolog

Expert Technologies, Inc.
   461 Melwood Ave., Pittsburgh, PA 15230
   Expert systems for the construction and publishing industries

Exsys, Inc.
   Tower 56, 126 East 56 St., New York, NY 10022
   Expert system development tools

Franz, Inc.
   2920 Domingo Ave., Berkeley, CA 94705
   Franz Lisp, OPS5, Flavors

Frey Associates, Inc.
   Chestnut Hill Road, Amherst, NH 03031
   Natural language systems

General Electric Co.
   1 River Road, Schenectady, NY 12345
   Expert system development tools

General Research Corp.
   7655 Old Springhouse Road, McLean, VA 22102
   Expert system development tools

Gold Hill Computers, Inc
   163 Harvard St., Cambridge, MA 02139
   Common Lisp, Expert system development tools

Gould, Inc.
   6901 West Sunrise Blvd., Ft. Lauderdale, FL 33313
   AI languages, Interfaces to Lisp machines

Hewlett-Packard Company
Fort Collins, CO 80525
AI workstations, languages, and environments

Human Edge Software Corp.
2445 Faber Place, Palo Alto, CA 94303
Expert system development tools

IBM Corporation
Local IBM Sales Office
Lisp, AI environments, and Expert system development tools

Inference Corp.
5300 West Century Blvd., Los Angeles, CA 90045
Expert system development tools, custom expert systems

Integral Quality, Inc.
P.O. Box 31970, Seattle, WA 98103
Lisp

IntelliCorp, Inc.
1975 El Camino Real West Mountain View, CA 94040-2216
Expert system development tools, custom and packaged expert systems

Jeffrey Perrone & Associates, Inc.
3685 17th St., San Francisco, CA 94114
Expert system development tools

KDS Corporation
934 Hunter Rd., Wilmette, IL 60091
Expert system developed tools

Knowledge Analysis, Inc.
174 Monsen Road, Concord, MA 01742
Knowledge engineering

Lisp Machine, Inc.
6 Tech Drive, Andover, MA 01810
Lisp Computers, Environments, Languages, and Tools

Logicware, Inc.
5000 Birch St., The West Tower, Newport Beach, CA 92660
Prolog

Lucid, Inc.
 1090 East Meadow Circle, Palo Alto, CA 94303
 Common Lisp

Management Decision Systems, Inc.
 200 Fifth Ave., Waltham, MA 02254
 Expert systems for decision support

Martin Marietta Data Systems
 44 Washington Rd., Princeton Junction, NJ 08540
 Natural language systems

McDonnell Douglas, Knowledge Engineering Products Division
 20705 Valley Green Drive, Cupertino, CA 95014
 Expert system development tools

Microdata Corp.
 17481 Red Hill Ave., Irvine, CA 92714
 Natural language systems

Microrim, Inc.
 1750 112th St. N.E., Bellevue, WA 98004
 Natural language systems

Mitchell Associates
 P.O. Box 6189, San Rafael, CA 94903
 Lisp

PA Computers & Telecommunications, Division of PA Consulting Services, Inc.
 707 Alexander Road, Princeton, NJ 08504
                                or

Rochester House
 33 Greycoat Street, London, England SW1 P2QF

Palladian Software, Inc.
 41 Munroe St., Cambridge, MA 02142
 Expert systems for financial applications

Perq Systems, Inc.
 2600 Liberty Ave., Pittsburgh, PA 15230
 AI computers

Persoft, Inc.
 600 West Cummings Park, Woburn, MA 01801
 Expert systems

Production Systems Technologies, Inc.
 642 Gettysburg St., Pittsburgh, PA 15206
 OPS5 and OPS83

Programming Logic Systems, Inc.
 31 Crescent Drive, Milford, CT 06460
 Prolog

Prologica, Inc.
 1150 1st Ave., King of Prussia, PA 19406
 Prolog

Quintus Computer Systems, Inc.
 2345 Yale St., Palo Alto, CA 94306
 Prolog and Prolog development environment

Radian Corp.
 P.O. Box 9948, Austin, TX 78766
 Expert system development tools

Semantic Microsystems
 1001 Bridgeway, Sausalito, CA 94965
 Lisp for the Apple Macintosh

Silogic, Inc.
 6420 Wilshire Blvd., Los Angeles, CA 90048
 Prolog, Expert system development environment and tools

Smart Systems Technology, Inc.
 6870 Elm St., McLean, VA 22101
 AI training

Software Architecture & Engineering, Inc.
 1500 Wilson Blvd., Arlington, VA 22209
 Expert system development tools

Sun Microsystems, Inc.
 2550 Garcia Ave., Mountain View, CA 94043
 Lisp and AI environments

Symantec
   10201 Torre Ave., Cupertino, CA 95014
   Natural language systems

Symbolics, Inc.
   11 Cambridge Center, Cambridge, MA 02142
   Lisp computers, Environments, Languages, and Tools

Syntelligence
   1000 Hamlin Court, Sunnyvale, CA 94088
   Expert systems for insurance companies

Systems Designers Software, Inc.
   444 Washington St., Woburn, MA 01801
   AI languages and tools

Teknowledge, Inc.
   525 University Ave., Palo Alto, CA 94301
   Expert system development tools, custom expert systems

Tektronix, Inc.
   Box 500, Beaverton, OR 97077
   AI computers, Languages, Environments, and Tools

Tenchstar/Metacomco
   201 Hoffman Ave., Monterey, CA 93940
   Lisp

Texas Instruments, Incorporated
   P.O. Box 809063, Dallas, TX 75240
   Lisp computers, Environments, Languages, Tools, and Custom expert systems

The Lisp Company
   POB 487, Redwood Estates, CA 95044
   Lisp and Logo

Thoughtware, Inc.
   2699 S. Bayshore Drive, Coconut Grove, FL 33133
   Knowledge-based systems

Xerox Corp., Artificial Intelliegence Systems
   250 North Halstead, P.O. Box 7018, Pasadena CA 91109
   Lisp computers, Environments, Languages, and Tools

Bibliography and References

"3600 Technical Summary," *Symbolics,* Feb. 1983.

Aikens, Janice S., and others, "Puff: An Expert System for Interpretation of Pulmonary Function Data," *Computers and Biomedical Research,* Vol. 16, 1983, pp. 199–208.

Barstow, David, "A Perspective on Automatic Programming," *AI Magazine,* Vol. 5, No. 1, Spring 1984, pp. 5–27.

Barstow, David, and others, *Interactive Programming Environments.* New York: McGraw-Hill Book Company, 1984.

Beckman, Frank S., *Mathematical Foundations of Programming,* Menlo Park, Calif.: Addison-Wesley Publishing Co., Inc., 1981.

Bonissone, Piero P., and Harold E. Johnson, Jr., "Expert System for Diesel Electric Locomotive Repair," *Journal on Forth Applications and Research,* Vol. 1, No. 1, Sept. 1983, pp. 7–16.

Bradshaw, Gary F., Patrick W. Langley, and Herbert A. Simon, "Studying Scientific Discovery by Computer Simulation," *Science,* Vol. 222, No. 4627, Dec. 2, 1983, pp. 971–975.

Charniak, Eugene, "Artificial Intelligence—An Introduction," Tutorial No. 1, AAAI Conference (1983).

Corley, Charles J., and Joyce A. Statz, "Lisp Workstation Brings AI Power to a User's Desk," *Computer Design,* Jan. 1985, pp. 155–162.

Elkind, David, *Interpretive Essays on Jean Piaget: Children and Adolescents,* New York: Oxford University Press, Inc., 1970.

"Evaluating Knowledge Engineering Applications," Knowledge Engineering, Teknowledge Inc., Palo Alto, CA, 1983.

Fallat, Robert J., and Michael G. Snow, "Micropuff—Will It Make Pulmonary Function Test Interpretations a Breeze?" *Education Perspectives,* Vol. 2, No. 3, May–June 1984, pp. 14–20.

Forgy, Charles L., "OPS5 Users Manual," Technical Report, Department of Computer Science, Carnegie–Mellon University, Pittsburgh, PA, July 1981.

Forgy, Charles L., "Overview of OPS83," Technical Report, Department of Computer Science, Carnegie–Mellon University, Pittsburgh, PA, Aug. 1983.

Fox, Mark S., "The Intelligent Management System: An Overview," Technical Report, Robotics Institute, Carnegie–Mellon University, Pittsburgh, PA, Aug. 1981.

Fox, Mark S., and others, "ISIS: A Constraint-Directed Reasoning Approach to Job Shop Scheduling," Technical Report, Robotics Institute, Carnegie–Mellon University, Pittsburgh, PA, June 21, 1983a.

Fox, Mark S., and others, "Techniques for Sensor-Based Diagnosis," Technical Report, Robotics Institute, Carnegie–Mellon University, Pittsburgh, PA, 1983b.

Gagne, Robert M., "The Learning Requirements for Enquiry," *Journal of Research in Science Teaching*, Vol. 1, 1963, pp. 144–153.

"Overview," The Robotics Institute, Carnegie–Mellon University, Pittsburgh, PA.

Gevarter, W. B., "An Overview of Computer-Based Natural Language Processing," U.S. Department of Commerce, NBSIR 83-2687, Apr. 1983.

Harris, Larry R., "Natural Language Simplifies Computer Access," *Systems & Software*, Jan. 1984, pp. 206–212.

Harris, Larry R., "Experience with Intellect: Artificial Intelligence Technology Transfer," *AI Magazine*, Vol. 5, No. 2, Summer 1984, pp. 43–50.

Hayes-Roth, Frederick, *Building Expert Systems*, Reading, Mass.: Addison-Wesley Publishing Co., Inc., 1983.

Hollan, James D., and others, "Steamer: An Interactive Inspectable Simulation-Based Training System," *AI Magazine*, Vol. 5, No. 2, Summer 1984, pp. 15–27.

Kaarsberg, Tina, "Artificial Intelligence: Software Sophistry," *Yale Scientific*, Spring 1981, pp. 25–29.

Kaplan, S. Jerrold, "The Industrialization of Artificial Intelligence: From By-Line to Bottom Line," *AI Magazine*, Vol. 5, No. 2, Summer 1984, pp. 51–57.

Knickerbocker, Carl, "Integrating AI and Unix Applications," *Systems & Software*, Nov. 1984, pp. 139–144.

Kowalski, Thaddeus J., and Donald E. Thomas, "The VLSI Design Automation Assistant: An IBM System/370 Design," *IEEE Design and Test*, Vol. 1, No. 1, Feb. 1984, pp. 60–69.

Kukich, Karen, "Design of a Knowledge-Based Report Generator," *Proceedings of the 21st Annual Meeting of the Association for Computational Linguistics*, Massachusetts Institute of Technology, Cambridge, MA, June 1983.

Kulikowski, Casimir A., "Expert Medical Consultation Systems," *Journal of Medical Systems*, Vol. 7, No. 3, 1983, pp. 229–234.

Kunz, John, Thomas P. Kehler, and Michael D. Williams, "Applications Development Using a Hybrid AI Development System," *AI Magazine*, Vol. 5, No. 3, Fall 1984, pp. 41–54.

"Machine Tool Technology," *American Machinist*, Vol. 124, No. 10, Oct. 1980, pp. 105–128.

McDermott, John, "R1: A Rule-Based Configurer of Computer Systems," Technical Report, Department of Computer Science, Carnegie–Mellon University, Pittsburgh, PA, Apr. 1980.

McDermott, John, "R1: The Formative Years," *AI Magazine*, Vol. 2, No. 2, Summer 1981, pp. 21–29.

McDermott, John, and Judith Bachant, "R1 Revisited: Four Years in the Trenches," *AI Magazine,* Vol. 5, No. 3, Fall 1984, pp. 21–32.

McDonald, Clement J., "Protocol-Based Computer Reminders: The Quality of Care and the Non-perfectability of Man," *New England Journal of Medicine,* Vol. 295, Dec. 9, 1976, pp. 1351–1355.

McDonald, Clement J., *Action-Oriented Decisions in Ambulatory Medicine.* Chicago: Year Book Medical Publishers, Inc., 1981, pp. 1–14.

McDonald, Clement J., and others, "A Computer-Based Record and Clinical Monitoring System for Ambulatory Care," *Am J. Public Health,* Vol. 67, No. 3, Mar. 1977, pp. 240–245.

McDonald, Clement J., and others, "Data Base Management, Feedback Control, and the Regenstrief Medical Record," *Journal of Medical Systems,* Vol. 7, No. 2, 1983, pp. 111–125.

McDonald, Clement J., and others, "The Regenstrief Clinical Laboratory System," *IEEE Proceedings of the Seventh Annual Symposium on Computer Applications in Medical Care,* 1983, pp. 254–257.

McDonald, Clement J., and others, "CARE: A Real World Medical Knowledge Base," *Proceedings of COMPCON,* Spring 1984a, pp. 187–191.

McDonald, Clement J., and others, "Reminders to Physicians from an Introspective Computer Medical Record: A Two-Year Randomized Trial," *Annals of Internal Medicine,* Vol. 100, 1984b, pp. 130–138.

Minsky, Marvin, "A Framework for Representing Knowledge," in *The Psychology of Computer Vision,* ed. Patrick Henry Winston. New York: McGraw-Hill Book Company, 1975.

Minsky, Marvin, "K-Lines: A Theory of Memory," unpublished AI Memo 516, Artificial Intelligence Laboratory, Massachusetts Institute of Technology, Cambridge, MA, June 1979.

Minsky, Marvin, "Learning Meaning," unpublished draft of essay, Artificial Intelligence Laboratory, Massachusetts Institute of Technology, Cambridge, MA, July 12, 1982.

"Natural Language Technology," Technical Report, Texas Instruments, Dallas, TX, 1983.

"Natural Language Toolkit," Technical Report, Texas Instruments, Dallas, TX, 1983.

Nelson, Ruth, "The First Literate Computers," *Psychology Today,* Mar. 1978.

Nestler, Eric, "Symbolic Processor Aids Design of Complex Chips," *Computer Design,* Jan. 1985, pp. 147–153.

O'Connor, Dennis E., "Using Expert Systems to Manage Change and Complexity in Manufacturing," Digital Equipment Corp., Apr. 1983.

O'Connor, Patrick J., "Tutoring the Computers," *Yale Alumni Magazine and Journal,* Dec. 1981, pp. 10–13.

Paseman, William G., "Data Flow Concepts Speed Simulation in CAE Systems," *Computer Design,* Jan. 1985, pp. 131–140.

Peters, Thomas J., and Robert H. Waterman, Jr., *In Search of Excellence,* New York: Harper & Row, Publishers, Inc., 1982.

Piaget, Jean, "Development and Learning," *Journal of Research in Science Teaching,* Vol. 2, 1964, pp. 176–186.

Pryor, T. A., R. M. Gardner, P. D. Clayton, and H. R. Warner, "The HELP System," *Journal of Medical Systems,* Vol. 7, No. 2, 1983, pp. 87–102.

Reddy, Y. V., and Mark S. Fox, "KBS: An Artificial Intellignece Approach to Flexible Simulation," Robotics Institute, Carnegie–Mellon University, Pittsburgh, PA, Feb. 1982.

Rich, Charles, and Howard Shrobe, "Initial Report on the Programmer's Apprentice," *IEEE Transactions on Software Engineering,* Vol. 4, No. 6, Nov. 1978.

Rieger, Chuck, "From Office Automation to Personal Automation: An AI Perspective," Technical Report TR-1085, Scion Corp./University of Maryland, Aug. 1981.

Schank, Roger, and Robert Abelson, *Scripts Plans Goals and Understanding.* Hillsdale, N.J.: Lawrence Erlbaum Associates Inc., 1977.

Schank, Roger C., with Peter G. Childers, *The Cognitive Computer,* Reading, Mass.: Addison-Wesley Publishing Co., Inc., 1984.

Sheil, Beau, "Power Tools for Programmers," *Datamation,* Feb. 1983, pp. 131–144.

Spoerl, James, "AI Environment Speeds Software Development," *Systems & Software,* Aug. 1984, pp. 111–118.

Stefik, Mark, and others, "Knowledge Programming in Loops: Report on an Experimental Course," *AI Magazine,* Vol. 4, No. 3, Fall 1983, pp. 3–12.

Stevens, Albert, and others, "The Use of a Sophisticated Graphics Interface in Computer-Assisted Instruction," *IEEE CG&A,* Mar.–Apr. 1983.

Stolfo, Salvatore J., and Greg T. Vesonder, "ACE: An Expert System Supporting Analysis and Management Decision Making," Technical Report, Computer Science Department, Columbia University, New York, Oct. 1982.

Thomas, Donald E., and others, "Automatic Data Path Synthesis," *Computer,* Vol. 16, No. 12, Dec. 1983, pp. 59–70.

Turing, Alan M., "Can a Machine Think?" in *The World of Mathematics,* Vol. 4, ed. J. R. Newman. New York: Simon and Schuster, 1954, pp. 2099–2123.

von Limbach, Geoffrey, and Michael B. Taylor, "Expert System Rules Read Natural Language," *Systems & Software,* Aug. 1984, p. 124.

Warner, Homer R., and others, "HELP—A Program for Medical Decision-Making," *Computers and Biomedical Research,* Vol. 5, 1972, pp. 65–74.

Waters, Richard C., "The Programmer's Apprentice: Knowledge-Base Programming Editing," *IEEE Transactions on Software Engineering,* Vol. 8, No. 1, Jan. 1982, pp. 1–12.

Waters, Richard C., "The Programmer's Apprentice: Knowledge Based Program Editor," Professional Program Session Record No. 16 on State-of-the-Art Interactive Software Tools, *IEEE Mini/MIcro Northeast-84,* Boston, May 1984, pp. 1–9. (Also printed in *Conference Record, IEEE Mini/Micro Northeast-84.*)

Wiederhold, Gio., "Knowledge and Database Management," *IEEE Software,* Vol. 1, No. 1, Jan. 1984, pp. 63–73.

Winograd, Terry, *Language as a Cognitive Process,* Vol. 1: *Syntax,* Reading, MA: Addison-Wesley Publishing Co., Inc., 1983.

Winston, Patrick Henry, *Artificial Intelligence,* 2nd ed. Reading, MA: Addison-Wesley Publishing Co., Inc., 1984.

Winston, Patrick H., and Richard Henry Brown, eds., *Artificial Intelligence: An MIT Perspective,* Vol. 1. Cambridge, MA: The MIT Press, 1979.

Winston, Patrick Henry, and Berthold Klaus Paul Horn, *Lisp,* 2nd ed. Reading, MA: Addison-Wesley Publishing Co., Inc., 1984.

Winston, Patrick H., and Karen A. Prendergast, eds., *The AI Business,* Cambridge, MA: The MIT Press, 1984.

Wong, Carla M., and others, "Application of Artificial Intelligence to Triple Quadrupole Mass Spectrometry (TQMS)," *IEEE Transactions on Nuclear Science,* Vol. NS-31, No. 1, pp. 804–810.

Zadeh, Lotfi A., "Making Computers Think Like People," *IEEE Spectrum,* Vol. 21, No. 8, Aug. 1984, pp. 26–32.

Zadeh, L. A., 1984, "Test-Score Semantics as a Basis for a Computational Approach to the Representation of Meaning," *Proceedings of the Tenth Annual Conference of the Association for Literary and Linguistic Computing,* 1983.

Zadeh, L.A., "Syllogistic Reasoning in Fuzzy Logic and Its Application to Reasoning with Dispositions," *Proceedings of the International Symposium on Multiple Valued Logic,* Winnipeg, Canada, 1984.

Index

A

Abdul-Ilana, 303–4
Access-oriented programming, 197, 211–12
Accounting, 65, 72
ACE, 7
Active sentences, 238
Active values, 196, 201–2, 211–12
Actor, 291, 292
Adaptive pattern recognition in Savvy, 242, 275–81, 282, 284
ADL. *See* Arthur D. Little, Inc.
ADR. *See* Applied Data Research
Advanced Reasoning Tool. *See* ART
Advice taking, 148
Advisory systems, 287, 294, 295–96
Agenda mechanism, 216, 219
Agent, 238
AI on UNIX machines, 191, 219
Air Force Office of Scientific Research, 42–43, 218
Alcoa, 42

Ambiguity, 4, 227–28, 234, 236–38, 241, 242, 244–45, 247, 249–50, 259, 261, 264, 265, 271, 277, 286, 288, 295
Analysis step, in building expert systems, 156, 183, 208
Analyzing sentences, 232–38, 247–50, 253, 256–57, 273–75, 282–84, 291–92, 297–99, 300–301
Analyzing stories, 300–303
Antecedent, 88
Apollo Computer, 32, 191
Apple Computer, 33
Applications of AI, 3, 4, 7–8, 10–14, 19–20, 26–27, 35–36, 43, 54–62, 65, 72, 75, 82, 91, 93–96, 127, 128, 154–56, 157–73, 179–94, 198–216, 218, 219
  accounting, 65, 72
  assets and liabilities management, 13
  automated programming systems, 14
  automobile-insurance agent advisor, 186–91

Applications of AI (*cont.*):
  banking advisor, 8
  circuit design, 26
  computer algebra, 8
  computer configuration, 3, 4, 10, 35, 43, 54–61, 62, 65, 82, 174–79, 218
  contract writing, 8
  crisis management, 13, 93–96
  database intermediaries, 13–14, 26
  design systems, 10–13, 26
  design of brushes in DC motors, 199
  design of springs in DC motors, 199
  diagnosis, 3, 6, 7, 13, 18, 19–20, 26, 65, 72, 74–75, 90, 91, 93–96, 127, 154–56, 157–72, 186–94, 202–14, 219
    of automobile faults, 19–20, 75, 154–56, 157–72
    of computer disk drive faults, 91
    of computer network problems, 13
    of locomotive faults, 19
    of mechanical equipment malfunctions, 6, 13, 65, 219
    of medical problems, 3, 65, 72, 74–75, 90
    of minicomputer system faults, 186–94
    of nuclear power plant malfunctions, 13, 93–96, 127, 202–14
    of telephone cable problems, 7
  education, 7–8, 117–27
  exploratory programming, 27–31, 103, 134–35, 139–41, 146, 208
  Federal Express services advisor, 183–86
  financial planning services, 13, 65
  gas turbine engine troubleshooting, 179–81
  insurance advisor, 8, 186–91
  interest rate swapping, 182
  interfaces:
    to control panels, 201–2
    to controlling instrumentation in nuclear power plants, 202–14
    to databases, 4, 13–14, 18, 26, 31, 32, 130–31, 223, 227, 230, 240–85, 287, 294–95, 299
    to design automation programs, 114–15
    to instrumentation in process control plants, 219
    to mechanical equipment, 13, 26
    to scientific instruments, 13, 199
    to software, 13, 65
  interpretation and analysis, 13, 19, 26
  investment planning, 8, 179–81, 182
  job shop scheduling, 8
  maintenance and diagnostic advisor, 202
  manager's assistant, 130–31
  medical diagnosis and consultation, 3, 65, 72, 74–75, 90
  natural language interfaces to databases, 4, 13–14, 18, 26, 31, 32, 130–31, 223, 227, 230, 240–85, 287, 294–95, 299
  oil exploration, 1, 2–3, 4, 19, 43, 65, 83–89, 91–93
  planning, 1–2, 13, 26
    experiments, 13
    financial services, 13
    production of printed circuit boards, 1–2
  portfolio management, 8, 179–82
  project management, 13
  real-estate recommendations, 181, 182
  sales, 3, 48, 61
  scheduling, 8, 13, 26, 43, 62, 65, 216, 218
    factories, 8, 13, 43, 62, 218
    helicopters, 216
  signal processing, 13, 26–27, 65
  simulation, 117–20, 124–25, 218

statistics, 128
stocks and bonds trading, 182
troubleshooting. *See* diagnosis
vision systems, 4–5, 8, 14, 18, 26
VLSI-design systems, 10, 26
weld scheduler, 199–201
Applications of AI: run-time hardware, 198, 201–2
Applied Data Research, 261
Applied Expert Systems Inc., 8, 199
Arborist, 31
ART, 214–16
Arthur D. Little, Inc., 198–99
Artificial intelligence:
   acceptance, 32–33, 48, 60–61
   branches, 3–5
   cautions, 36–37, 153, 182
   definition, 2, 3, 6–7
   education, 40, 42, 48–49, 50–52, 151
   importation at DEC, 54–62
   market trends, 6, 33–36
   resistance, 36, 45–47, 60
Artificial Intelligence Corp., 242, 247
ASCII code, 8–9
Assertion, 130
Assets and liabilities management, 13
AT&T Bell Labs, 127, 128
Atari, 22
ATNs, 231–34, 236, 239, 248–50, 268–71
ATRANS, 291
Augmented transition networks. *See* ATNs
Austin, Howard, 143
Automated programming systems, 14
Automotive diagnostic systems, 19–20, 75, 157–72

B

B&W. *See* Babcock & Wilcox
Babcock & Wilcox, 199–201
Backtracking, 215
Backward chaining, 88–89, 93–96, 103, 156, 157–58, 161–62, 174, 212–14, 221
Battelle Memorial Institute Inc., 199
Begin, Menachem, 303
Beliefs, 300
Biological organism pattern recognition mechanisms, 242
Birnbaum, Lawrence, 304
Bolt Beranek and Newman, 117, 118, 144
Brattle Research Corp., 8
Britton Lee, 131
Building-a-prototype step, in building expert systems, 146, 157

C

C (programming language), 191, 219
Cardinality, 207
Cardinality facet, 207
Carnegie Group Inc., 216, 218, 287, 297, 299
Carnegie-Mellon University, 8, 22, 42–43, 54, 59–61, 148, 217, 218
Case frames, 297–99
Case grammars, 238–39
Case statements, 140–141
CATS-1, 19, 32, 127
Causal agent, 238
Causal models, 75–76, 104–5, 115
Certainty factors, 88, 91, 159, 167, 177, 194
Chomsky, Noam, 235
Choosing a natural language system, 242–46
Choosing an expert system application, 65–70
Circuit design, 26, 108–15

Classes, 135, 196, 205–8
Class hierarchies, 51, 135–39, 196, 205–8
Clout, 265–75
　application dictionary, 273–74
　ATNs, 268–71
　database searches, 271
　displaying data, 272–73, 275
　heuristic rules, 265, 267, 270–73
　interactive definition capability, 266–67
　lexicon, 273–74
　parser, 267–69, 270, 271, 275
Cluster analysis in Savvy, 281–82, 284
CMU. *See* Carnegie-Mellon University
Coagent, 238
Cobol, 82, 252, 261
Coding an expert system, 146, 156–57
Cognitive Systems Inc., 294–96
Common Lisp, 201–2
Compound symbols, 258
Computational processing, 8–9 (*See also* Numeric processing)
Computer-aided engineering, 108, 112
Computer configuration. *See* Configuration of computers
Computer design, 108–9
Computer vision systems, 4–5, 8, 14, 18, 26
Computerized Yale Retrieval and Updating System. *See* Cyrus
Conceptual dependencies, 288–91
Confidence factors, *See* Certainty factors
Configuration of computers, 3, 4, 10, 35, 43, 54–61, 62, 65, 82, 97–103, 174–79, 218
Conflict resolution, 101–3
Conjunctions, 244–45
Consequent, 88, 96
Context-free grammar, 234–36
Contexts, 99–103, 174–77
Control blocks, 91, 173
Control mechanism, 71–72, 90–91, 97, 156, 163–67, 173

Counter-agent, 238
Cullinet, 247
Cyrus, 302–3

D

DADM, 130–31
Daisy Modeling Language, 115
Daisy Systems Corp., 46–47, 108, 112
Data dictionary, 247
Data-driven programming, 196, 211–12
Data-driven reasoning, 88, 97–103
Data General Corp., 32
Database, 4, 7, 9–10, 13–14, 18, 73–76, 77, 97
Database interfaces, 4, 13–14, 18, 26, 31, 32, 130–31, 218–19, 223, 227, 230, 240–85, 287, 294–95, 299
Database intermediaries, 13–14, 26, 130–31
Database management features in knowledge systems, 216–19
Debugging an expert system, 167–69, 191
DEC. *See* Digital Equipment Corp.
DEC System 10s and 20s, 31–32, 54
Decision support systems, 31
Decision tree, 31, 181, 186–88, 191–92, 194
Deductively Augmented Data Management. *See* DADM
Delco Products, 199
Density of coverage, 242–43, 248–49
Design automation, 113–15
Design of brushes in DC motors, 199
Design of springs in DC motors, 199
Design step, in building expert systems, 153–56
Design systems, 10–13, 26
Determiner, 231–32
Diagnosis systems, 3, 6, 7, 13, 19–20, 26, 65, 72, 74–75, 90–91,

93–96, 127, 157–72, 191–94, 202–14, 219
automotive faults, 19–20, 75, 157–72
computer disk drive faults, 91
computer network problems, 13
locomotive faults, 19
mechanical equipment malfunctions, 6, 13, 65, 219
medical problems, 3, 65, 72, 74–75, 90
minicomputer system faults, 186–94
nuclear power plant malfunctions, 13, 93–96, 127, 202–14
telephone cable problems, 7
Dictionary, 227–28, 229–30, 232–34, 247, 256, 258, 259–60, 273–74, 284, 286, 297
Differential pressure, 85, 92
Digital Equipment Corp., 3, 31, 32, 35, 42–43, 47–48, 52, 54–62, 81, 82, 201, 218
Digital Research Inc., 201
Dipmeter Advisor, 19, 35, 43, 144
Disk storage management. *See* Database management features in knowledge systems
Dowe, Jim, 281
Drill bit sticking problems, 83–85, 92–93
Drilling Advisor, 83–89, 91–93
Drilling assembly, 84–85
Drilling supervisors, 86, 92–93
DS engineering workstations, 32

E

Eclipse computers, 32
Education in AI, 40, 42, 48–49, 50–52, 151
Electronic spreadsheets, 33, 40
Elf Aquitaine, 83, 85, 92–93
ELIZA, 229–30
Encapsulation of procedures, 134–35, 140–41
English, 261–63
Escort, 219
Excalibur Technologies Corp., 241, 275
Expanding a knowledge system, 168–69
Expectations, 291, 292, 299, 300–301
Expert-Ease, 157, 182–91, 194
building a knowledge system, 183–85, 188
testing the knowledge system, 191
Expert system. *See* Knowledge systems
Explanations in expert systems, 124–27, 159–60, 175, 177, 191, 194
Exploratory programming, 27–31, 82, 134–35, 139–41, 146, 208, 213
Explorer natural language system, 294–95

F

Factory management system, 217, 218
Factory scheduling system, 8, 13, 43, 218
Fairchild, 22
Fast Reading Understanding and Memory Program. *See* Frump
Federal Express services system, 183–86
Field testing, 149–50, 156, 167–69, 175, 177, 191
Financial services planning, 13, 65
Finegold, Aryeh, 46–47
Finite state automaton, 231
Flavors, 134
Fluency of expression, 245–46, 248
Focus, 33
Forgy, Charles, 101
Formal grammars, 230–32, 234–36
Formal logic, *See* Logic
Formal programming languages, 226, 244, 245, 261

Forth (programming language), 32
Fortran, 82, 194, 252, 261
Forward chaining, 96–103, 200
Fourth generation programming
    languages, 33, 40, 246–47,
    261–63
Frames, 77–78, 105–15, 117, 122–25,
    152, 196, 200, 202–5, 207–9,
    211–12, 214, 217, 221
  definition of, 105–6
  generic frames, 109–11, 122–23,
    125, 205–6
  hierarchies, 108–9, 111–12, 115,
    122–24, 125, 205–8
  inheritance, 111–12, 115, 123–24,
    125, 207–8
  in KEE, 202–5, 207–9, 211–12, 214
  in Language Craft, 297–99
  in the Logician, 109–11, 113–14
  languages, 218
  specific frames (instance frames),
    109–11, 123–24, 205–6, 207,
    208
  in Steamer, 117, 120–25, 205–7
Frey Associates, 252
Frump, 300–302
Fuller, Sam, 59
Functions, 76, 221
Fundamental symbol, 258
Fuzzy logic, 74, 153, 194

G

Games for AI education, 50–52
Garbage collection, 217
Gatemaster, 108, 113
GEM, 201–2
GEN-X, 179, 181, 182
General Electric Co., 19, 32, 182
General Motors, 199
General Problem Solver (GPS), 24
General Telephone & Electronics, 22

Generator, 289–90
Generic frames, 109–11, 122–23, 125,
    205–7
Generic grammar, 221
Generic procedures, 124–27
Goal, 88, 89, 90, 96–97, 157–59,
    163–64, 165, 173, 175, 178–79,
    300
Goal-driven reasoning, 88–89, 93–96
Goal Hill Computers Inc., 182
Gould Inc., 191
Graceful degradation of expert systems,
    105
Grammar, 230–32, 234–36, 247,
    256–58, 259, 260
  Chomsky grammars, 235
  context-free grammar, 234–35
  in Intellect, 247
  in NaturalLink, 247, 256–58
  specification of, 257–58
Grammarian, in NaturalLink, 258–59
Grammatical cases, 238–39
Graphical environments, 52–54, 195,
    196, 198, 201–2
Graphical image knowledge bases, 196,
    211–12
Gulf Oil Corp., 43

H

Harris, Larry, 242, 243, 244, 245
Hearsay II, 72
Hearts, 148
Heuristic rules in natural language, 265,
    267, 270–73
Heuristics, 17, 64, 71, 79, 194, 242,
    265, 267, 270–73
Hewlett Packard, 32
Hierarchical links, 205–6
Hierarchies:
  of classes, 51, 135–39
  of contexts, 174–77

Index

of frames, 77–78, 108–9, 111–12, 115, 122–24, 125, 205–8
of viewpoints, 215–16
Human Edge Software, 182

I

IBM, 31, 32, 191, 198, 201–2, 247, 281
IKE, 221–22
Implied meaning, 239, 242, 288, 290–91, 292, 295, 296, 299, 300, 303
Incremental modification of expert systems, 64–65, 103, 146, 156, 160–72, 175, 178, 191, 208
Indexing structure in expert systems, 90, 97, 101, 178–79
Inducing rules, 179, 181, 186–88, 191–92, 194
Inference Corp., 8, 214, 218
Inference mechanism, 63, 71–73, 78, 81, 88–89, 93–103
Inferring information with conceptual dependencies, 290–91
Information Builders Inc., 247
Information Sciences Institute, 144
INGEST, 290
Inheritance, 76, 78, 111–12, 115, 123–24, 125, 132–39, 152, 196, 205–8, 212, 215–16
  in ART, 215–16
  in frames, 78, 111–12, 115, 123–24, 125, 207–8
  in KEE, 207–8, 212
  in the Logician, 111–12, 115
  in object-oriented programming, 135–39, 196
  of procedures in Steamer, 124–27
  in semantic networks, 76, 132–33
  in Steamer, 123–25
  in viewpoints, 215–16

Instance, 206
Instance frames (specific frames), 109–11, 123–24, 205–6, 207, 208
Instrument, 238
Insurance agent advisor, 186–91
Integrated AI development environments, 29, 195–96, 198
Integrated AI programs, 61–62, 201–2, 219–22
Integrated Knowledge Environment. *See* IKE
Integrated Partial Parser. *See* IPP
Intellect, 242, 247–52
  ambiguity handling, 249–50
  application-specific lexicon, 247
  ATNs, 248–49
  density of coverage, 248–49
  dictionary, 247
  grammar, 247
  navigating the database, 249
  parser, 248–49
  preference ratings, 249–50
  root lexicon, 247
  semantic information, 247
  series information, 248
  syntactic information, 247
IntelliCorp, 53–54, 93, 196, 198, 201, 219
Interest rate swapping, 182
Interfaces:
  to control panels, 201–2
  to controlling instrumentation in nuclear power plant, 202–14
  to databases, 4, 13–14, 18, 26, 31, 32, 130–31, 223, 227, 230, 240–85, 287, 294–95, 299
  to design automation programs, 114–15
  to mechanical equipment, 13, 26
  to process control plant instrumentation, 219
  to scientific instruments, 13, 199
  to software, 13, 65

International terrorism analysis program, 303
Interpretation and analysis systems, 13, 19, 26
Investment planning, 8, 179–81, 182
IPP, 303
Irregular nouns, 232
Irregular verbs, 232
ISIS, 8, 43, 218
Iterative testing, 156, 160–62, 178, 191, 212

J

Jeffrey Perrone & Associates, Inc., 182, 183

K

K: Base, 181–82
Kaarsberg, Tina, 302, 303, 304
KEE, 53–54, 196, 198–214
  active images, 196, 201–2, 211–12
  assertion/retrieval language, 212
  building an expert system, 208–12
  external form of rules, 203–5, 207
  facets, 207
  frames, 202–5, 207–9, 211–12, 214
  generic frames, 205–6
  hierarchies of frames, 205–8, 212
  inference strategies, 212–14
  inheritance, 207–8
  instance frames (specific frames), 205–6, 207, 208
  internal form of rules, 203, 205
  knowledge bases, 202, 208, 214
  legal values, 207
  logical form of rules, 205
  procedural attachments, 196, 201–2, 211–12
  rule debugger, 204–5
  rule system, 203–5, 208–9, 212–14
  run-time system, 201–2
  units (frames), 202–5, 207–9, 211–12, 214
  variables, 205, 209, 212, 214
Key seating, 85, 92
Knowledge, 10, 73–74, 75–76, 146–47
Knowledge acquisition, 15, 67–68, 142–48, 154, 156, 179 (*See also* Knowledge engineering)
Knowledge base, 63, 71–75, 76, 77, 78, 81, 88, 97
Knowledge base management system, 216–17, 218–19
Knowledge-bottlenecks, 65–66, 68–69, 85
Knowledge Craft, 216–18, 299
  agenda mechanism, 216, 218
  disk storage management system, 216–17
  knowledge representation languages, 216, 218
  modeling capabilities, 217–18
  schema, 218
  viewpoint mechanism, 216, 218
Knowledge engineering, 21, 67–68, 69, 142–48, 154, 156, 179
Knowledge Engineering Environment. *See* KEE
Knowledge Network, 61–62
Knowledge system architecture, 28–29, 63–64, 71–73, 81, 113–14
Knowledge system characteristics, 65
Knowledge system prerequisites, 69–70

L

Lambda machine, 219, 221
Language Craft, 287–88, 297–99
  case frames, 297–99
  dictionary, 297
  parser, 297–98
  semantic analysis, 297–99

semantic constraints, 297
sentence structure, 297, 298
syntactic analysis, 297–98, 299
Large-scale knowledge system
    development tools, 151–52,
    195–223
Lawrence Livermore Laboratory, 49,
    199
Layout and design, 112–14
LDS Hospital, 3
Learning, (computer programs that
    learn), 22
Legal values, 160, 161, 168, 175, 207
Lehman Brothers/Shearson/American
    Express, 30, 182
Lexicographer, in NaturalLink, 259–60
Lexicon, 229–30, 232–34, 247, 256,
    258, 259–60, 273–74, 284, 286,
    297
Lisp, 20, 31, 82, 173, 174, 196, 201–2,
    204, 250, 252
Lisp computers, 20–21, 30, 31–32, 35,
    52–54, 151–52, 195, 198, 199
Lisp Machine Inc., 30, 32, 219, 221
Lisp processor boards, 201
Lisp programs on conventional
    computers, 30, 34–35
LMI. *See* Lisp Machine Inc.
Locomotive diagnosis system, 19, 127
Logic, 78, 115, 129–30, 152
Logic Workbench, 219
Logician, 108–15
  architecture, 113–14
  frames, 109–11, 113–14
  software, 113–15
Loops, 50, 196, 199

M

M.1, 157–73, 174
  certainty factor, 159, 169
  control rules, 163–67
  explanations, 159–60
  goal, 157–59, 163–64, 165, 173
  inference strategy, 158, 161–67
  legal values, 160, 163, 168
  variables, 163, 166
Machine fault diagnosis, 219
Macintosh computer, 201
Management's role in importing AI, 43,
    44, 47–48
Manager's assistant, 130–31
Market trends, 5–6, 33–36
Martin Marietta Data Systems, 261
Massachusetts Institute of Technology,
    22
Match-rules-and-perform-action cycle.
    See Recognize-act cycle
Mathematica. *See* Martin Marietta Data
    Systems
Mathematical logic. *See* Logic
McCarthy, John, 24
McDermott, John, 54, 59–61, 149
McDonnell-Douglas, 148
Means-end analysis, 24–25
Medical diagnostic and consultation
    systems, 3, 65, 72, 74–75, 90
Megalogician, 108, 113
Messages, 134–35, 136, 140–41
Meta-rules, 90–91, 153
Methods, 134–35, 136, 140–41, 202,
    208
Michie, Donald, 186
Microcomputer-based AI tools, 151–94
Microcomputer-based natural language
    systems, 254–61, 264–85
Micropuff, 32
Microrim, 265
MicroVAX, 201
Military systems, 6, 13, 25–26
Minsky, Marvin, 105–6
Mione, Joseph, 188
MIT. *See* Massachusetts Institute of
    Technology
Modifiability of knowledge systems,
    27–31, 71–73, 75, 81–82, 103,
    146, 156, 160–72, 175, 212

Modularity in the Logician, 113–15
Modularity of AI systems, 27–28, 63, 71–73, 81–82, 103, 105, 113–15, 146, 191
Monitoring programs, 13, 202, 218
MOPS, 293–94, 303
Motivation analysis, 228, 300, 304
Motorola 68010, 219
Multiple paradigm tools, 196–98, 200, 202–23
Multi-valued logic, 175, 194
Munson, Jack, 45
Mycin, 72, 74, 90

N

Natural language, 26, 31, 32, 108, 125, 221, 224–304
  ambiguity, 241, 244–45, 247, 249–50, 271, 277, 286, 288, 295
  flexibility, 227, 230, 259, 261, 264, 265, 271
  fluency of expression, 245–46
  formal grammars, 230–32, 234–36
  heuristic rules, 242, 265, 267, 270–73
  interactive definition capabilities, 252–53, 266–67, 276–77
  interface to applications, 247, 250, 299
  interface to databases, 4, 13–14, 18, 26, 31, 32, 130–31, 223, 227, 230, 240–85, 287, 294–95, 299
  interface to knowledge acquisition systems, 221, 288, 299
  interfacing to databases (how to), 256–60
  limitations, 227–29, 239
  key word-based, 227, 229–30
  menu-based, 221, 254–55

system components, 242, 247–49, 253, 256, 273–74, 275, 287, 288, 297
system selection criteria, 242–46
NaturalLink, 31, 254–61, 264
  consistency checking of grammars, 256, 258–59, 260–61
  coordinator toolkit, 260
  error checking, 256, 258–59, 260–61
  grammar, 256, 257–58, 259, 260
  Grammarian, 258–59
  interface definition tools, 256
  Lexicographer, 259–60
  lexicons, 256, 259–60
  parsing, 256–57, 259, 260
  production rules, 257–58
  screenbuilder, 260
  toolkit, 255–61
  translator, 256–57, 259
  windows, 254–56, 259, 260–61
  writing a grammar, 257–59
Navigating the database, 242, 245, 247–48, 249, 257, 258, 267, 270–71, 274–75
Navy Dept., 300
Nelson, Ruth, 300
Newell, Allen, 24
Newspaper reading programs, 300–303
Nomad, 33
Non-deterministic parsing, 234, 249–50, 286
Noun phrase network, 231–34
Noun phrase production rules, 230, 234–36
Nuclear power plant diagnosis, 93–96, 127, 201–14
Numeric processing, 7, 8–10, 16–18

O

Object-oriented programming, 134–41, 152, 196, 201–2, 205–6

Object-oriented programming languages, 133–34
O'Connor, Dennis, 54
O'Connor, Patrick, 301, 304
Ohio State University, 199
Oil exploration applications, 1, 2–3, 4, 19, 43, 65, 83–89, 91–93, 127
On-line English, 247
OPS5, 61, 218

P

PA Computers and Telecommunications, 219
Pacific Medical Center, 3
Pam, 300
Paraphrasing, 247, 250, 286, 287, 289
Parent-child links, 136–39, 205–6
Parse trees, 221–22, 234–38, 259
Parsing, 203, 205, 221–22, 231–38, 248, 249, 256–57, 259, 260, 267–69, 270, 271, 275, 277, 284, 286, 291, 292, 297–98
Pascal, 82, 194
Passive sentence, 238
Pattern matching:
  in natural language systems, 227, 229–30 (*See also* Adaptive pattern recognition in Savvy)
  in rule interpreters, 81, 98–103
PDP-10s and 20s, 31–32, 54
PDP-11s, 32, 61
Perception systems, 4–5, 8, 14, 18, 26
Perkin-Elmer, 191
Personal computer-based AI tools, 31, 151–94
Personal computer-based natural language systems, 31, 254–61, 264–85
Personal computers, 30, 31, 32, 151–53, 182, 191, 254, 264–65, 275, 281
Personal Consultant, 174–79
  certainty factor, 177
  English translation of rule, 175, 177
  explanations, 175
  graphics access, 174
  inference strategy, 174, 178–79
Peters, Thomas J., 30
Picon, 219–21
PL/1, 250, 252, 261
Plan Applying Mechanism. *See* Pam
Planning systems, 1–2, 13, 26, 65
  experiments, 13
  financial services, 13
  production of printed circuit boards, 1–2
Predicate calculus, 129
Predicates, 76, 129, 221
Preference ratings of interpretations, 249–50
Premises, 177
Prepositional phrase, 231–32, 235–36
Procedural attachments, 196, 211–12
Procedural tools, 191–94
Procedure-oriented paradigm, 78, 91, 115, 117, 124, 152, 173, 196
Production memory, 98–103
Production rules (*See also* Rules)
  for grammars, 230, 235–36, 257–58
  for knowledge systems, 88–89, 93–96, 98–103
Project management, 218
Prolog, 20, 218, 219
Prolog application development system, 219
Pronouns, 228–29, 244, 266, 270–71
Proposition, 129
Prototyping in Lisp, 27–31, 82, 134–35, 139–41, 146, 212
Pruning, 90
PTRANS, 289, 291
Puff, 32

Q

Quality control, 14
Quinlan's ID3 algorithm, 186

R

R1. *See* XCON
R:Base, 265–66
Radial, 191
Radian Corp., 157, 191
Ramis, 33, 261–63
Randomized bit buffer, 279–81
Rapid prototyping. *See* Exploratory programming
Reactors, 201–14
Real-estate recommendations, 181
Real-time process control, 219–21
Reasoning in parallel, 215–16
Recognize-act cycle, 98–103
Recognizing sentences, 232–34, 282–84
Recognizing words, 231–32
Reconstructive theories of past knowledge, 287, 303
Record, 75, 77, 265
Referents, 228–29, 244, 266, 270–71
Regenstrief Institute for Health Care, 3
Regression EXpert. *See* REX
Reimplementation of Lisp programs on conventional computers, 31, 32, 201–2
Relational database capabilities in Prolog, 219
Relational database management system, 265–66
Relations, 265–66, 271
Requests, in sketchy scripts, 300–301
Requirements specifications, 27–28
Resistance to AI, 36, 45–47, 60
Restaurant script, 292–93
Reveal, 148
Rewrite rules, *See* Production rules

REX, 127–28
Root class, 135–36
Root context, 175–77
Rule induction, 179, 181, 183, 186–91, 192, 194
Rule interpreters, 81, 90
Rule-based languages, 78, 81–82
Rules:
  in expert systems, 50–51, 78–82, 88–90, 91–92, 93–96, 97, 98–103, 104–5, 106, 108, 130, 131, 152, 158–73, 174–75, 177–79, 181, 182, 196, 199, 200, 203–5, 208–10, 212–16, 218, 221
  heuristic rules in natural language, 265, 267, 270–73
  production rules in natural language grammars, 230, 235–36, 257–58
RuleMaker, 191–92
RuleMaster, 157, 191–94
Run-time hardware for commercial AI applications, 201–2

S

S.1, 173, 199
Sales applications, 3, 48, 61
Sam, 300
Sarah the chimp, 224–25
Savvy, 275–85
  adaptive pattern recognition techniques, 275–81, 282, 284
  bit buffer, 279–81
  cluster analysis, 281–82, 284
  defining synonyms, 276–77, 284–85
  extending Savvy, 276, 284
  mathematical transformation, 276, 281
  parsing, 277, 284
  pseudo-randomization, 281, 282, 284
  recognizing sentences, 282–84

semantic processing, 275, 277, 278, 284
syntactic processing, 275, 277, 278, 284
training Savvy, 282–85
Schank, Roger, 132, 287, 288, 289, 292, 294, 298, 299
Scheduling, 8, 13, 26, 43, 62, 65, 216, 218
  factories, 8, 13, 43, 62, 218
  helicopters, 216
Schema, 218
Schema Representation Language. *See* SRL
Schematic capture, 108–9, 221
Schlumberger, 2–3, 19, 43, 143, 144, 146
Script Applying Mechanism. *See* Sam
Script-based natural-language systems, 287, 288, 292–96, 300–304
  advisory systems, 287, 294, 295–96
  geology database interfaces, 294–95
  interfaces to databases, 294
  story understanding programs, 300–304
Scripts, 78, 132, 265, 288, 292–93, 294, 295, 296, 297, 298, 299, 300–302
Search intersection, 245
Search space, 27, 90, 97
Search union, 245
Security in DADM, 131
Seismic data interpretation, 19
Semantic approach to natural language, 236, 239, 242, 265, 270–73, 287–304
Semantic information in syntactic analysis systems, 227, 229, 230, 232, 236, 242, 247, 253, 264–65, 267, 270–73, 275, 277, 278, 284
Semantic network, 76, 78, 132, 232
Sentence analysis:
  using case frames, 297–99
  using conceptual dependencies, 291
  using scripts, 292–94
  using syntax analysis, 230, 231–39
Sentence structure, in Language Craft, 297–98
Sentence understanding. *See* Understanding sentences
Series information, 245–46, 248
Shaw, Clifford, 24
Shearson/Lehman Brothers/American Express, 30, 182
Signal processing, 13, 26–27, 65
Silogic, Inc., 219
Simon, Herbert, 26
Simulation systems, 117–20, 124–25, 199, 218
Single-paradigm tools, 198
Single-valued parameters, 175
Situation-action, 78, 88, 98–99, 104, 108
Sketchy scripts, 300–302
Slade, Stephen, 301
Sloan, Kenneth, 261
Slots, in frames, 77–78, 106, 108–11, 120–25, 127–28, 196, 202–5, 207–9, 211–12, 214
Sloughing, 85, 92
Smalltalk, 134
Software engineering:
  classical techniques, 27–28
Sparse coverage, 243
Specialization strategy. *See* Specificity
Specific frames (instance frames), 109–11, 123–24, 205–6, 207, 208
Specificity, 97, 102–3
Spoerl, James, 138
SRL, 217–18
Steamer, 7–8, 117–27, 144
  explanations, 124–27
  frames, 117, 120–25
  generic frames, 122–23, 125
  generic procedures, 124–27
  inheritance, 123–24, 125

Steamer (*cont.*):
  simulation capabilities, 117–20, 124–25
  specific frames (instance frames), 123–24
  specific procedures, 124–27
  teaching steam plant operation, 118–20, 124–27
Stereotypical situations, 288, 292–94, 296, 298, 303
Stocks and bonds trading, 182
Story understanding programs, 300–304
Subclasses, 135–36, 196, 205–8
Subgoal, 89, 93–96, 163–67, 178–79, 212–14
Sumex, 32
Sun Microsystems, 191
Symbolic processing, 6–7, 8–10, 16–18, 75–76, 78
Symbolics' computers, 199, 201
Symbolics, Inc., 32, 201
Symbols, 7
Syntactic processing, 227, 229, 230–38, 242, 247–49, 253, 256–59, 264, 265, 268–70, 271, 273, 275, 277, 278, 284, 287, 296, 297
Syntactic structure, 234–35
Syntelligence, 8
System Development Corp., 45, 130
System.car, 157–72

T

Table-based AI tools, 152, 179–94
Taylor, Michael, 272
Teaching steam plant operation with Steamer, 117–20, 124–27
Teaching steam plant operation traditionally, 118
Technology transfer, 38, 40–45, 47–52, 54–61

Teknowledge, 47, 68–69, 83, 93, 157, 173, 199, 218
Tektronix, 30, 32
Terrorism analysis program. *See* International terrorism analysis program
Testing an expert system, 149–50, 156, 161–62, 175, 191
Texas Instruments, 31, 32, 157, 174, 254, 255, 260
Themis, 252–53
  defining synonyms, 252–53
  syntax analysis, 253
  thematic analysis, 253
TI. *See* Texas Instruments
Time-series data, 245–46, 248
Time tags, 97, 102
Titan expert system, 191–92
Tools, 5–6, 20, 29–30, 31, 49–50, 53–54, 151–223
  backward chaining tools, 157–79
  cautions, 153
  in conventional environments, 30–31, 151–53, 198, 201–2, 218–19
  knowledge system development tools, 5–6, 49–50, 53–54, 151–223
  large-scale tools, 195–223
  microcomputer-based tools, 151–94, 195
  table-based tools, 179–94
  training, 49, 199–200
  users, 5–6, 49–50, 198–201
  vertical market tools, 219–23
Top-level control block, 173
Top-level goal, 158, 163–67
Transition network, 231–34, 236, 239, 248–50, 268–71
Triple Quadripole Mass Spectrometer, 49, 199
Troubleshooting. *See* Diagnosis systems
Truckin', 50–52, 138
Turing, Alan M., 23
Turing test, 23–24

Turnkey AI applications, 39–40

U

Uncertainty factors. *See* Certainty factors
Understanding implied meaning, 239, 242, 288, 290–91, 292, 295, 296, 299, 300, 303
Understanding sentences:
   in syntax analysis systems, 238–39
     (*See also* Analyzing sentences)
   with case frames, 297–99
   with conceptual dependencies, 291
   with scripts. 292–94
Unique frames. *See* Instance frames
Units. *See* KEE frames
Users:
   of knowledge system development tools, 5–6, 49–50, 198–201
   of turnkey AI applications, 39–40
University of Southern California Information Sciences Institute, 144
UNIX, 191, 194, 219
UNIX machines that run AI, 30, 32, 191, 219
UNIX pipes, 194

V

Vance, Cyrus, 302–3
VAX, 32, 52, 54, 59, 60, 61, 149, 191, 198, 199, 201
Vehicle-accident sketchy script, 301
Verb-phrase network, 231–34
Verb-phrase production rules, 230, 235–36
Viewpoints, 214–16, 218
Virtual memory, 216–17, 219

VisiCalc, 25, 33
Vision systems. *See* Computer vision systems
VLSI, 26, 108–9
von Limbach, Geoffrey, 272

W

Washoe the chimp, 224–25
Waterman, Robert H., 30
Weld scheduler, 199–201
Well-formed formula, *See* Wff
Westinghouse Electric Corp., 8, 42–43, 218
Wff, 205
What-if questions, symbolic, 40, 120, 130–31
Witch-doctor syndrome, 16, 66
Word processing, 8–9
Working memory, 98–103

X

XCON, 3, 4, 10, 35, 43, 48, 54–61, 62, 82, 97, 149, 218
Xerox, 32, 138, 196, 199
XSEL, 3, 48, 61, 218

Y

Yale University, 287, 289, 301, 304

Z

Zadeh, Lotfi, 194
Zetalisp, 201–2